Snort 2.0
Intrusion Detection

Jay Beale

James C. Foster

Jeffrey Posluns Technical Advisor

Brian Caswell Technical Editor

KEY	SERIAL NUMBER
001	PK9HFQRD43
002	Q2PLNYUCVF
003	8JASTRQX3A
004	Z2B76ELRQY
005	JUDYT5R33S
006	XG3QRGEES6
007	JAN3EPQ2AK
008	9BSPACELY7
009	FREDP7V6FH
010	5BVFBRN3YZ

PUBLISHED BY
Syngress Publishing, Inc.
800 Hingham Street
Rockland, MA 02370

Snort 2.0 Intrusion Detection

Printed in the United States of America

1 2 3 4 5 6 7 8 9 0

ISBN: 1-931836-74-4

Technical Editor: Brian Caswell
Technical Advisor: Jeffrey Posluns
Acquisitions Editor: Catherine B. Nolan
CD Production: Michael Donovan

Cover Designer: Michael Kavish
Page Layout and Art: Shannon Tozier, Patricia Lupien
Copy Editor: Beth A. Roberts
Indexer: Nara Wood

Distributed by Publishers Group West in the United States and Jaguar Book Group in Canada.

Acknowledgments

We would like to acknowledge the following people for their kindness and support in making this book possible.

Karen Cross, Lance Tilford, Meaghan Cunningham, Kim Wylie, Harry Kirchner, Kevin Votel, Kent Anderson, Frida Yara, Jon Mayes, John Mesjak, Peg O'Donnell, Sandra Patterson, Betty Redmond, Roy Remer, Ron Shapiro, Patricia Kelly, Kristin Keith, Jennifer Pascal, Doug Reil, David Dahl, Janis Carpenter, and Susan Fryer of Publishers Group West for sharing their incredible marketing experience and expertise.

The incredibly hard working team at Elsevier Science, including Jonathan Bunkell, AnnHelen Lindeholm, Duncan Enright, David Burton, Rosanna Ramacciotti, Robert Fairbrother, Miguel Sanchez, Klaus Beran, and Rosie Moss for making certain that our vision remains worldwide in scope.

David Buckland, Wendi Wong, Daniel Loh, Marie Chieng, Lucy Chong, Leslie Lim, Audrey Gan, and Joseph Chan of STP Distributors for the enthusiasm with which they receive our books.

Kwon Sung June at Acorn Publishing for his support.

Jackie Gross, Gayle Voycey, Alexia Penny, Anik Robitaille, Craig Siddall, Darlene Morrow, Iolanda Miller, Jane Mackay, and Marie Skelly at Jackie Gross & Associates for all their help and enthusiasm representing our product in Canada.

Lois Fraser, Connie McMenemy, Shannon Russell, and the rest of the great folks at Jaguar Book Group for their help with distribution of Syngress books in Canada.

David Scott, Tricia Wilden, Marilla Burgess, Annette Scott, Geoff Ebbs, Hedley Partis, Bec Lowe, and Mark Langley of Woodslane for distributing our books throughout Australia, New Zealand, Papua New Guinea, Fiji Tonga, Solomon Islands, and the Cook Islands.

Winston Lim of Global Publishing for his help and support with distribution of Syngress books in the Philippines.

Contributors

Jay Beale is a security specialist focused on host lockdown and security audits. He is the Lead Developer of the Bastille project, which creates a hardening script for Linux, HP-UX, and Mac OS X. He is also a member of the Honeynet Project and a core participant in the Center for Internet Security. A frequent conference speaker and trainer, Jay speaks and trains at the Black Hat and LinuxWorld conferences, among others. Jay writes the Center for Internet Security's UNIX host security tool, currently in use worldwide by organizations from the Fortune 500 to the Department of Defense. He maintains the Center's Linux Security benchmark document and, as a core participant in the non-profit Center's UNIX team, is working with private enterprises and United States agencies to develop UNIX security standards for industry and government. Aside from his CIS work, Jay has written a number of articles and book chapters on operating system security. He is a columnist for *Information Security Magazine* and previously wrote a number of articles for SecurityPortal.com and SecurityFocus.com. He is the author of the *Host Lockdown* chapter in *UNIX Unleashed* and the security section in *Red Hat Internet Server*. He is currently finishing the book entitled, *Locking Down Linux*. Jay also served as the Security Team Director for MandrakeSoft, helping set company strategy, design security products, and pushing security into the third largest retail Linux distribution. He now works to further the goal of improving operating system security. He makes his living as a security consultant and trainer through Baltimore-based JJBSec, LLC.

Anne Carasik is a system administrator at the Center for Advanced Computational Research (CACR) at the California Institute of Technology. She is in charge of information security at CACR, which includes every aspect of information security including intrusion detection (running Snort, of course), network security, system security, internal IT auditing, and network security policy. Her specialties include Linux, Secure Shell, public key technologies, penetration testing, and network security architectures. Anne's background includes positions as a Principal

Security Consultant at SSH Communications Security, and as an Information Security Analyst at VeriSign, Inc.

Aidan Carty (CCSA, CCSE, CCNA) is a Senior Systems and Security Architect for Entropy Ltd., which is based in Ireland. His specialties include the designing and building of intrusion detection systems, firewall architecture, integration, and UNIX system security. Aidan also teaches a number of courses in the areas of intrusion detection, firewalls and TCP/IP. Aidan would like to thank his wife, Bettina, his friends, colleagues and the engineers he works with on a daily basis: Dave, Joe, Angela, Niall, Sarah and Dan, and finally thanks to Mr. Marty Roesch for putting together a very cool program... Snort.

Scott Dentler (CISSP, CCSE, CCSA, MCSE, CCNA) is an IT consultant who has served with companies such as Sprint and H&R Block, giving him exposure to large enterprise networks. Scott's background includes a broad range of Information Technology facets, including Cisco Routers and Switches, Microsoft NT/2000, Check Point firewalls and VPNs, Red Hat Linux, network analysis and enhancement, network design and architecture, and network IP allocation and addressing. He has also prepared risk assessments and used that information to prepare business continuity and disaster recovery plans for knowledge-based systems.

Adam M. Doxtater (CUSA, MCSE) is a computer engineer for MGM MIRAGE in Las Vegas, NV. Prior to MGM MIRAGE, he was employed as a computer consultant in the greater Las Vegas area. Aside from his full-time work, Adam has contributed to the Open Sound System digital audio architecture, allowing it to be ported to a larger UNIX/Linux audience. His Linux-related efforts and columns have been featured in such magazines as *eWeek* and *Network World*, as well as Web sites such as Linux.com, NewsForge.com, and LinuxWorld.com. Adam is responsible for the launch of the MadPenguin.org Linux portal and currently handles most of the design, writing, and organizational tasks for the site. Since its launch in early January 2003, MadPenguin.org has gathered an impressive following and user base. Over the past two and a half years, Adam has also contributed to several Syngress/Osborne McGraw-Hill certification publications and is truly thankful for the opportunity to reach an audience of that magnitude. Adam owes his accomplishments to his wife, Cristy, and daughter, Amber Michelle.

Wally Eaton (Security+, CNX, BSCS, CCNP, CCDP, MCSE, MCP+I, Network+, FCC) is Chief Security Officer for the City of Jacksonville, FL. Previously Wally held the position of Senior Systems Field Engineer for the Unisys Corporation, retiring after 20 years of service. At Unisys his duties included installing, debugging, and maintaining hardware and system software for Unisys mainframe computers. Wally is a contributing author to *Sniffer Pro Network Optimization & Troubleshooting Handbook* (Syngress Publishing, ISBN: 1-931836-57-4). He is currently enrolled in the graduate program at Capitol College of Maryland, pursuing a master's of Science in Network Security (MSNS).

Jeremy Faircloth (Security+, SSCP, CCNA, MCSE, MCP+I, A+) is a Senior IT Engineer for Gateway, Inc., where he develops and maintains enterprise-wide client/server and Web-based technologies. He also acts as a technical resource for other IT professionals, using his expertise to help others expand their knowledge. As an analyst with over 10 years of real world IT experience, he has become an expert in many areas including Web development, database administration, enterprise security, network design, and project management. Jeremy is a contributor to several Syngress publications including *Hack Proofing XML* (ISBN: 1-931836-50-7), *ASP .NET Developer's Guide* (ISBN: 1-928994-51-2), *SSCP Study Guide & DVD Training System* (ISBN: 1-931836-80-9), and *Security+ Study Guide & DVD Training System* (ISBN: 1-931836-72-8). Jeremy currently resides in Denver, CO and wishes to thank Christina Williams and Austin Faircloth for their support in his various technical endeavors.

James C. Foster (CISSP, CCSE) is the Director of Research and Development for Foundstone, Inc. and is responsible for all aspects of product, consulting, and corporate R&D initiatives. Prior to joining Foundstone, James was a Senior Consultant and Research Scientist with

Guardent, Inc. and an adjunct author at *Information Security Magazine*, subsequent to working as an Information Security and Research Specialist at Computer Sciences Corporation. With his core competencies residing in programming, Web-based applications, cryptography, and wireless technology, James has conducted numerous code reviews for commercial OS components, Win32 application assessments, Web-based application assessments, wireless and wired penetration tests, and reviews on commercial-grade cryptography implementations. James is a seasoned speaker and has presented throughout North America at conferences, technology forums, security summits, and research symposiums with highlights at the Microsoft Security Summit, MIT Wireless Research Forum, SANS, MilCon, TechGov, InfoSec World 2001, and the Thomson Security Conference. He is also commonly asked to comment on pertinent security issues and has been sited in *USAToday, Information Security Magazine, Baseline, Computer World, Secure Computing*, and the *MIT Technologist*. He is a contributor to *Special Ops: Host and Network Security for Microsoft, UNIX, and Oracle* (Syngress Publishing, ISBN:1-931836-69-8). James holds degrees and certifications in Business, Software Engineering, Management of Information Systems, and numerous computer-related or programming-related concentrations and has attended or conducted research at the Yale School of Business, Harvard University, Capitol College, and the University of Maryland.

Vitaly Osipov (CISSP, CCSE, CCNA) is co-author of Syngress Publishing's *Check Point Next Generation Security Administration* (ISBN: 1-928994-74-1) *Cisco Security Specialist's Guide to PIX Firewalls* (ISBN: 1-931836-63-9), *Special Ops: Host and Network Security for Microsoft, UNIX, and Oracle* (ISBN: 1-931836-69-8), and *Managing Cisco Network Security, Second Edition* (ISBN: 1-931836-56-6). Vitaly resides in Australia and has spent the last six years working as a consultant for companies in Eastern, Central, and Western Europe. His specialty is designing and implementing information security solutions. Currently Vitaly is the team leader for the consulting department of a large information security company. In his spare time, he also lends his consulting skills to the antispam company, CruelMail.com. Vitaly would like to extend his thanks to his many friends in the British Isles, especially the one he left in Ireland.

Technical Advisors

Jeffrey Posluns (SSCP, CISSP, CISA, CCNP, CCDA, GSEC) is the Founder of SecuritySage, a leading-edge information security and privacy consulting firm. Jeffrey oversees and directs the professional services teams, product reviews, and innovative product development. Jeffrey has over 11 years experience specializing in security methodologies, audits and controls. He has extensive expertise in the analysis of hacker tools and techniques, intrusion detection, security policies, forensics and incident response. Jeffrey is an industry-recognized leader known for his ability to identify trends, resolve issues, and provide the highest quality of customer service, educational seminars and thought-provoking presentations.

Prior to SecuritySage, Jeffrey founded and co-founded several e-commerce and security initiatives, where he served as President and/or Chief Technology Officer. His responsibilities included such areas as the strategy and implementation of corporate initiatives, project management, professional and managed services, as well as research and development. He has also authored a variety of security-specific books, including the *SSCP Certification Study Guide & DVD Training System* (Syngress Publishing, ISBN: 1-931836-80-9), as well as whitepapers, financial and security-related software, and security toolkits.

Jeffrey is looked to as an authority to speak on IT security related issues and trends at conferences, in the media and law enforcement forums. He is a regular speaker at industry conferences organized by such groups as the Information Systems Audit and Control Association (ISACA) and the Association of Certified Fraud Examiners (ACFE). Jeffrey is also a trainer for the CISSP certification course.

Ryan Russell has worked in the IT field for over 13 years, focusing on information security for the last seven. He is the primary author of *Hack Proofing Your Network: Internet Tradecraft* (Syngress Publishing, ISBN: 1-928994-15-6), and is a frequent technical editor for the Hack Proofing series of books. Ryan founded the vuln-dev mailing list, and moderated it for three years under the alias "Blue Boar." He is a frequent lecturer at security conferences, and can often be found participating in security mailing lists and Web site discussions. Most recently, Ryan has been writing Enforcer, an anti-worm product that uses Snort as its sensor technology. Ryan is the Director of Software Engineering for AnchorIS.com.

Technical Editor

Brian Caswell, a highly respected member of the Snort Community, is the Webmaster for the Snort.org site and the primary individual responsible for maintaining the rules that drive the Snort intrusion detection system. He is highly experienced in deploying intrusion detection systems in both small businesses and enterprise-sized environments, and has spoke on the topic multiple times at the CanSecWest conferences in 2002 and 2003. Brian is an employee of Sourcefire, provider of one of the world's most advanced and flexible intrusion management solutions based on the Snort IDS and founded by the original developer of Snort. In 2002, Sourcefire was recognized as one of the most influential vendors in the IT security marketplace by *Information Security Magazine*.

Contents

Foreword

In our world of ever-increasing Internet connectivity, there is a constant threat of intrusion, denial of service attacks, or countless other abuses of network resources. In the face of these challenges, scores of companies have scrambled to produce software to block and detect network-based attacks. But while intrusion detection software can easily cost thousands or even tens of thousands of dollars, there remains a strong contender in this market: Snort. It's efficient, stable, and has an ever-growing community of users. Best of all, it costs nothing.

The creator of Snort, Marty Roesch, has labeled Snort as a lightweight intrusion detection system; however, Snort is anything but lightweight. Snort is capable of performing real-time IP traffic analysis and packet logging for both the small home user, or even the busiest corporate networks. Its rule-based detection engine is capable of identifying an impressive variety of attacks, including CGI scans, buffer overflows, SMB probes, and can even help track down unauthorized server services across your network. It is even capable of identifying obfuscation and other techniques hackers use to avoid detection.

Snort runs on numerous hardware platforms and OS configurations. Its extensible architecture and open source distribution has long made it a popular choice for intrusion detection. It is not uncommon to see administrators who have already invested thousands of dollars on intrusion detection systems using Snort to fill in the gaps.

At its core, Snort is a network packet sniffer. Run Snort without specifying a ruleset and you will be able to see all of the traffic traversing a network on the same network segment. But it is the rule processor that gives Snort its real power. The flexible and powerful rules language allows a sophisticated analysis of all network traffic, to determine how to handle any particular packet. Snort can choose to ignore, record, or even alert an administrator of specific network traffic. It is capable of utilizing any number of logging or alerting methods, including Syslog, plain text or XML files, and even WinPopup messages to Windows clients. As new types of attacks emerge, updating Snort is simply a matter of adding a new rule.

Although Snort was designed for simplicity, it is not a plug-and-play solution. To use Snort you must become familiar with the power of Snort. The authors of this *Snort 2.0 Intrusion Detection* have gone to great lengths to teach you how to use

Snort, from the basics of getting started to advanced rule configuration, and covers all aspects of using Snort, including basic installation, preprocessor configuration, and optimization of your Snort system. The authors provide a rare and valuable collection of experience and insight to this simple yet powerful tool. Nowhere will you find such complete, in-depth documentation on how to install, configure, and use Snort.

Snort does not try to be everything and by no means tries to compete with commercial intrusion detection applications. But when it comes to the spotting malicious traffic, it performs remarkably well. But to do so requires a solid knowledge of how to configure Snort rules. Chapter 5, *Playing by the Rules*, breaks down the components of Snort rules and teaches how to build effective and efficient rules, detailing every variable, option, and action available.

Chapters 6 and 7 *Preprocessors* and *Implementing Snort Output Plug-Ins* discuss in great detail the preprocessing and output options that allow easy customization and integration of Snort into your existing network environment. The last few chapters provide excellent information on advanced optimization and usage of Snort.

Snort does not provide an easy-to-use graphical interface, flashy reports, or online help. What it does is detect intrusions and it does that well. With its powerful rules engine and simple architecture, it undoubtedly can complement or even replace any commercial IDS you may already have. Snort is an indispensable network security tool; and the *Snort 2.0 Intrusion Detection* book is an indispensable reference for anyone using this tool to protect their networks.

— *Mark Burnett*

## Chapter 1

Intrusion Detection Systems

Solutions in this chapter:

- **What Is Intrusion Detection?**
- **A Trilogy of Vulnerabilities**
- **Why Are Intrusion Detection Systems Important?**
- **What Else Can Be Done with Intrusion Detection Systems**

☑ **Summary**

☑ **Solutions Fast Track**

☑ **Frequently Asked Questions**

Introduction

"Intruder Alert! Intruder Alert! Warning, Will Robinson!" When we heard that ominous announcement emanating from a robot as it twisted and turned with arms thrashing and head spinning, we sat galvanized to our televisions waiting for the intruder to reveal itself. Would this be the end of Will Robinson, as we knew him?

All right, this might be a bit dramatic for a prelude to a discussion of intrusion detection, but with most security administrators, when a beeper goes off there is a moment of anxiety. Is this the big one? Did they get in? Do they own my network? Do they own my data?

These and many other questions flood the mind of the well-prepared security administrator. On the other hand, the ill-prepared security administrator, being totally unaware of the intrusion, experiences little anxiety. For him, the anxiety comes later.

Okay, so how can a security-minded administrator protect his network from intrusions? The answer to that question is quite simple, with an intrusion detection system.

What Is Intrusion Detection?

Webster's dictionary defines an intrusion as "the act of thrusting in, or of entering into a place or state without invitation, right, or welcome." When we speak of intrusion detection, we are referring to the act of detecting an unauthorized intrusion by a *computer* on a *network*. This unauthorized access, or intrusion, is an attempt to compromise, or otherwise do harm, to other network devices.

An Intrusion Detection System (IDS) is the high-tech equivalent of a burglar alarm—a burglar alarm configured to monitor access points, hostile activities, and known intruders. The simplest way to define an IDS might be to describe it as a specialized tool that knows how to read and interpret the contents of log files from routers, firewalls, servers, and other network devices. Furthermore, an IDS often stores a database of known attack signatures and can compare patterns of activity, traffic, or behavior it sees in the logs it is monitoring against those signatures to recognize when a close match between a signature and current or recent behavior occurs. At that point, the IDS can issue alarms or alerts, take various kinds of automatic action ranging from shutting down Internet links or specific servers to launching backtraces, and make other active attempts to identify attackers and actively collect evidence of their nefarious activities.

By analogy, an IDS does for a network what an antivirus software package does for files that enter a system: it inspects the contents of network traffic to look for and deflect possible attacks, just as an antivirus software package inspects the contents of incoming files, e-mail attachments, active Web content, and so forth to look for virus signatures (patterns that match known malware) or for possible malicious actions (patterns of behavior that are at least suspicious, if not downright unacceptable).

To be more specific, intrusion detection means detecting unauthorized use of or attacks on a system or network. An IDS is designed and used to detect and then to deflect or deter (if possible) such attacks or unauthorized use of systems, networks, and related resources. Like firewalls, IDSs can be software based or can combine hardware and software (in the form of preinstalled and preconfigured stand-alone IDS devices). Often, IDS software runs on the same devices or servers where firewalls, proxies, or other boundary services operate; an IDS *not* running on the same device or server where the firewall or other services are installed will monitor those devices closely and carefully. Although such devices tend to operate at network peripheries, IDS systems can detect and deal with insider attacks as well as external attacks.

IDS systems vary according to a number of criteria. By explaining those criteria, we can explain what kinds of IDSs you are likely to encounter and how they do their jobs. First and foremost, it is possible to distinguish IDSs by the kinds of activities, traffic, transactions, or systems they monitor. IDSs can be divided into network-based, host-based, and distributed. IDSs that monitor network backbones and look for attack signatures are called *network-based IDSs*, whereas those that operate on hosts defend and monitor the operating and file systems for signs of intrusion and are called *host-based IDSs*. Groups of IDSs functioning as remote sensors and reporting to a central management station are known as Distributed IDS (DIDS).

In practice, most commercial environments use some combination of network, and host, and/or application-based IDS systems to observe what is happening on the network while also monitoring key hosts and applications more closely. IDSs can also be distinguished by their differing approaches to event analysis. Some IDSs primarily use a technique called *signature detection*. This resembles the way many antivirus programs use virus signatures to recognize and block infected files, programs, or active Web content from entering a computer system, except that it uses a database of traffic or activity patterns related to known attacks, called *attack signatures*. Indeed, signature detection is the most widely used approach in commercial IDS technology today. Another approach is called *anomaly detection.* It uses rules or predefined concepts about "normal" and "abnormal" system activity (called *heuristics*) to distinguish anomalies from normal system behavior and to monitor, report on, or block anomalies as they occur. Some anomaly detection IDSs implement user profiles. These profiles are baselines of normal activity and can be constructed using statistical sampling, rule-base approach or neural networks.

Literally hundreds of vendors offer various forms of commercial IDS implementations as well as an advanced method for interpreting IDS output. Most effective solutions combine network- and host-based IDS implementations. Likewise, the majority of implementations are primarily signature based, with only limited anomaly-based detection capabilities present in certain specific products or solutions. Finally, most modern IDSs include some limited automatic response capabilities, but these usually concentrate on automated traffic filtering, blocking, or disconnects as a last resort. Although some systems claim to be able to launch counterstrikes against attacks, best practices indicate that automated identification and backtrace facilities are the most useful aspects that such facilities provide and are therefore those most likely to be used.

IDSs are classified by their functionality and are loosely grouped into the following three main categories:

- Network-Based Intrusion Detection System (NIDS)
- Host-Based Intrusion Detection System (HIDS)
- Distributed Intrusion Detection System (DIDS)

Network IDS

The NIDS derives its name from the fact that it monitors the entire network. More accurately, it monitors an entire network segment. Normally, a computer network interface card (NIC) operates in nonpromiscuous mode. In this mode of operation, only packets destined for the NICs specific media access control (MAC) address are forwarded up the stack for analysis. The NIDS must operate in promiscuous mode to monitor network traffic not destined for its own MAC address. In promiscuous mode, the NIDS can eavesdrop on all communications on the network segment. Operation in promiscuous mode is necessary to protect your network. However, in view of emerging privacy regulations, monitoring network communications is a responsibility that must be considered carefully.

In Figure 1.1, we see a network using three NIDS. The units have been placed on strategic network segments and can monitor network traffic for all devices on the segment. This configuration represents a standard perimeter security network topology where the screened subnets housing the public servers are protected by NIDSs. When a public server is compromised on a screened subnet, the server can become a launching platform for additional exploits. Careful monitoring is necessary to prevent further damage.

Figure 1.1 NIDS Network

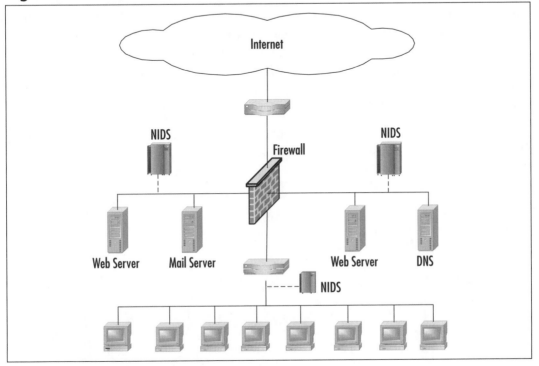

The internal host systems are protected by an additional NIDS to mitigate exposure to internal compromise. The use of multiple NIDS within a network is an example of a defense-in-depth security architecture.

Host-Based IDS

HIDS differ from NIDS in two ways. HIDS protects only the host system on which it resides, and its network card operates in nonpromiscuous mode. Nonpromiscuous mode of operation can be an advantage in some cases, because not all NICs are capable of promiscuous mode. In addition, promiscuous mode can be CPU intensive for a slow host machine.

Another advantage of HIDS is the ability to tailor the ruleset to a specific need. For example, there is no need to interrogate multiple rules designed to detect Domain Name Services (DNS) exploits on a host that is not running. Consequently, the reduction in the number of pertinent rules enhances performance and reduces processor overhead.

Figure 1.2 depicts a network using HIDS on specific servers and host computers. As previously mentioned, the ruleset for the HIDS on the mail server is customized to protect it from mail server exploits, while the Web server rules are tailored for Web exploits. During installation, individual host machines can be configured with a common set of rules. New rules can be loaded periodically to account for new vulnerabilities.

Figure 1.2 HIDS Network

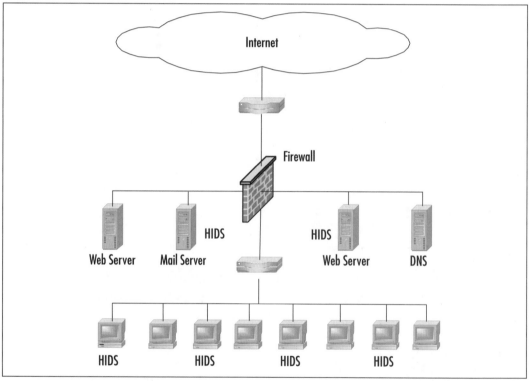

Distributed IDS

The standard DIDS functions in a Manager/Probe architecture. NIDS detection sensors are remotely located and report to a centralized management station. Attack logs are periodically or continuously uploaded to the management station and can be stored in a central database; new attack signatures can be downloaded to the sensors on an as–needed basis. The rules for each sensor can be tailored to meet its individual needs. Alerts can be forwarded to a messaging system located on the management station and used to notify the IDS administrator.

In Figure 1.3, we see a DIDS system comprised of four sensors and a centralized management station. Sensors NIDS 1 and NIDS 2 are operating in stealth promiscuous mode and are protecting the public servers. Sensors NIDS 3 and NIDS 4 are protecting the host systems in the trusted computing base.

Figure 1.3 DIDS Network

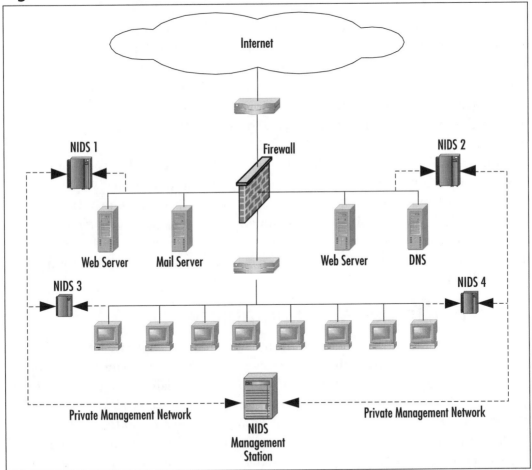

The network transactions between sensor and manager can be on a private network, as depicted, or the network traffic can use the existing infrastructure.

When using the existing network for management data, the additional security afforded by encryption, or VPN technology, is highly recommended.

In a DIDS, complexity abounds. The scope and functionality varies greatly from manufacturer to manufacturer, and the definition blurs accordingly. In a DIDS, the individual sensors can be NIDS, HIDS, or a combination of both. The sensor can function in promiscuous mode or nonpromiscuous mode. However, in all cases, the DIDS' single defining feature requires that the distributed sensors report to a centralized management station.

A Trilogy of Vulnerabilities

The year 2001 will forever live in infamy. The tragic events of the terrorist attack on the World Trade Center had a devastating effect on the American people and on the populace of the entire world. This horrifying occurrence catapulted Americans into a war on terrorism that has redefined our government's position on national security. The newly formed Homeland Security agency's initiatives have profoundly affected the way we view both our daily lives and the security of our country.

Although overshadowed by the terrorist attack, the global Internet community experienced its own moment of truth in 2001, for during that single year the number of Internet attacks exceeded all previous years combined. Barely recovering from one exploit, we were immediately confronted with another.

In this section, we are going to cover three major intrusions of the year 2001. The combined reported incidents numbered in the millions, with a cleanup cost in the billions.

Directory Traversal Vulnerability

In February of 2001 an article authored by Steven Shields appeared on the SANS reading room. Shields wrote that on October 10, 2000 an anonymous user posted a message to the Packetstorm forum in which the user claimed that by the use of a specific URL, he (or she) could execute the DIR command. Thus was born the "Web Server Folder Traversal" vulnerability. The article went on to say that, although an easy fix, this vulnerability is still in use today and is likely to be the access method of choice for most of the attacks against Internet Information Servers (IISs).

This was a true statement then and, to some degree, still is. But perhaps a little history is in order. On August 10, 2000, Microsoft Security Bulletin (MS00-057) was released. This bulletin informed the world that a patch had become available for the "File Permission Canonicalization" vulnerability. We remember that day quite well, for we all sprang from our desks and immediately downloaded and installed the patch, realizing how important "Canonicalization" was to our company. Didn't you?

The MS00-57 bulletin summary stated that Microsoft had released a patch that eliminates security vulnerability in the Microsoft IIS. Under very restricted conditions (known only to the entire hacking community), the vulnerability could allow a malicious user to gain additional permissions to certain types of files hosted on a Web server, should the server be running Microsoft IIS 4.0 or 5.0.

In defense of the determination not to install the patch immediately, there were other entries in the bulletin that cast doubt on the actual dangers of this vulnerability. For example, under the heading "*What's the scope of the vulnerability*" it stated that it could not be used to set arbitrary permissions, that it could only be used to impose the permissions from the bona fide folder's parent, grandparent, and so forth. At the time, no one thought of the Scripts folder as a member of the family. In addition, the scope included the comforting statement—"The vulnerability would not provide a way for the malicious user to locate files on the server."

The scope statement of MS00–057 did not take into account the ability of the Directory Traversal vulnerability to copy the CMD.exe utility into the Scripts directory. The Sadmind/IIS worm used this functionality very effectively. The worm defaced thousands of America's computers with Chinese propaganda and a not very flattering reference to the hacker PoizonBox. The exact GET request used by Sadmind/IIS is as follows:

```
GET/ scripts/../../winnt/system32/cmd.exe /c+
copy+\winnt\system32\CMD.exe+root.exe
```

The GET request uses the Traversal vulnerability and copies CMD.exe as root.exe.

OINK!

For complete details on the Solaris Sadmind/IIS worm and its use of the Directory Traversal vulnerability, access the following URL: www.cert.org/advisories/CA-2001-11.html.

The bulletin concluded with a brief section labeled "*What is canonicalization?*" which consisted of just four lines. To date, there have been thousands of lines written about the subject and its infamous dot dot slash. A part of history now, the dot dot slash, or ..\, is of extreme importance in our discussion of IDSs. The pattern can be used as a *footprint*, or *signature*, and will be discussed in more detail later in this chapter.

CodeRed Worm

On June 19, 2001, the *CERT Advisory CA-2001-13 Buffer Overflow in IIS Indexing Service DLL* was released. As usual, it had very little impact on the information community and went relatively unnoticed by system administrators. However, this small but costly programming oversight would prove to be only the beginning of what would become a billion-dollar exploit.

The advisory stated that a vulnerability existed in the indexing service used by Microsoft IIS 4.0 and IIS 5.0 running on Windows NT, Windows 2000, and beta versions of Windows XP. This vulnerability allows a remote intruder to run arbitrary code on the victim's machine. The advisory description stated that there was a remotely exploitable buffer overflow in one of the ISAPI extensions installed with most versions of IIS 4.0 and 5.0. The specific Internet/Indexing Service Application Programming Interface was IDQ.DLL. The failure of the programmer to check the input would result in one of the most pervasive exploits in history.

On July 19, 2001, just one month later, the world was informed that someone had found a use for the Indexing Service besides indexing. The *CERT Advisory CA-2001-19 "CodeRed" Worm Exploiting Buffer Overflow in Indexing Service DLL* was released. The overview stated that CERT/CC had received reports of a new self-propagating malicious program that exploits IIS systems susceptible to the vulnerability described in *Advisory CA-2001-13*. The report explained that two variants of the CodeRed worm had already affected more than 250,000 servers.

OINK!

CERT The Coordination Center (CERT/CC) is a center of Internet security expertise located at the Software Engineering Institute, a federally funded research and development center operated by Carnegie Mellon University.

Nimda Worm

In September of 2001, an industrious hacker not desirous of reinventing the wheel (or the exploit) developed what would become one of the most devastating Internet worms to date. Said hacker simply bundled together some of the better current exploits and added a few new tricks of his own. The resulting worm would soon be known around the globe as *Nimda*.

On September 18, 2001, an advisory describing the third in a related group of exploits was posted on the CERT.org site. At that time, no one knew this exploit would cost over a billion dollars to clean up. The *CERT Advisory CA-2001-26 Nimda Worm* overview stated that CERT had received reports of a new malicious program known as the W32/Nimda worm. This new worm appeared to spread by multiple vectors.

- Client to client via e-mail
- Client to client via network shares
- From Web server to client via browsing of compromised Web sites
- Client to Web server via active scanning for and exploitation of various IIS 4.0/5.0 Directory Traversal vulnerabilities
- Client to Web server via scanning for the backdoors left by the CodeRed II and Sadmind/IIS worms

Talk about a Swiss army knife of exploits! This one raised the bar on the art of hacking and created a new awareness in network security. The apprehension and paranoia experienced by most system administrators was to be proven justified.

The three historical exploits detailed previously resulted in major financial losses for many organizations; the exploits intruded on corporate, government, and private entities worldwide. The flow of malicious packets knew no boundaries, crossing continents and circumnavigating the globe in a matter of hours. Ill-prepared system administrators suffered enormous damages, loss of data, and extended downtime. In a dark time in American history, with smoke still bellowing from the disaster of the World Trade Center, it was inconceivable for someone to unleash the destruction that Nimda would cause. Nevertheless, someone did.

What Is an Intrusion?

At the scene of a crime, one of the first tasks of the forensic evidence technician is the gathering of fingerprints. These fingerprints can be used to determine the identity of the criminal. Just as in criminal forensics, network forensics technicians gather fingerprints at the scene of a computer crime. The fingerprints are extracted from the victim computer's log and are known as *signatures* or *footprints*. Almost all exploits have a unique signature. Let's look at the signatures of our three: Directory Traversal, CodeRed, and Nimda.

- **Directory Traversal footprint** The Directory Traversal exploit or dot "../" could be used against IIS 4.0 and 5.0 if extended Unicode characters were used to represent the "/" and "\". For example, if a hacker entered the string in Figure 1.4 into his browser, the contents of a directory on the victim's computer would be displayed on the hacker's system. The important part of this example is the uniqueness of the pattern /..%c1. The pattern can be used as a digital fingerprint or signature/footprint in an IDS.

Figure 1.4 Directory Traversal Footprint

```
http://Victim.com/scripts/..%c1%1c../winnt/system32/cmd.exe?/c+dir
```

- **CodeRed footprint** For the CodeRed exploit, the system footprint was provided by *Advisory CA-2001-19* and stated that the CodeRed worm activity can be identified on a machine by the presence of the entry in the Web server log files (Figure 1.5). The footprint of Figure 1.5 is extremely important from an intrusion detection point of view. It represents the information necessary to detect the intrusion before it can do damage to your network.

Figure 1.5 CodeRed Footprint

```
/default.ida?NNNNNNNNNNNNNNNNNNNNNNNNNNNNNNNNNNNNNNNNNNNNNNNNNNNNNNNNNNNNNNNNN
NNNNNNNNNNNNNNNNNNNNNNNNNNNNNNNNNNNNNNNNNNNNNNNNNNNNNNNNNNNNNNNNNNNNNNNNNNNNNN
NNNNNNNNNNNNNNNNNNNNNNNNNNNNNNNNNNNNNNNNNNNNNNNNNNNNNNNNNNNNN%u9090%u6858%ucbd
3%u7801%u9090%u6805%ucbd3% u7801 etc.
```

- **Nimda footprint** The numerous footprints described in the *CERT Advisory CA-2001-26* read like a dictionary of exploits. Within Figure 1.6 are displayed a few of the exploits delivered in its payload. When one is building an *intrusion detection rule*, Nimda's system footprints offer many signatures from which to choose. Furthermore, because the zombie machines or hacker scripts cycle through the complete list, any entry could be used to detect the intrusion. The most obvious one to use (from a security administrator's point of view) is GET /scripts/root.exe. GET root.exe in an HTML request is very suspicious, especially on a Windows machine.

Figure 1.6 Nimda Footprint

```
GET /scripts/root.exe?/c+dir
GET /c/winnt/system32/cmd.exe?/c+dir
GET /d/ winnt/system32/cmd.exe?/c+dir
GET /scripts/..%5c../..%5c../winnt/system32/cmd.exe?/c+dir
GET /_mem_bin/..%5c….%5c../winnt/system32/cmd.exe?/c+dir
GET /_vti_bin/..%5c….%5c../winnt/system32/cmd.exe?/c+dir
```

Using Snort to Catch Intrusions

Snort is an open source network intrusion detection system capable of performing real-time traffic analysis and packet logging on IP networks. Snort can perform protocol analysis, content searching/matching, and can be used to detect a variety of attacks and probes—such as buffer overflows, stealth port scans, CGI attacks, SMB probes, OS fingerprinting attempts, and much more. Snort is rapidly becoming the tool of choice for intrusion detection.

There are three main modes in which Snort can be configured: sniffer, packet logger, and network intrusion detection. Sniffer mode simply reads the packets off the network and displays them in a continuous stream on the console. Packet logger mode logs the packets to the disk. Network intrusion detection mode is the most complex and configurable, allowing Snort to analyze network traffic for matches against a user-defined ruleset and to perform one of several actions, based on what it sees.

Let's take a brief look at Snort's ability to detect the trilogy of intrusions we discuss in this chapter.

Directory Traversal Detection Using Snort

In IDS mode, Snort can be configured to send alerts when a network packet matches the rule stored in its configuration file. As our first example in Figure 1.7, an alert has been generated by Snort for a Directory Traversal exploit. The first line displays the message "WEB-IIS cmd.exe access". The source and destination IP addresses are displayed in line four and are 172.16.60.112 (hacker) and 172.16.60.111 (victim), respectively. The last line of the alert provides a source of information concerning this exploit.

Figure 1.7 Snort Directory Traversal Alert

```
[**] [1:1002:5] WEB-IIS cmd.exe access [**]
[Classification: Web Application Attack] [Priority: 1]
11/25-08:27:24.603264 0:60:8:3:48:D0 -> 0:6:29:15:B4:76 type:0x800 len:0x12E
172.16.60.112:1047 -> 172.16.60.111:80 TCP TTL:128 TOS:0x0 ID:62467
IpLen:20 DgmLen:288 DF
***AP*** Seq: 0x2CE2F8  Ack: 0xBFA3664  Win: 0x2238  TcpLen: 20
```

Figure 1.8 shows the accompanying log entry for this intrusion. The first line displays the message "WEB-IIS cmd.exe access". The second line displays the date, time, type, and length of the packet. The third line displays the source and destination IP addresses. For this example, the box on the end of the sixth line contains the signature data that generated this alert. We recognize from previous discussion the Directory Traversal footprint Get /scripts/..%c1%c1../winnt/system32/cmd.exe?/c+dir.

Figure 1.8 Snort Directory Traversal Log

```
[**] WEB-IIS cmd.exe access [**]
11/25-08:27:24.603264 0:60:8:3:48:D0 -> 0:6:29:15:B4:76 type:0x800 len:0x12E
172.16.60.112:1047 -> 172.16.60.111:80 TCP TTL:128 TOS:0x0 ID:62467
IpLen:20 DgmLen:288 DF
***AP*** Seq: 0x2CE2F8  Ack: 0xBFA3664  Win: 0x2238  TcpLen: 20
47 45 54 20 2F 73 63 72 69 70 74 73 2F 2E 2E 25   GET /scripts/..%
63 31 25 63 31 2E 2E 2F 77 69 6E 6E 74 2F 73 79   c1%c1../winnt/sy
73 74 65 6D 33 32 2F 63 6D 64 2E 65 78 65 3F 2F   stem32/cmd.exe?/
63 2B 64 69 72 20 48 54 54 50 2F 31 2E 31 0D 0A   c+dir HTTP/1.1..
41 63 63 65 70 74 3A 20 2A 2F 2A 0D 0A 41 63 63   Accept: */*..Acc
65 70 74 2D 4C 61 6E 67 75 61 67 65 3A 20 65 6E   ept-Language: en
2D 75 73 0D 0A 41 63 63 65 70 74 2D 45 6E 63 6F   -us..Accept-Enco
64 69 6E 67 3A 20 67 7A 69 70 2C 20 64 65 66 6C   ding: gzip, defl
61 74 65 0D 0A 55 73 65 72 2D 41 67 65 6E 74 3A   ate..User-Agent:
20 4D 6F 7A 69 6C 6C 61 2F 34 2E 30 20 28 63 6F    Mozilla/4.0 (co
6D 70 61 74 69 62 6C 65 3B 20 4D 53 49 45 20 35   mpatible; MSIE 5
2E 30 3B 20 57 69 6E 64 6F 77 73 20 39 38 3B 20   .0; Windows 98;
44 69 67 45 78 74 29 0D 0A 48 6F 73 74 3A 20 31   DigExt)..Host: 1
37 32 2E 31 36 2E 36 30 2E 31 31 31 0D 0A 43 6F   72.16.60.111..Co
6E 6E 65 63 74 69 6F 6E 3A 20 4B 65 65 70 2D 41   nnection: Keep-A
6C 69 76 65 0D 0A 0D 0A                            live....

=+=+=+=+=+=+=+=+=+=+=+=+=+=+=+=+=+=+=+=+=+=+=+=+=+=+=+=+=+=+=+=+
=+=+=+=+=+=+=+=+=+=+
```

CodeRed Detection Using Snort

In Figure 1.9, we see the Snort alert for CodeRed. The first line displays the message "WEB-IIS ISAPI .ida attempt". Line 2 classifies this attack as a Priority of 1. The last line of the alert provides a source of information concerning this exploit.

Figure 1.9 Snort CodeRed Alert

```
[**] [1:1243:6] WEB-IIS ISAPI .ida attempt [**]
[Classification: Web Application Attack] [Priority: 1]
11/25-09:02:48.930399 0:60:8:3:48:D0 -> 0:6:29:15:B4:76 type:0x800 len:0x1E2
172.16.60.112:1051 -> 172.16.60.111:80 TCP TTL:128 TOS:0x0 ID:5636 IpLen:20
DgmLen:468 DF
***AP*** Seq: 0x4D4E13  Ack: 0x2B98C5A9  Win: 0x2238  TcpLen: 20
[Xref => cve CAN-2000-0071][Xref => bugtraq 1065][Xref => arachnids 552]
```

Figure 1.10 show the accompanying log entry for this intrusion. The first line includes the message "WEB-IIS .ida attempt". The signature for the CodeRed exploit can be seen in the box at the end of line six. The display is truncated and includes only a few of the necessary 254 "N" characters. The "N" characters have no particular significance except to overflow the buffer. The CodeRed II exploit used the same overflow mechanism with two hundred fifty four "X" characters.

Figure 1.10 Snort CodeRed Log

```
[**] WEB-IIS ISAPI .ida attempt [**]
11/25-09:02:48.930399 0:60:8:3:48:D0 -> 0:6:29:15:B4:76 type:0x800 len:0x1E2
172.16.60.112:1051 -> 172.16.60.111:80 TCP TTL:128 TOS:0x0 ID:5636 IpLen:20
DgmLen:468 DF
***AP*** Seq: 0x4D4E13  Ack: 0x2B98C5A9  Win: 0x2238 TcpLen: 20
47 45 54 20 2F 47 65 74 25 32 30 2F 64 65 66 61   GET /Get%20/defa
75 6C 74 2E 69 64 61 3F 25 32 30 4E 4E 4E 4E 4E   ult.ida?%20NNNNN
4E 4E 4E 4E 4E 4E 4E 4E 4E 4E 4E 4E 4E 4E 4E 4E   NNNNNNNNNNNNNNNN
4E 4E 4E 4E 4E 4E 4E 4E 4E 4E 4E 4E 4E 4E 4E 4E   NNNNNNNNNNNNNNNN
4E 4E 4E 4E 4E 4E 4E 4E 4E 4E 4E 4E 4E 4E 4E 4E   NNNNNNNNNNNNNNNN
4E 4E 4E 4E 4E 4E 4E 4E 4E 4E 4E 4E 4E 4E 4E 4E   NNNNNNNNNNNNNNNN
```

Nimda Detection Using Snort

Figure 1.11 shows the Snort alert for the Nimda worm. The alert contains the pertinent information for this exploit, including source and destination IP addresses as well as a reference to the *CERT Advisory CA-2001-26*.

Figure 1.11 Snort NIMDA Alert

```
[**] [1:1256:7] WEB-IIS Nimda access [**]
[Classification: Web Application Attack] [Priority: 1]
11/25-09:24:07.903678 0:60:8:3:48:D0 -> 0:6:29:15:B4:76 type:0x800 len:0x19E
172.16.60.112:1052 -> 172.16.60.111:80 TCP TTL:128 TOS:0x0 ID:7940 IpLen:20
DgmLen:400 DF
***AP*** Seq: 0x60D2AA  Ack: 0x3EA1743B  Win: 0x2238  TcpLen: 20
[Xref => url www.cert.org/advisories/CA-2001-26.html]
```

As mentioned earlier, the Nimda worm produced a virtual cornucopia of signatures, each intended to perform a specific exploit. The Snort log display of Figure 1.12 shows only one, the "scripts/root.exe" signature. The file used for this signature was left behind by the CodeRed II worm and is the result of copying the Windows CMD.exe as root.exe. Snort has detected Nimda's attempt to access this backdoor and has generated both an alert and a log entry.

Figure 1.12 Snort NIMDA Log

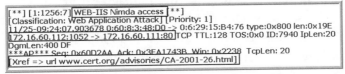

```
[**] WEB-IIS Nimda access [**]
11/25-09:24:07.903678 0:60:8:3:48:D0 -> 0:6:29:15:B4:76 type:0x800 len:0x19E
172.16.60.112:1052 -> 172.16.60.111:80 TCP TTL:128 TOS:0x0 ID:7940 IpLen:20
DgmLen:400 DF
***AP*** Seq: 0x60D2AA  Ack: 0x3EA1743B  Win: 0x2238  TcpLen: 20
47 45 54 20 2F 47 65 74 25 32 30 2F 73 63 72 69   GET /Get%20/scri
70 74 73 2F 72 6F 6F 74 2E 65 78 65 3F 2F 63 2B   pts/root.exe?/c+
64 69 72 20 48 54 54 50 2F 31 2E 31 0D 0A 41 63   dir HTTP/1.1..Ac
```

OINK!

Did I mention that Snort is free? That's right, free.

Why Are Intrusion Detection Systems Important?

Everyone is familiar with the oft-used saying, "What you don't know can't hurt you." However, anyone who has ever bought a used automobile has learned, first hand, the absurdity of this statement. In the world of network security, the ability to know when an intruder is engaged in reconnaissance, or other malicious activity, can mean the difference between being compromised and not being compromised. In addition, in some environments, what you don't know can directly affect employment—yours.

IDSs such as Snort can detect ICMP and other types of network reconnaissance scans that might indicate an impending attack. In addition, the IDS can alert the admin of a successful compromise, which allows him the opportunity to implement mitigating actions before further damage is caused.

IDSs provide the security administrator with a window into the inner workings of the network, analogous to an X-ray or a blood test in the medical field. The ability to analyze the internal network traffic and to determine the existence of network viruses and worms is not altogether different from techniques used by the medical profession. The similarity of network viruses and worms to their biological counterparts has resulted in their medical monikers. IDSs provide the microscope necessary to detect these invaders. Without the aid of intrusion detection, a security administrator is vulnerable to exploits and will become aware of the presence of exploits only after a system crashes or a database is corrupted.

Why Are Attackers Interested in Me?

"The Attack of the Zombies"—sounds a lot like an old B-grade movie, doesn't it? Unfortunately, in this case, it is not cinema magic. Zombie attacks are real and cost corporations and consumers billions. Zombies are computerized soldiers under the control of nefarious hackers, and in the process of performing distributed denial-of-service (DDoS) attacks, they blindly carry out the will of their masters.

In February 2000, a major DDoS attack blocked access to eBay, Amazon.com, AOL-Time Warner, CNN, Dell Computers, Excite, Yahoo!, and other e-commerce giants. The damage done by this DDoS ranged from slowdown to complete system outages. The U.S. Attorney General instructed the FBI to launch a criminal investigation. This historical attack was perpetrated by a large group of compromised computers operating in concert.

The lesson to be learned from this event is that no network is too small to be left unprotected. If a hacker can use your computer, he will. The main purpose of the CodeRed exploit was to perform a DDoS on the White House Web site. It failed, due only to the author's oversight in using a hard-coded IP address instead of DNSs. The exploit compromised over a million computers, ranging from corporate networks to home users.

In light of the war on terrorism and taking into account government-sponsored hacking, the use of an IDS such as Snort can prove crucial in the protection of the world's network infrastructure.

As will be detailed in later chapters, Snort has many rules that can alert the system administrator to the presence of zombies.

Where Does an IDS Fit with the Rest of My Security Plan?

IDSs are a great addition to a network's defense-in-depth architecture. They can be used to identify vulnerabilities and weaknesses in your perimeter protection devices; for example, firewalls and routers. The firewall rules and router access lists can be verified regularly for functionality. In the event these devices are reconfigured, the IDS can provide auditing for change management control.

IDS logs can be used to enforce security policy and are a great source of forensic evidence. Inline IDSs can halt active attacks on your network while alerting administrators to their presence.

Properly placed IDSs can alert you to the presence of internal attacks. Industry analysis of percentages varies. However, the consensus is that the majority of attacks occur from within.

An IDS can detect failed administrator login attempts and recognize password-guessing programs. Configured with the proper ruleset, it can monitor critical application access and immediately notify the system administrator of possible breaches in security.

Doesn't My Firewall Serve as an IDS?

No! Having said that and said it emphatically, we shall try to stop the deluge of scorn from firewall administrators who might take exception to the statement. Admittedly, a firewall can be configured to detect certain types of intrusions, such as an attempt to access the Trojan backdoor SubSeven's port 27374. In addition, it could be configured to generate an alert for any attempt to penetrate your network. In the strictest sense this would be an IDS function. However, it is asking enough of the technology to simply determine what should and shouldn't be allowed into or out of your network without expecting it to analyze the internal contents of every packet. Even a proxy firewall is not designed to examine the contents of all packets; the function would be enormously CPU intensive. Nevertheless, a firewall should be an integral part of your defense-in-depth, with its main function being a gatekeeper.

Where Else Should I Be Looking for Intrusions?

When computers that have been otherwise stable and functioning properly begin to perform erratically and periodically hang or show the Blue Screen of Death, a watchful security administrator should consider the possibility of a *buffer overflow attack*.

Buffer overflow attacks represent a large percentage of today's computer exploits. Failure of programmers to check input code has led to some of the most destructive and costly vulnerabilities to date.

Exploits that are designed to overflow buffers are usually operating system (OS) and application software specific. Without going into detail, the input to the application software is manipulated in such a manner as to cause a system error or "smash the stack" as it is referred to by some security professionals. At this point in the exploit, malicious code is inserted into the computer's process stack and the hacker gains control of the system.

In some cases, for the exploit to be successful, the payload, or malicious code, must access OS functions located at specific memory addresses. If the application is running on an OS other than that for which the exploit was designed, the results of overflowing the buffer will be simply a system crash and not a compromise; the system will appear to be unstable with frequent resets. Interestingly, in this situation the definition of the exploit changes from a system compromise to a DoS attack.

IDSs can alert you to buffer overflow attacks. Snort has a large arsenal of rules designed to detect these attacks; the following are just a few:

- Red Hat lprd overflow

- Linux samba overflow

- IMAP login overflow

- Linux mountd overflow

We discuss these rules, along with many more, in detail later in this book.

Backdoors and Trojans

Backdoors and Trojans come in many flavors. However, they all have one thing in common—they are remote control programs. Some are malicious code designed to "zombiefy" your computer, drafting it into a hacker's army for further exploits. Others are designed to eavesdrop on your keystrokes and send your most private data to their authors. Programs such as Netbus, SubSeven, and BO2k are designed to perform these tasks with minimal training on the part of the hacker.

Remote control programs can have legitimate purposes, such as *remote system administration*. PCAnywhere, Citrix, and VNC are examples of commercial and free remote control programs. However, it should be pointed out that commercial products, in the hands of hackers, could just as easily be used for compromise. The legitimate use of these tools should be monitored, especially in sensitive environments.

Snort has many rules to aide the security administrator in detecting unauthorized use of these programs.

Notes from the Underground....

The Unpatriotic Computer

Being alerted when an attempt to compromise your network is taking place provides valuable information. Such information allows you to take proactive steps to mitigate vulnerabilities, then to take steps to secure your perimeter from further attempts. Equally valuable information, and perhaps even more important, is confirmation that you have been compromised. In other words, while the knowledge of an attempt might be useful, the knowledge of a successful compromise is crucial.

In the early hours of the CodeRed attack, the information available to construct an attack signature was sketchy. The global Internet community

Continued

was reeling from the sheer volume of attacks and trying to cope with the network destruction. During those initial hours, we became aware of the intent of CodeRed. One of its main purposes was to perform a DoS attack on the White House Web site. Thousands of computer zombies operating in concert would have flooded www.whitehouse.gov with 410MB of data every four and a half hours per instance of the worm. The amount of data would quickly have overwhelmed the government computer and rendered it useless.

Armed with this knowledge, at our site we immediately built an attack signature using the White House's IP address of 198.137.240.91 and configured Snort to monitor the egress to the Internet. Any attempt to access this address would generate an alert, plus the log provided us with the source address of the attacking computer. Essentially, what we accomplished was a method of remotely detecting the presence of compromised systems on our internal network.

The author of CodeRed hard-coded the Internet address into the payload, thereby allowing the White House networking administrators to simply change the Internet address and thwart the attack. We continued to use our signature that was built on the old IP address and it proved to be invaluable on many occasions, alerting us to newly compromised systems.

What Else Can Be Done with Intrusion Detection?

The name Intrusion Detection System conjures up a vision of a device that sits on the perimeter of your network alerting you to the presence of intruders. While this is a valid application, it is by no means the only one. IDS can also play an important role in a defense-in-depth architecture by protecting internal assets, in addition to acting as a perimeter defense. Many internal functions of your network can be monitored for security and compliance.

In this section, we look at various internal IDS applications and reveal how Snort can be used to protect your most valuable resources.

Monitoring Database Access

When pondering the selection of a candidate for the "Crown Jewels" of a company, there is no better choice than the company's database. Many times, an organization's most valuable assets are stored in that database. Consider the importance of data to a pharmaceutical research company or to a high-tech software developer. Think the unthinkable—the theft of the U.S. military's launch codes for the nation's Intercontinental Ballistic Missile System. The importance of data confidentially, integrity, and availability in such situations cannot be stressed strongly enough.

Admittedly, database servers are usually located deep within a network and are only accessible by internal resources. However, if one considers the FBI's statistics for internal compromise, this location is not as safe as one might assume. A NIDS, when properly configured on the same segment with your database server, can go a long way in preventing internal compromise.

Snort includes a comprehensive ruleset designed to protect from database exploits. The following are a few examples:

- ORACLE drop table attempt
- ORACLE EXECUTE_SYSTEM attempt
- MYSQL root login attempt
- MYSQL show databases attempt

Monitoring DNS Functions

What's in a name? For our discussion, the important question is, "What's in a name server?" The answer is, "Your network's configuration." The entries in your domain name server might include internal network component names, IP addresses, and other private information about your network. The only information a hacker requires to map your network can be gleaned from a DNS zone transfer. The first step in a DNS reconnaissance probe is to determine the version of your DNS server. Snort detects this intrusion by invoking the rule "DNS Name Version Attempt." The second step in the exploit will be detected by the Snort rule "DNS Zone Transfer Attempt."

IDSs placed at key locations within your network can guard against DNS exploits. Snort offers many rules to protect your namespace.

E-Mail Server Protection

When taking into account e-mail protection, we often resort to e-mail virus-scanning software to mitigate exposure. These programs have matured over the years and have become a formidable defense against attacks stemming from e-mail. Snort has many rules that can detect e-mail viruses such as the QAZ worm,

NAVIDAD worm, and the newest versions of the ExploreZip. In response to a brand new threat or a revision of an existing virus, Snort rules can be modified immediately. Viruses are often in the wild for a considerable amount of time before virus-scanning companies respond with updates; this delay can prove to be a costly one.

In addition, one should develop a comprehensive approach to e-mail security by considering the possibility of an attack on the server itself. Snort has the ability to detect viral e-mail content while simultaneously protecting the e-mail server from attack. It is this added functionality that makes Snort stand out. Snort can be configured to detect and block e-mail bombers, as well as other exploits that might disable your e-mail services.

Using an IDS to Monitor My Company Policy

In today's litigious society, given the enormous legal interest in subjects such as downstream litigation and intellectual property rights, it would be prudent to con-sider monitoring for compliance with your company's security policy. Major motion picture companies have employed law firms specializing in Internet theft of intellectual property. Recently, many companies were sued because their employees illegally downloaded the motion picture *Spiderman*. Some of the employees involved were not aware that their computers were taking part in a crime. Nevertheless, the fines for damages were stiff—up to $100,000 in some cases.

Many file-sharing programs, such as KaZaA and Gnutella, are often used to share content that is federally prohibited. Computers are networked with com-puters in other countries that have differing laws. In the United States, the pos-session of child pornography is a federal offense. One is liable under the law simply for possessing it and can be held accountable whether one deliberately downloaded the content or not.

Summary

IDSs can serve many purposes in a defense-in-depth architecture. In addition to identifying attacks and suspicious activity, you can use IDS data to identify security vulnerabilities and weaknesses.

IDSs can enforce security policy. For example, if your security policy prohibits the use of file-sharing applications such as KaZaA, Gnutella, or messaging services such as Internet Relay Chat (IRC) or Instant Messenger, you could configure your IDS to detect and report this breach of policy.

IDSs are an invaluable source of evidence. Logs from an IDS can become an important part of computer forensics and incident-handling efforts. Detection systems are used to detect insider attacks by monitoring outbound traffic from Trojans or tunneling and can be used as incident management tools to track an attack.

A NIDS can be used to record and correlate malicious network activities. The NIDS is stealthy and can be implemented to passively monitor or to react to an intrusion.

The HIDS plays a vital role in a defense-in-depth posture; it represents the last bastion of hope in an attack. If the attacker has bypassed all of the perimeter defenses, the HIDS might be the only thing preventing total compromise. The HIDS resides on the host machine and is responsible for packet inspection to and from that host only. It can monitor encrypted traffic at the host level, and is useful for correlating attacks that are detected by different network sensors. Used in this manner it can determine whether the attack was successful. The logs from an HIDS are a vital resource in reconstructing an attack or determining the severity of an incident.

Solutions Fast Track

What Is Intrusion Detection?

☑ Unauthorized access, or intrusion, is an attempt to compromise, or otherwise do harm, to your network.

☑ Intrusion detection involves the act of detecting unauthorized and malicious access by a computer or computers.

☑ IDSs use footprints or signatures to identify malicious intrusions.

☑ IDSs can be network based, host based, or distributed systems.

A Trilogy of Vulnerabilities

☑ **Directory Traversal** The Directory Traversal exploit or "../" might be used against IIS 4.0 and 5.0 if extended Unicode characters were used to represent the "/" and "\". If a hacker entered the string using this pattern into his browser, he could force the victim's computer to execute any command he wanted.

☑ **CodeRed** On July 19, 2001, the *CERT Advisory CA-2001-19 "CodeRed" Worm Exploiting Buffer Overflow in Indexing Service DLL* was released. The overview stated that CERT/CC had received reports of a new self-propagating malicious code that exploits IIS systems susceptible to the vulnerability described in *Advisory CA-2001-13*. By the time the second advisory was released, the CodeRed worm had already infected more than 250,000 servers.

☑ **NIMDA** On September 18, 2001, an advisory describing the third in a related group of exploits was posted on the CERT.org site. The *CERT Advisory CA-2001-26 Nimda Worm* overview stated that CERT had received reports of a new malicious code known as the W32/Nimda worm. A virtual Swiss army knife of exploits, this new worm appeared to spread by multiple vectors.

Why Are Intrusion Detection Systems Important?

☑ No network is too small to be left unprotected. If a hacker can use your computer, he will.

☑ Multiple computers operating in concert perform DDoS attacks. Hacker masters need zombies.

☑ Internet pirates use any system available on the Web to store contraband and to distribute stolen software or pornographic content.

☑ Without your knowledge or consent, your system can be used as a relay for nefarious, and oftentimes illegal, activities.

☑ Logs from IDSs are an important part of computer forensics and incident-handling efforts.

☑ IDSs keep you informed of your network's health and security.

☑ IDSs can detect failed administrator login attempts and recognize password-guessing programs.

☑ Inline IDS systems can halt active attacks on your network while alerting administrators to their presence.

☑ IDSs can be used to identify vulnerabilities and weaknesses in your perimeter protection devices; in other words, firewalls and routers.

☑ IDS logs can be used to enforce company policy.

☑ Inline IDSs can halt active attacks on your network while alerting administrators to their presence.

☑ Firewall rules and router access lists can be verified regularly for functionality.

☑ Buffer overflow attacks represent a large percentage of today's computer exploits. Snort has a large arsenal of rules designed to detect these attacks.

☑ Backdoors and Trojans are remote control programs that are malicious code designed to take control of your computer. Snort can detect the communications of these Trojans and alert you to their presence.

☑ E-mail servers are prime targets for intrusions. They must be accessible from the Internet, and thus are vulnerable to attack. Snort has many signatures that guard against direct attacks on the server, as well as detect e-mail borne viruses.

What Else Can Be Done with Intrusion Detection?

☑ IDSs can be used for a variety of functions in addition to detection of intrusions, including monitoring database access, monitoring DNS services, protecting your e-mail server, and monitoring corporate policies.

Frequently Asked Questions

The following Frequently Asked Questions, answered by the authors of this book, are designed to both measure your understanding of the concepts presented in this chapter and to assist you with real-life implementation of these concepts. To have your questions about this chapter answered by the author, browse to **www.syngress.com/solutions** and click on the **"Ask the Author"** form.

Q: I have a firewall. Do I need an IDS?

A: Yes. Firewalls perform limited packet inspection to determine access to and from your network. IDSs inspect the entire packet for malicious content and alert you to its presence.

Q: What is promiscuous mode operation?

A: Normally, when a NIC receives a packet addressed to another device it drops the packet. This type of operation is known as nonpromiscuous mode. In promiscuous mode, the entire packet will be processed regardless of its address. A NIDS must operate in promiscuous mode.

Q: How many IDSs do I need?

A: The number of IDSs in an organization is determined by policy and budget. Network topologies differ greatly; security requirements vary accordingly. Public networks might require minimal security investment, whereas highly classified or sensitive networks might need more stringent controls.

Q: Can an IDS cure a virus?

A: No. Although IDS can detect the signatures of some e-mail viruses, curing a virus is the function of antivirus software.

Q: Can an IDS stop an attack?

A: Yes. An inline IDS can detect and block an intrusion.

Q: Do I need both HIDS and NIDS to be safe?

A: While the use of both NIDS and HIDS can produce a comprehensive design, network topologies vary. Some networks require only a minimum investment in security, while others demand specialized security designs.

## Chapter 2

Introducing Snort 2.0

Solutions in this chapter:

- **What Is Snort?**
- **Snort System Requirements**
- **Exploring Snort's Features**
- **Using Snort on Your Network**
- **Security Considerations with Snort**

☑ **Summary**

☑ **Solutions Fast Track**

☑ **Frequently Asked Questions**

Introduction

You probably picked up this book because you've heard of Snort as an open-source network security solution. However, Snort is more than that. Snort is a full-fledged, open-source, Network-based Intrusion Detection System (NIDS) that has many capabilities. These capabilities include packet sniffing and packet logging in addition to intrusion detection. In addition to all of the basic Snort Features, you can set up Snort to send real-time alerts. This provides you with the ability to receive alerts in real time, rather than having to continuously monitor your Snort system.

Snort is like a vacuum that takes particular items (in this case, packets) and allows you to do different things. You can either watch the items as they get sucked up (packet sniffer), put the items into a container (packet logger), or it can sort them and let you know when a particular item has gone through your NIDS.

So why is Snort so popular? Providing packet sniffing and logging functions is an elementary part of Snort, but Snort's beefiness comes from its intrusion detection capabilities—which matches packet contents to an intrusion rule. Snort might be considered a lightweight NIDS. A "lightweight" intrusion detection system (IDS) is one that has a small footprint and can run on various operating systems (OSs). Additionally, Snort provides functionality only before found in commercial-grade network IDSs such as Network Flight Recorder (NFR) and ISS RealSecure.

Snort's popularity runs parallel to the increasing popularity of Linux and other free OSs such as the BSD-based OSs NetBSD, OpenBSD, and FreeBSD. Just because Snort's roots are in open source does not mean that it's not available for other commercial OSs. On the contrary, you can find ports of Snort available for Solaris, HP-UX, IRIX, and even Windows.

Snort is a signature-based IDS, and uses rules to check for errant packets in your network. A rule is a set of requirements that would trigger an alert. For example, one snort rule to check for peer-to-peer file sharing services checks for the GET string not connecting to a service running on port 80. If a packet matches that rule, that packet creates an alert. Once an alert is triggered, the alert can go a multitude of places, such as a log file, a database, or to an SNMP trap.

Oink!

Snort's logo is a pig, and many references are piggish in nature.

In this chapter, you'll get an understanding of what Snort is, what its features are, and how to use it on your network. Additionally, you'll learn about the history of Snort, and how it came to be such a popular IDS. You'll also learn the importance of securing your Snort system, and some of the pitfalls of Snort. However, Snort's advantages far exceed its pitfalls.

> **OINK!**
>
> There are commercial solutions for Snort as well, but they are out of scope for this chapter. Although Snort is available for free under the GNU Public License (GPL), there are commercial solutions available for Snort through Sourcefire. More information is available about the commercial offerings in Appendix A, "Commercial Options."

What Is Snort?

In short, Snort is a packet sniffer/packet logger/network IDS. However, it's much more interesting to learn about Snort from its inception rather than just to take the in-short answer.

Snort was originally intended to be a packet sniffer. In November 1998, Marty Roesch wrote a Linux-only packet sniffer called APE. Despite the great features of APE, Marty also wanted a sniffer that also does the following:

- Works on multiple OSs

- Uses a hexdump payload dump (TCPDump later had this functionality)

- Displays all the different network packets the same way (TCPDump did not have this)

Marty 's goal was to write a better sniffer for his own use. He also wrote Snort as a libcap application, which gives Snort portability from a network filtering and sniffing standpoint. At the time, only TCPDump was also compiled with libcap, so this gave the system administrator another sniffer with which to work.

Snort became available at Packet Storm (www.packetstormsecurity.com) on December 22, 1998. At that time, Snort was only about 1600 lines of code and had a total of two files. This was about a month after Snort's initial inception, and was only used for packet sniffing at this point. Marty's first uses of Snort included monitoring his cable modem connection and for debugging network applications he coded.

OINK!

The name Snort came from the fact that the application is a "sniffer and more." In addition, Martin said that he has too many programs called a.out, and all the popular names for sniffers called TCP-something were already taken.

Snort's first signature-based analysis (also known as rules-based within the Snort community) became a feature in late January 1999. This was Snort's initial foray down the path of intrusion detection, and Snort could be used as a lightweight IDS at the time.

By the time Snort version 1.5 came out in December 1999, Martin had decided on the Snort architecture that is currently being used until version 2.0. After version 1.5 was released, Snort was able to use all the different plug-ins that are available today.

However, Snort took a backseat to another IDS Marty was working on for a commercial IDS startup. That startup took a sharp nosedive and Marty found himself unemployed. Because of Snort's increasing popularity, Marty thought that it was time to work on Snort and make it easier to configure and get it working in an enterprise environment.

While working on Snort, Marty discovered that between coding and support, Snort was becoming a full-time job. In addition, Marty knew that if he could make Snort work for the enterprise, people would invest money in Snort and support for it. Marty started Sourcefire from this idea. Sourcefire hired most of the core team who developed Snort. However, Snort is still open source and will always be open source. The latest version of Snort is 2.0, which is a rework of the architecture and at press time contains approximately 75,000 lines of code.

Although Sourcefire writes and supports Snort in a commercial release, there will be a GNU release of Snort available.

Even though Snort 2.0 is a complete rewrite and an improvement over the current Snort implementation, Snort has gone though a more in-depth evolution. Snort did not start out with preprocessing ability, nor did it start out with plug-ins. Over time, Snort grew to have improved network flow, plug-ins for databases such as MySQL and Postgres, and preprocessor plug-ins that check RPC calls and port scanning *before* the packets are sent to the rules to check for alerts.

Snort keeps everyone on the latest version by supporting the latest rules only on the latest revision. As of press time, the latest revision is 2.0.0, so the rules only work with those versions.

Speaking of rules, as time progressed, so did the number of rules. The size of the latest rules you download is increasing with the number of exploits available. As a result, the rules became organized by type as they are now. The rule types include P2P, backdoor, distributed denial of service (DDoS) attacks, Web attacks, viruses, and many others. These rules are mapped to a number that is recognized as a type of attack or exploit known as a Sensor ID (SID). For example, the SID for the SSH banner attack is 1838.

Because of Snort's increasing popularity, other IDS vendors are adopting a Snort rule format. TCPDump adopted the hex encoding for packets, and community support is ever increasing. There are at least two mailing lists for Snort:

- **http://lists.sourceforge.net/lists/listinfo/snort-users** A discussion of Snort's usage and application

- **http://lists.sourceforge.net/lists/listinfo/snort-sigs** Dedicated entirely to the Snort rules

Snort System Requirements

Before getting a system together, you need to know a few things. One, Snort data can take up a lot of disk space, and two, you'll need to be able to monitor the system remotely. The Snort system we maintain is in our machine room (which is cold, and a hike downstairs).

Because we're lazy and don't want to hike downstairs, we would like to be able to maintain it remotely *and* securely. For Linux and UNIX, this means including Secure Shell (SSH) and Apache with Secure Sockets Layer (SSL). For Windows, this would mean Terminal Services (with limitation on which users and machines can connect, and Internet Information Servers [IIS]).

Hardware

One of the most important things you'll need, especially if you're running Snort in Network-based Intrusion Detection System (NIDS) mode, is a really big hard drive. If you're storing your data as either syslog files or in a database, you'll need a lot of space to store all the data that the Snort's detection engine uses to check for rule violations.

Another highly recommended hardware component for Snort is a second Ethernet interface. One of the interfaces is necessary for typical network connectivity (SSH, Web services, and so forth), and the other interface is for Snorting. This sensing interface that does the "snorting" is your "Snort sensor."

Snort does not have any particular hardware requirements that your OS doesn't already require to run. Running any application with a faster processor usually makes the application work faster. However, you will be limited in the amount of data you collect by your network connection and by your hard drive.

However, you will need to have a reasonable size network interface card (NIC) to collect the correct amount of network packets. For example, if you are on a 100MB network, you will need a 100MB NIC to collect the correct amount of packets. Otherwise, you will miss packets and be unable to accurately collect alerts.

In addition, you will need a good size hard drive to store your data. If your hard drive is too small, there is a good chance that you will be unable to write alerts to either your database or log files. For example, our current setup for a single Snort sensor is a 9GB partition for /var.

Operating System

Snort was designed to be a lightweight network intrusion system. Currently, Snort can run on x86 systems such as Linux, FreeBSD, NetBSD, OpenBSD, and Windows. Other systems supported include Sparc Solaris, PowerPC MacOS X and MkLinux, and PA-RISC HP-UX. Snort will run on just about any modern OS today.

Oink!

People can get into religious wars as to which OS is best, but *you* have to be the one to administer the system, so you pick the OS that best suits your needs, skills, and environment.

There is an ongoing argument regarding the best OS on which to run Snort. A while back, the *BSDs had the better IP stack, but since Linux has gone to the 2.4 kernel, the IP stacks are comparable. Our favorite is NetBSD, but your mileage might vary.

Other Software

Once you have the basic OS installed, you're ready to go. Make sure that you have the prerequisites before you install:

- autoconf and automake★
- gcc★
- lex and yacc (or the GNU implementations flex and bison, respectively)
- The latest version of libcap from tcpdump.org

OINK!

These are only necessary if you're compiling from source code. If you are using Linux RPMs or Debian packages, you do not need these.

There is other optional software you can install. This includes:

- MySQL, Postgres, or Oracle (SQL databases)
- smbclient if using WinPopup messages
- Apache or another Web server
- PHP or Perl, if you have plug-ins that require them
- SSH for remote access (or Terminal Server with Windows)
- Apache with SSL capabilities for monitoring (or IIS for Windows)

There's more detail on installation in Chapter 3, "Installing Snort."

Exploring Snort's Features

Snort has several features that make it very powerful: packet sniffing, packet logging, and intrusion detection. Before getting into Snort's features, you should understand Snort's architecture. Snort has several important components, most of which take plug-ins to customize your Snort implementation. These components include preprocessors and alert plug-ins, which enable Snort to manipulate a packet to make the contents more manageable by the detection engine, and the alert system, which can send its output through various methods.

Snort can perform several simple tasks; however, if you understand the architecture, Snort makes a lot more sense. Snort consists of four basic components:

- The sniffer
- The preprocessor
- The detection engine
- The output

In its most basic form, Snort is a packet sniffer. However, it is designed to take packets and process them through the preprocessor, and then check those packets against a series of rules (through the detection engine).

Figure 2.1 offers a high-level view of the Snort architecture. In its simplest form, Snort's architecture is similar to a mechanical coin sorter.

1. It takes all the coins (packets from the network backbone).

2. Then it sends them through a chute to determine if they are coins, and how they should roll (the preprocessor).

3. Next, it sorts the coins according to the coin type. This is for storage of quarters, nickels, dimes, and pennies (on the IDS this is the detection engine).

4. Finally, it is the administrator's task to decide what to do with the coins—usually you'll roll them and store them (logging and database storage).

Figure 2.1 Snort Architecture

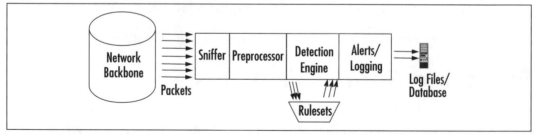

The preprocessor, the detection engine, and the alert components of Snort are all plug-ins. Plug-ins are programs that are written to conform to Snort's plug-in API. These programs used to be part of the core Snort code, but were separated out to make modifications to the core source code more reliable and easier to accomplish.

Packet Sniffer

A packet sniffer is a device (either hardware or software) used to tap into networks. It works in a similar fashion that a telephone wiretap does, but it is used for data networks instead of voice networks. A network sniffer allows an application or a hardware device to eavesdrop on data network traffic. In the case of the Internet, this usually consists of IP traffic, but it can be other traffic such as IPX and AppleTalk network protocols.

Because IP traffic consists of many different types of network traffic, including TCP, UDP, ICMP, routing protocols and IPSec, many sniffers analyze the various network protocols to interpret the packets into something human-readable.

Packet sniffers have various uses:

- Network analysis and troubleshooting

- Performance analysis and benchmarking

- Eavesdropping for clear-text passwords and other interesting tidbits of data

Encrypting your network traffic can prevent people from being able to sniff your packets into something readable. Like any network tool, packet sniffers can be used for good and evil.

As Marty said, he named the application because it does more than sniffing—it snorts. The sniffer needs to be set up to obtain as many packets as possible. As a sniffer, Snort can save the packets to be processed and viewed later as a packet logger. Figure 2.2 illustrates Snort's packet sniffing ability.

Figure 2.2 Snort's Packet Sniffing Functionality

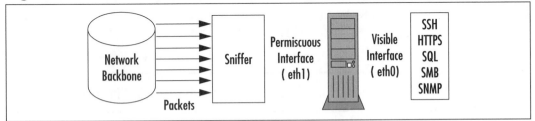

Preprocessor

At this point, our coin sorter has obtained all the coins it can (packets from the network), and is ready to send the packets through the chute. Before rolling the coins (the detection engine), the coin sorter needs to determine if they are coins.

This is done through the preprocessor. The preprocessor takes the raw packets and checks them against certain plug-ins (like an RPC plug-in and a port scanner plug-in). These plug-ins check for a certain type of behavior from the packet. Once the packet is determined to have a particular type of "behavior," it is then sent to the detection engine. From Figure 2.3, you can see how the pre-processor uses its plug-ins to check a packet.

Figure 2.3 Snort's Preprocessor

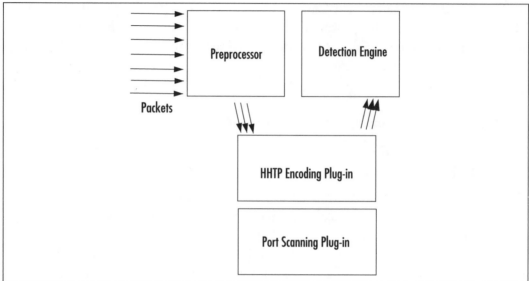

This is such a great feature for an IDS because other plug-ins can be enabled and disabled as they are needed at the preprocessor level. For example, you can say you don't care about RPC traffic coming into your network for whatever reason. You can disable this plug-in and use the others.

OINK!

More information on the preprocessors is in Chapter 6, "Preprocessors."

Detection Engine

The detection engine is the meat of the IDS in Snort. The detection engine takes the data that comes from the preprocessor and its plug-ins, and that data is checked through a set of rules. If the rules match the data in the packet, then they are sent to the alert processor.

Earlier in this chapter, we described Snort as a signature-based IDS. The signature-based IDS function is accomplished by using various rulesets. The rulesets are grouped by category (Trojan horses, buffer overflows, access to various applications), and are updated regularly.

The rules themselves consist of two parts:

- **The rule header** The rule header is basically the action to take (log or alert), type of network packet (TCP, UDP, ICMP, and so forth), source and destination IP addresses, and ports

- **The rule option** The option is the content in the packet that should make the packet match the rule.

The detection engine and its rules are the largest portion (and steepest learning curve) to learn and understand with Snort. Snort has a particular syntax that it uses with its rules. Rule syntax can involve the type of protocol, the content, the length, the header, and other various elements, including garbage characters for defining butter overflow rules.

Once you get it working and learn how to write Snort rules, you can fine-tune and customize Snort's IDS functionality. You can define rules that are particular to your environment and customize however you want.

The detection engine is the part of the coin sorter that actually rolls the coins based on the type. The most common American coins are the quarter, dime, nickel, and penny. However, you might get a coin that doesn't match, like the Kennedy half-dollar, and discard it. This is illustrated in Figure 2.4.

For more on Snort's rules, please refer to Chapter 5, "Playing by the Rules."

Alerting/Logging Component

After the Snort data goes through the detection engine, it needs to go out somewhere. If the data matches a rule in the detection engine, then an alert is triggered. Alerts can be sent to a log file, through a network connection, through UNIX sockets or Windows Popup (SMB), or SNMP traps. The alerts can also be stored in an SQL database such as MySQL and Postgres.

Additionally, there are all sorts of additional tools you can use with Snort here. These include various plug-ins for Perl, PHP, and Web servers to display the logs through a Web interface. Logs are stored in either text files (by default in /var/log/snort) or in a database such as MySQL and Postgres.

Figure 2.4 Snort's Detection Engine

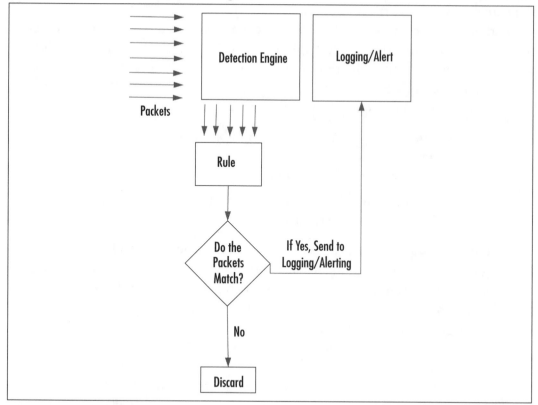

Like the detection engine and the preprocessor, the alert component uses plug-ins to send the alerts to databases and through networking protocols such as SNMP traps and WinPopup messages. See Figure 2.5 for an illustration of how this works.

Additionally, with syslog tools such as Swatch, Snort alerts messages can be sent via e-mail to notify a system administrator in real time so no one has to monitor the Snort output all day and night.

Table 2.1 lists a few examples of various useful third-party programs and tools. For more on how to handle Snort's data, see Chapter 8, "Exploring the Data Analysis Tools."

Figure 2.5 Snort's Alerting Component

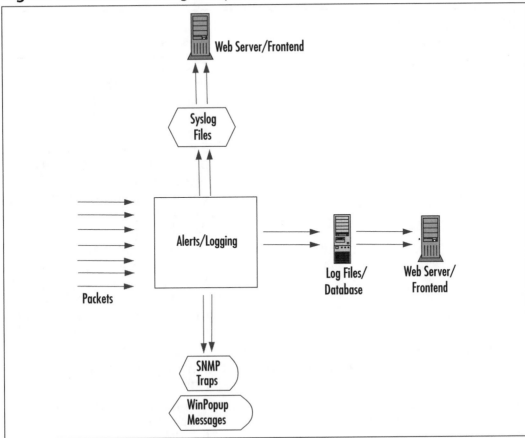

Table 2.1 Useful Snort Add-Ons

Output Viewer	URL	Description
SnortSnarf	www.silicondefense.com/ software/snortsnarf	A Snort analyzer by Silicon Defense used for diagnostics. The output is in HTML.
Snortplot.php	www.snort.org/dl/contrib/ data_analysis/snortplot.pl	A Perl script that will graphically plot your attacks.
Swatch	http://swatch.sourceforge.net	A real-time syslog monitor that also provides real-time alerts via e-mail.

Continued

Table 2.1 Useful Snort Add-Ons

Output Viewer	URL	Description
ACID	http://acidlab.sourceforge.net	The Analysis Console for Intrusion Databases. Provides logging analysis for Snort. Requires PHP, Apache, and the Snort database plug-in. Since this information is usually sensitive, it is strongly recommended that you encrypt this information by using mod_ssl with Apache or Apache-SSL.
Demarc	www.demarc.com	A commercial application that provides an interface similar to ACID's. It also requires Perl, and it is also strongly recommended that you encrypt the Demarc sessions as well.
Razorback	www.intersectalliance.com/ projects/RazorBack/index.html	A GNOME/X11-based real-time log analysis program for Linux.
Incident.pl	www.cse.fau.edu/~valankar/ incident	A Perl script used for creating incident reports from a Snort log file.
Loghog	http://sourceforge.net/ projects/loghog	A proactive Snort log analyzer that takes the output and can e-mail alerts or block traffic by configuring IPTables rules.
Oinkmaster	www.algonet.se/~nitzer/ oinkmaster	A tool used to keep your rules up to date.
SneakyMan	http://sneak.sourceforge.net	A GNOME-based Snort rules configurator.
SnortReport	www.circuitsmaximus.com/ download.html	An add-on module that generates real-time intrusion detection reports.

Using Snort on Your Network

Your IDS can use just one Snort system, or more than one if you need redundancy. For example, it is possible to divide the task of network monitoring across multiple hosts. The chief benefit of dividing tasks is redundancy—if one element of the system goes down, the network can still be monitored and protected.

The previously outlined network structure can be used for *passive monitoring* or *active monitoring*. Passive monitoring is simply the ability to listen to network traffic and log it. Active monitoring involves the ability to either:

- Monitor traffic and then send alerts concerning the traffic that is discovered

- Actually intercept and block this traffic

Snort is primarily used for active auditing. Don't intrusion detection applications also do signature-based and anomaly-based detection? Signature-based detection means that you predefine what an attack looks like, and then configure your network monitoring software to look for that signature. Anomaly based detection requires the IDS to actually listen to the network and gather evidence about "normal" traffic. Then, if any traffic occurs that seems different, the IDS will respond by, for example, sending out an alert to the network administrator.

After dealing with a post-mortem on a compromised system, it's amazing how helpful a Snort NIDS can be. On the flip side, it's also frustrating when your Snort system does not log a possible attack. Let's take a possible attack: the IMAP login overflow attack. In this case, an attacker tries a buffer overflow to cause a remote root exploit.

Snort can let you know that someone is sending an IMAP packet that contains the signature of an IMAP login overflow. Depending on how you have Snort set up, you can either monitor the output or you can be notified by e-mail. Great, now you can yank the Ethernet cable from the wall and look at the corpse and find some tools used to break into the system and what they plan on doing on your machine.

The rule for detecting this attack is:

```
alert tcp $EXTERNAL_NET any -> $HOME_NET 143 (msg:"IMAP login buffer \
    overflow attempt"; flow:established,to_server; content:"LOGIN";    \
    content:"{"; distance:0; nocase;                                   \
    byte_test:5,>,256,0,string,dec,relative; reference:bugtraq,6298;   \
    classtype:misc-attack; sid:1993; rev:1;)
```

This rule checks for any packet originating from the external network (defined by EXTERNAL_NET) to any system on the internal network (defined by HOME_NET) to port 143, which is the IMAP port. The *msg* variable defines what is sent to the Snort alert, and the rest of the information of the packet is content based. There are definitions on the type of attack (*misc-attack*), the SID number (1993), and the Bugtraq (www.securityfocus.com) reference on the attack *6298* (which you can find at www.securityfocus.com/bid/6298).

OINK!

More information on rules and the detection engine is in Chapter 5.

Then, there's the flip side: Snort does not detect an attack on your system. Take another UNIX system you have running. This one is running Apache with FrontPage extensions (gasp!). Someone finds a new overflow on FrontPage for which there is no Snort rule yet, and then he has your box. Not to mention, your security solution did not provide any assistance with the attack.

Snort's Uses

Snort has three major uses:

- A packet sniffer
- A packet logger
- A NIDS

All the uses relate to each other in a way that builds on each other. However, it's easiest to put the packet sniffer and the packet logger together in the same category—basically, it's the same functionality. The difference is that with the logging functionality; you can save the packets into a file. Conversely, you can read the packet logs with Snort as well.

Using Snort as a Packet Sniffer and Logger

In its simplest form, Snort is a packet sniffer. That said, it's the easiest way to start. The command-line interface for packet sniffing is very easy to remember:

```
# snort -d -e -v
```

Note that the *-v* option is required. If you run Snort on a command line without any options, it looks for the configuration file (.snortrc) in your home directory. Snort configuration files are discussed in detail in Chapter 3.

Table 2.2 lists Snort options and their function.

Table 2.2 Basic Snort Options for Packet Sniffing and Logging

Option	What It Does
-v	Put Snort in packet sniffing mode (TCP headers only)
-d	Include all network layer headers (TCP, UDP, and ICMP)
-e	Include the data link layer headers

You cannot use options *−d* and *−e* together without also using the *−v* option. If you do, you get the same output if you use *snort* without any options:

```
florida:/usr/share/doc/snort-doc# snort -de
Log directory = /var/log/snort


Initializing Network Interface eth0
using config file /root/.snortrc
Parsing Rules file /root/.snortrc


+++++++++++++++++++++++++++++++++++++++++++++++++++++
Initializing rule chains...
ERROR: Unable to open rules file: /root/.snortrc or /root//root/.snortrc
Fatal Error, Quitting..
```

Now, if you run snort with the *−v* option, you get this:

```
florida:/usr/share/doc/snort-doc# snort -v
Log directory = /var/log/snort

Initializing Network Interface eth0

    --== Initializing Snort ==--
Decoding Ethernet on interface eth0

    --== Initialization Complete ==--
```

```
01/22-20:27:44.272934 192.168.1.1:1901 -> 239.255.255.250:1900

UDP TTL:150 TOS:0x0 ID:0 IpLen:20 DgmLen:297

Len: 277

=+=+=+=+=+=+=+=+=+=+=+=+=+=+=+=+=+=+=+=+=+=+=+=+=+=+=+=+=+=+=+=+=+=+=+

01/22-20:27:44.273807 192.168.1.1:1901 -> 239.255.255.250:1900

UDP TTL:150 TOS:0x0 ID:1 IpLen:20 DgmLen:353

Len: 333

=+=+=+=+=+=+=+=+=+=+=+=+=+=+=+=+=+=+=+=+=+=+=+=+=+=+=+=+=+=+=+=+=+=+=+

[]
```

After a while, the text scrolls off your screen. Once you press **Ctrl-C**, you get an output summary that summarizes the packets that Snort picked up, by network type (TCP, UDP, ICMP, IPX), data link information (including ARP), wireless packets, and any packet fragments.

```
Snort analyzed 56 out of 56 packets, dropping 0(0.000%) packets
Breakdown by protocol:          Action Stats:
      TCP: 0      (0.000%)        ALERTS: 0
      UDP: 44     (78.571%)       LOGGED: 0
     ICMP: 0      (0.000%)        PASSED: 0
      ARP: 1      (1.786%)
    EAPOL: 0      (0.000%)
     IPv6: 0      (0.000%)
      IPX: 0      (0.000%)
    OTHER: 11     (19.643%)
  DISCARD: 0      (0.000%)
===========================================================================
Wireless Stats:
Breakdown by type:
   Management Packets: 0    (0.000%)
   Control Packets:    0    (0.000%)
   Data Packets:       0    (0.000%)
===========================================================================
Fragmentation Stats:
Fragmented IP Packets: 0   (0.000%)
   Fragment Trackers: 0
   Rebuilt IP Packets: 0
```

```
      Frag elements used: 0
Discarded(incomplete): 0
    Discarded(timeout): 0
   Frag2 memory faults: 0
========================================================================
TCP Stream Reassembly Stats:
      TCP Packets Used: 0        (0.000%)
      Stream Trackers:  0
      Stream flushes:   0
      Segments used:    0
      Stream4 Memory Faults: 0
========================================================================
Snort received signal 2, exiting
```

Since this isn't very useful for checking the data of the packets, we'll run snort with the *–dev* option to give us the most information:

```
florida:/usr/share/doc/snort-doc# snort -dev
Log directory = /var/log/snort


Initializing Network Interface eth0


    --== Initializing Snort ==--
Decoding Ethernet on interface eth0


    --== Initialization Complete ==--


01/22-20:28:16.732371 0:4:5A:F2:F7:84 -> 1:0:5E:7F:FF:FD type:0x800 len:0x5B
131.215.183.30:57535 -> 239.255.255.253:427 UDP TTL:254 TOS:0x0 ID:26121
IpLen:20 DgmLen:77
Len: 57
02 01 00 00 31 20 00 00 00 00 73 70 00 02 65 6E  ....1 ....sp..en
00 00 00 17 73 65 72 76 69 63 65 3A 64 69 72 65  ....service:dire
63 74 6F 72 79 2D 61 67 65 6E 74 00 00 00 00 00  ctory-agent.....
00


=+=+=+=+=+=+=+=+=+=+=+=+=+=+=+=+=+=+=+=+=+=+=+=+=+=+=+=+=+=+=+=+=+=+=+=+
```

```
01/22-20:28:18.354830 0:4:5A:F2:F7:84 -> 1:0:5E:0:0:2 type:0x800 len:0x3E
131.215.184.253:1985 -> 224.0.0.2:1985 UDP TTL:2 TOS:0x0 ID:0 IpLen:20
DgmLen:48
Len: 28
00 00 10 03 0A 78 01 00 63 69 73 63 6F 00 00 00   .....x..cisco...
83 D7 B8 FE                                       ....


=+=+=+=+=+=+=+=+=+=+=+=+=+=+=+=+=+=+=+=+=+=+=+=+=+=+=+=+=+=+=+=+=+=+=+=+
```

If you've used TCPDump before, you will see that Snort's output in this mode looks very similar. It looks very typical of a packet sniffer in general.

```
{date}-{time} {source-hw-address} -> {dest-hw-address} {type}
{length} {source-ip-address:port} -> {destination-ip-address:port}
{protocol} {TTL} {TOS} {ID} {IP-length} {datagram-length} {payload-length}
{hex-dump} {ASCII-dump}
```

This is all great information you're gathering, and Snort can collect it into a file as well as display it to standard output. Snort has built-in packet logging mechanisms that you can use to collect the data as a file, sort it into directories, or store the data as a binary file.

To use the packet logging features, the command format is simple:

```
# snort -dev -l {logging-directory} -h {home-subnet-slash-notation}
```

If you wanted to log the data into the directory /var/adm/snort/logs with the home subnet 10.1.0.0/24, you would use the following:

```
# snort -dev -l /var/adm/snort/logs -h 10.1.0.0/24
```

However, if you log the data in binary format, you don't need all the options. The binary format is also known as the TCPDump formatted data file. Several packet sniffers use the TCPDump data format, including Snort.

The binary format for Snort makes the packet collection much faster because Snort doesn't have to translate the data into a human readable format immediately. You only need two options: the binary log file option *-L* and the binary option *-b*.

For binary packet logging, just run the following:

```
# snort -b -L {log-file}
```

For each log file, Snort appends a timestamp to the specified filename.

It's great that you're able to collect the data. Now, how do you read it? What you need to do is parse it back through Snort with filtering options. You also have the option to look at the data through TCPDump and Ethereal, as they use the same type of format for the data.

```
# snort [-d|e] -r {log-file} [tcp|udp|icmp]
```

The last item on the line is optional if you want to filter the packets based on packet type (for example, TCP). To take further advantage of Snort's packet logging features, you can use Snort in conjunction with the Berkeley Packet Filter (BPF).

```
# snort -vd -r <file> <bpf_filter>
```

The BPF allows packets to be filtered at the kernel level. This can optimize performance of network sniffers and loggers by eliminating packets with the best performance because it happens at such a low level in the operating system.

The following are some examples of BPF filters. They are commonly used for ignoring packets, and work with expressions (and, or, not).

If you want to ignore all traffic to one IP address:

```
# snort -vd -r <file> not host 10.1.1.254
```

If you want to ignore all traffic from the 10.1.1.0 network to destination port 80:

```
# snort -vd -r <file> src net 10.1.1 and dst port 80
```

If you want to ignore all traffic coming from host 10.1.1.20 on port 22:

```
# snort -vd -r <file> not host 10.1.1.20 and src port 22
```

Using Snort as an NIDS

Now that you understand the basic options of Snort, you can see where the IDS comes into play. To make Snort an IDS, just add one thing to the packet logging function: the configuration file.

```
# snort -dev -l /var/adm/snort/logs -h 10.1.0.0/24 -c /root/mysnort.conf
```

Your rules are in the configuration file, and they are what trigger the alerts. We discuss rules in depth in Chapter 5.

Snort and Your Network Architecture

So, how do you make Snort as useful as possible? You put the Snort system(s) on your network where it will be most usefulness. Where this is depends on several factors: how big your network is, and how much money you can get your management to spend on Snort systems.

If you cannot get enough money to acquire enough Snort systems to achieve the optimal designs shown in Figure 2.6, you'll need to see what you can use from a practical sense. If you need to limit your spending, forego the system inside the router and just make sure you have the Snort systems inside the subnets you want to protect.

Figure 2.6 An IDS Network Architecture with a Screening Router

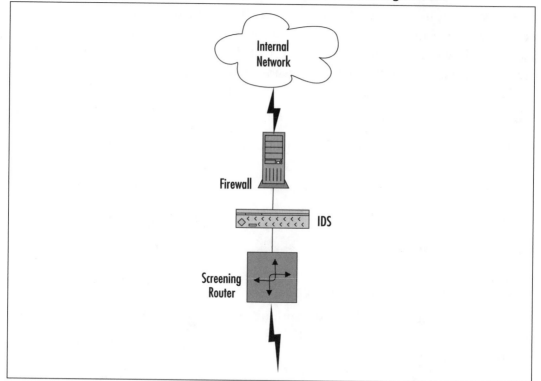

Many network administrators set up a screening router. This enables the router to act as a poor-man's firewall and stop packets at the network level, usually by their well-known ports. The problem with this is that many packets can be rerouted through other ports.

However, if a packet gets past your screening router, this might be a good place to put your IDS. This enables you to detect what you deem as attacks while enabling some filtering to hopefully catch some of the problems with the router. Figure 2.6 shows the IDS network architecture with a screening router.

In this case, you would want to put an IDS system on the inside of your firewall and another in between your outside router and your firewall. Here we're also assuming that your router is filtering some traffic through the access lists as well. You do not want your Snort system on the outside of your network because it will increase your false positive rate, and it leaves your Snort system more vulnerable to attack. This is illustrated in Figure 2.7. Most important is the Snort system inside your firewall. This is the one you should monitor frequently for attacks. This system should only trigger alerts from possible legitimate attacks, and produce much fewer false alerts, or a false positive. However, the Snort system in between your router and your firewall will also provide you with useful information—especially for a postmortem on a compromised system.

Figure 2.7 A Firewalled Network with Snort Systems

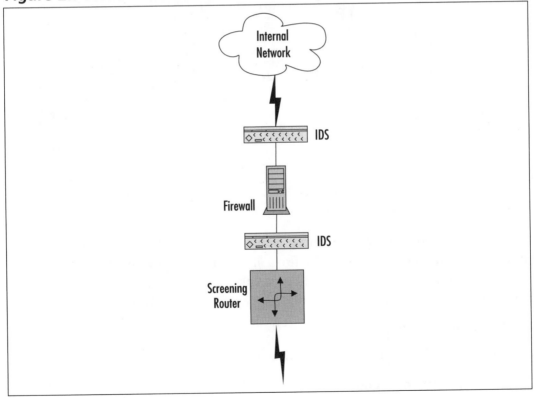

However, many network architectures do have a Demilitarized Zone (DMZ) for providing public services such as Web servers, FTP servers, and application servers. DMZs can also be used for an extranet (which is a semi-trusted connection to another organization), but we'll stick to the public server DMZ architecture in this example. This is illustrated in Figure 2.8.

Figure 2.8 A Firewalled Network with a DMZ

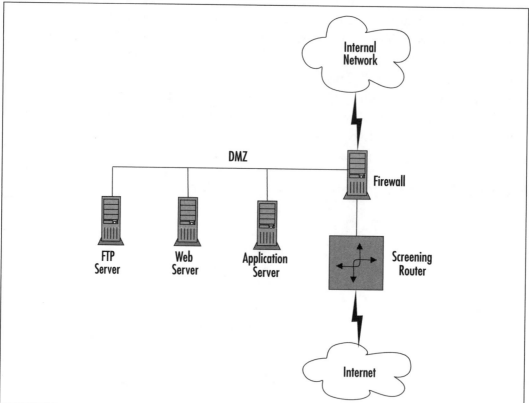

In this case, you would want three Snort systems: one inside the router, one inside the DMZ, and one inside the firewall. The reason for the additional IDS machine is because you have an additional subnet to defend. Therefore, a good rule of thumb for an optimal situation for your Snort systems is:

- One inside the router
- One inside each subnet you want to protect

This is illustrated in Figure 2.9.

Figure 2.9 A Firewalled Network with a DMZ and Snort

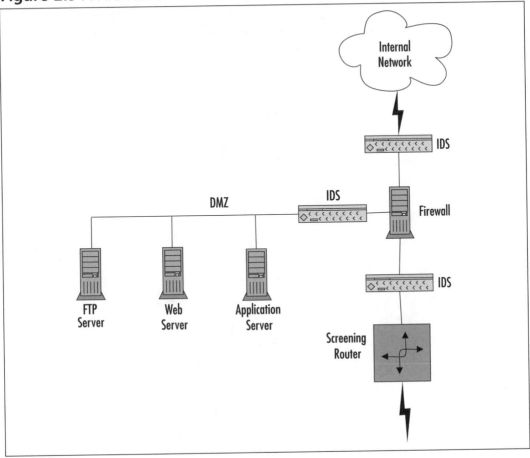

Snort and Switched Networks

Snort can be used on a switched network as well. As switches become increasingly popular, monitoring them with Snort (or any other IDS) becomes more and more critical. Your switch can either be inside your router or inside your firewall.

A switch provides you with Layer 2 (Data Link layer of the OSI seven layer model) configurability, including virtual LANs (VLANs), which allows you to subnet directly at the switch. Switches have also been used as overpriced routers. In this case, you'll want to save your money if you're not using your switch's features.

In this case, you can connect the Snort system directly to the switch. The switch has a Switch Port ANalyser port (SPAN) port, which is where the Snort system will be connected. The Snort system then takes "copies" of the packets to be analyzed. This is illustrated in Figure 2.10.

Figure 2.10 A Switched Network

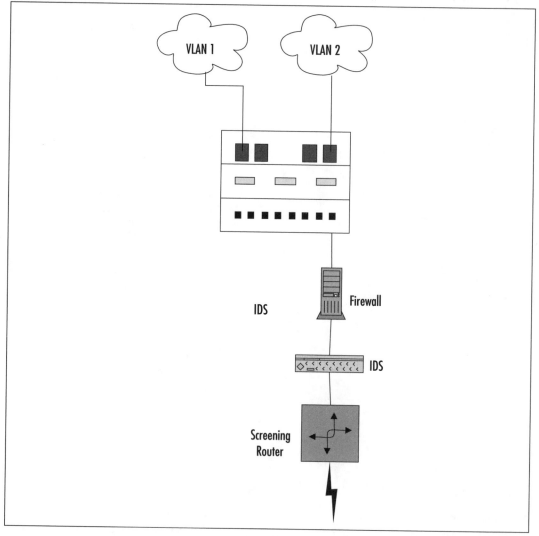

In this case, you'll have to decide which other ports on your switch you want to monitor with the SPAN port. Usually, you will monitor just one port; otherwise, you can flood the SPAN port. This might kill the performance of both your switch and your IDS. This is illustrated in Figure 2.11.

Figure 2.11 A Switched Network with Snort Systems

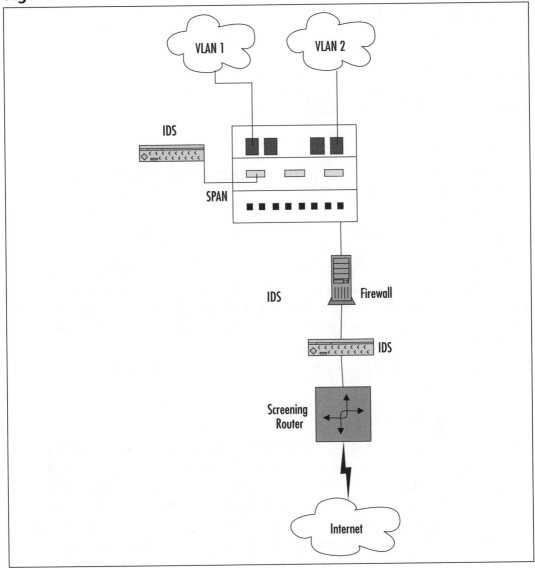

Pitfalls When Running Snort

Snort is a wonderful tool; however, like all tools, it has its pitfalls. Snort has three major pitfalls:

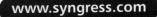

- Not picking up all the packets
- False positive alerts
- False negative alerts

Snort might not pick up all packets because of the speed of the network and the speed of the promiscuous interface. This can also be dependent on the network stack implementation of the operating system.

False Alerts

False positives are when Snort gives you a warning when it shouldn't. Basically, a false positive is a false alarm. If you go with a default ruleset with Snort, then you will definitely get many false alarms. This can trigger a lot of alerts until you decide what is relevant to your network. The more open your network is, the more alarms you'll want to monitor.

On the opposite end, you can get false negatives. In other words, someone compromises a Snort-monitored system and your Snort system doesn't detect it. You might think that this doesn't happen, but when you get an e-mail from another system administrator describing a suspicious activity and your Snort system didn't pick it up, well, this is a very real scenario. Make sure you keep your Snort rulesets up to date, and your expectations on what you expect from your Snort system.

Upgrading Snort

Upgrading Snort can be quite painful for two reasons: the ruleset syntax might change, and the interface to the alert logs. We have found both to be obstacles when trying to upgrade Snort systems, and can be quite a pain to deal with.

Additionally, Snort has changed its architecture with Snort 2.0 to increase performance and hopefully make the rulesets easier to handle. However, it will also mean a possible painful upgrade to make sure that Snort still can read your custom rulesets and use your alert interface.

Security Considerations with Snort

Even though you are using Snort to improve your security, making sure that your Snort system is as secure as possible will make the data trustworthy. If someone breaks into your Snort system, there is no reason to trust the alerts it sends, thereby making the system completely useless until after you wipe the disks and reinstall everything.

Snort Is Susceptible to Attacks

With that said, a typical Snort installation is subject to attacks. Why? You'll want to get in remotely (SSH) and you'll probably want to store the alerts in a database (MySQL or Postgres). In addition, you'll probably want to view the alerts with a spiffy interface that might require a Web server (Apache or IIS).

This makes your Snort system just like any other application, so stay on top of security vulnerability announcements and OS security announcements.

Now, based on this information, you have several ports open on your Snort system: SSH (port 22), HTTP (port 80), HTTPS (port 443), and possibly MySQL (port 3306) or Postgres (port 5432). Now, anyone with access to a network can use NMAP and portscan your sniffer directly on its nonpromiscuous interface.

This is something that needs to be addressed because all of the preceding applications have had quite a few serious security issues, even as recently as last year (2002). In addition to making sure that your applications are up to date, you need to make sure that your kernel is configured properly and also up to date. You didn't think that running Snort allows you to disregard basic system administration practices, did you?

Notes from the Underground....

Snort Security Vulnerabilities

All applications end up with some discovered vulnerability; however, Snort's are minimal. For a security application, SSH seems to have the lead on the amount of security vulnerabilities discovered.

Snort, however, has very few in its few years of existence. It's nice to see a security application practice good security. The Snort core has never had a network-based vulnerability, excluding a DoS attack if Snort was configured in a nonstandard manner. Third party plug-ins can be vulnerable, but they aren't part of the Snort core, which helps keep Snort itself secure. Table 2.2 lists Snort's vulnerabilities to date.

Continued

Table 2.2 Snort's Vulnerabilities to Date

Version	Vulnerability	Fixed
1.8	Snort dumps core. This was a bug in the stream preprocessing.	1.8.1
Prior to 1.8.1	Unicode HTTP encoding to IIS can be used to bypass Snort.	1.8.1
1.8.3	DoS attack from incorrect ICMP handling.	1.8.4
1.8.6	State problems were generated by fragroute.	1.8.7 beta1
1.9.0 and earlier	Buffer overflow in the RPC preprocessor plug	1.9.1

Securing Your Snort System

Even though your Snort implementation is locked down, your system itself might not be. Make sure you do the basics. There are some things you need to do; no excuses.

- **Turn off services you don't need.** Services like Telnet, the Berkeley R services, FTP, NFS, and NIS should not be running on your system In addition, make sure you don't have any of the useless services running; for example, echo, discard, and chargen.

- **Maintain system integrity.** Tripwire is a freeware application that checks for those backdoors and Trojans you don't suspect. There are plenty of other freeware applications like Tripwire—AIDE and Samheim are two worth mentioning.

- **Firewall or TCP Wrap the services you do use.** Services like SSH and MySQL should be TCP wrapped or firewalled, as they have their own security holes as well. For services that you can't TCP Wrap such as Apache, make sure you have it configured as securely as possible. IPTables is the latest version of the Linux firewall, and there are plenty of references on how to implement it.

- **Encrypt and use public key authentication as much as you can.** You should enable public key authentication only for OpenSSH. Another thing you might want to consider doing for Apache for using it to view logs is to use Apache-SSL and use digital certificates for client-side authentication. This helps keep the obvious people out of your system through the usual compromisable channels.

■ **Patch, patch, patch.** We cannot stress this enough. Make sure you keep your patches and packages up to date as much as possible. Stay on top of applications you use and their security announcements—the same goes for any operating system you use. For FreeBSD/NetBSD/OpenBSD, make sure you keep your ports and packages up to date. For Red Hat Linux, make sure you stay on top of the updated RPMs. For those of you who are using Debian, you'll have the easiest time as long as you remember to run *apt-get update && apt-get upgrade* on a regular basis.

Summary

This chapter provided practical knowledge of the open-source IDS Snort, and how it can help you with your security concerns. You learned about the history of Snort, how the Snort architecture works, and system requirements.

Additionally, you learned about Snort's different uses. These include using Snort as a packet sniffer, a packet logger, and an IDS. You also learned about some pitfalls with Snort, including false positives.

Finally, this chapter also touched on some security considerations you should have when running a Snort system. It's critical to keep the system as secure as possible, especially as an active packet logger or IDS.

Solutions Fast Track

What Is Snort?

☑ Snort is a packet sniffer, a packet logger, and a network IDS.

☑ Snort runs on various operating systems and hardware platforms, including many UNIX systems and Windows. Hardware platforms include Intel-based systems, PA-RISC, PowerPC, and Sparc.

☑ It is highly recommended to have a large hard disk for data storage. Additionally, it is recommended to have two network interfaces on the system: one to run in promiscuous mode, and the other for typical networks connectivity (for example, SSH and HTTPS).

Exploring Snort's Features

☑ Snort's major components are the preprocessor, the detection engine, and the alert/logging components. All of Snort's components are implemented as plug-ins to increase flexibility.

☑ The preprocessor is used to take the packet data and process it before the data gets checked against the rules in the detection engine.

☑ The detection engine works by checking the data in each packet against a ruleset. Snort comes with a standard set of rules, but administrators can write their own as well.

☑ The alert/logging component takes the output of the data after it gets checked against the ruleset. The data can go straight into a log file in text or binary (TCPDump data) format. In addition, the data can be stored in SQL databases, or sent over the network through SNMP traps or WinPopup messages.

Using Snort on Your Network

☑ Snort can be used in various ways on your network. You can use it as a packet sniffer or a packet logger in addition to network intrusion detection.

☑ Snort can write packets in both text and binary mode. Binary mode is also known as TCPDump data format. This is not human-readable, but it is a standard that Snort, TCPDump, and Ethereal all use to read and write network data. In addition to writing data, Snort can also filter the data to human-readable format from the binary format.

☑ Snort as an IDS needs to go on each of the private subnets you plan to monitor. It also helps to be able to place a Snort system behind the screening router as well.

Security Considerations with Snort

☑ Like any other application, Snort is subject to security vulnerabilities, including buffer overflows and DoS attacks.

☑ Snort should be upgraded on a regular basis to keep up to date with the latest signatures and the latest bug fixes with the application itself.

☑ In addition to securing the Snort application, you also need to secure the OS. This includes disabling unnecessary services, regularly applying patches, and proper configuration. It also includes encrypting sensitive traffic, such as login sessions with SSH and HTTP traffic with SSL.

Frequently Asked Questions

The following Frequently Asked Questions, answered by the authors of this book, are designed to both measure your understanding of the concepts presented in this chapter and to assist you with real-life implementation of these concepts. To have your questions about this chapter answered by the author, browse to **www.syngress.com/solutions** and click on the **"Ask the Author"** form.

Q: What OS can I run Snort on? Which one is best for performance?

A: Snort runs on many UNIX distributions, including Linux, FreeBSD, OpenBSD, NetBSD, HP-UX, and Solaris. It also runs on Windows. The ★BSD distributions are known for the good implementations of the TCP/IP stack; however, Linux is comparable in kernel version 2.4.*x* and higher.

Q: Why log the Snort data in binary format? What can I gain from this?

A: Snort's binary format is also known as the TCPDump data format. Logging the packets to binary format makes packet collection faster. It also means that later you can look through the data and filter it after collection instead of during. Logging in binary format saves time because Snort does not have to translate the data from binary to human-readable format on-the-fly.

Q: How does Snort use plug-ins?

A: Snort uses plug-ins in various ways. The preprocessor can take plug-ins to translate data such as HTTP data into a more readable format, or it can take plug-ins that check for patterns such as checking for portscans. The detection engine can take rulesets of various types, but can also take plug-ins. The alerting/logging component is the most obvious place you'll see plug-ins. The plug-ins for alerting/logging include functionality for SQL databases, SNMP traps, and WinPopup messages.

Q: How do I keep my Snort system secure?

A: Keeping your Snort system secure is just a matter of good system administration. This includes proper configuration, disabling unnecessary services, regular updates, and encrypting sensitive data.

## Chapter 3

Installing Snort

Solutions in this chapter:

- **A Brief Word on Linux Distributions**

- **Installing PCAP**

- **Installing Snort**

☑ **Summary**

☑ **Solutions Fast Track**

☑ **Frequently Asked Questions**

Introduction

In this chapter, we will cover all of the steps necessary to complete a functioning Snort intrusion detection system (IDS) install. Due to the overwhelming amount of Linux distributions available today, installation instructions can vary from distribution to distribution, and are beyond the scope of this chapter. For this reason, we will cover the information specific to installation on the Red Hat 8.0 platform for the Linux portions of the chapter. We have chosen Red Hat because it is the most commonly used Linux distribution in the world, and serves as a good starting point on which to base further installations. Most of what we cover here should apply to most other popular distributions without a huge amount of modification; if the instructions do vary, it will be minimal. We will go into a bit more detail later in this introduction. As a side note, if you would like to acquire Red Hat Linux to use as a test bed for the exercises in this book, you can download it from one of their mirrors free of charge at www.redhat.com/download/mirror.html. Alternately, you can purchase the full package, complete with support, from most computer software retailers. As advocates of Linux and free software, we recommend the latter if you really enjoy the product. Your contributions help to keep the whole thing going, and at less than $40.00 USD, you can't go wrong.

Let's take a moment to introduce you to the way we approached this chapter. We know that not everyone is a Linux guru, and we do not expect you to understand everything (*we* don't even understand everything), so we tried to approach almost every subject as if we were learning it for the first time. Our only assumption is that you do have a basic understanding of the operating system (OS) and how to use it. Knowing that this can be redundant information for those of you who are already comfortable with the terminology and procedures, we made the step-by-step instructions for each install easy to find and read. This chapter will serve as an excellent *skimming* reference for that crowd. The only time we get wordy with the procedures is when there is possibly some pitfall to watch for, or maybe some side notes that might be helpful. We keep all of our lengthy descriptions and discussions *outside* of the chapter instructions.

As with any other common package installation, it is best to start with a solid OS installation. Please make sure that your OS is current and error free. For this installation, you must first verify that your networking setup on the target machine is up to date and functioning properly.

The packages you will need for installing Snort IDS are all available free of charge on the Internet at their respective Web sites. We have also included the latest release (as of press time) of each package on the CD-ROM that accompanies this book to save you some effort when it comes time to build the programs. If you would like to download the latest version of the software before beginning, feel free to do so; just make sure to substitute package names when necessary. For example, if we reference the file snort-2.0.0.tar.gz and you have snort-2.0.3.tar.gz, use your filename because it's newer. You can also find a README file on the accompanying CD-ROM in the snort-2.0.0 folder, which has the same list for your convenience.

A Brief Word about Linux Distributions

As stated earlier, we will be focusing, for the most part, on the Red Hat Linux 8.0 platform for all of our examples and walk-throughs. Many of you might not use Red Hat as your preferred distribution, so we would like to stop and acknowledge a few of the more prevalent versions out there and some variations you will find in the documentation you are about to read. We are going to look at just a few of the distros not based on the Red Hat Package Manager (RPM) management system. The following distributions rely on either source-based distribution, or proprietary methods of package management. Other releases that use RPM as their system of choice include SuSE, Mandrake, Turbolinux, and Conectiva.

Debian

Debian GNU/Linux (currently in stable version 3.0) has been around forever and is known to many as the most secure and stable version of Linux available. apt-get, the package management system on Debian, is second to none in terms of ease of use. The *apt-get* syntax goes something like this

- ***apt-get install <packagename>*** (where *<packagename>* is the name of the software package) installs new packages. These packages can come from the Debian CD-ROM, an NFS share, or straight from the Debian mirrors on the Internet, and download and install in one simple step.
- ***apt-get remove <packagename>*** uninstalls software already on the machine.

Slackware

Slackware Linux (currently in stable version 9.0) is a favorite among hardcore Linux users, and understandably so. The support base for it is huge, and the system itself is stable, fast, and secure. Although this distribution is not for the faint of heart, we recommend it to anyone ready for the challenge. Slackware Linux also has a package management system based on the compile-from-source tarball model. Its packages can be easily identified by their .tgz extension. There is a built-in utility called pkgtool that allows for easy package management, or you can simply add, remove, oredit packages right from the command line. For example:

- *installpkg <packagename>* will install the package you choose onto your system.

- *removepkg <packagename>* will uninstall the package of your choice.

- *upgradepkg oldpackage%newpackage* is the quick-and-dirty way to upgrade your packages on-the-fly.

One other thing we would like to point out about the Slackware distro is the rpm2targz utility. This program converts RPM files to a format usable on a system without RPMs. The syntax for rpm2targz is:

```
rpm2targz packagename.rpm.
```

Gentoo

Gentoo Linux (currently in pre-release 1.4rc3) is an interesting distribution unlike any other available today. The only thing close that we are aware of is the *Linux From Scratch* (LFS) project. The idea behind Gentoo Linux is to provide users with a minimal (45.3MB according to their FTP mirrors) CD-ROM that you boot to and connect to the Internet to download the rest of the distribution. Gentoo then builds the entire OS to be optimized for your specific hardware. For package management, Gentoo uses the emerge system. Emerge works much like *apt-get*, but is slower because it builds and compiles each package optimized for your system. The way in which emerge works is fairly straightforward: It downloads the source code for the software package you request, compiles it, and installs it into the running system. Like we said, it's a close cousin of *apt-get*, and the only noticeable difference is that *apt-get* doesn't compile the software it downloads. Emerge, like *apt-get*, pulls its software index from what is called the *Portage tree*. The Portage tree is basically a database containing information about every package ready to run on Gentoo Linux. To give you an idea of how emerge works, including syntax, we have included an example shown next. In this example, we will download and install the Snort 2.0 package. (Sounds like a proper choice considering the material we are going over, doesn't it?)

First, we will find out if Snort is available in the Portage tree by querying it with the following syntax:

```
emerge -p snort
```

This tells emerge that we want to pretend to install Snort (you guessed it… —*p* means pretend). Emerge will then present us with a list of software that will be downloaded to satisfy Snort and its dependencies. It will look something like this (this is not actual output… it's fictitious, but you get the idea):

```
Calculating dependencies........ done!
[ebuild    U] sys-libs/lib-1.1.3-r2 to /
[ebuild    U] sys-libs/glib_not-1.2.9 to /
[ebuild N  ] snort-libs/fakelibs-1-a2 to /
[ebuild N  ] snort-base/snort-2.0.0 to /
```

If we are satisfied with the output, simply enter the command *emerge snort,* and Gentoo will gladly install Snort for you. To uninstall a package, the command is *unmerge snort*. Enough said—Emerge is that simple, and an excellent package tool.

Installing PCAP

libpcap is a packet capture library for Linux systems. What is unique about this library is that it can capture packets destined for the local hosts, and can also pick up packets destined for other hosts on the network. This, in essence, means that you can place a machine in a strategic location on your network and have it analyze the packets that travel through (for a quick example, see Figures 3.1 and 3.2). Snort requires this library to function, and it is best to download the newest version of it every time you install or upgrade Snort. The benefits of getting the newest release are twofold: You will realize increased stability *and* speed running the program. Even if your system already has a version of PCAP (such as Red Hat Linux) you should follow this advice.

OINK!

Some operating systems (such as Red Hat) include a modified PCAP library. It is usually worth the effort to install the latest version of libpcap every time you install a new version of Snort. Installing the latest version of libpcap provides two major benefits: Increased stability and speed.

The current version of libpcap can be found at www.tcpdump.org. We have included libpcap 0.7.2 (current release at the time of writing this book) on the CD-ROM accompanying this book.

Figure 3.1 Snort IDS Monitoring Internal Traffic

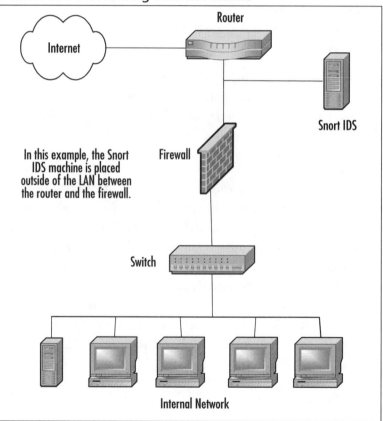

Figure 3.2 Snort IDS Monitoring External Traffic

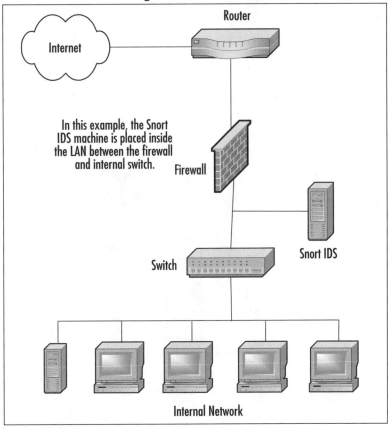

Installing libpcap from Source

Installing libpcap from the source tarball is relatively simple, especially for those familiar with compiling source code. The only thing you really need to make sure of is that you have chosen to install development tools into your original OS install. These tools should include the following, and probably more depending on your distribution of choice. As noted previously, we are going to be using Red Hat Linux 8.0 for the purpose of demonstration.

- **gcc** The GNU cc and gcc C compilers. This is the core of your development tools; nothing else functions without it.

- **automake** The GNU utility for creating makefiles on-the-fly.

- **autoconf** The GNU utility for configuring source code on-the-fly.

- **binutils** GNU binary utilities.

- **make** The GNU tool for making life easier for the individual compiling the code. It automates much of the process by using the makefile.

In Red Hat Linux 8.0, you can add these tools by performing the following:

1. As root, open the panel menu and select **System Settings | Packages**
   (Figure 3.3).

Figure 3.3 Selecting the Packages Utility from the Panel Menu

2. The **Package Management** dialog will open.

3. Scroll down to the **Development** section and select the check box next
   to **Development Tools** (Figure 3.4).

Figure 3.4 The Package Management System

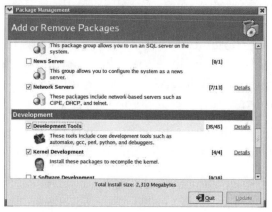

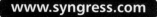

4. Click **Update** in the bottom-right corner of the window.

5. The OS will calculate the required packages and dependencies.

6. When it is complete, it will present you with a dialog confirming your package selection choices (Figure 3.5). You can always double-check your selections by clicking **Show Details** in this dialog.

7. Simply click **Continue** and the system will proceed with the installation. This is the last dialog you will see, unless you are prompted for CD-ROM media, or if there are errors during the install. On a successful operation, there are no further visual or audible prompts.

Figure 3.5 Completing the Package Install

Now that your system is complete with all of the tools necessary for package compilation, we will continue with the configuration and build stages. Again, if you have any experience compiling software on Linux, you will be able to get through this section fairly quickly. We will be following the common **configure | make | make install** format for building the package into the system. For those of you who are new at this, don't be afraid; this is pretty simple as long as your system has the tools described in the last section.

For those of you who are not familiar with the source code compilation/installation of packages from tarballs (a tarball is a compressed set of files similar to a zip file created in Windows using WinZip or PKZip), we have given you a little history on the subject. Please see the sidebar "Notes from the Underground" for information.

Notes from the Underground…

Configure, *Make,* and *Make Install* Defined

Most of you might already be familiar with this time-tested method of software installation on Linux, but I think it might be a good idea for those new to the scene to cover the definition. At first glance, Linux can be an intimidating beast, but first impressions are not always accurate. Although this might seem like a long process just to install a piece of software, it really is worth the effort. Unlike shrink-wrapped software, compiling from source code is almost always better because it is being made specifically for your system. Prepackaged software is always built for the lowest common denominator, so if the programmer's target *lowest* machine is a 100MHz Pentium, that is what you get … software built to run on a 100MHz Pentium. If you have a 2GHz processor, you will not be taking advantage of all of the optimizations for your processor. When you compile software on Linux, it is being made by you, and for you. Each machine you compile it on will have its own unique setup. We are not saying that all prepackaged software is bad, because it's not. We have run a ton of it, but we just wanted to point out the benefits of doing it the Linux way. You'll thank us for it later.

Let's get on with the show…

Most software developed for Linux is distributed in what is known as a *tarball*. A tarball is nothing more than a compressed file containing other files and/or directory structures. We like to equate it to a zip file created with WinZip (for those of us familiar with the Windows OS). Tarballs can come in several formats, the most popular end with the extensions of tgz, tar.gz, or tar.bz2. Each extension signifies a specific compression algorithm that was used to create the file. Depending on the source, the extensions might differ, but they are all capable of being extracted by modern versions of the *tar* program. Tar is a console program designed to create and extract compressed archives. You can read more about tar and its features at *www.gnu.org/software/tar/.* It comes as a standard package with almost every Linux distro, but you can get the latest version at that address as well.

When you receive a tarball, the first step is to extract it into a temporary directory where you can work with it. **/tmp** is usually a good place to accomplish this task. Once the tarball is extracted, verify that the archive created a new directory (they usually do) with its contents.

In some cases, it might extract into your current working directory. In any case, locate a file named *configure*. The configure file is always located in the "root" (this directory is usually named after the package name) directory of the files you just extracted. This is the main directory you will be working from to install your software package. You will almost always use these three commands successively:

- **./configure** The *configure* file is a script that contains code designed to essentially "figure out" the machine on which it is running. It looks at environment variables, dependencies, and verifies what software, if any, is missing. If you watch the screen when it is running, you will see a lot of questions and answers flying by. This is exactly what is going on. It is checking to make sure that everything is where it is supposed to be. The *configure* script is responsible for generating the makefile, which will become important in the next step. If you see any errors here, you will need to tend to them before continuing. Most issues will be cleared up by installing what-ever dependency the *configure* script was missing. When all dependencies are fulfilled, you can run *configure ure* again.

- **make** The *make* command is a part of almost every UNIX/Linux installations in existence today. It is not a script like *configure* is, but an actual utility. *Make* will use the makefile created by the *configure* script in the last step. The primary function of *make* is to compile the code to be used during the final install. It accomplishes this by reading and executing the code in the makefile in a specific order deter-mined by the *configure* script. The makefile is similar in layout to an initialization file in that it has "headings" or cat-egories for each step of the *make* process. One of these headings is *install*, which is used in the next step by *make install*. Again, it is important to note any errors during the compilation process to make sure you take care of them before continuing.

- **make install** This is the final step of the installation process. What *make install* does is fairly simple: it reads the informa-tion from the install section of the makefile and distributes the executables and other files created by *make* to the proper locations in the machine's directory structure. Once this step is complete (without error), the software is installed and ready to use.

Now when you are ready to tackle your next big software installation, you will be armed with the knowledge of what all of the syntax and commands actually mean. This has always been helpful to me ... to be able to understand the meaning behind what I'm doing, and not just going through the motions presented to me via documentation. I sincerely hope that this has been helpful to you.

Simply issue the following commands at the prompt:

1. As the root user, open a terminal using the panel menu by selecting **System Tools | Terminal**, or by using **Ctrl+Alt+F2** to open a new full-screen console. (You can alternately choose any key from **F1** through **F6** for opening full-screen consoles, but for this exercise, we will use the **F2** key.)

2. If your system does not have automount enabled, mount the accompanying CD-ROM by entering the command **mount /dev/cdrom /mnt/cdrom** and pressing **Enter**.

OINK!

The location of your CD-ROM drive might differ depending on your setup and/or Linux distribution. Please check the documentation that came with your OS. For example, SuSE Linux uses the /media directory instead of the standard /mount like most other distributions. If you have a CD-RW drive, your device might be named cdrecorder instead of cdrom. Please be aware of these differences and substitute where necessary.

3. Change the working directory to the location of the package on the CD-ROM by typing **cd/mnt/cdrom/Snort-2.0.0/Linux/PCAP** and pressing **Enter**.

4. Copy libpcap-0.7.1.tar.gz to your **/tmp** directory by typing **cp libpcap-0.7.2.tar.gz/tmp/libpcap-0.7.2.tar.gz** and press **Enter**.

5. Change directories to **/tmp**, extract the contents of the file by typing **cd /tmp && tar −zxvf libpcap-0.7.2.tar.gz**, and press **Enter**. This will create a new directory in **/tmp** called **libpcap-0.7.2**.

Let's take a moment to define the variables we used for the tar command in the last statement:–*z, -x, -v,* and –*f* as options.

■ The –*z* option specifies that the file needs to be processed through the gzip filter. You can tell if an archive was created with gzip by the .gz extension.

■ The –*x* option dictates that you want the contents of the archive to be extracted. By default, this action will extract the contents into the current working directory unless otherwise specified.

■ The –*v* option stands for verbose, which means that tar will display all files it processes on the screen. This is a personal preference and is not critical to the extraction operation.

■ The –*f* option specifies the file that tar will process. In our current example, this would be libpcap-0.7.1.tar.gz. Sometimes it might be necessary to specify a full path if the file you want to work with is located in another directory.

6. Change directories to the new folder by typing **cd libpcap-0.7.1** and pressing **Enter**.

7. At the command prompt, type **./configure** and press **Enter**. This will run the *configure* script for libpcap (Figure 3.6).

Figure 3.6 Running the *configure* Script

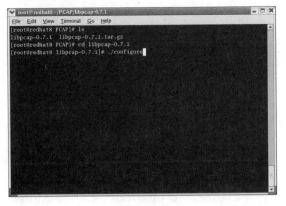

8. When the *configure* script has completed its operation, you should be returned to a prompt. Make sure you have no errors on screen. Everything should look okay if you installed your development tools from earlier in the chapter. At the prompt, type **make** and press **Enter**.

9. The *make* command will also bring you back out to a prompt when it has completed its work. Again, you need to check the output that *make* has displayed onscreen to verify that the operation was trouble-free. At the prompt, type **make install** and press **Enter**.

10. After *make* command finishes the installation of the software, you will be returned to the command prompt—and with luck, free of error.

Installing libpcap from RPM

You can also install libpcap from an RPM package if your distribution supports it. At the time of writing, www.rpmfind.net returned 57 results (spanning 11 Linux distributions) when presented with a query for libpcap. Frankly, we believe that this is the best place to find custom-compiled RPMs for your distribution of choice. We have included RPMs for the following distributions on the accompanying CD-ROM. They are located in the /Snort-2.0.0/Linux/pcap/ rpms directory.

- **Conectiva**   Version 6.2 (RPM and SRPM)
- **Mandrake**   Version 6.2 (RPM), version 7.1 (RPM and SRPM)
- **Red Hat (7.2, 7.3, 8.0)**   Version 6.2 (RPM only)
- **SuSE Linux**   Version 7.1 (RPM only)

The procedures involved in installation via RPM are, more often than not, much easier than an installation that uses source code—if there are no dependency problems. The RPM system, while an excellent package management tool, is fraught with problems regarding dependencies. It understands and reports what the specific package requires to install, but is not yet capable of acquiring and installing the packages necessary to fulfill its requirements.

If you are not familiar with the term, *dependencies* are packages and/or libraries required by other packages. The Linux OS is built on dependencies, which you can visualize as an upside-down tree structure. At the top of the tree are your basic user-installed programs, such as Snort. Snort depends on libpcap to operate, and libpcap requires other libraries to function.

Installing Snort

Now we can get into the actual installation of Snort. So far, we have covered the basics of Linux package management, including RPM installs, source compilation, and installing libpcap, so this next section should be fairly easy for us to get through. Luck for us, the installation of Snort is painless, so we can save all of our energy for the setup, configuration, and rules management.

First, you need to get Snort. Whether you choose to get it from the Web site at www.snort.org or on the accompanying CD-ROM is entirely up to you. The version on the CD-ROM is 2.0.0, so we will use it in our example install. This is the most current stable version available at press time. Please note that we strongly recommend going to www.snort.org and downloading the very newest stable release, as you will benefit from new functionality, bug fixes, stability, and speed enhancements. This software is constantly changing, growing, and getting better every day.

Installing Snort from Source

There is something to be said about installing software from source code. In our opinion, it is the easiest and best way to install a properly functioning software package. In this section, we will be installing the Snort 2.0.0 package from a source tarball located on the accompanying CD-ROM. To install Snort, simply follow these simple steps:

1. As root, browse to the **/Snort-2.0.0/Linux/src** folder located in the Chapter 3 directory (03) on the CD-ROM.

2. Copy the tarball to the **/tmp** directory by typing **cp snort-2.0.0.tar.gz /tmp** at the command line.

3. Change directories to **/tmp** by typing **cd /tmp** at the command line.

4. Extract the tar archive by issuing the command **tar –zxvf snort-2.0.0.tar.gz**.

5. Change directories into the newly created Snort directory by typing **cd snort-2.0.0**.

6. At the command line, type **./configure** to configure the package. You should see text start to scroll by (similar to the example in Figure 3.7).

Figure 3.7 Running the Snort *configure* Script

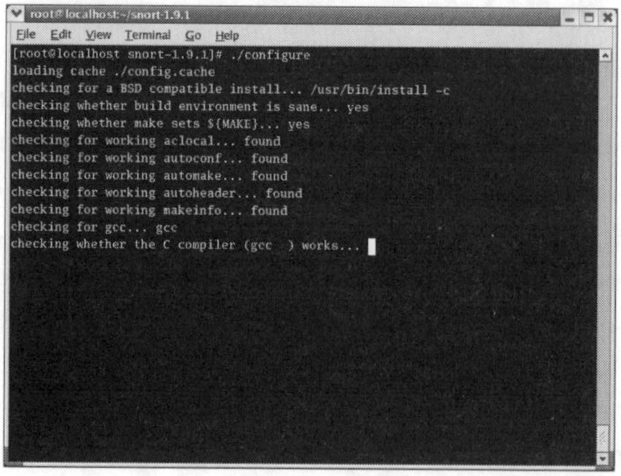

7. Next, type **make** at the command line. This will create the makefile.

> **OINK!**
>
> This might take some time depending on the speed of the target machine.

8. As the final step in the build process, type **make install** at the command prompt. This action will deliver the package and its files to where they belong in the system. The Snort install is now officially complete. We can now move on to basic customization.

Customizing Your Installation: Editing the snort.conf File

The first order of business after completing the Snort install is to customize it to your needs. We are going to begin with the snort.conf file located in the /etc/snort directory. This file contains the configuration settings that Snort will use every time it is invoked. This configuration file is lengthy, but the sample file that the developers provided us is complete with basic instructions on syntax and use. Although it is very thorough in its descriptions, we would still like to cover a few basic settings that will allow Snort to function properly.

First, we will need to change the *var HOME_NET* variable in the snort.conf file. What this variable signifies is the internal network address of your LAN. In most textbook cases, this value will be an entire subnet, but it can also be in the form of a single IP address. In this example, we are going to use the subnet of our internal network card. In this case, it will be 192.168.0.0/24, which means that the address space of 192.168.0.1–192.168.0.254 will be represented, using a subnet mask of 255.255.255.0 (Figure 3.8).

The next variable we need to look at is *var EXTERNAL_NET*. You can set this to whatever subnet your external network adapter is answering requests (or in this case, listening) on. In this example, we will use *var EXTERNAL_NET any*. This tells Snort to listen for all addresses on the external network. In our opinion, this value should be left at the default state of *any*.

Figure 3.8 Editing the snort.conf File in gedit

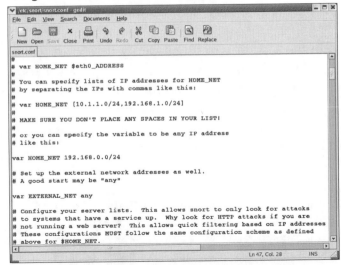

If you scroll down further into the config file, you will see a section dedicated to server-specific variables. These variables will look similar to *var HTTP_PORTS 80* or *var ORACLE_PORTS 1521*. These variables (or vars) specify specific ports on which Snort should watch for attacks. The only downside to the current implementation is that you either have to list ports in succession (for example, 80:82, which means 80 through 82 inclusive) or on separate lines. Work is underway to add support for port lists.

Other areas of initial interest should include the preprocessors, output plug-ins, and ruleset sections. Preprocessors are the filters that Snort puts the incoming data stream through before it actually processes the data. In the example snort.conf file, notice that IP defragmentation is turned on. This helps to detect fragmentation and denial-of-service (DoS) attacks. You can also enable other pre-processors in this section to fit your particular scenario.

The output plug-ins section defines whether Snort will use various logging and alert features, and tells it what format to use to dump the data. The ruleset section defines what the system will consider "suspicious" activity. Based on this alone, you should visit www.snort.org *frequently* to download the latest rulesets to ensure that your IDS is doing the job you meant for it to do—without an up-to-date ruleset, your machine will be nothing more than an expensive paperweight. It is also a good practice to comment out rules that do not apply to your organization and/or needs. Unnecessary and extra rules can lead to false positive alerts from the system.

Also you should make note that you can alter the path to your rulesets, by changing the *include $RULE_PATH/rule.rules* line to reflect the location of your updated rules.

The final step in this section is to simply verify that Snort will actually run without error. To accomplish this, we will run Snort with a generic configuration/ruleset and no options. To do this, open a terminal window, type **snort −v**, and verify that the program loads without error. You will see a screen similar to the one in Figure 3.9. All we are doing here is running Snort in *verbose* mode (hence the *−v* flag). Since everything looks good, let's move on to the next section.

Figure 3.9 Running Snort with the Verbose Option Enabled

Enabling Features via *configure*

During the build process (more specifically, during the *configure* script portion), we can pass options to the installer to customize it to whatever specific situation or needs we might have. These were harvested from the INSTALL file in the Snort 2.0.0 tarball (which is on the accompanying CD-ROM, so if you ever need to reference them, you can find them there).

- ■ **--enable-debug** Enable debugging options (bug reports and developers only).

- ■ **--with-snmp** Enable SNMP alerting code.

- ■ **--enable-smbalerts** Enable the SMB alerting code, which is somewhat unsafe because it executes a *popen()* call from within the program (which runs at root privs). You've been warned, use it with caution!

- ■ **--enable-flexresp** Enable the "Flexible Response" code, which allows you to cancel hostile connections on IP-level when a rule matches. When you enable this feature, you also need the libnet-library that can be found at www.packetfactory.net/libnet. See README.FLEXRESP for details. This function is still alpha, so use with caution.

- ■ **--with-mysql=DIR** Support for MySQL; turn this on if you want to use ACID with MySQL.

- ■ **--with-odbc=DIR** Support for ODBC databases; turn this on if you want to use ACID with a nonlisted DB.

- ■ **--with-postgresql=DIR** Support for PostgreSQL databases; turn this on if you want to use ACID with PostgreSQL.

- ■ **--with-oracle=DIR** Support for Oracle databases; turn this on if you want to use ACID with Oracle.

- ■ **--with-openssl=DIR** Support for OpenSSL (used by the XML output plug-in).

- ■ **--with-libpq-includes=DIR** Set the include directories for PostgresSQL database support to DIR.

- ■ **--with-libpq-libraries=DIR** Set the library directories for PostgresSQL database support to DIR. Setting both of these values enables the Postgres output plug-in module.

- *--with-libpcap-includes=DIR* If the configuration script can't find the libpcap include files on its own, the path can be set manually with this switch.

- *--with-libpcap-libraries=DIR* If the configuration script can't find the libpcap library files on its own, the path can be set manually with this switch.

Installing Snort from RPM

Depending on your distribution and release number, there might not be RPMs available. In most cases, you can probably find contributed source RPMs from a Web site such as www.rpmfind.net, and then you can build your own. We recommend building your own because all systems are inherently different and have their own file system structure and environments. We will cover installation via RPM and source RPM in this section. This should seem pretty easy to you in comparison to installation by tar archives.

Let's start with the RPM installation. The installation is simple. All you have to do is browse to the **/Snort-2.0.0/Linux/RPM** folder on the accompanying CD-ROM and do one of two things:

- **In console mode** At a console prompt, just enter the command **rpm –Uvh snort-2.0.0-snort.i386.rpm**. This will complete the installation routine for you. Note that we used the *–U* (upgrade) option versus *–i* (install)—it will install with either. We are always concerned that if we use *–i*, the installer will not upgrade files properly (if there are any files to upgrade to newer versions), but if we use the *–U* flag, it will do a more thorough job of installing the software. What we're trying to say is that you can install the software simply by typing **rpm –i snort-2.0.0-1snort.i386.rpm**.

- **Inside X Windows** If you are using KDE, GNOME, or one of the many X Window systems out there, this set of instructions is for you. Inside the **/Snort-2.0.0/Linux/RPM** folder on the accompanying CD-ROM, double-click the **snort-2.0.0-1snort.i386.rpm** file. Under Red Hat Linux 8, you will be prompted with a dialog asking if you would like to proceed. All you have to do is click **Continue** and RPM will install the package. As stated earlier, depending on your distribution instructions might vary; so make sure to consult the documentation or man files that came with your distribution. Most of the RPM-based distributions are not much different from what we have witnessed here. Another point that is distribution dependent is that you might not get a confirmation that the package was successfully installed onto the system. In true UNIX/Linux fashion, some distributions do not waste time displaying unnecessary information to the screen. The only time you might ever hear Linux speak is when something went dreadfully wrong (and we all hope that day never comes).

Now we will look at the source RPM (or SRPM) as a means of a more solid installation. This is the preferable way to install packages if you use RPM-based distributions such as Red Hat, and the SRPMs are readily available to you. Usually, sites such as www.freshrpms.net and www.rpmfind.net will have these available for most packages and almost all RPM-based distros.

Recompiling a source RPM is not as daunting as it might sound. RPM takes care of all the minute details involved in a recompile and rebuild. Let's start with the SRPM located in the **/Snort–2.0.0/Linux/srpm** folder on the accompanying CD-ROM. It is the most current version of Snort and is ready for rebuilding into your system. Depending on the version of RPM you are using, the syntax can vary slightly. The first example we will give you will run on RPM version 4.1 or higher (Red Hat 8.0 includes this version). At a console prompt, all you have to do is navigate to the **/Snort–2.0.0/Linux/srpm** folder and enter **rpmbuild —rebuild snort-2.0.0-1snort.src.rpm**. This will prompt RPM to rebuild the file into a regular RPM specifically designed for your system.

The second example is for versions lower than 4.1. For these systems, just enter **rpm —rebuild snort-2.0.0-1snort.src.rpm**. This command will do exactly the same thing as in the previous example, but in a slightly different syntax. Both versions will place the completed RPM package in a subfolder under the **/usr/src/** directory. On a Red Hat 8.0 system, the completed builds are located under **/usr/src/redhat/RPMS/i386**.

OINK!

The only drawback to building a package from an SRPM is that all of the package's dependencies must be met, even though you are not *actually* installing the program. In the case of Snort, you must have MySQL, PostgreSQL, and UCD-SNMP installed (including devels and libraries). The reason for this is simple: With Snort, the developers have coded the software to support a variety of databases. When you attempt to rebuild the

SRPM, it looks for all of the various dependencies required for *all* database systems it was built to run with. This is true even if you don't ever intend to use all of the options. The fact of the matter is that they are present and must be rebuilt into the final package for it to function properly. If you do not satisfy all of the program's dependencies, the rebuild will fail. One good thing is that it will explain what components it is missing to allow you to install them and try the rebuild again.

Installation on the Microsoft Windows Platform

All you Microsoft users were probably wondering when we were going to get to the section designated for you. Well, we are here. Sorry for the delay. Please keep in mind that we have not pushed the Microsoft portion to the end for any reason other than for the simple fact that it is an easier task installing on this system than on its Linux counterparts. This is going to be much shorter in terms of installation steps. Configuration should be a breeze as well. As a personal opinion, we always recommend installing on Linux (rather than Windows) if you have the resources to do so—for reasons of stability and pure speed. Linux is also far superior at performing network-related tasks.

Let's get started with the installation. First, we'll need to install the packet capture library for Windows, WinPcap, which is on the accompanying CD-ROM. You can find it under the **Snort-2.0.0/Win32/winpcap2.3** directory, or you can also install it from the GUI that is included on the CD-ROM. The installation is very simple and should go smoothly. Here is how to install WinPcap manually by browsing the CD-ROM:

1. Browse to the **Snort-2.0.0/Win32/winpcap2.3** folder on the CD-ROM.

2. Double-click **WinPcap-2-3.exe** to launch the installer.

3. The installer will present you with a Welcome dialog as in Figure 3.10. Click **Next**.

Figure 3.11 The Snort Installer Welcome Screen

4. The next dialog is a simple notification that lets you know that the installation was completed successfully (Figure 3.11). Click **OK**.

Figure 3.11 Confirming a Successful WinPcap Installation

5. The next screen is another confirmation that the installation has finished on your computer (Figure 3.12). Click **Finish**.

Figure 3.12 Completing the WinPcap Install

Congratulations! The WinPcap installation was a success. Although it is not noted during the installation, we recommend rebooting the machine for any changes to take effect, as Windows always seems to need a little extra coaxing. If you ever need to uninstall WinPcap, it places an entry in the *Add/Remove Programs* applet in the Windows Control Panel. Simply remove it from there if something goes wrong.

The latest version of Snort (as of press time) is included on the accompanying CD-ROM. You are also encouraged to visit www.snort.org to download the latest and greatest version. For this exercise, we will be installing from the CD-ROM.

1. To begin, navigate to the **Snort–2.0.0/Win32** folder on your CD-ROM and double-click the **Snort–2.0.0.exe** file. This will start the installer. Optionally, you can also start the installer through the graphical

interface we have provided (this will start automatically when the CD-ROM is inserted into the drive).

2. Once the installer launches, you will be presented with the GNU General Public License (GPL). We strongly recommend reading this in its entirety if you have the patience and the time. It is a wonderful piece of literature and has remained unchanged since its inception in 1991. This is the license under which most open-source software is distributed, including Linux. When you have finished reading the license, click **I Accept** (Figure 3.13).

Figure 3.13 The GNU GPL Agreement for Snort

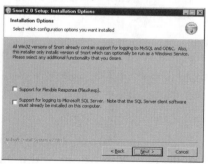

3. The next screen to appear is the Installation Options dialog (Figure 3.14). Here, you will be able to select optional components to fit your unique situation. As the software states, if you choose the SQL option, make sure that the SQL client software is already installed on the target machine. Click **Next** when you are ready to continue.

Figure 3.14 Snort 2.0 Installation Options Window

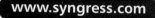

4. Next, you are presented with the screen shown in Figure 3.15. This window presents you with a list of components to install. Again, you can choose what you would like to install here to fit your needs. Please note that it is pretty important to make sure that Snort is one of your choices—it might make for an interesting installation without it. Your component options are as follows:

- **Snort** Installs Snort, configuration files, and rules.

- **Documentation** Installs the Snort documentation.

- **Contrib** Copies additional user-contributed add-on modules and tools.

5. Click **Next** when you are satisfied with your choices.

Figure 3.15 Choosing Components for Your Snort Install

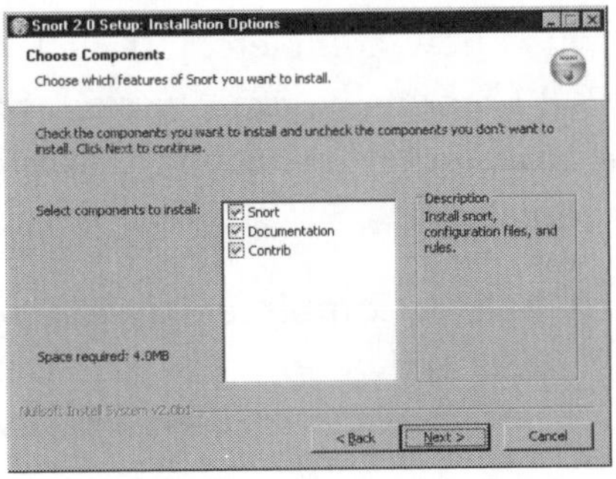

6. Now you are prompted with an installation location (Figure 3.16). The default is fine unless you're feeling creative. Click **Install**.

Figure 3.16 Installation Location Window

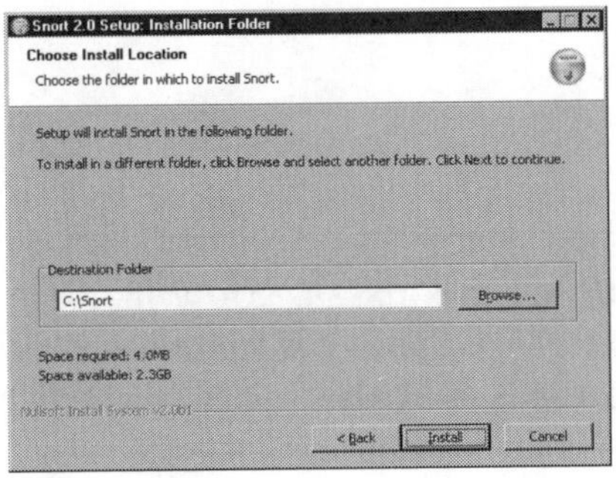

7. The installer will start copying files to your hard drive. It doesn't take long, so don't go anywhere. When it is complete, you will be presented with a screen like the one shown in Figure 3.17.

Figure 3.17 Your Snort Installation Is Now Complete

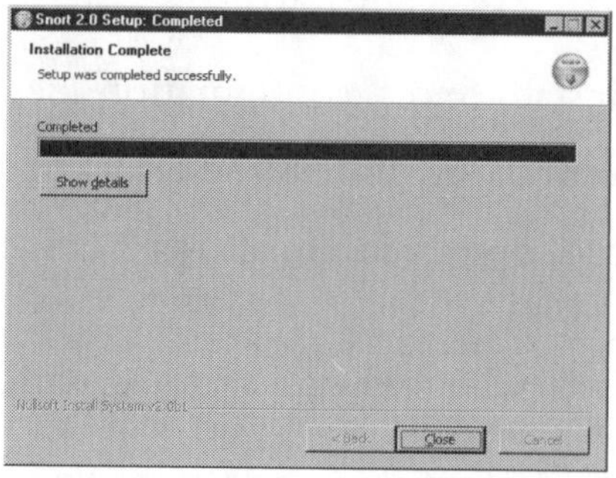

8. The installation is now complete. Just click **Close** and consider Snort to be ready to use! Optionally, you can click **Show Details** to view the output of the installer (Figure 3.18). This is especially helpful if something goes wrong.

Figure 3.18 Installation Complete Screen with the Show Details Option Activated

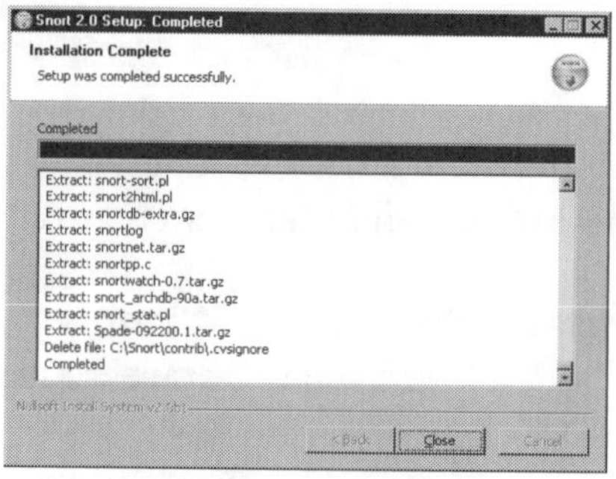

OINK!

Upon completion of the install, you will see a final window prompting you to verify that WinPcap2.3 is installed on your machine, and that you will need to manually edit the snort.conf file to ensure proper operation.

Notes from the Underground…

Detailed Component Selection Options

During the install of the Win32 version of Snort (when the custom install option is chosen), we are presented with more a detailed selection of choices. Here, we will attempt to discuss, in general terms, what each option does and how it will affect your installation.

- **Snort-Barebones** This is the installation we are performing in this chapter, and is subsequently the base, or "bare," version of Snort.
- **Snort-Flexresp** This will install Snort with flexible response (session sniping) activated.
- **Snort-MySQL-Flexresp** This will install Snort with added support for MySQL and Flexresp.
- **Snort-MSSQL-MySQL-Flexresp** This will install Snort with added support for Microsoft SQL, MySQL, and Flexresp.
- **Snort-MSSQL-MySQL** This will install Snort with added support for Microsoft SQL and MySQL.
- **Snort-MySQL** This will install Snort with added support for MySQL.

Please note that in order to install most of these custom options with Snort, you will need to have a fully functioning dependency tree. For example, if you want to install Snort with MySQL support, you must have a functioning MySQL database server before you attempt to install Snort. If you don't, Snort will fail miserably and your network security needs will go unattended.

Installing Bleeding-Edge Versions of Snort

If you are one of those types who like to live life to the fullest, you might want to just go out and get the latest version of the software directly from the developers, and they are always happy to provide you with what you need and crave. For this reason, they make their daily Concurrent Version System (CVS) (see the following "Tools & Traps" sidebar) snapshots available for download. You can find them at www.snort.org/dl/snapshots if you would like to try them out. Keep in mind that CVS builds are the equivalent to beta builds and must be approached as such. They can contain bugs, and there is not a reasonable amount of support for these types of installations.

Tools & Traps....

The CVS System

The CVS is a versioning system that allows many developers to work on the same project simultaneously, while keeping track of what changes have been made, who made them, and most importantly, what versions exist and keeping them separated. You will generally find many versions of a project in a CVS tree.

You will find that CVSs exist on many Web sites for almost every open-source project. For example, SourceForge (www.sourceforge.net) has CVS repositories for all of the projects it contains. To browse most CVS trees, you will need a CVS client application. However, SourceForge has a Web interface for browsing as well, which is a nice feature if you need to quickly get some information or code from a CVS tree. Here are a couple of GUI applications for CVS:

- If you would like a CVS front-end app for Linux, VisualCVS (www.scentech.ch/products/visualcvs) is a client worth checking out.

- If you would like a CVS application for Windows, WinCVS (www.wincvs.org) is a pretty good client.

Summary

In this chapter, we covered the basics of package management, including RPM and source code packages. We also covered complete installs of the PCAP libraries for Linux and Windows systems, Snort IDS for Linux and Windows. You are now armed with the knowledge and software necessary to continue with this book.

As stated several times in this chapter, it is important to keep your Snort installation up to date. This includes the packet capture libraries and the Snort system itself. You should also visit the Snort site frequently for updated rulesets. Computer security is a fast-paced sector, and it is necessary to keep on top of things so that your systems are not easily compromised.

We also strongly recommend that you keep your OS up to date as well, especially when it comes to security updates and patches. Windows makes this easy through the Windows Update interface. Red Hat Linux has the option for Red Hat Network (RHN), which, in our opinion, is far better than its Windows counterpart.

All of these parts will come together to form a solid IDS that will server you well for years to come.

Solutions Fast Track

A Brief Word about Linux Distributions

☑ Debian GNU/Linux (currently in stable version 3.0) has been around forever and is known to many as the most secure and stable version of Linux available.

☑ Slackware Linux (currently in stable version 9.0) is a favorite among hardcore Linux users, and understandably so. The support base for it is huge, and the system itself is stable, fast, and secure.

☑ Gentoo Linux (currently in pre-release 1.4rc3) is an interesting distribution unlike any other available today. The only thing close that we are aware of is the *Linux From Scratch* (LFS) project. The idea behind Gentoo Linux is to provide users with a minimal (45.3MB according to their FTP mirrors) CD that you boot to and connect to the Internet to download the rest of the distribution.

☑ As with any other common package installation, it is best to start with a solid OS installation. Please make sure that your OS is current and error free.

Installing PCAP

☑ libpcap is a packet capture library for Linux systems. Windows uses WinPcap.

☑ Always install the newest version of libpcap before installing Snort.

☑ libpcap is a necessary requirement before you attempt to install Snort IDS.

Installing from Source

☑ Snort is available through online downloads and is included on the accompanying CD-ROM.

☑ You can use CVS to get the latest, bleeding-edge version of Snort.

☑ Snort is available for UNIX, Linux, and Windows systems.

☑ Snort can be downloaded as a tarball (or tar archive), which contains the source code.

☑ Installation is accomplished with the *./configure, make, make install* routine.

☑ After Snort is installed, you must edit the snort.conf configuration file.

Frequently Asked Questions

The following Frequently Asked Questions, answered by the authors of this book, are designed to both measure your understanding of the concepts presented in this chapter and to assist you with real-life implementation of these concepts. To have your questions about this chapter answered by the author, browse to **www.syngress.com/solutions** and click on the **"Ask the Author"** form.

Q: What operating systems will Snort run on?

A: Snort will run on UNIX, Linux, and Microsoft Windows

Q: Does Snort have any software requirements and/or dependencies?

A: Yes. First, you must have the pcap packet capture libraries installed. You will also need to have some form of database available to you if you intend to use Snort's database integration features.

Q: What major databases will Snort work with?

A: Snort will work well with MySQL, PostgreSQL, and Microsoft SQL.

Q: How can I get Snort?

A: You can get Snort on the CD-ROM that comes with this book, download binaries online at their Web site, or get the latest version from their CVS tree.

Q: Does Snort act as a firewall for my network?

A: No. Snort is an IDS, designed to detect a wide variety of network intrusions (for example, DoS attacks) defined in the rulesets and alert when it finds anything. It does not block any type of attack or intrusion.

Q: Can I specify which ports Snort should pay particular attention to?

A: Yes. You need to edit the snort.conf file and add lines similar to *var HTTP_PORTS 80* for each port you need to monitor. Alternately, you can stack multiple ports in one line in the form *var HTTP_PORTS 80:82*.

Snort: The Inner Workings

Introduction

This chapter explains the internal workings of Snort, the components used, and why they are used. Snort is currently at version 2.0.0 and has progressed significantly through the years. It has now reached the point of being an extremely stable and high-quality intrusion detection system (IDS).

This chapter focuses on the internal workings of Snort version 2.0.0, which is available for many platforms via the Snort homepage at www.snort.org and on the CD-ROM that accompanies this book in the Chapter 3 directory). Throughout this book, we will be focusing on the UNIX version of Snort in our examples, but rest assured that the command lines work just as well with the Windows version of Snort.

This chapter provides an overview of the entire Snort process, from packet capture to detection and logging. We will be referencing functions and sections from within the Snort source code. The Snort source code is documented (in most cases), and we recommend that, if you are a coder, you look through it while reading this chapter. If you do not have any coding experience, you will probably still pick up some useful information from the source code. The following files are a good place to start:

- **snort.c** Main Snort code
- **decode.c** Packet decoder
- **rules.c** Rules engine
- **detect.c** Detection engine
- **log.c** Logging engine

While the source code is vast, it is definitely worth reviewing to get a flavor of the Snort development process and open-source coding at its best.

Oink!

Buried in the source code are little amusing comments by Marty Roesch and the other developers, probably written late at night while stuck on difficult debug problems.

Snort Components

When discussing the internals of Snort, Figure 4.1 often helps to clarify the components at work and offers a high-level view of the Snort process.

Figure 4.1 Snort Component Overview

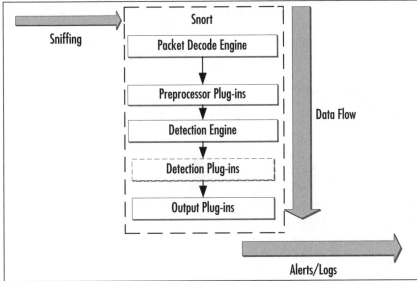

The following are the four main components of Snort and the Snort process:

1. **Packet capture/decoder engine** First, traffic is acquired from the network link via the libpcap library. Packets are passed through the decode engine that first fills out the packet structure for the link-level protocols, which are then further decoded for higher-level protocols such as TCP and UDP ports.

2. **Preprocessor plug-ins** Packets are then sent through a set of preprocessors. Packets are examined and manipulated before being handed to the detection engine. Each preprocessor checks to see if this packet is something it should look at, alert on, or modify.

3. **Detection engine** Packets are then sent through the detection engine. The detection engine checks each packet against the various options listed in the Snort rules files by performing single, simple tests on an aspect or field of the packet. The detection plug-ins provide additional

detection functions on the packets. Each of the keyword options in the rule is linked to a detection plug-in that can perform additional tests.

4. **Output plug-ins** Snort then outputs the alerts from the detection engine, preprocessors or the decode engine.

Capturing Network Traffic

Snort needs a way to capture network traffic, and does so through two mechanisms:

- Setting the network card into promiscuous mode.
- Then grabbing the packets from the network card using the libpcap library.

We discuss *promiscuous mode* and the libpcap library later in the "Packet Sniffing" section. For now, let's take quick refresher on the OSI model and the TCP/IP protocol suite. It's important, as we will be referencing them both throughout this chapter.

The OSI and TCP/IP Models

The Open Systems Interconnection (OSI) model was originally designed to be a standard for developing network communication protocol suites. By strictly adhering to the OSI model, different network vendors could write code that would interoperate with other competing network vendors. Unfortunately, the network industry didn't fully comply with the OSI model, and the TCP/IP protocol suite was no exception.

The most powerful part of the OSI model is the "layering" concept. Each layer consists of a number of components, separated into seven layers. Each layer is responsible for a particular part of the communication process. During communication, the layers receive data formatted by the layers above, manipulate the data, and then send it down to the layer below. When receiving data, the layers receive the data from the layer below, unpack the data, and then pass it up one level.

The layering concept has the following advantages:

- Major code rewrites of a protocol are not necessary if a particular component needs to be changed. For example, if you want to change the IP component at Layer 3, it won't affect the other layers.

- It allows for the breakdown of complex network processes into more manageable sublayers.

- Industry–standard interfaces provide interoperability between different vendors. A vendor can write a piece of code for the network layer, for example, and other vendors can then use it seamlessly.

- Layering allows for easier troubleshooting, because the protocols are separated into layers. When troubleshooting, you don't have to tackle the complete protocol, only the layer with the problem.

In this chapter, we also talk about Snort decoding, and significant actions at the different layers of the OSI model. Figure 4.2 shows where Snort's activities lie in the OSI model.

Figure 4.2 The OSI Model and Snort

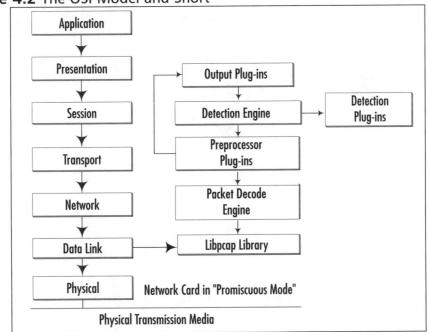

OINK!

The OSI model provides a useful method of describing how a protocol suite such as TCP/IP works. When learning about a new protocol or protocol suite, you will tend to refer back to the OSI model, as it helps us understand where a protocol fits in and what other protocols interoperate with it.

TCP/IP

Originally a governmentally funded research project, TCP/IP has grown to be the most popular protocol suite in the world. TCP/IP is a combination of suites of different protocols at different layers of the OSI model, as you will see later in the chapter. While Snort can decode other protocols, it is primarily focused on the TCP/IP suite. The TCP/IP suite doesn't exactly following the OSI model, and in some cases differs depending on the operating system. Therefore, using the OSI model as a blueprint, Figure 4.3 illustrates the TCP/IP protocol suite.

Figure 4.3 The TCP/IP Model and Snort

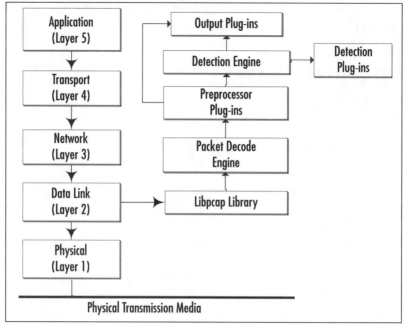

The five layers of TCP/IP are as follows:

- **Application layer** For example, Web-based HTTP protocol, e-mail SMTP-based protocol

- **Transport layer** For example, TCP and UDP

- **Network layer** For example, ICMP and IP

- **Data Link layer** For example, Ethernet, Token Ring, and ARP

- **Physical layer** For example, a network card or modem

OINK!

Further information on TCP/IP and OSI model can be found in the book *TCP/IP Illustrated Volume 1* by W. Richard Stevens. Originally published in 1994, it is still relevant today and is an excellent resource on TCP/IP, one of our favorites.

Packet Sniffing

Snort needs a mechanism to get the traffic as it passes along the network. Figure 4.4 shows a sample design network, which we will be using as a reference throughout the chapter.

Figure 4.4 Sample Network

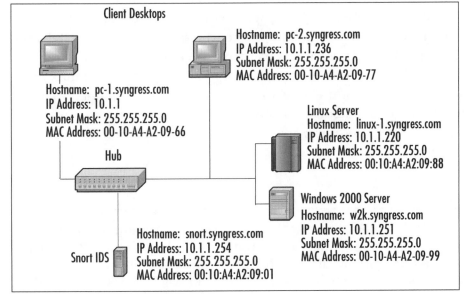

Taking as an example a user on the desktop machine pc-1 (IP address: 10.1.1.1), the user opens his Web browser and types **http://10.1.1.220**, which starts a connection to the Linux server. Within the TCP/IP stack of pc-1, the request travels down the five layers of the TCP/IP model, encapsulating along the way. When the request reaches Layer 3 (network layer), the desktop machine requires a mechanism to discover the hardware address of the Linux machine's network card (this is called the Media Access Control, or MAC, address). It does so using the Address Resolution Protocol (ARP). The desktop machine sends out an ARP request for the machine with the IP address 10.1.1.220, and the Linux machine will answer with its MAC address.

OINK!

A MAC address is in the format 00:10:A4:A2:09:88, and is a unique address burned into every network card. We can see the MAC address of our network card by running the command *ifconfig -a* in Linux, and *ipconfig /all* on Windows 2000.

Once the pc-1 machine has the MAC address of the Linux server (00:10:A4:A2:09:88), it will encapsulate the traffic into an Ethernet frame (Layer 2) and send the packet to the Linux machine. When the Linux server receives the packet, it will decode the packet through the different layers of the TCP/IP model. The Linux server will re-encapsulate its response back down the layers of the TCP/IP model, and the packets will travel back to the desktop machine.

While the desktop machine pc–1 is communicating with the Linux server, the traffic is seen by all of the network cards connected to the hub. Each network card then examines the destination MAC address of the Ethernet frame (00:10:A4:A2:09:88), sees if it matches against its MAC address, and ignores it if it doesn't.

OINK!

In Figure 4.4, all of the machines are connected using a *hub*. Hubs are a broadcast medium, where all of the traffic is broadcast out to each of the ports on the hub. In a switched environment, the switch will learn which ports have which MAC address, and will only send the traffic destined for those MAC address to the particular ports. Even if the Snort machine is in *promiscuous mode*, it still won't see all the traffic because the switch will not pass the traffic to it. Modern switches have a mechanism to *mirror* or *span* the traffic, which involves making a copy of the traffic and sending it to a special port. By plugging our Snort server into this port, we will be able to see all of the network traffic that travels across the switch.

A Network Card in Promiscuous Mode

The default behavior of a network card is to ignore traffic that is not destined for its particular MAC address. We need to change this behavior so that it doesn't check the destination MAC address. By placing the network card in promiscuous mode, we have a mechanism for seeing all of the traffic as it's placed on the hub.

Referring back to our previous example, the Snort server has a network card in *promiscuous mode*. When the packet from the desktop machine pc-1 to the Linux server (or for that matter, any packet on the network) is seen by our machine running Snort, the network card will make that packet available at the data link layer (refer to Figure 4.3 for the position of Layer 2 of the TCP/IP model). Snort then needs a mechanism to get packets from the network card at the data link layer and into its packet decoder. Snort does this using the libpcap library.

What Is the libpcap Library?

The libpcap library was written as part of a larger program called TCPDump. The libpcap library allowed developers to write code to receive link-layer packets (Layer 2 in the OSI model) on different flavors of UNIX operating systems without having to worry about the idiosyncrasy of different operating systems' network cards and drivers. Essentially, the libpcap library grabs packets directly from the network cards, which allowed developers to write programs to decode, display, or log the packets. The TCPDump program did just that. A cross-platform sniffer, originally written by Van Jacobson, Craig Leres, and Steven McCanne at Lawrence Berkeley Labs to analyze TCP performance problems, TCPDump allowed you to capture packets and then decode and display them. One day, frustrated with the limitations and output formats of TCPDump, Marty Roesch wrote Snort as a replacement to TCPDump. The original version of Snort did not have preprocessors or fancy plug-ins; it was simply a better TCPDump.

Pieces of TCPDump have been borrowed by Snort. The following is the header of an early version of Snort's source code:

```
/*
 * Program: Snort
 * Purpose: Check out the README file for info on what you can do with Snort.
 *
 * Author: Martin Roesch (roesch@clark.net)
 *
```

```
* Comments:
* Ideas and code stolen liberally from Mike Borella's IP Grab program.
Check out his stuff at http://www.borella.net. I also have ripped some
* util functions from TCPdump, plus Mike's prog is derived from it as well.
* All hail TCPdump....
*/
```

How Does Snort Link into libpcap?

Looking inside the snort.c source code, when Snort starts up it checks a number of settings and configurations. It calls the libpcap library, which, among other things, checks the interface and puts it into promiscuous mode. When Snort calls the libpcap functions and initializes the interfaces, it enters what is called the *primary execution loop*, or pcap_loop.

In this endless loop, the pcap function waits until it has received packets from the network card device driver, and then calls the *ProcessPacket()* function. The *ProcessPacket() function* links into Data-Link layer decode routine decode.c. More information on this topic can be found in the section *Decoding Packets* later in this chapter.

So, why use libpcap? libpcap is a cross-platform library that works on all major UNIX systems and Windows, so there's no need to reinvent the wheel for decoding and packet capture. Writing your own sniffer is straightforward, and information on libpcap and writing libpcap code can be found at www.tcpdump.org/pcap.htm.

Snort is only one of many programs that use the libpcap library and components of TCPDump; a full list is at www.tcpdump.org/related.html. One of our personal favorites (besides Snort, of course) is Ethereal (www.ethereal.com). Ethereal is an excellent GUI-based open-source packet sniffer with a massive decode plug-in set that can decode over 335 different network protocols. It also reads pcap formatted log files, so looking through large outputs from Snort or TCPDump is easy.

The original TCPDump and libpcap versions were UNIX only. However, a research and development group in Italy have put together a Windows version of libpcap called winpcap, which can be found at http://netgroup-serv.polito.it/winpcap. Like the UNIX libpcap, winpcap is used by a number of Windows-based sniffer programs, including Snort and Ethereal. Versions of these programs can be found on the accompanying CD-ROM in the Chapter 3 and Chapter 5 directories, respectively.

> **OINK!**
>
> Snort requires that the libpcap or WinPcap libraries be installed before Snort is installed; the libpcap libraries are a separate entity to Snort. For more information on this topic, please refer to Chapter 3 "Installing Snort."

Decoding Packets

Now that the packets have arrived from the network card and have been passed to the Snort decode engine by the libpcap library, Snort needs to decode the raw Data-Link layer packets (Layer 2 of the OSI model). Snort can recognize different protocols, including Ethernet, 802.11, Token Ring, and other higher layer protocols such as IP, TCP, and UDP. During the decode process, Snort links the raw data to structures for later analysis by the preprocessors and detection engine. (see the section *Storage of Packets* later in the chapter).

Referring back to the network example in Figure 4.4, the desktop machine pc-1 connects to the Linux server via a Web browser, and the following actions occur. When Snort starts up, the network card is placed into promiscuous mode by the libpcap library. As the packet travels on the hub, from pc-1 to the Linux server, the network card gets the packet and copies it to the network driver. The libpcap library enabled by Snort is in an endless loop watching for packets. When it receives the packets from the network card driver, it then runs the *ProcessPacket()* function (in the decode.c source code).

The *ProcessPacket* function calls the *DecodeEthPkt* function, which decodes the Ethernet frame. From within the *DecodeEthPkt* function, the *DecodeIP* function decodes the IP protocol. Finally, the *DecodeTCPPkt* function is called, which decodes the TCP packet. So, we have decoded the TCP packet and linked it to the appropriate data structures, and are now ready for detection. Figure 4.5 illustrates the different decode functions and the order in which they are processed.

Figure 4.5 Snort Decode Structure

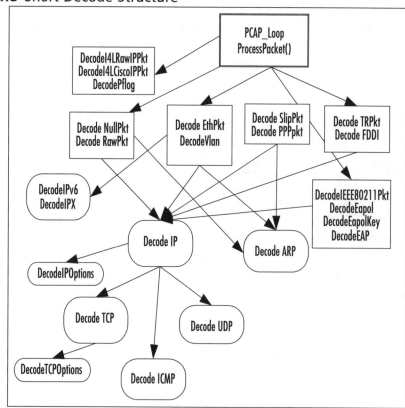

> **OINK!**
>
> Snort supports a number of protocols, but some are simply recognized and nothing is done to them. An example of this is IPX. Snort recognizes IPX, but does not decode it above Layer 2—Snort only uses it for statistics.

Storage of Packets

As we move through the Snort functions, you might be asking, "Where does Snort store the actual packets?" The answer is in pointers and data structures held in memory. If you look at the code in decode.h, you will see data structures that define all of the protocols used by Snort; for example, TCP, IP, and Ethernet. Snort overlays these structures onto the raw packets using pointers that represent the protocol. For example, the pointer to the raw data that comes from libpcap as an Ethernet frame is the _EthrHdr_ header. In the case of higher-level protocols such as TCP, it will overlay further data structures onto them. The following example shows the Ethernet and the TCP header structures.

```
/*
 * Ethernet header
 */
typedef struct _EtherHdr
{
    u_int8_t ether_dst[6];
    u_int8_t ether_src[6];
    u_int16_t ether_type;
}


typedef struct _TCPHdr
{
    u_int16_t th_sport;        /* source port */
    u_int16_t th_dport;        /* destination port */
    u_int32_t th_seq;          /* sequence number */
    u_int32_t th_ack;          /* acknowledgement number */
    u_int8_t th_offx2;         /* offset and reserved */
    u_int8_t th_flags;         /* flags */
    u_int16_t th_win;          /* window */
    u_int16_t th_sum;          /* checksum */
    u_int16_t th_urp;          /* urgent pointer */
}
```

The core of all of these structures is _Packet_. From within _Packet_, all of the Snort data structures are created and built as shown in the following _Packet_ structure:

```
typedef struct _Packet
{
    struct pcap_pkthdr *pkth;   /* BPF data */
    u_int8_t *pkt;                   /* base pointer to the raw packet data */
    EtherHdr *eh;                    /* standard TCP/IP/Ethernet/ARP headers */
    VlanTagHdr *vh;
    WifiHdr *wifih;              /* wireless LAN header */
    EtherARP *ah;
```

```
     IPHdr *iph, *orig_iph; /* and orig. headers for ICMP_*_UNREACH family
*/
     u_int32_t ip_options_len;
     u_int8_t *ip_options_data;

     TCPHdr *tcph, *orig_tcph;
     u_int32_t tcp_options_len;
     u_int8_t *tcp_options_data;

     UDPHdr *udph, *orig_udph;…
```

Processing Packets 101

Now that we have obtained some data packets and decoded them into the different protocols, what is the next step in processing? There are three phases to this next step:

1. Preprocessors
2. Detect engines and plug-ins
3. Output plug-ins

Preprocessors

Before the packets are sent to the detection engine, they are first sent to the preprocessors. The preprocessor concept originated in Snort v1.5. The main idea behind the introduction of preprocessors was to provide a framework to allow for alerting, dropping, and modification of the packets before they reached Snort's main detection engine.

OINK!

For a more detailed look at preprocessors, please refer to Chapter 6, "Preprocessors."

Referring back to Figure 4.4, the desktop machine pc-2 decides to connect to the Windows 2000 Web server. The user opens the browser and enters the following:

```
http://10.1.1.251/%73%63%72%69%70%74%73/%68%61%63%6B%6D%65.%65%78%65
```

The HTTP protocol specifies that binary characters can be passed within the Universal Resource Identifier (URI) by using *%xx* notation, where *xx* is the hex value of the character. When the URI arrives at the Web server, it converts it to http://10.1.1.251/scripts/hackme.exe.

Within Snort, the pattern matcher is looking for a pattern of */scripts/hackme.exe*, but we have effectively mangled the URI so it does not trigger an alert.

The _decode Family of Preprocessors

One task of the preprocessor is to normalize packets before sending them to the detection engine. In the case of our HTTP request, the *http_decode* preprocessor changes the URI before it reaches the detection engine. We can still write signatures as we normally do; the preprocessor normalizes them into a standard format.

> **OINK!**
>
> An excellent white paper on the IDS evasion of Web attacks can be found at www.wiretrip.net/rfp/pages/whitepapers/whiskerids.html. The author, Rain Forest Puppy, was one of the key developers of the http_decode preprocessor.

The *telnet_decode*, *ftp_decode*, and *rpc_decode* preprocessors follow the same lines as *http_decode*. However, instead of normalizing URIs, these preprocessors normalize Telnet, FTP, and RPC traffic before it is sent to the detection engine.

The frag2 Preprocessor

Let's take this concept one step further. What if we fragmented the packets? Fragmentation is a necessary function of the TCP/IP suite, as different routers on the Internet (or internally) have different sized network links. Fragmentation dissects the packets into smaller pieces so that they can fit the smaller links as they travel the network. However, as helpful as fragmentation is, fragmenting packets can also be an extremely effective way of bypassing pattern-based IDSs. One of the most famous tools for doing this is fragrouter.

OINK!

The existence of fragmented packets is normal on a network, especially if it's connected to the Internet. However, a large number of fragmented packets on a network would be classified as suspicious. You can block fragmented packets on most modern firewalls or routers, but in doing so, you might block access to systems for certain users who are traveling over a number of router hops or small links. It's definitely a trade-off between security and usability that needs careful review.

The fragrouter program takes network traffic and fragments it into small pieces before putting it onto the network, thus effectively evading pattern-matching systems. The pattern-based IDSs would only see portions of the packets as they travel across the network. At the far side, the TCP/IP stack on the Web server would reassemble the packets and interpret the results. One downside of fragmentation is that it can be used as an effective denial-of-service (DoS) attack. If your fragmented packets are exceptionally small, the Web server is using valuable system resources to reassemble them, thus clogging up the bandwidth available to your network. An IDS also has to reassemble the fragmented packets, which also requires a significant amount of memory and resources. Thus, if traffic volume is high enough and many fragmented packets are on the network, the IDS might be too busy reassembling fragmented packets to notice an attack on the Web server. Moreover, if the IDS is under load just watching normal traffic, it might miss a single packet that would make the signature invalid.

This brings us to the frag2 preprocessor. Using the frag2 preprocessor, fragmented packets are reassembled before they get to the detection engine, so signatures can be applied to the full sessions, not just the individual small packets. The frag2 preprocessor will also write alerts when fragmentation thresholds are reached.

Finally, what if we could trigger thousands of false-positives, thereby overloading the IDS, and as in a fragmentation attack make the IDS blind due to lack of resources? The stick (www.eurocompton.net/stick) program was released with this in mind. stick takes all of the signatures files in Snort and generates packets that trigger alerts on the IDS. In our previous HTTP example, stick would generate a packet that contained the "/scripts/hackme.exe" string on the HTTP port and then place it on the network. The IDS would see the traffic containing the pattern and alert.

The stream4 Preprocessor

The stream4 preprocessor was designed to make Snort *stateful*. At over 2000 lines of code, and able to handle up to 64,0000 connections, stream4 is one of the largest components of Snort. By making Snort stateful, it can avoid the problems created by stick and provide better signature-matching capabilities. In addition, as a byproduct, the stateful properties allow Snort to detect operating system finger-printing techniques and scans using *out of state* packets, typically used by the NMAP program (www.insecure.org/nmap).

When a TCP connection (Layer 3 of the TCP/IP) from a client to a server is made, a number of events take place. An initial conversation is carried out; this is known as the three-way handshake. Once the connection is set-up, data is transferred. When the data has been transferred, the conversation ends. Using the stream4 preprocessor, during these conversations Snort builds internal tables to represent these sessions and tears them down after each session ends.

By making Snort capable of keeping its own state table, it becomes aware of a full session, not just individual SYN, ACK, and FIN flags to a particular server. This is important when we try to apply signatures, as in the example of a user opening a connection to a Web server. In this case, Snort monitors the conversation between the client (the user's browser) and the server (Web server), and will build internal tables for each session. When the detection engine matches a packet, it checks to see if it is part of an established session, rather than blindly matching packets against signatures (which the stick program exploited). Snort is now capable of only alerting on matched signatures to established sessions.

Another advantage of Snort being stateful is that out-of-sequence scanning techniques can also be detected (for example, a *stealth FIN scan*, a popular scanning method using Nmap). According to the TCP protocol, FIN packets are only seen during the closing sequence of a connection (see Figure 4.6). If a FIN packet is sent to a closed TCP port, the server should send back an RST packet to the other side. The stream4 preprocessor will alert on the event of a FIN packet sent for a session that was never established.

Figure 4.6 TCP Session

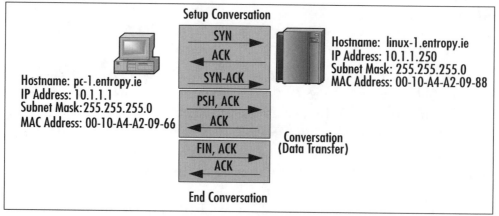

In the following output from the stream4 preprocessor, the final line shows the SF (SYN FIN) flag set on the packet.

```
[**] [111:13:1] (spp_stream4) STEALTH ACTIVITY (SYN FIN scan) detection
[**]
07/09-19:49:16.000000 10.1.1.236:1034 -> 10.1.1.220:6000
TCP TTL:255 TOS:0x0 ID:31377 IpLen:20 DgmLen:40
******SF Seq: 0xFFFFFFFF  Ack: 0x0  Win: 0x1000  TcpLen: 20
```

The portscan Family of Preprocessors

An important part of an IDS is the ability to detect portscans. Portscans are a regular occurrence on any network connected to the Internet, and are used by potential intruders to identify servers and the ports that are open. Once the attacker discovers which ports are open, he attempts to exploit the services provided on those ports. Referring back to Figure 4.6, a typical TCP portscan works by sending a initial SYN to a server. The server replies with a SYN/ACK if the port is open, and a SYN/RST if the port is not listening. By sending SYNs to multiple ports and watching for the return SYN-ACK, we can map which ports are open on a server. Snort detects portscans through the use of preprocessors. The current 2.0.0 version of Snort, has two portscan preprocessors available:

- portscan preprocessor
- portscan2 preprocessor

There are some differences in the way in which each preprocessor works. The portscan preprocessor is watching for a single machine (client) connecting to multiple ports on a single server over a period of time. It also detects UDP portscans the same way and Stealth scans (see the section *Stealth Portscanning*).

The portscan2 preprocessor is effectively the bigger brother of portscan. It has the same functionality as the original portscan preprocessor, but is now a complete rewrite of code. At its core it uses the conversation plug-in, similar to stream4, which tracks connection states. Therefore, portscan2 can determine if a SYN-ACK (see Figure 4.6) is part of a legitimate current connection or an actual scan. portscan2 also has a new output format that provides more information on the portscan, and supports separate thresholds for ports and machines hit in a given time. Going forward, the portscan2 preprocessor will be the standard portscan detector for Snort.

OINK!

The limitation in portscan detectors is, of course, the concept of "slow scans." If you scan a machine over the course of a week—say, one port per hour—it won't trigger the portscan detectors, as they would have to store details on every connection made throughout the day. On a busy or large network, it's a daunting task.

So, which preprocessor should you run? The portscan preprocessor is a simple and stable portscan detector. The portscan2 preprocessor is new, but does have some additional tuning options, thresholds, and better stealth scan detection. If your Snort server has the system resources in terms of memory and CPU processing power, run both over a period of time to see which gives the best results. In addition, you might run a few portscans yourself and see the results (with permission from your system administrator, of course).

OINK!

The default configuration of both portscan preprocessors will always throw up false positives; the usual suspects are DNS servers and Web proxy servers. The portscan preprocessors can be configured to ignore traffic from certain hosts, and in the case of portscan2, certain ports to and from a server. We show the configuration of the portscan preprocessors later in Chapter 6.

Stealth Portscanning

Nowadays, the "bad guys" are trying to be stealthy in their port scanning attempts. Figure 4.7 is a representation of the TCP header.

Figure 4.7 TCP Header

Source Port		Destination Port	
Sequence Number			
Acknowledgement Number			
Offset	Reserved	Flags	Window
Checksum		Urgentpointer	
Options			
Data			

Within the TCP header are flags that denote the state of the packet. These flags can be URG, ACK, PSH, RST, SYN, and FIN, and represent different states of the session (see Figure 4.6). By mixing up the TCP flags, the attacker is hoping to elicit a response from the server to allow him to map open services. More importantly, however, the attacker is trying to avoid detection by portscan detection programs.

OINK!

You can also reference the earlier section *Storage of Packets*; the TCP Header structure is a representation of Figure 4.7.

A number of scans rely on setting different TCP flags; for example:

- **Full XMAS scan** Sets the TCP flags to FIN, URG, PSH. The target server should send back an RST on all closed ports.

- **TCP FIN scan** Sets the TCP flag to be FIN. As with the XMAS scan, the target should send back an RST.

- **NULL scan** Sets the TCP flag to have no options. Again, the target should send back an RST.

portscan Output

The portscan and portscan2 preprocessors both send alerts using the standard Snort output alerting mechanism (see the section *Output and Logs* later in the chapter). However, they do have their own in-built logging system that's separate from the main Snort output plug-ins. The logging system is configured in snort.conf under the relevant portscan or portscan2 preprocessor section.

The following alerts are generated from portscan and portscan2, and would be sent to the Snort output facility:

```
[**] [100:1:1] spp_portscan: PORTSCAN DETECTED to port 1 from 192.168.1.53
(STEALTH)
[**] [117:1:1] (spp_portscan2) Portscan detected from 192.168.1.53: 6
targets 14 ports in 11 seconds
```

The following are sample contents of portscan.log and scan.log:

- **Portscan.log** Sample data is from a Full XMAS scan.

  ```
  Oct  6 20:35:47 192.168.1.53:52645 -> 192.168.1.1:40936 XMAS
  **U*P**F
  ```

- **Scan.log** A full XMAS scan, but contains more data than portscan.log does.

  ```
  10/06-20:35:47.000000  TCP src: 192.168.1.53 dst: 192.168.1.1
  sport: 52645 dport: 40936 tgts: 3 ports: 59 flags: **U*P**F
  event_id: 1298
  ```

OINK!

Because the portscan preprocessors only send alerts to Snort, if you are configuring Snort to "Log to Database," none of the events will be written. No logs will be written either, as the preprocessors will be using their own log format.

Other Preprocessors

A number of other preprocessors ship with Snort version 2.0.0. Some of these are in the experimental stage of development. Table 4.1 lists the preprocessors that are available and a brief description of their functionality.

Table 4.1 Other Snort Preprocessors

Preprocessors	Function
rpc_decode	Decodes RPC, similar to the HTTP decoder
telnet_decode	Decodes Telnet and FTP, similar to the HTTP decoder
conversation	Provides basic conversation status on protocols (used by the portscan2 preprocessor)
Back Orifice detector	Decodes Back Orifice network traffic
arpspoof	Experimental ARP misuse detection code
asn1_decode	Experimental ASN1 detection code
fnord	Polymorphic shellcode analyzer and detector

Understanding Rule Parsing and Detection Engines

We now have the packets from the network, we've decoded them and placed them into our data structures, and have organized, filtered, and decoded the packet streams. The next part of the journey is the detection engine.

The rules engine can be translated into two components:

- Rules builder/translator
- Detection engine based on the built rules

Rules Builder

Snort rules are text based and usually stored in a directory or subdirectory from the Snort binary. The rules files are categorized into different groups; for example, the file ftp.rules contains a selection of FTP attacks and exploits.

On startup, Snort reads all of the rules files, and creates a three-dimensional (3D) linked list. Snort then uses this list to match packets against for detecting. The importing and reading of these files is done by the *ParseRulesFile()* function in the parser.c source code referenced from the main snort.c source code.

The building of the linked list is initiated from the main snort.c source code. On startup, Snort reads the snort.conf configuration file, and at the section "Step 4—Customize your rule set," links to each of the specified rules files. Contained in each of the rules files are the Snort rules that are parsed and the linked list created.

Step 4 of snort.conf:

```
###################################################################
# Step #4: Customize your rule set
#
.
include $RULE_PATH/bad-traffic.rules
include $RULE_PATH/exploit.rules
include $RULE_PATH/scan.rules
include $RULE_PATH/finger.rules
include $RULE_PATH/ftp.rules
include $RULE_PATH/telnet.rules
include $RULE_PATH/rpc.rules
.
```

OINK!

The following sections are a brief introduction to Snort rules. For a more detailed discussion of this topic, please refer to Chapter 5, "Playing by the Rules."

Rule Format

Before talking about how the linked list is created, let's look at a simple sample Snort FTP rule (Figure 4.8). The following rule detects an old FTP exploit on a Linux machine. This rule is stored in the ftp.rules file. Snort rules are in text format all on one line, and can be broken into two sections:

- The rule header

```
alert tcp $EXTERNAL_NET any -> $HOME_NET21
```

- The rule options

```
(msg:"FTP EXPLOIT wu-ftpd 2.6.0 site exec format string overflow
Linux"; flow:to_server, established; content:
"|31c031db31c9b046cd8031c031db|"; reference:bugtraq,1387;
reference:cve,CAN-2000-0573; reference arachnids,287;
classtype:attempted-admin; sid:344; rev4;)
```

Rule Header

The following is a detailed description of the syntax used in the rule header:

- **alert** This will be the output format used. For more information, refer to the subsequent section *Output and Logs* later in this chapter. This output format will match to the top parts of the linked list tree header (*ListHead*). Other options for this position in the rule include *log, pass, dynamic,* and *activate.*

- **TCP** This part of the syntax is the protocol being used; in this case, TCP. This will match to the top part of the linked list. Other options for this position in the rule include UDP, IP, and ICMP.

- **$EXTERNAL_NET** This part of the syntax is the source IP address (by default set to *any*).

- **any** This is the source port set to *any* source port.

- **->** This arrow indicates direction of the conversation; in this case, *$EXTERNAL_NET* on *any* port going to *$HOME_NET* on port 21.

- **$HOME_NET** When defining rules in Snort, *$Variables* are used. A variable is defined once at the start of the snort.conf file and is used throughout the rules. The *$HOME_NET* variable would be defined as our network (in our example, 10.1.1.0/24), and the *$EXTERNAL_NET* variable would be set to *any*, which can be translated to "any network." On initialization, the Snort rules parser will substitute the *$HOME_NET* variable with the value set in the snort.conf. If you change your network address, rather than having to change all the rules, just change the *$HOME_NET* variable.

- **21** This is the destination port of the attack. In our rule header we can see that we are looking for any potential attacks on port 21. Port 21 is the port typically used for FTP action.

Rule Options

The following is a detailed description of the syntax used in the rule option:

- **_msg_** "FTP EXPLOIT wu-ftpd 2.6.0 site exec format string overflow Linux." This is the message displayed by the alert.

- **_flow:to_server,established_** Snort contains keywords that link to detection plug-ins in the options part of a rule. The *flow* option is the third dimension of the linked list, and is a pointer to the clientserver detection plug-ins (see the source code sp_clientserver.c). The clientserver plug-ins link to the stream4 preprocessor to check if the packet is part of an established session.

- **_content_** "*|31c031db 31c9b046 cd80 31c031db|*" If the packet is matched against the Rule Tree node, then the session is an established one. Snort will take the following content and try to match it against the packet using the Boyer-Moore search algorithm (see the section *How a Packet Is Matched* later in the chapter.)

- **_Reference_** This keyword allows you to include references to third-party attack identification information; for example, URLs to Bugtraq, McAfee, and the manufacturer or identification codes from vendors.

- **_Classtype: misc-attack_** Attacks are given a classification to allow users to quickly understand and prioritize each attack. Each classification has a default priority, which allows the user to prioritize what events he looks at via a simple number: 1 for High, 2 for Medium, and 3 for Low.

- **_Sid344_** This is the Snort rule unique identifier. All of the rules in Snort have a unique identification number. Information on the rule can be checked at www.snort.org/snort-db. The SID is also used by reporting programs to easily identify rules.

- **_Rev:4_** This section of the options refers to the version number for the rule. When Snort rules are submitted by the open-source community, the rules go through a revision process. Over time, this process allows the rules to be fine-tuned and to avoid false-positives.

OINK!

Updating the Snort rule descriptions is a community effort. A number of signatures do not have descriptions, so if you have some spare time, pick a signature and write a description (www.snort.org/snort-db/help.html).

What Is a 3D Linked List?

While we are processing the rules files, we need a way to store them for matching against the incoming packets. Snort uses a 3D linked list (see Figure 4.8). In software development terms, a *linked list* is an algorithm for storing a list of items; in our case, the Snort rules and their options. Snort stores rules and their options in the linked list and then searches the list for a rule header match. Then, within the header match, it searches for a pattern match or a match using a detection plug-in.

Figure 4.8 The Snort Rule Tree

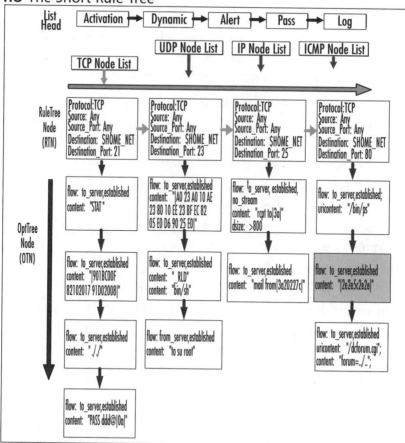

Components of the Snort Rule Tree

There are five separate chains of rules. These chains are the list headings at the top of Figure 4.8.

- **Activation** Alert and then turn on another dynamic rule.
- **Dynamic** Log the traffic when called by the above activation rule.
- **Alert** Generate an alert and then log the packet.
- **Pass** Ignore this packet.
- **Log** Log the traffic (don't alert).

For each of the five chains of rules, there are separate linked lists, broken down by protocol. This level of the tree is referred to as the Rule Tree Nodes (RTN). The four protocols supported by the Rule Tree are:

- **TCP** TCP protocol; for example, SMTP, HTTP, FTP
- **UDP** UDP protocol; for example, DNS lookups
- **ICMP** ICMP protocol; for example, ping, traceroute
- **IP** IP protocol; for example, IPSec, IGMP

Within each of the protocol linked lists are the Rule options, which are referred to as the Option Tree Nodes (OTN). An example of these options would be:

- **Content** Content checked by the Boyer-Moore pattern matching algorithm
- **Flow** Link to detection plug-in

On initialization, Snort reads the rule files and populates the linked lists. Figure 4.8 shows a populated *OptionTreeNode* for the TCP *RuleTreeNode* off the Alert chain.

How a Packet Is Matched

Once we have built our linked lists, we need a method to navigate the list to look for a match to the packets. The following Snort HTTP rule is present in the middle-right portion of the following output.

```
alert tcp $EXTERNAL_NET any -> $HTTP_SERVERS $HTTP_PORTS
(msg:"WEB_IIS..\.. acess";flow:to_server,established; content:
"|2e2e5c2e2e|"; reference: bugtraq,2218; reference:cve, CAN-199-0299;
classtype:web-application-attack; sid:974; rev:6;)
```

When the packet arrives at the detection engine, Snort will navigate through the rule headers in the following order: *Activation, Dynamic, Alert, Pass,* and *Log*. Within each of the rule headers, the RTNs and the OTNs will be checked. In our example, the action is *alert*; therefore, the first two nodes *Activation* and *Dynamic* have been checked but no matches returned.

Snort then moves to the Alert chain. The search method is dependent on the protocol of the packet (in our example, TCP), so we start on the TCP node list. Traveling along the RTNs from left to right, it tries to match the packet by the following parameters:

- Source IP address

- Destination IP address

- Source port

- Destination port

When Snort finds a match, the algorithm moves down the columns looking for a match inside each of the OTNs. There might be a number of HTTP rules, so Snort checks the options of each. When we get to our HTTP exploit, Snort will do the following:

Within our particular option node are two items:

- A pointer to a detection plug-in, which is the third dimension of the linked list, the first two being the RTN and OTNs. The flow plug-in checks to see if the packet matches an established session.

- A pattern we want to search for using the Boyer-Moore Fast String Searching Algorithm.

OINK!

There are currently 35 individual options you can have in the Options part of a rule (OTN). As long as the rule doesn't exceed 8k, you could use them all, but we are keeping our example simple.

One of the most efficient string pattern-matching algorithms is the Boyer-Moore Fast String Searching Algorithm (www.cs.utexas.edu/users/moore/best-ideas/string-searching/index.html). This searching algorithm is extremely efficient at matching patterns in a string. When a rule contains a *content:* option, the algorithm is used to search the contents. The contents can be in a number of formats, binary or text, or a mixture of the two; in our HTTP-based example, it's in binary "|2e2e5c2e2e|".

Now that we have found a match, we exit the tree structure and return to the Alert tree head. We alert via the output format (see the section *Output and Logs*) specified and then exit. Snort uses a fast exit strategy; once it matches a packet, it doesn't check it against any other rules.

OINK!

Snort version 2.0 gives users the ability to choose from three completely different pattern-matching algorithms depending on their use of Snort: Aho-Corasick, Wu-Manber, and Boyer-Moore search algorithms. Further information can be found in the "High Performance Multi-Rule Inspection Engine" white paper (see the section *Snort 2.0 Rule Design* later in the chapter).

Pass Rules

Sometimes you want to ignore traffic from a particular server. There are two options for this:

- Use BPF filter language on Snort startup (see later section "Using Snort as a quick sniffer")
- Use a Pass Rule (pass rules can be set up to ignore particular traffic)

If we want to ignore the traffic from a particular server for a particular signature, we can use the Pass rule; see the changes we made to the previous HTTP exploit rule. The pass rule will ignore any traffic that matches the following signature:

```
pass tcp $EXTERNAL_NET any -> $HTTP_SERVERS $HTTP_PORTS
(flow:to_server,established; content "|2e2e5c2e2e|";)
```

OINK!

To enable the Pass rule, you have to change the mechanism Snort uses to process rules (Activation, Dynamic, Alert, Pass, Log). This is done with the –o command-line switch, which changes it to (Pass, Activation, Dynamic, Alert, Log). Be careful when using this switch, because it is possible to set up a Pass rule that will pass all traffic and alert on nothing.

Log Rules

The *log* option is for logging of all packets that match a rule. The *log* option does not alert; it just logs to the defined output format (see the section *Output and Logs*). The *log* option doesn't work when enabled with Snort in binary mode.

```
log tcp $EXTERNAL_NET any -> $HTTP_SERVERS $HTTP_PORTS
(flow:to_server,established; content"|2e2e5c2e2e|";)
```

Dynamic and Activation rules

The *dynamic* and *activation* rules allow you to alert on a packet, similar to the *alert* option, but then log a number of packets after it. In our next example, we are alerting to the output facility when the packet matches, and then we are linking to the dynamic rule, which logs the next 128 packets coming from *$EXTERNAL_NET* on any port going to the *$HTTP_SERVERS* on the *$HTTP_PORTS*.

```
activate tcp $EXTERNAL_NET any-> $HTTP_SERVERS $HTTP_PORTS (msg:"WEB-
IIS..\..access"flow:to_server,established: activates: 1;
content"|2e2e5c2e2f|"; reference:bugtraq,2218;reference:cve,CAN-199-0229;
classtype:web-application-attack; sid:974;rev6;)

dynamic tcp $EXTERNAL_NET any -> $HTTP_SERVERS $HTTP_SEVERS $HTTP_PORTS
(activated_by: 1; count 128;)
```

OINK!

The *activate* and *dynamic* options are being phased out by a new tagging option available as the *tag* keyword.

Detection Plug-Ins

Snort has a plug-in architecture for the detection engine; the current version 2.0.0 of Snort has 22 built-in detection plug-ins. The files are contained in the detection-plug-ins subdirectory from the main SRC directory.

The detection plug-in architecture allows other developers to write plug-ins that link into the Snort rules. An example of a third-party detection plug-in is the snortsam program, available at www.snortsam.net/index.html. This program provides a link between detecting an exploit (our FTP exploit) and the ability to reconfigure your firewall to block the source IP address. If we take our original FTP rule and modify it for snortsam, the rule would look like the following:

```
alert tcp $EXTERNAL_NET any -> $HOME_NET 21
(msg:"FTP EXPLOIT wu-ftpd 2.6.0 site exec format string overflow Linus";
flow:to_server,established; content: "|31c031db31c9b046cd80 31c031db|";
reference:bugtraq,1387; reference:cve,CAN-2000-0573;
reference:arachnids,287; classtype:attempted-admin; sid:344; rev:4; fwsam:
src, 1 hour;)
```

The extra option is *fwsam: src, 1 hour;*, which translates into "block the source IP address of the attack for 1 hour."

OINK!

Snort also has the capability to tear down TCP connections and send "ICMP destination unreachable" for UDP connections using the *REACT* keyword.

Snort 2.0 Rule Design

A number of white papers on the design features of Snort 2.0 are available at www.sourcefire.com/technology/whitepapers.htm.
Of particular interest are the following papers:

- Snort 2.0—"Detection Revisited"

- Snort 2.0—"Multi-Rule Inspection Engine"

- Snort 2.0—"Rule Optimizer"

- Snort 2.0—"Protocol Flow Analyzer"

Output and Logs

Now that we have, sniffed, decoded, and detected events, we need a mechanism to write or display them in a meaningful fashion. This is where the output plug-ins become necessary. The output plug-ins differ from the other components of Snort, as there is no single entry point into the output plug-ins. Different components use the output plug-ins at different stages.

- The packet decode engine will use the output plug-ins; for example, output to TCPDump format or ASCII decode format.

- The preprocessor will use the output plug-ins to alert on events, but some have their own output format; for example, the portscan2 preprocessor.

- The detection engine will use the output plug-ins to alert and log.

Output modules are similar to the Snort preprocessors in that they allow Snort to be more flexible about how it presents its alerts and logs.

OINK!

Long term, the output stage will be moving to a separate process (see the section *Barnyard and Unified Output* later in the chapter). The main reason for this is that while monitoring high-speed networks, you don't want to have to wait for an output plug-in to write its alerts to a database.

The logging engine code mostly resides in the log.c file. Output plug-ins are defined in the output-plugins directory; the plug-ins start with the extension spo_. Deciding on the strategies for output is dependent on how you want to use Snort. There are multiple options you can use, including:

- **Snort as a quick sniffer** Using Snort as a quick sniffer to troubleshoot network issues.

- **Intrusion detection mode** Enabling Snort for intrusion detection.

- **Snort for honeypot capture and analysis** Using Snort's capability for packet capture and intrusion detection.

- **Logging to databases** Logging of alerts to an Enterprise database.

- **Alerting using SNMP** Integrating Snort into your network monitoring station (NMS) using the Simple Network Management Protocol (SNMP).

- **Barnyard and unified output** Separate program to process alerts and logs, created by Snort in unified mode output.

Snort can also do combinations of the preceding options; for example, writing to a database and alerting using SNMP to your NMS. You can also defined custom outputs for individual rules; for example, on a particular HTTP exploit alert to the NMS, all others log to a database. Multiple output plug-ins can be defined; each is run in turn on alerting

Snort as a Quick Sniffer

If you run Snort with the command *snort -v*, Snort will start up and then print out the IP/TCP/UDP/ICMP headers of the packets it's sniffed to the screen. Referring back to our sample network (Figure 4.4), if we are connected to pc-2 and want to Telnet onto our Linux server, Snort would see the following:

```
[root@linuxtest snort]# snort -v
Initializing Output Plugins!
Log directory = /var/log/snort
Initializing Network Interface eth0
        --== Initializing Snort ==--
Decoding Ethernet on interface eth0
        --== Initialization Complete ==--


<Header omitted for brevity>


06/04-23:34:49.280177 10.1.1.236:1056 -> 10.1.1.220:23
TCP TTL:64 TOS:0x10 ID:59230 IpLen:20 DgmLen:60 DF
******S* Seq: 0x46382934  Ack: 0x0  Win: 0x16D0  TcpLen: 40
TCP Options (5) => MSS: 1460 SackOK TS: 927387242 0 NOP WS: 0
=+=+=+=+=+=+=+=+=+=+=+=+=+=+=+=+=+=+=+=+=+=+=+=+=+=+=+=+=+=+=+=+
```

The first thing to notice is that Snort outputs to a standard format for each packet. In the preceding output, we can see our pc-2 desktop client (10.1.1.236)

on source port (1056) connecting to the Linux server (10.1.1.220) on port 23 (Telnet). Snort shows the IP and TCP protocol information, including the first SYN (***S).

Output Format

The *-v* switch shows basic IP/TCP/UDP/ICMP headers. If we want to see more information, we can use two other switches:

- The *-d* switch will show the application data in HEX and ASCII (Layer 7 of the OSI model).

- The *-e* switch will show the Data Link layer headers (Layer 2 of the OSI model).

```
06/04-23:39:05.288734 0:50:DA:42:B:9E -> 0:1:3:48:78:BA type:0x800 len:0x87

10.1.1.220:23 -> 10.1.1.236:1059 TCP TTL:64 TOS:0x10 ID:15596 IpLen:20
DgmLen:121 DF

***AP*** Seq: 0xB06E41D6  Ack: 0x56DB2709  Win: 0x16A0  TcpLen: 32

TCP Options (3) => NOP NOP TS: 115899727 927412845

FF FB 01 52 65 64 20 48 61 74 20 4C 69 6E 75 78   ...Red Hat Linux

20 72 65 6C 65 61 73 65 20 37 2E 33 20 28 56 61    release 7.3 (Va

6C 68 61 6C 6C 61 29 0D 0A 4B 65 72 6E 65 6C 20   lhalla)..Kernel

32 2E 34 2E 31 38 2D 33 20 6F 6E 20 61 6E 20 69   2.4.18-3 on an i

36 38 36 0D 0A                                            686..

=+=+=+=+=+=+=+=+=+=+=+=+=+=+=+=+=+=+=+=+=+=+=+=+=+=+=+=+=+=+=+=+=+=+=+=+
```

In the preceding output, the first line is the MAC address (Layer 2) of the client (0:50:DA:42:B:9E), and the last line is the ASCII decode of the Telnet. The rows in between are the IP and TCP protocol information.

As you can see, we are logging on to a Red Hat Linux machine.

Berkeley Packet Filter Commands

If you are connected to a busy network, it won't be long before your computer screen quickly fills up with decoded network traffic from Snort. When TCPDump was originally designed, the developers had a similar issue, so they filtered traffic using a command language called the Berkeley Packet Filter (BPF) commands. The BPF commands allow you specify protocols, hosts, and ports; basically, any field that can be decoded can be searched on or filtered by. With the BPF commands we can set up Snort to log to the screen but only for certain servers. For example, in Figure 4.4, if we only want to see traffic to and from the Linux machine on the Telnet port 23, we would apply the following BPF logic on Snort startup:

```
[root@linuxtest snort]# snort -vde host 10.1.1.220 and port 23
```

This will run Snort, display to the screen, and decode the Layer 7 and Layer 2 traffic, but only for the host 10.1.1.220 and only on the port 23 (Telnet). Further information on the BPF language can be found at www.tcpdump.org/tcp-dump_man.html.

Log to Disk

What if you want to log the traffic to disk for review later? If this is the case, you would use the following command:

```
[root@linuxtest snort]# snort -de -l /var/snort_logs
```

Note the missing *–v* option. This means that Snort will not log to the screen. The previous command puts Snort into sniffer mode, it creates files in the /var/snort_logs directory for each of the clients initiating connections (our pc-2 [10.1.1.236]), and then creates a file for each unique session. Contained in each file is the decoded traffic in ASCII representation format. Therefore, in the 10.1.1.236 subdirectory is a file called TCP:1059-23 (this refers to TCP the protocol, 1059 the source port, and 23 the destination port). Inside the file are the decoded packets similar to the information we saw in the *Output Format* section.

```
[root@linuxtest 10.1.1.236]# ls -la
drwx------       2 root       root          4096 Jun   4 23:58 .
drwxr-xr-x       7 root       root          4096 Jun   4 23:58 ..
-rw-------       1 root       root         27848 Jun   4 23:58 TCP:1059-23
```

Log In to a pcap Format

The previous configuration creates text-based files with the decode traffic inside. Using the following command:

```
[root@linuxtest snort]# snort -l /var/snort_logs -b
```

all traffic is logged in binary mode, and the output is written into a single file in pcap format in the /var/snort_logs directory.

This has a number of advantages:

- It allows review using open-source or commercial sniffer programs; for example, Ethereal.

- It allows playback into Snort or sniffers.

- It is extremely quick; basically, Snort takes all the traffic and writes it to a file.

Now, what if we wanted to read back into Snort the pcap formatted log file we just created, and for Snort to decode the packets as in the previous examples? The following command reads the file back into Snort for decode:

```
[root@linuxtest snort]# snort -de -r snort.log.1046008361
```

Alternatively, you can also apply BPF filters and use the *–v* switch to display the traffic to the screen:

```
[root@linuxtest snort]# snort -v -de -r snort.log.1046008361 host
10.1.1.220 and port 23
```

OINK!

If you have snort.log in binary mode, you can use Ethereal (See the earlier section *How Does Snort Link into libpcap*?) to import the file. Ethereal gives you a GUI-based sniffer, and you can review the traffic at your leisure.

Intrusion Detection Mode

When we start up Snort in default IDS mode, the default output is to alert to a text file called "alerts" in a subdirectory called "log," and then create a subdirectory structure similar to the previous *Log to Disk* section.

Snort Logging

Before we discuss output with Snort in IDS mode, we need to talk about the different Snort output modes:

- Alerting mode
- Logging mode

Alerting Mode

When an Alert rule is matched (see the section *How a Packet Is Matched* earlier in the chapter), the Alert action in Snort is hard-coded to do two things:

- Output an event to what is called the *alert facility*.
- Log as much as possible/desired to the configured Logging mode.

The *alert facility* controls the actual format of the alert and, to a certain degree, its destination. The alert facility options are as follows.

- **Full** Full alerts format will have the alert messages in addition to the full packet headers (default).
- **Fast** Alert is in a simple format with a timestamp, alert messages, source and destination IPs/ports.
- **Syslog** Logs to syslog; the default alerting facilities are LOG_AUTH-PRIV and LOG_ALERT.
- **Unixsock** Sets up a UNIX domain socket and sends alerts to it.
- **SMB** Send WinPopup messages.

The default alert facility for Snort is Full; this can be changed from the command line on startup of Snort.

Logging Mode

The *Logging mode* just logs full packet information to the various sources without generating an alert. The logging mode can be called directly using the *log, dynamic* keywords in a Snort rule, or as a secondary action from the *alert* keyword. By default, logs are put into /var/log/Snort (but this can be changed using the –*l* switch).

The default logging mechanism writes logs in the same fashion as the output format discussed earlier in the section *Log to Disk*. Within the subdirectory defined by the –*l* switch (-l /var/log), a subdirectory is created for each client machine IP address. In the following example, a subdirectory for pc-1 has been created, and inside each subdirectory are alerts, which contain the alert messages and a packet decode. The scan.log is the output from the portscan2 preprocessor, and the alert file was created by the "Alert facility."

```
[root@linuxtest log]# ls -la
drwxr-xr-x   15 root      root         4096 Jun  5 23:31 .
drwxr-xr-x    6 root      root         4096 Jun  2 11:13 ..
drwx------    2 root      root         4096 Jun  5 23:31 10.1.1.1
drwx------    2 root      root         4096 Jun  5 23:31 127.0.0.1
drwx------    2 root      root         4096 Jun  5 23:31 192.168.1.1
drwx------    2 root      root         4096 Jun  5 23:31 10.1.1.220
drwx------    2 root      root         4096 Jun  5 23:31 192.168.1.150
drwx------    2 root      root         4096 Jun  5 23:31 192.168.1.64
-rw-------    1 root      root       622502 Jun  5 23:31 alert
-rw-------    1 root      root        17732 Jun  5 23:31 scan.log
```

Logging Formats

A number of logging plug-ins are available to Snort, and are configured in the logging section of the snort.conf file (see the following example). Multiple output formats are possible, so you can log to a particular syslog "logging facility" and output to a CSV format.

```
###################################################################
# Step #3: Configure output plugins
# Uncomment and configure the output plugins you decide to use.
```

The best way to support multiple output plug-ins is to specify them in the Snort configuration file (snort.conf). This is preferable, as the command-line switches will always override the options in the snort.conf, giving the message "WARNING: command line overrides rules file alert plugin!"

The following output plug-ins are available to Snort:

- **CSV** (Comma Separated Values) This output format allows alert data to be written in format easily importable to a database or spreadsheet.

- **Syslog** Similar to the option from the *alert facility*, this option provides more customization on the actual syslog facility output.

- **Database** One of the more popular output plug-ins, it allows data to be written into the following databases: MySQL, PostgreSQL, unixODBC, Oracle, and MS-SQL Server.

- **Null** This allows Snort to alert via the Alert facility, but not create any log files.

- **Tcpdump** This allows Snort to output log files in TCPDump format.

- **SnmpTrap** This allows Snort to send SNMP traps into NMSs.

- **Unified** This plug-in is the future of Snort, and is the fastest possible method of logging Snort events. It will log into a binary format with FAST alerting. The Barnyard program will read the files from the Unified format, process them, and then output to a number of formats.

- **XML** The XML plug-in enables Snort to log in SNML (Simple Network Markup Language, a.k.a. Snort Markup Language) to a file or over a network.

OINK!

If you are compiling Snort from the source code, you need to specify the links to third-party output libraries. For example, when compiling Snort with MySQL support, you need to install MySQL and its client libraries before Snort is installed, and also configure Snort to use the libraries while compiling itself. To add MySQL support, use the *./configure —with-mysql=/usr/local/mysql* switch.

The following will configure Snort to run in its most basic intrusion detection mode, Snort will start up, log everything "Full" to the log directory, and use the snort.conf file for configured options.

```
[root@linuxtest snort]# snort -l ./log -c snort.conf
```

Snort for Honeypot Capture and Analysis

A honeypot provides security researchers with information on the latest attacks and exploits being used by the attackers. The honeypot involves placing servers on the Internet and then watching them being hacked. During this process, the researchers need to gather as much network information as possible, and then have the ability to replay the attacks or review the network traffic.

The following will configure Snort to capture all the traffic in binary format:

```
[root@linuxtest snort]# snort -l /var/snort_logs -b
```

Once we have collected a large amount of data over a one-week period, for example, we want to read it back into Snort and apply signatures to it.

```
[root@linuxtest snort]# snort -r snort.log.1046008362 -l /var/snort_logs/
-c snort.conf
```

OINK!

A customized snort.conf is available at http://project.honeynet.org/ papers/honeynet/tools/ for use in honeynet projects.

Logging to Databases

The database plug-ins (spo_database.c and spo_database.h) use a slightly different methodology when writing alerts and logs (see the previous section *Snort Logging*). Normally, the *log* keyword in the Snort rule links to the log facility, and the *alert* option attaches it to the alert facility, but also writes to the log facility. The database plug-ins are slightly different: if the database plug-in is configured for *alert*, it will only receive output from alert rules, whereas if it's configured for *log*, it will receive output from both log and alert rules.

The following is an example configuration in the snort.conf:

```
output database: alert, mysql, user=snort password=x dbname=snort
host=mysql
```

OR

```
output database: log, mysql, user=snort password=x dbname=snort host=mysql
```

The "alerts" from preprocessors (for example, portscan2) will be written to the database only if the database plug-in is set to "alert." In that case, the actual decoded packets for alerts are created in a subdirectory in the same manner as in the section *Logging Mode*. If the database plug-in is set to "log," then preprocessor alerts will not be sent to the database plug-in, but the packet decodes for the alerts will be sent (used by ACID for Layer 3 and Layer 4 decodes). This means that in "log" mode, a third-party reporting tool such as snortsnarf (www.silicon-defense.com) is needed to report on the preprocessors output, because the events are not written to the database.

The database plug-in currently supports the following databases:

- **MySQL** www.mysql.org
- **PostgreSQL** www.postgresql.org
- **unixODBC** www.unixodbc.org
- **Oracle** www.oracle.com
- **MS-SQL Server** www.microsoft.com

Snort Reporting Front Ends

Once a database has been created and the data is being logged into it, we will need a mechanism to query the database and generate reports. We can use the Analysis Console Engine for Intrusion Detection (ACID) at www.cert.org/kb/acid. ACID is a PHP-based analysis engine that can search and process the data from databases written to them by Snort. ACID supports the following features:

- Query-builder and search interface for finding alerts matching on alert meta information (for example, signature, detection time), as well as the underlying network evidence (for example, source/destination address, ports, payload, or flags).

- Packet viewer (decoder) will graphically display the Layer 3 and Layer 4 packet information of logged alerts.

- Alert management by providing constructs to logically group alerts to create incidents (alert groups), deleting the handled alerts or false positives, exporting to e-mail for collaboration, or archiving of alerts to transfer them between alert databases.

- Chart and statistic generation based on time, sensor, signature, protocol, IP address, TCP/UDP ports, or classification.

Building the Database

Before the databases can be used, tables within the database need to be created to store the Snort data. Contained in the *contrib* directory are database creation scripts; for example, *create_mysql* or *create_oracle*. These scripts create the tables and fields within each specific type of database. To set up the database plug-in for MySQL, follow these steps:

1. Install MySQL.

2. Compile Snort with MySQL support.

3. Create a Snort user in the MySQL database and set up security.

4. Create the MySQL tables using the *create_mysql sql* script; this creates the Snort tables used to store the data.

5. Configure the snort.conf database line
   output database: log, mysql, user=snort password=xxx dbname=snort host=mysql-server the username is Snort, the database to log to is called Snort, and the MySQL server is called mysql-server).

6. Start up Snort. During initialization, Snort will call the output plug-ins that will make a connection to the database.

OINK!

The database plug-in author Roman Danyliw has an excellent Web site that contains lots of information about the database plug-in— www.andrew.cmu.edu/~rdanyliw/snort/snortdb/snortdb_faq.html.

Alerting Using SNMP

SNMP is a de-facto standard for inter-network management of devices. The Snort SNMP plug-in (spo_SnmpTrap.c and spo_SnmpTrap.h) can send SNMP traps and SNMP informs to NMSs. The SNMP plug-in requires the net-snmp libraries available at http://net-snmp.sourceforge.net to be installed first, and Snort to be compiled with SNMP support (./configure –with-snmp). The plug-in will support SNMP version 2.0 and SNMP version 3.0.

OINK!

The main developers of the SNMP plug-in have a detailed overview of the Snort SNMP process at www.cysol.co.jp/contrib/ snortsnmp/snortSnmpGuide.html.

Barnyard and Unified Output

The unified output plug-in (spo_unified.c and spo_unified.h) allows Snort to write *alerts* and *logs* into a single binary formatted file (unified format), which allows Snort to output alerts and logs quickly and efficiently. The Barnyard program reads the unified formatted file and then outputs it in a number of formats.

The separation of the output-processing component of Snort allows Snort to monitor the traffic, write to the unified format on alert, and then continue monitoring traffic. The output plug-ins that normally slow Snort down are now moved to Barnyard, which processes the unified file and outputs to the following formats:

- *Alert_Fast* Writes output in a similar fashion to the current "Alert Fast" format.

- *Log_Dump* Writes output into a decoded ASCII packet dump.

- *Alert_Html* Creates a series of HTML pages for alerts.

- *Alert_CSV* Writes alerts into a CSV format (similar to the current CSV output plug-in).

- *Alert_Syslog* Writes alerts out to syslog facilities (similar to the current syslog output plug-in).

- *Output_pcap* Writes data out to pcap format.

- *Acid_DB* Writes alerts/data into the database scheme used by ACID.

Summary

In this chapter, we reviewed both the OSI and TCP/IP models. Understanding these models is necessary when discussing network-based technologies. Once we had a clear understanding of network protocol layouts, we then moved on to how Snort gets packets from the network with a network card in *promiscuous mode*. We then discussed the libpcap library, which provides a mechanism to get the packets off the *promiscuous mode* card and into Snort.

Once Snort has the packets from libpcap, it creates data structures for the packets, decodes them by protocol, and starts the detection process. The detection process involves first passing the packets on to the preprocessor plug-ins such as stream4 and frag2. The preprocessor plug-ins provide a mechanism to check or mangle the packets before they get to the main decoder plug-ins. The stream4 plug-in gives Snort *stateful inspection* capabilities, and frag2 reassembles fragmented packets. After passing the packets through the preprocessor plug-ins, the packets arrive at the main decode engine, which will match the packets against its 3D linked list of signatures and decoder plug-ins and then alert or log. When we match a signature, Snort needs a mechanism to output its results, either by logging to disk or to the numerous other formats such as databases or SNMP. Snort has a multitude of uses, including as a network sniffer and IDS, or for packet capture and review in honeypot projects.

Solutions Fast Track

Snort Components

☑ At the core of Snort's network capture capability is the libpcap library and a network card in promiscuous mode.

☑ A promiscuous-mode network card captures all of the network traffic it sees, unlike other network cards that filter on the MAC address contained within the Ethernet frame. The libpcap library provides Snort with a cross-platform method of linking into the network cards of most major UNIX and Windows platforms.

Decoding Packets

- ☑ Snort can decode a large number of protocols, from Ethernet, Token Ring ,and Wireless to the higher-layer protocols such as IP, TCP, and UDP.

- ☑ Snort doesn't decode protocols such as IPX and IPv6. It merely recognizes them and uses them later for statistics.

- ☑ Snort stores the packets in data structures, which form pointers to the raw data from libpcap.

Processing Packets 101

- ☑ The preprocessors mangle, alert, and drop packets before they arrive at the main detection engine in Snort.

- ☑ The frag2 preprocessor reassembles fragmented packets, while stream4 gives Snort stateful inspection functionality.

Understanding Rule Parsing and Detection Engines

- ☑ The core detection engine uses text-based rules stored in a 3D linked list. The third dimension of the list links to detection plug-ins, which the first and second dimensions link to the Rule Header and Rule Options fields of the rule.

- ☑ The detection plug-ins provide additional tests that can be performed on a packet.

- ☑ The Pass rule is used to ignore certain types of traffic or signatures, while the Log rule merely logs traffic without alerting.

Output and Logs

- ☑ Snort has a number of uses: as a sniffer, for intrusion detection, and for the capture of network traffic in a honeypot scenario.

- ☑ Snort has two different output modes: Alerting and Logging. Within the Alerting and Logging modes, further options are available.

☑ Logging to a database involves setting up the database structures beforehand and then configuring the snort.conf to connect and write to that database.

Frequently Asked Questions

The following Frequently Asked Questions, answered by the authors of this book, are designed to both measure your understanding of the concepts presented in this chapter and to assist you with real-life implementation of these concepts. To have your questions about this chapter answered by the author, browse to **www.syngress.com/solutions** and click on the **"Ask the Author"** form.

Q: How do I go about writing one of my own preprocessor or detection plug-ins?

A: There are template files contained in the template subdirectory from the main src directory. There is a template set for detection plug-ins (sp_template.c and sp_template.h), and a template set for preprocessors (spp_template.c and spp_template.h). You need to write quality preprocessor and detection plug-ins; poorly written plug-ins can slow Snort down and, in some cases, cause Snort to crash. Scott Campbell has written a nice little DNS preprocessor (www.geocities.com/axonpotential/snort/19/). It's clearly documented and we recommend that you have a look at it.

Q: In Snort ver 2.0.0, do fragrouter and stick still cause problems?

A: During a recent IDS vendor test by http://nss.co.uk, they used both stick and fragrouter to test the detection as part of their overall testing strategy. Snort version 1.8.6 performed well in these test, missing only one or two types of stick and fragrouter attacks. However, with version 2.0.0 of Snort, improvements were made to fix these shortcomings. The "IDS Group Test Report Edition 3" is well worth reading; the testers in NSS wrote an excellent unbiased report on a number of IDS vendors. The testing equipment they use to put the IDS under heavy load is quite cool too.

Q: How fast is the decode engine?

A: One of the most popular questions asked of Marty Roesch is, "How fast is Snort?" A properly configured Snort machine can handle 100MB of network traffic (dependant on the number of rules and preprocessor configurations). At the higher levels around the 200 to 350MB per-second mark, libpcap is reading packets from the network card at a large rate and then calling the *ProcessPacket()* function within Snort. Calling *ProcessPacket()*uses up CPU cycles, which at high speed overloads the system. The decode engine will get the traffic, but with on average a 50-percent packet loss. (On Linux, an optimized version of libpcap can be downloaded to increase performance—http://public.lanl.gov/cpw/.) Even with an optimized libpcap driver, the preprocessors will need to be finely tuned to handle 200 to 350MB of traffic, or in some cases should be turned off.

Q: Is the use of the libpcap model going to change for high-speed networks?

A: The Snort 2.0 architecture allows for what are called "acquisition plug-ins." These plug-ins allow a developer to write a specific packet-capture network card driver for a particular operating system (Linux), and this plug-in would provide Snort with packet capture at much higher speeds. By doing this, you will lose the portability aspect of Snort, as it will be tied to one particular net-work card and operating system. However, you will gain much higher packet capture speeds because of the tight integration with the network card, which would then link directly to Snort, thereby reducing the overheads on the system because of the libpcap library.

Q: How do I enable Barnyard?

A: Barnyard can be downloaded from www.snort.org/dl/barnyard. Once down-loaded, follow these steps:

1. Compile the Barnyard source code and install.
2. Configure your snort.conf configuration file, and set up Snort for "Unified mode" (see the earlier section *Barnyard and Unified Output*).
3. Configure your Barnyard.conf configuration file with the desired output format.
4. Start up Snort and then start up Barnyard.

Remember that Barnyard is still in beta, so report any bugs or errors to the Barnyard mailing list at barnyard-users@lists.sourceforge.net. More detailed information regarding Barnyard can be found in Chapter 11, "Mucking Around with Barnyard."

## Chapter 5

Playing by the Rules

Solutions in this chapter:

- **Understanding Configuration Files**
- **The Rule Header**
- **The Rule Body**
- **Components of a Good Rule**
- **Testing Your Rules**
- **Tuning Your Rules**

- ☑ **Summary**
- ☑ **Solutions Fast Track**
- ☑ **Frequently Asked Questions**

Introduction

It might come as a surprise to you, but intrusion detection systems (IDSs) are not a bleeding-edge technology, and Snort is no exception. In fact, Snort is the one of the oldest IDSs that is still supported. So, why are you reading this book? We are about to tell you. Snort is the most popular and widely used packet sniffer and intrusion detection engine in the world. Its rules-based engine (notice that we did not say signature-based engine) collects and correlates packets based on rules. The term *signature* refers to nothing more than a basic definition of an attack, akin to the footprint left in the mud by the shoe of someone breaking into a house. A rule defines the attack methodology in terms of identifying the intruder, analogous to identifying how the robber broke into the house in hopes of catching the robber.

When technologists discuss IDSs, Snort always stands apart from the crowd because of two key differentiators: flexibility and simplicity. These features were two of the initial design goals during the development of Snort and carried through during the design of the rule schema and engine support modules of the application. Many Snort rules can be written in one line of text, and before version 1.8, it was mandatory that rules be only one line. A tremendous number of Snort users do not use Snort to its fullest potential. Throughout this chapter, you will learn the importance of proper rule creation and how you could potentially use these rules to leverage logging and alert features during wireless attacks, network-based attacks, and Web assessments.

By the end of this chapter, you should be able to read, understand, and write Snort intrusion detection rules for your IDS sensors. The rule format and testing in combination with a few performance tips and tricks will ensure that you implement the best possible set of rules for your environment, the goal for any IDS administrator or engineer.

Snort rules can be written in multiple ways and can "flag" or generate alerts in several more ways; however, you should know the driving factor behind all rules. The Snort feature set acts as a collection of tools wrapped up into a single application. It has a packet capture tool, a parsing tool to analyze packets, and multiple input and output modules. When Snort captures a packet that matches the signature of a rule that you have included within your effective set of rules, it triggers that as a hit. This is an important aspect to understand before you learn the format of a rule and then how to implement rules.

A Snort rule can be divided into two main sections, the rule header and rule body. In this chapter, you will learn the intricacies and particulars for writing the rule header and body.

Understanding Configuration Files

Due to Snort's built-in capabilities, it is possible to define and use features that make it easier to use in a large or distributed environment via configuration files. Other valuable features allow objects to be reused in multiple instances of sensors locally or remotely. Snort configuration files allow the engine to include variables, additional configuration files, and additional linked include files.

Defining and Using Variables

Snort provides users the ability to define custom variables for use within the rulesets. Defining variables is straightforward, as they use a one-to-one substitution method. The syntax for this command is:

```
var <desired_variable_name> <variable_value>
```

These variables should be included in the rules file and can be used in place of IP addresses and networks. This first example instruction is used to define a single IP address; it defines the variable *DNS_SERVER* to be the address 10.1.1.2.

```
var DNS_SERVER 10.1.1.2
```

The next example rule is used to define a network address. It defines the variable *INTERNAL_NET* to be the class B network 10.2.0.0.

```
var INTERNAL_NET 10.20.0.0/16
```

The following example differs from the first two, because it is used to define multiple network addresses. It sets the variable *INTERNAL_NETS* to include a class B, class C, and single IP address.

```
var INTERNAL_NETS [10.1.0.0/16, 10.2.1.0/24, 10.1.1.8]
```

Defining and using variables in the rules is an excellent method for creating portable rules and rulesets for your organization.

The Snort engine currently lets you take variables to the next level of sophistication by defining dynamic variables. Dynamic variables might be based on another variable that can be set in other parts of the configuration file, or additional include files. When declaring dynamic variables such as *desired_variable_name*, you would reference a previously declared variable, *variable*. The following are examples of dynamic variables being declared:

```
var EXTERNAL_WEB $DMZ_WEB
var 2PHP $INTRANET_WEBS
```

In the case that *variable* has not been defined or is illegitimate, *desired_variable_name* would inherit the *static_default_address* value. In the case that you do not want to include a backup static route, you might include an error message to display when the included variable is undefined.

As you can see in the following rule examples, the second section of the variable definition is separated by a colon, ":". The area preceding the colon is used for defining the initial variable to be used, whereas the area following the colon is used to notify the engine of what to do if the variable is undefined. Examples of the allowed formats are as follows:

```
var <desired_variable_name> $<variable:static_default_address>
var <desired_variable_name> $<variable:?Error: the variable was undefined>
```

This next rule defines a single dynamic IP address. Specifically, it defines the variable *DNS_SERVER* to have a single dynamic IP address of variable *ORG_DNS_SERVER*. If *ORG_DNS_SERVER* is undefined, then *DNS_SERVER* will have the value of 10.1.1.2.

```
var DNS_SERVER $(ORG_DNS_SERVER:10.1.1.2)
```

This next example uses undefined variables. It depicts a user who has selected to configure the system to print out an error message instead of statically assigning a variable.

```
var ENTIRE_INTERNAL_COMPANY $(INTERNAL_NETS:?Gabe, you forgot to define
INTERNAL_NETS)
```

As a general note, using print statements is an excellent method for debugging your rules and rulesets. Print statements can be used when debugging your Snort configuration and are specified with question marks. The text that follows the questions as seen in the previous example would be printed if the *$INTERNAL_NETS* variable had not been previously defined within one of the Snort configuration files.

Defining multiple addresses within a dynamic variable is just as easy as defining a single address or network. First, you must predefine a variable to encompass multiple systems, and then simply reference that variable from the dynamic variable format. In following our two-step example, the first task defines a multiple address variable, while the second task defines the dynamic variable *BOSTON_ZONE* to equal the value of the multi-address variable *DMZ*.

```
var DMZ [10.1.1.1, 10.1.1.2, 10.1.1.3]
```

Snort incorporates numerous methods for controlling engine-related configurations to ensure that the engine and rules are tailored for each environment. Most of these configuration choices can be made in one of two ways. The first would be to directly specify the desired configuration option via the command line when executing Snort. The second method (and a more efficient and manageable method for enterprise environments) is defining Snort configurations in a configuration file and just telling Snort to use that configuration file when starting. Snort grabs that configuration file and reads all of the configuration options and values individually, just as if they were specified via the command line. It is highly recommended that you create and use configuration files when deploying Snort sensors in your environment, unless you are merely testing rules and engine capabilities.

Instructions for Snort configuration have a very specific format, consisting of identifying the desired configuration and its corresponding value. The values might vary; however, the format leaves no room for error. The format for defining Snort instructions is *config <instruction>:<value>*. The *config* variable informs Snort that you are about to provide an instruction to configure Snort in a specific manner. The *instruction* is the desired configuration you want to make with the value of *value*.

Using Variables for Instructions

Snort includes a robust set of instructions that you can specify to tweak each individual sensor installation for its respective environment and threat base. The following section describes each of the available instructions that can be used when defining Snort configurations via configuration files or the command line when there is a matching command line option. Not all options can be set from the command line. The *alert_with_interface_name* feature allows you to append the interface name that received the packet onto the alert notice. This is especially helpful when your Snort engine is located on a multihomed system, or has multiple network interface cards (NICs) connecting the system to multiple networks simultaneously. The appropriate interface name value for this instruction is the corresponding system name of the network card. The command line operator is *−I*. A common example would be *eth0*.

- *alertfile*   The alert file instruction allows you to designate the file to be used to store all of the Snort triggered alerts. It is a helpful instruction that can allow you to make backups of the file on a routine basis or use it as input for correlation applications. There is no command-line operator for this instruction. An example value is *local_alerts.log*.

- *bpf_file*   The Berkeley Packet Filter (BPF) file instruction allows you to designate a file for Snort to use containing the BPF-formatted filters. The command-line operator is –*F*, and any filename would be an appropriate value for this instruction.

- *checksum_mode*   The checksum mode allows Snort to designate the types of packets that will be checked for proper packet checksums. No corresponding command-line operator exists, and the values are limited to all, *none, noicmp, noip, notcp*, and *noudp*. As you might have gleaned, you can directly specify to use all or none of the packets, or identify protocols to disregard.

- *chroot*   Similar to the UNIX command *chroot*, Snort's modified *chroot* instruction can be used to specify the new desired Snort home directory. By default, Snort's root directory is that in which the Snort executable resides. The command-line operator for this instruction is –*t*.

- *classification*   Defining Snort rule's classification schemas are covered later in this chapter. Additional information on this option can be found later in the chapter.

- *daemon*   The daemon instruction allows you to fork the Snort process just as you would fork any other system-level process. To terminate processes that have been forked, you would merely use the *kill* command. The command line operator is –*D* for the daemon instruction.

- *decode_arp*   A valuable feature within Snort is the fact that it permits you to decode and analyze multiple types of protocols. The decode ARP instruction enables ARP decoding on the engine. The command line operator is –*a*. No corresponding value is required.

- *decode_data_link*   Similar to the ARP decoding instruction, the Data Link Decoding instruction decodes data link layer packet data to be included in the analysis engines, alerts, and logs. The command-line operator for the decoding data link layer instruction is –*e*, and no corresponding value is required.

- *disable_decode_alerts* This instruction allows you to disregard the alerts generated during Snort's decoding phase. The disabling decode alerts instruction does not require any corresponding value and has no corresponding command-line operator.

- *dump_chars_only* In the case that you only want to retrieve characters, you can use the dump characters only instruction using the command-line operator *−C*. This instruction doesn't need an appended value and should be used with caution because it disregards anything that is not a character.

- *dump_payload* The dumping payload instruction can also be executed via the command-line operator *−d*. The feature allows you to dump all of the application layer data from the captured packets. This instruction does not require any corresponding value.

- *dump_payload_verbose* The dumping verbose payload data instruction has the command-line operator *−v* and is the same as the *dump_payload* instruction, except that the verbose instruction dumps the entire packet starting at the Data Link layer.

- *interface* Interface declaration is an essential feature for multihomed enterprise IDSs. Multihomed systems, or systems including multiple network cards, can be connected to multiple networks simultaneously and thus potentially require that you use different sets of rules for different interfaces. The command-line operator *−i* requires as a value the name of the NIC.

- *logdir* Setting the Snort log directory is beneficial for customizing installations for multiple environments. It allows you to define the directory for outputting Snort logs. The command-line operator is *−l* and it takes as an argument the desired log directory. A suitable example would be C:/Snort/logs.

- *min_ttl* The minimum Time-To-Live (TTL) instruction permits you to define sensor-wide TTL values. If a packet did not meet the defined minimum requirement, that packet would be dropped and no further rule analysis would occur on that packet. No equivalent command-line operator exists. The value is equal to the number of hops you want to declare. For example, in Snort if you defined the minimum TTL as 3, then any packet with a TTL value less than 3 would be ignored. As an additional note, configuring the minimum TTL to equal 1 would pass or accept almost all-legitimate network-based traffic. This rule can assist in dropping locally generated traffic.

- **no_promisc** Snort allows you to directly disable promiscuous mode on your NIC; however, this function should be used with care because you will not receive all of the packets destined for other systems when you execute this command. Promiscuous mode enables your card to capture all packets on the wire. The command-line operator is *−p* and it does not require a corresponding value.

- **nolog** This instruction allows you to disable all Snort logging, but does not affect the other rule action types such as alert, activate, pass, or dynamic. This configuration instruction is rarely used, because in just about all cases you will want to log certain potentially malicious packets. The instruction does not take any parameters and has a command-line equivalent of *−N*.

- **obfuscate** The obfuscate instruction allows you to obfuscate IP addresses for alert and logging action events. You do not have to provide additional values since it will affect the entire sensor. The command-line operator is *−O*.

- **order** You can change the order for passing or ignoring specified packets using the order instruction with a corresponding command-line operator of *−o*. This allows you to modify the hierarchy for rules analyzed the by sensor's defined rulesets.

- **pkt_count** Snort provides you with the capability of exiting or shutting down after a specified number of packets has been captured. For example, if you are conducting benchmarks or stress tests, this instruction is extremely helpful in identifying the transmission rate and level of bandwidth consumption. To use this instruction, you only need to provide it the desired total number of packets that you want to analyze via the command-line operator *−n*.

- **quiet** One method to minimize user and system interaction is to enable the quiet instruction. The quiet instruction disables two main categories of system contact: banners and status reports. Enabling this instruction potentially alleviates a great deal of system clutter, and the command line operator is *−q*.

- *reference_net* The reference net is analogous to the system's home network and can be set with the reference net instruction. You can set your default home network with this instruction and its corresponding command line operator –*h*. To define the network, you only need to provide the desired network address as the value.

- *set_gid* The Snort group can be modified with the set group ID instruction. This instruction is a bit outdated and rarely used since it was created to mimic the UNIX user and group schemas. It does have a command-line operator, –*g*.

- *set_uid* The command-line operator to set or change the Snort user ID is –*u*. Along with the set group ID function, the set user ID instruction is also outdated and seldom used, since scenarios in which you would want to modify the Snort user during sensor configuration are "few are far between."

- *show_year* Including the year field in the timestamp is defined within the show year instruction. It is rarely used in Snort because in most cases, logging packets by year is not necessary and impractical. The corresponding command-line operator –*y* requires no additional values during configuration.

- *stateful* The stateful instruction allows you to analyze a stream of packets or traffic sessions. Stateful inspection is implemented in Snort via preprocessor plug-ins, specifically the Stream4 preprocessor option. There is no corresponding command-line operator for this command. Please refer to Chapter 6, "Preprocessors," for more information on how to use the stateful option and Snort preprocessors.

- *umask* The umask option permits you to inform Snort to umask during runtime. The command-line option for this command is –*m*, and if you want to specify this in the config file, the syntax is *config umask: VALUE*.

- *utc* Snort allows you to decide which type of time reference can be associated with the captured packets and action events. By default, the local system time is referenced; however, you can choose to use the Coordinated Universal Time (UTC) as the reference point. The command line operator is –*U* and it does not require any additional parameters for successful implementation, as the decision inherits to all of the corresponding events.

- **verbose** In most cases, more information is better than less when referring to logging potential malicious activity. The verbose instruction
  informs the system to log all of the packets in detail from the link layer
  to STDOUT. No additional parameters are necessary with the command-line operator *–v*.

Including Rule Files

Snort allows you to specify include files containing collections of rules that you
can use when implementing rules. The format is similar to that of C & C++
include files *#include*. You must be careful when using include files, because variables and rule types defined within the include files will substitute predefined
values for those variables. This means that if you used the same name for a variable locally and in an include file, then in most cases, the value for that variable
will be wrong when one of the two signatures gets triggered. The format for
defining include files is as follows:

```
include: <complete_path_and_filename>
```

The Rule Header

Snort rule headers should be considered the main portion of the signature, since
the header identifies what should be done when the rule is flagged, what protocol to use, and source and destination information including ports, IP address,
and networks. The mere data in the rule, or the *body*, has the potential to be
somewhat small in comparison. The rule header can be divided into four main
categories:

- Rule action
- Protocol
- Source information
- Destination information

Figure 5.1 is a depiction of the rule header.

While source and destination are key virtual fields in the rule header, it is
important to note that these fields are declared with a direction instruction. The
direction instruction informs the interpreter engine which of the variable fields is
the source and which is the destination. Details and direction instruction specifics
are covered later in this chapter.

Figure 5.1 A Snort Rule Header

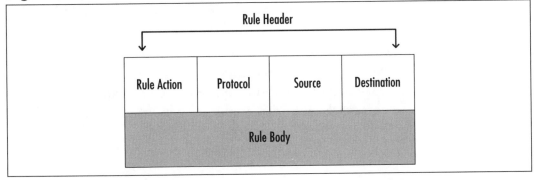

Rule Action Options

Snort currently has five rule options from which to choose when writing a rule to be implemented in your signature. The rule actions indicate to the engine what operation should take place when the rule is matched during the packet analysis phase. The rule actions are highly significant because they each have a different goal and result. When determining what rule action should be specified for your rule, you must ask yourself, "what is the goal of the rule and what is the level of importance if it were to occur?" If the rule were to be triggered, would you have a reasonable amount of accuracy that a malicious user had obtained unauthorized access to a system or information? If so, then it might be best served as an Alert action, or possibly even a custom action, which we detail later in this section. If you noticed a portscan, then it might best to merely log the packet. Determining the rule action is critical and should be carefully thought out before designation. The five rule actions created by default are:

- **Pass** The *pass* action simply ignores the packet, and then analysis continues to execute on further captured packets.

- **Log** The *log* rule action allows you to log the packet in a manner that you can specify during the configuration of your Snort sensor.

- **Alert** The *alert* rule action logs the packet in the same manner as the Log action, and then alerts the user in a manner specified during configuration time. Alerts can be powerful actions and should be used efficiently. An alert log that is too large might prove be a nuisance or an ineffective mechanism for protecting your network.

- **Dynamic** The *dynamic* action is unique in that it remains dormant until an Activate rule triggers it "on." After it is triggered, it then acts like a Log action rule.

- **Activate** The *activate* action is the most powerful rule action created by default within Snort, because when triggered, it generates an alert and then starts the specified dynamic rule. These can be an excellent for catching complex attacks, intruders using a variety of tools, or even for categorizing data in a different manner.

OINK
_____

In most cases, you will never need to use the *pass* action on a corporate or enterprise network. However, it does come in handy when you want to ignore traffic from a certain system, such as the internal DNS server or network.

In addition to these five rule options, you can create custom rule types. These rule types determine how other applications output the data to other types of output plug-ins. The format is straightforward. First, designate the rule type, and then the actions that you want to occur when the rule action is specified. For example, the following rule provides for the creation of a text file log when a defined hacker anomaly is detected:

```
ruletype hacker_log
{
    type log
    log_tcpdump: hacker.txt
}
```

This rule is written to send an alert to two different logs when the Gabriel virus is detected:

```
ruletype gabriel_virus
{
    type alert output
    alert_syslog: LOG_AUTH LOG_ALERT
    log_tcpdump: gabriel_virus.log
}
```

The following rule is written so that NetBIOS scans are logged to a specific log:

```
ruletype netbios_scanning_log
{
    type log output
    log_tcpdump: netbios.scan
}
```

Finally, this rule will update a remote database:

```
ruletype update_database
{
    type alert output
output database: log, mysql, user=GJF password=badpass (continued)
dbname=lauryn host=10.100.2.53
}
```

Defining custom rule types is an excellent way to modularize your Snort sensor, and can be an efficient tool to aid with multiple sensor installations. If it helps, an analogy comparing rule types toobject oriented programming (OOP) objects can be drawn, since you can create custom rule types that can be easily transferred and reused for multiple sensors; the rule types are reusable objects.

Tools & Traps…

Fidelis Snort Enhancements

Fidelis Security Systems Inc. (www.fidelissec.com) creates intrusion detection products, technologies, and tools that according to Fidelis "lower the total cost of intrusion detection ownership." The four tools or Snort enhancement applications that Fidelis has created extend the original functionality of Snort and can increase the overall speed of the engine (Fidelis claims a speed enhancement of up to four times the normal operating speed).

- **SNORTRAN** was designed to be an optimizing compiler for Snort's rules and encompasses three main techniques: string

Continued

set clustering, decision trees, and precompilation of pattern matching.

- **MudPit** is arguably the most significant Fidelis Snort add-on and was created as a complementary feature to Snort's new unified alert and log output plug-ins. In general, it provides users the ability to process both the unified alert and log output streams simultaneously, while only actually outputting to the user one single collaborative dataset. Unfortunately, the one drawback to MudPit is that it can only be implemented on UNIX and Linux-based platforms.

- **SplitSnort**, used in Fidelis' commercialized Snort appliances, creates two platform-internal preprocessors out of Snort's detection cycle that receives and analyzes separated traffic. The tool is usually implemented on Fidelis' multi-CPU systems. The obvious benefit of this feature is increased processing thresholds.

- **DirectWire** is a package that was created to increase packet-capturing speeds. The package uses real-time packet scheduling in combination with enhanced traffic queues to minimize packet loss during periods of high bandwidth consumption.

Supported Protocols

The current free version of Snort was designed to support the analysis of four different protocols: ICMP, TCP, IP, and UDP. When designating the protocol for the rule, you simply include the type after the rule action separated by a single while space. At the time of publishing, there were additional modules created for the analysis of different types of protocols, such as 802.11, HTTP, and ARP. More information on these modules can be found on the Web, but are not covered in this chapter because of the amount of available information and lack of enterprise adoption. Please refer to Snort.org for more information on currently available protocol plug-ins or Snort information.

OINK

You can only specify one protocol per rule!

Assigning Source and Destination IP Addresses to Rules

The third portion of the rule header field is used to assign source and destination IP addresses pertinent to that specific rule. There are two available options for including system addresses in the rule: using individual IP addresses, or Classless Inter Domain Routing addresses (CIDR). CIDR addresses are easy to specify in a rule; however, you must first understand the format of a CIDR address block. If you wanted to write a rule that covered a class B address range for the 10.2.0.0 through 10.2.255.255 address space, you would only need to write 10.2.0.0./16. If you are ambitious, you could include the IP address 10.123.123.54 as 10.123.123.54/32 using CIDR notation. Table 5.1 lists some of the most common CIDR block notations with their corresponding subnet masks, number of corresponding class C addresses, and number of included hosts. The subnet masks are included for educational purposes and are not required or supported within Snort rules.

Table 5.1 CIDR Block Addressing

CIDR Block	Subnet Mask	Number of Class C Addresses	Hosts
/14	255.252.0.0	1024	262144
/15	255.254.0.0	512	131072
/16	255.255.0.0	256	65536
/17	255.255.128.0	128	32768
/18	255.255.192.0	64	16384
/19	255.255.224.0	32	8192
/20	255.255.240.0	16	4096
/21	255.255.248.0	8	2048
/22	255.255.252.0	4	1024
/23	255.255.254.0	2	512
/24	255.255.255.0	1	256
/25	255.255.255.128	?	128
/26	255.255.255.192	?	64
/27	255.255.255.224	1/8	32
/28	255.255.255.240	1/16	16
/29	255.255.255.248	1/32	8

Continued

Table 5.1 CIDR Block Addressing

CIDR Block	Subnet Mask	Number of Class C Addresses	Hosts
/30	255.255.255.252	1/64	4
/31	255.255.255.254	1/128	2
/32	255.255.255.255	1/256	1

OINK

You can find more information on the CIDR block addressing specification at www.rfc-editor.org/rfcsearch.html in RFCs 1517, 1518, and 1519.

It is pertinent that you understand CIDR block addressing, because you cannot use domain names such as gabe.snort.org, internal.mycompany.com, or regular expressions for reference in the source or destination fields. Similar in most programming and scripting languages, the negation operator or "!" can be used in combination with an IP address or set of addresses to negate the value. For example, if you would like to create a rule that is valid for any system not included in your local network, you would write !10.100.4.0/24, where 10.100.4.0/24 is equivalent to your internal network space. This is an excellent method for specifying the address space for an external malicious user. A common addressing schema is to use a negated source and non-negated destination as follows:

```
var INTERNAL_NET 10.20.0.0/16
log tcp !INTERNAL_NET any -> $INTERNAL_NET any
```

The rule header will log any packet not originating from the internal network with an internal network destination address. We discuss the variable declaration statement in previous schema and declaring variables in general later in this chapter.

In addition to using CIDR notation and single IP addresses, you can also specify address ranges in a list format using brackets to enclose the IP ranges. There is no reasonable limit of commas that you can use when declaring lists within your rules; however, it might make more sense for you to declare address variables to use within the rules. Variable declarations are a sensible mechanism for minimizing rule size and reusing code.

The following shows a rule header that uses the list brackets [] to log TCP traffic from 10.100.2.3, 10.100.3.0 through 10.100.3.255, and 10.101.0.0 through 10.101.255.255 going to the single IP address 10.1.1.5.

```
log tcp [10.100.2.3,10.100.3.0/24,10.101.0.0/16] any -> 10.1.1.5
```

The last unique object that you can use in the IP source and destination fields is the *any* command. As you might have assumed, the *any* command is a special wildcard reference that lets you quickly assign the entire range of possibilities. It is most commonly used in highly technical vulnerability identification rules, such as identifying a potential Unicode or buffer overflow attack. It is useful because in these scenarios, you might not want to limit the source of the attack to only external entities, and might want to include internal addresses. In most circumstances, you would want to identify all specific attacks on your systems; whether they are internal or external is initially inconsequential. The following demonstrates a common rule seen within Snort that turns it from an IDS to a packet logger. If you follow the format for the rule header, you will see that the rule logs all TCP packets from any source to any destination. A rule such as this would not need a body, since the entire rule is defined within the header. Later in this chapter, you will see how similar rules are created using the BPF schema.

```
log tcp any any -> any any
```

Assigning Source and Destination Ports

Source and destination ports are somewhat similar in the method of declaration to that of the source and destination IP addresses within the Snort rule format. You can still use the *any* wildcard and the *!* negation reference in the rules with the exact same usage as IP fields. It is also in that you can define single ports by directly including that port number in the following rule. Specifically, this syntax details a rule that generates an alert for TCP traffic arriving from any source, destined for port 12345 any IP. Just for your own edification, port 12345 is a common port used for the popular backdoor and remote administration program NetBus.

```
alert tcp any any -> any 12345
```

One of the obvious differences with the port's declaration is that you do not have the option to use CIDR notation to define blocks of addresses. Moreover, Snort does not allow you to list out specific ports in brackets separated by commas similar to the case in the IP schema. However, Snort does allow you to include ranges of ports with a predefined minimum and maximum port number. If you choose to leave out the minimum and maximum port number, then the default minimum port number is 0 and the maximum number is 65535. The following rule defines a rule that logs all UDP traffic from any IP and port source, destined to any *LOCAL_NET* variable on ports 1 through 100.

```
log udp any any -> $LOCAL_NET 1:100
```

The next rule we'll examine has the alert action for TCP traffic from any source IP with a source port of 0 to 1024 destined for any IP with a destination port of 0 to 1024. Another way to verbally describe this rule would be to say that it alerts all TCP traffic spawned from and destined toward a privileged port. The term *privileged* when referencing to computers and ports refers to ports 0 to 1024.

```
alert tcp any :1024 -> any :1024
```

The last method for writing ranges in Snort rules is to specify the beginning port number with an empty maximum port. This rule logs any TCP traffic destined for an unprivileged port, or ports 1025 and higher. It is important to understand the rule format and be able to dictate the rules in plain English, because the colon operator means equal to or greater than in the following rule, and equal to or less than in the previous rule:

```
log tcp any any -> any 1025:
```

A good hint would be to read the statement aloud just to double-check your logic stream. For example, the rule that defines port negation would read as "log all UDP traffic originating from port 21 destined for any port that is not 21."

```
log udp any 21 -> any !21
```

OINK

One important detail to note is that ports are only used in TCP- and UDP-based rules. The other Snort-supported protocols do not use the port fields; however, the Snort engine requires something to be specified. The wildcard any is generally the accepted value for non-TCP/UDP rules.

Understanding Direction Operators

The direction operators tell the Snort engine the proper way to read the rules. It is an effortless way to redefine the source and destination of the rule, or in some cases to disregard source and destination. Currently, there are only two direction operators: -> and <>. Note that there is no <- operator since it would only be a reverse of the -> operator, and thereby serve no real purpose. The -> operator tells the Snort engine that the source information for the rule is on the left side of the arrow, and the destination side of the rule is on the right side. The following rule alerts any external IP address that transmits any TCP packets to internal systems on port 139:

```
alert tcp $EXTERNAL_NET any -> $INTERNAL_NET 139
```

It is important to understand that this next rule is not the same rule as the one we just examined, although at first glance it appears to have the same logic. Since there is no <- operator, it would throw an error in Snort.

```
alert tcp $INTERNAL_NET 139 <- $EXTERNAL_NET any
```

The next example illustrators a rule that logs all TCP data transferred on privileged ports between the *$INTERNAL_NET* and *$RESEARCH_NET* variables:

```
log tcp $INTERNAL_NET :1024 <> $RESEARCH_NET :1024
```

It does not dictate nor does it care where the traffic initiates, as long as it is either the internal or research network and is destined toward the other. The <> operator is a bit more tricky and can cause quite a bit of turmoil if used improperly. As written, this rule could log quite a bit of data, thereby clogging IDS logs. It is recommended that you limit these types of rules to specific IP addresses or rules that you believe would not receive a tremendous response, because they could have negative log and performance implications.

Activate and Dynamic Rule Characteristics

Snort provides users with a very powerful tool by allowing them to define activate and dynamic rule scenarios, thereby creating a chaining set of rules. When an activate rule is triggered, it launches the defined dynamic rule to start executing based on a few configuration specifics within that dynamic rule. As an example, it might be against company policy to use Telnet externally because login credentials are transmitted in clear text and the subsequent policy is to use Secure Shell (SSH). In this case, you might find it necessary to log all Telnet login credentials using Snort, probably not a common use but an adequate example nonetheless. The following is an example of the activate and dynamic rules that trigger upon the use of data being sent to port 23, a port most commonly used by Telnet. Once the dynamic rule is triggered from the activate rule, it logs the next 20 packets as designated by the count object:

```
activate tcp any any -> any 23 (activates: 23; msg:" Potential Telnet Login
Credentials Logged";)dynamic tcp any any -> any 23 (activated_by: 23;
count: 20;)
```

A slight hybrid of the previous example would be to log credentials and any commands or instructions sent to the system that was being accessed via Telnet. The following does not trigger on Telnet usage, it triggers when a user attempts to su to root after gaining local access to the system. The count has been increased to 100 because in this case, you want to log some of the actions conducted on the system.

```
activate tcp any any -> any 23 (activates: 24; msg:"SU – Root Attempt";
content:"su – root";)
dynamic tcp any any -> any 23 (activated by: 24; count: 100;)
```

There are a couple key differentiators for each type of action. The activate rule is exactly like the alert rule that we identified earlier in the chapter, and the dynamic action is similar to that of a log rule. The activate rule does require one additional object, the *activates* object, specified within the body of the message. The *activates* object informs the engine to look for and trigger the dynamic rule that executes or is *activated_by* the same numerical reference. The dynamic rule takes two additional objects: *activated_by* and *count*. The *activated_by* object specifies the number that must be triggered to execute the rule, and the *count* object informs the engine the maximum number of times the dynamic rule will be executed. In this case, it will run 20 additional times once triggered, thereby logging the first 20 packets of a Telnet session and in most cases capturing the clear-text authentication credentials. Notice that the activate rule "activates" the number 23, and the dynamic rule is *activated_by* 23. That is the connection that binds those two rules, not the fact that by coincidence the rules have identical headers minus the action.

```
activate tcp any any -> any 139 (activates: 2;
    msg:"poor example of linked rules";)
dynamic udp any any -> any any (activated_by: 2;
count: 200;)
```

The preceding rule, while having the proper format and specification, is a poor example and potential wasteful method for using a dynamic rule. Any TCP traffic destined for NetBIOS port 139 will activate a dynamic rule to log the next 200 UDP that the Snort sensor captures. The important aspect here is that the activate rule can spawn any type of dynamic rule that you define.

Snort's Protocol Flow Control, first piloted in version 1.9, was designed to provide the user or administrator with greater capabilities when it came to designing complicated rules, especially at the application layer. It will allow the user to specify the direction in which the rule is supposed to trigger actions; specifically, whether it was sent from a client-server, or vice versa. Protocol Flow Control is a powerful tool that does not solely rely on the IP layer for rule specification. It will continue to launch a new large and technical subset of Snort IDS signatures. Refer to www.snort.org for up-to-date Snort information on this key feature.

The Rule Body

First, let it be known that Snort rules do not require the body field to be complete rule definitions. The body of the rule is an excellent addition that extends the breadth of rule definition beyond simply logging or alerting based on packet source and destination. With this said, we don't want to disregard the importance of the rule body, because it can be considered the "meat and potatoes" for rules identifying complex attack sequences. The body format is broken down into sections separated by semicolons. Each section defines an option trailed by the desired option value. The rule options that can be included in range from protocol specifics and fielding, including IP, ICMP, and TCP. Other applicable options include messages that print out as reference points for the system administrator, keywords to search on, Snort IDs to use as a filing system for Snort rules, and case-insensitivity options.

The rule options are separated by semicolons within the main body of the Snort rule:

```
alert tcp any any -> any 12345 (msg:" Test Message";)
```

As you can see, the rule's body (in bold) is confined by the parentheses. In this case, the body of the message contains two content values. The first value is a message to display when the alert is triggered, and the second is the *nocase* option, which allows you to specify case-insensitive specific rules. In addition to the Snort specific rules and body syntax, Snort also allows you to write "pre-analysis" packet filters in BPF format. We discuss BPF-formatted rules in more detail later in the chapter.

Rule Content

When writing Snort rules, the most powerful and important set of options that you can include within the body of the rule revolves around analyzing the payload of the packet. You can analyze payloads via binary and ASCII values in addition to specifying multiple other types of options that assist in identifying potentially malicious packet content.

ASCII Content

Similar to the method for including binary content strings in the body, ASCII content strings are included with quotations without the pipe characters. In this case, you should only include one string per rule. Later in this section, we discuss how to include lists of multiple strings to match on in a single rule. The format for using this option is the same as the binary content option *content: "STRING"*, and you can negate the string with the exclamation point. In the following rule, the rule searches for the bad string *malicious string /etc/passwd* and displays the following message string:

```
alert tcp any any -> any any (content: "malicious string /etc/passwd";
msg:"Searching for ASCI Garbage!";)
```

OINK!

If you want to use the colon, pipe character, or quotation mark, you must first escape the character within encapsulating quotes.

Including Binary Content

To include binary content within your content string, you merely need to encapsulate the HEX equivalent data between pipe characters (|). Binary data can be easily captured and incorporated into rules using network sniffers such as TCPDump, Ethereal, and Iris to capture raw data strings. Snort implements the Boyer-Moore pattern searching and matching algorithm to identify included content strings from captured packets. You can use the negation operator—

exclamation point—to specify content that you do not want to match on. The format for using this option is *content: "STRING";*. The following rule shows the proper syntax for including binary/HEX data into the rule.

```
alert tcp any any -> any any (content: "|0000 0101 EFFF|"; msg:"Searching
for Garbage!";)
```

The three tools mentioned to assist in capturing binary strings can be downloaded at the following addresses:

- **TCPDump** www.tcpdump.org
- **Ethereal** www.ethereal.org
- **Iris** www.eeye.com

ASCII and Binary Content Rules

In addition to adding ASCII and binary content individually, you have the ability to combine the two types of strings in a single rule. Combining strings is not a complicated task, but you must remember to use the same rules for including ASCII and binary strings in the rule. Including mixed content is different from including multiple strings in a single rule. In the following rule, the content string is broken up into a binary, then ASCII, and then back to binary. The rule will interpret the content string as a single string, and then use that single instance of the string for packet matching.

```
alert tcp any any -> any any (content: "|0101 FFFF|/etc/passwd|E234|";
msg:"Searching for Mixed Garbage!";)
```

The depth Option

The *depth content option* modifier allows you to statically set the number of bytes that the rule should analyze when searching for the defined content string. To minimize CPU cycles and optimize speed for your sensor, you should use this option in conjunction with your content option. The format for the command is *depth: <NUMBER_OF_BYTES>;*.

OINK
_____

The average server header in HTTP 1.0 can be obtained in the first 200 bytes of a packet.

_____

The offset Option

The *offset option content* modifier informs the Snort engine to begin searching for the supplied content string at the offset byte. It is especially useful when you know that you are searching for a specific string that might be included as a subset of other strings. For example, if you know that you can write a rule based upon a specific Web server version and you also know that the Web server version appears in the response header from a Web server, it might be best to use an offset of 0. It is important to note that this one of the most important options to use, and one of the most dangerous because, if set improperly, you could miss an attack. The format for setting the content modifier is *offset: <NUMBER_OF_BYTES>;*.

The nocase Option

You have the ability to disregard text case within rule content by using the *nocase* option. For this option to work, you must have previously defined a content string within the rule. In this example, the rule will trigger on any TCP packet destined for the Telnet service with the word *administrator* in the payload of the packet. This rule example is helpful if you are attempting to sniff pertinent authentication credentials. As you might have gleaned from the example, the format to use this option is *nocase;*.

```
alert tcp any any -> any 23 (content: "administrator"; nocase;)
```

The session Option

The *session* option is one of the most useful options if you use Snort in an attack capability. It allows you to grab clear-text data from protocol sessions and output that data to the screen. As you can imagine, the ability to log and view only usernames, passwords, and executed commands is extremely useful. This rule generates an alert and then prints the entire FTP session transmission to standard output.

```
alert tcp any any -> any 21 (content: "FTP Session Data"; session:
printable;)
```

The format to use the session command is *session: PRINTABLE (or) ALL;*. You must either use the *printable* or the *all* modifier with the *session* command, but not both. In our example, we used the session option modifier *printable*.

Uniform Resource Identifier Content

The *Uniform Resource Identifier (URI)* content option allows you to analyze traffic from the requesting system. Instead of matching the rule body and content strings against the entire packet, you can specify it to only match the rule's content string(s) in the URI section of a request instead of the packet's payload. The format of the URI content option is *uricontent: "STRING";*. Here is the correct option syntax:

```
log tcp any any -> any 80 (content: "Logging PHF"; uricontent:"/cgi-
bin/phf";)
```

The stateless Option

In early versions of Snort, the capability to allow rules to analyze stateless data was provided in the *stateless* option. The latest versions of Snort, post versions 1.8, have included this functionality in the *flow* option. The format for the stateless option is *stateless*. Reference section "Flow Control" in this chapter for more information on stateless rules and including stateless content.

Regular Expressions

It is extremely important to note that the *regular expressions* option is still considered an "in-development" function and is actively being tested and debugged. The option implements a quasi-rendition of the standard regular expressions standard. Currently, you have the ability to use one of two wildcards: the question mark and the asterisk. The question mark, *?*, can be used to replace any single character in an attack string, while the asterisk, ***, is used to define one or many characters. For example, if you were searching for the string *c?t*, the rule would trigger on the words *cat*, *cut*, and, like it or not, *czt*. Now, in the case that you searched for the string *m*n*, you would receive positive matches for the words *main*, *men*, *mountain*, and *m234@#$n*. In addition to the using the wildcards in the content string, you must add the *regex;* modifier in the body of the rule as seen here:

```
alert tcp $OUTSIDE any -> $DMZ 80 (content: "../*../"; regex; msg:" Bad
Example of a dot dot Attack";)
```

Flow Control

The *flow control* configuration option, first introduced in Snort version 1.9, allows users to define the packet's direction in reference to client-server communication streams. It dramatically increases the functionality of Snort because you do not have to define packet direction at the IP layer. The flow functionality works in coordination with Snort's TCP reassembly module and allows rules to distinguish packet content and direction in regard to client-server architecture. One of the most notable benefits for this feature is allowing rules to be written on potential client attack data streams toward the server, and then analyzing the server's response to see if an attack was successful.

The data in Table 5.2 represents the flow control's modifying configuration options with a brief corresponding description. All of the current options supported in Snort's flow control are based on the TCP protocol and reassembling TCP sessions.

Table 5.2 Flow Control Options

Option Instructions	Brief Description
to_server	Passes true on packets sent to the server.
from_server	Passes true on packets sent from the server.
to_client	Passes true on packets sent to the client.
from_client	Passes true on packets sent from the client.
only_stream	Only activates on reconstructed packets or packets within an established stream.
no_stream	This instruction is the opposite of the previous example and does not pass packets that are reconstructed or within an established stream.
established	The *established* instruction will activate on packets that are part of an established TCP connection or session.
stateless	Modified from the original Snort *stateless* instruction, the Flow Control's *stateless* option is geared toward activating on packets regardless of state. Various static attacking tools such as stick send stateless packets in hopes of executing a system- or network-wide denial-of-service (DoS) attack. The *stateless* option must be used without the *flow:* prefix.

The *flow control* options are used in a manner similar to that of other common Snort configuration instructions. Within the body of the rule, define *flow: <OPTION>*, where *OPTION* is one of the option instructions in Table 5.2. The following example Snort rule will flag on TCP packets sent from the client in a TCP stream transmitting toward the server with a confirmed attack string overflow.

```
alert tcp any any -> $DMZ_WEBS 80 (msg:"Client Attacking Server Example";
flow:from_client; content:"/cgi-
bin/handler/something;cat\t/etc/group|?data=Download";)
```

Conversely, the following example flags on packets sent from a server with a potential string that can be found when a UNIX password file is viewed. With this rule, flagging packets only from servers will minimize false positives.

```
alert tcp $DMZ any -> $EXTERNAL any (msg: "Server Potentially Sending
Sensitive Info"; flow:from server; content:"root:: ";)
```

IP Options

The *IP* options are key in identifying numerous IP-based types of attacks in addition to other types of more complex attacks. Many of the IP options are used in writing rules to identify network device attacks, attempts to map a network, and protocol-based DoS attacks.

Fragmentation Bits

Generic fragmentation rules should be applied within your environment to protect against the more complex types of attacks. The *fragment bit* option allows you to analyze the fragment and reserved bits within an IP header. You have three available flags within the *fragmentation bits* option that you can specify:

- **D**: "Don't Fragment"
- **M**: "More Fragments"
- **R**: "Reserved Bit"

The preceding flags were included by the Snort development team with the corresponding naming convention logic. In addition to the bit flags, there are five operator flags:

- ***** As with the other Snort options that implement that operator flags, the asterisk stands as an all wildcard.
- **!** The exclamation point is used for negation.
- **+** The addition sign for a specified bit flag plus either of the other bits that are implemented.
- **–** The minus sign for any bit
- **, , ,** The format for this option is *fragbits: <BIT VALUE>;*.

Equivalent Source and Destination IP Option

The feature to check equivalent IP addresses was a late addition and only serves one purpose: to identify forged, or spoofed, packets. Sending packets with the same source and destination used to be a common method for testing packet filter firewalls. The technique is outdated as commercial vendors ensure that their products do not build in this flaw. The format for this rule is *sameip;*.

This rule checks for a equivalent source and destination IP address within an IP packet and should be included in all enterprise rulesets:

```
alert ip any any -> any any (msg:" Same Source and Destination IP Address";
sameip;)
```

IP Protocol Options

Snort allows you to specify IP options within a packet that you would like to match or negate a packet upon. Due to the nature of the IP options and a development flaw within Snort, you can only include one option in a rule. This is not critical, because IP options are not commonly used within commercial network applications. The format to use this option in the configuration file is *ipopts: <IP_OPTION>;*. Table 5.3 lists the IP options available within Snort.

Table 5.3 Snort IP Options

IP Options	Brief Overview
eol	Used to specify the end of an IP list
lsrr	IP loose source routing
nop	Used when there is no IP option set
rr	Record route
satid	The IP stream identifier
sec	The IP security option, also known as IPSec
ssrr	IP strict source routing
ts	The timestamp field

ID Option

The *ID* option permits you to identify static IP ID values within an analyzed packet. Conventionally, it has little use, but is another of the options added within Snort in case it ever becomes tremendously essential in identifying a type of attack. The format to use the IP *ID* option is *ID: "VALUE"*.

Type of Service Option

Initially, the *Type-of-Service (TOS)* option was added for future use and to complete the IP rule API. However, multiple attacks were released in the summer of 2002 relating to malicious use of the IP TOS field. In most cases, the TOS field value is zero, and in the case of some old Cisco equipment, the incoming TOS field must be set to zero. The format to use the TOS option is *tos: "VALUE";*. The following rule alerts on external traffic bound for Cisco devices with the TOS field not set to zero:

```
alert tcp $EXTERNAL any -> $CISCO any (msg:" Cisco TOS Example"; tos:!"0";)
```

Time-To-Live Option

The *Time to Live (TTL)* option's core value comes in identifying network mapping queries via tools such as traceroute, tracert, and netroute. It compares the defined value to that of the analyzed packets in search for a direct match. The format to use this option is *TTL: "VALUE"*. TTL also supports >, <, and =.

TCP Options

There are three TCP specific options that you can use within the body of your Snort rules. Each triggers upon a different static value within the TCP header of a packet. The sequence and ACK options are rarely used, but the TCP flags option is considered a value-add for numerous rules.

Sequence Number Options

The *sequence number* option is used to check for static TCP sequence numbers within analyzed packets, and therefore is rarely used. Static communication programs and flooding tools are two of the rare example programs that can be identified by guessable sequence numbers. According to Marty Roesch, "it was added for the sake of completeness." The format to use this option is:

```
seq: <sequence_number_value>;.
```

TCP Flags Option

The *TCP flags* option is comprehensive; it allows you to determine if each potential flag is set, unset, or used in combination with another flag. The alphanumeric flags are used to determine what specific flags are set within the packets, while the special characters such as the addition, asterisk, and exclamation mark are used as wild cards and as a negate option, respectively. In addition to the flags, you can use the reserved bit options to detect atypical network activity such as multiple types of fingerprinting techniques. Table 5.4 lists all of the TCP flags currently available within Snort.

Table 5.4 Snort TCP Flags

TCP Flags	Brief Flag Description
A	The option to check if the ACK flag is set.
F	The option to check if the FIN flag is set.
P	The option to check if the PSH flag is set.
R	The option to check if the RST flag is set.
S	The option to check if the SYN flag is set.
U	The option to check if the URG flag is set.
0	A unique option to detect if no TCP flag has been set within the packet.
1	The 1 option determines if the reserved bit 1 is set within the packet.
2	The 2 option determines if the reserved bit 2 is set within the packet.
+	The addition sign is used to determine if a specific flag is set and followed by other TCP flags. Ex: A+ triggers on any packet with the ACK flag set in addition to other flags.
*	The asterisk is a wild card character that you can use to specify any flag that matches on any specified flags. Ex: *AS triggers on all packets that have the ACK or SYN flag set
!	Likewise to most negation commands, this checks to see if the packet does not have the specified flag set. Ex: !S triggers on all packets that do not have the SYN flag set.

TCP flags and options can be combined within the body to create a more powerful and accurate rule. The format to use this option is *flags: <TCP_VALUE(s)>;*.

TCP ACK Option

The *TCP ACK* option within Snort is used to determine if the ACK field has been set to a NON-TRUE value. In nearly all implementations of the TCP stack and protocol, the field is TRUE upon transmission of a valid TCP ACK packet.

One noted exception does exist: the NMAP tool sets the field to FALSE or zero for TCP packets that it transmits during a NMAP TCP ping scan. Therefore, this option could help potential malicious NMAP-generated traffic. The format to use this option is *ack: <ACK_NUMERICAL_VALUE>*.

OINK!

Additional information on NMAP and NMAP TCP ping scans can be found at www.insecure.org/nmap.

ICMP Options

Snort has four different ICMP-related options that can be used in the body of the rule for creating specific attack signatures. Each option has distinct techniques for triggering on precise fields within an ICMP packet, including ICMP code, type, ID, and values. It is important to understand that the following options only add value when used in ICMP designed rules, not TCP- or UDP-based rules.

ID

Different from the IP ID option and field, the *ICMP ID* option triggers upon a specific field value within an ICMP ECHO packet. According to the Snort development team (www.snort.org), the option was written to identify rogue applications that use ICMP as the means of transporting communication. An example of this would be a chat client that sends data in the payload field of the ICMP packet. In multiple cases, these chat clients do not randomize or even use dynamic ICMP IDs, therefore allowing them to be easily identified with Snort rules. In addition to rogue ICMP programs, the option can be used to identify any type of program using static ICMP IDs. The format to use this option is *icmp_id: value*.

Sequence

Similar to the ICMP ID option, the motivation behind developing this option was to identify static ICMP communication programs. Refer to the previous description for more detailed information. The format to use this option is *icmp_seq: value*.

The icode Option

The *icode* option allows you to specify a single value for the ICMP code value of the packet. There are two general options for configuring the icode option within the rule. The first is to set the specific option you would like to trigger if an identical icode value is analyzed in the packet. The second option is to set an invalid code value for ICMP packets. If you define an invalid code value, then the rule will trigger when another invalid ICMP code value is analyzed. Identifying invalid ICMP options is helpful in identifying spoof, flood obfuscation, and DoS attacks. The format to use the option is *icode: value*.

The itype Option

The *itype* option examines the value of the itype field within the ICMP packet. Similar to the icode option, you can set an incorrect itype value to trigger upon the detection of invalid ICMP type values. Additionally the itype option can also be set to trigger upon other specific options. The format to use the option is *icode: value*.

Rule Identifier Options

Snort has several options that can be used to further identify, provide corresponding documentation, and categorize Snort's set of rules. These options should not be confused with threat detection options, as they serve to simply enhance the reporting and configuration features within Snort.

Snort ID Options

The *Snort ID* option was included to serve as a method to categorize, distinguish, and identify single Snort ID rules. The simple schema allows manual and automated systems to use specific rules. The format is *sid: <ID_VALUE>;*. Table 5.5 lists the ranges that can be used as Snort ID values.

Table 5.5 Snort ID Ranges

Range Values	Usage Overview
Less than 100	Reserved for future use
100 to 1,000,000	For use by Snort within the www.snort.org distribution ruleset
Greater than 1,000,000	For use by custom Snort rules

Rule Revision Number

The Snort rule revision number is used in the case that edits are done to an original rule. Organizations most commonly use this when grammatical and technical revisions are made to a rule. The format to use this option is *rev: <REVISION_NUMBER>;*. The following is an example of a rule with the rule revision set to 2:

```
alert tcp any any -> any 79 (rev:2; msg:" Revision";)
```

Severity Identifier Option

The *severity identifier* option allows you the ability to manually override the default rule priority set by the classification option. The option permits you to increase or decrease the priority of the rule and the format for the severity identifier option is *priority: <PRIORITY_VALUE>;*. The following rule has a priority of 1 because it triggers when UDP traffic is sent to the fictitious worm backdoor on port 21974.

```
alert udp any any -> $INTERNAL 21974 (priority:1; msg: "Bad Worm
Backdoor";)
```

Classification Identifier Option

The *classification identifier* option permits you to set a class attack-type or meaningful categorization for the rule. Rule classifications have classification IDs, corresponding priorities, and documentation. The classtypes have corresponding values, 1 being the most severe. The format for the option is *classtype: <NAME_OF_CLASSIFICATION>;*. Tables 5.6, 5.7, and 5.8 list the default classtype IDs that are available within Snort, along with their corresponding priority and description. It is important to note that there are only three classtype severities initially defined, but the engine allows you to create additional priorities.

Table 5.6 Critical Classifications (Priority 1)

Classtype	Brief Description
attempted-admin	Attempted administrator privilege gain
attempted-user	Attempted user privilege gain
shellcode-detect	Executable code was detected
successful-admin	Successful administrator privilege gain

Continued

Table 5.6 Critical Classifications (Priority 1)

Classtype	Brief Description
successful-user	Successful user privilege gain
trojan-activity	A network Trojan was detected
unsuccessful-user	Unsuccessful user privilege gain
web-application-attack	Web application attack

Table 5.7 Intermediate Classifications (Priority 2)

Classtype	Brief Description
attempted-dos	Attempted DoS
attempted-recon	Attempted information leak
bad-unknown	Potentially bad traffic
denial-of-service	Detection of DoS attack
misc-attack	Miscellaneous attack
non-standard-protocol	Detection of a nonstandard protocol or event
rpc-portmap-decode	Decode of an RPD query
successful-dos	Denial of service
successful-recon-largescale	Large-scale information leak
successful-recon-limited	Information leak
suspicious-filename-detect	A suspicious filename was detected
suspicious-login	An attempted login using a suspicious user name was detected
system-call-detect	A system call was detected
unusual-client-port-connection	A client was using an unusual port
web-application-activity	Access to a potentially vulnerable Web application

Table 5.8 Low-Risk Classifications (Priority 3)

Classtype	Brief Description
icmp-event	Generic ICMP event
misc-activity	Miscellaneous activity
network-scan	Detection of a network scan

Continued

Table 5.8 Low-Risk Classifications (Priority 3)

Classtype	Brief Description
not-suspicious	Not suspicious traffic
protocol-command-decode	Generic protocol command decode
string-detect	A suspicious string was detected
unknown	Unknown traffic

External References

Another excellent resource you have within the body of the rule to categorize and provide relevant information about the rule is the *external reference* option. The external reference IDs can be modified via the provided plug-in to specify systems and their corresponding URLs, which might provide additional information to output plug-ins.

The format to use a single instance of the command is *reference: <SYSTEM>, <ID VALUE>;.* Multiple instances of the command can be chained together, as long as a semicolon separates each reference call. The following is an example of a rule using multiple instances of the reference command:

```
log tcp any any -> any 12345 (reference:CVE, CAN-2002-1010; reference:URL,
www.poc2.com; msg:" NetBus";)
```

Miscellaneous Rule Options

In addition to the protocol-specific rule options, options geared for enhanced reporting and categorization, and content identifiers, some options clearly have no adequate parent category. These options range from technical anomalies to logging-related features as explained in the following option descriptions.

Messages

One of the most commonly used and beneficial rule options is the *message* option. It is the primary method to inform Snort administrators of the potential vulnerabilities, threats, and attacks that were identified. This option provides you the ability to include the specified message with the generated alerts, logs, and dumps. The message text is defined by quotes "" to allow the interpreter to distinguish message characters such as the parenthesis ")" and semi-colon ";" from rule body characters. The format to use this option is *msg: "EXAMPLE ATTACK MESSAGE";*. The following has a bold message of "Finger":

```
alert tcp $EXTERNAL any -> $INTERNAL 79 (msg:" Finger";)
```

Logging

The logging capabilities of Snort can be viewed as a significant advantage over many of Snort's competitor IDSs. The logging option informs Snort that all corresponding packets related to that specific instance of the rule to be logged to the specified file. Organized logging permits Snort to subdivide rule logs based on perceived tool usage, attack types, source locations, and destinations. The format to use this option is:

```
logto: "PATH/FILE.extension";
```

TAG

In addition to the logging option, the *tag* option permits you to log additional packets relevant to a triggered rule. This provides you the ability to define rules that analyze and log traffic from a specific source or traffic, related to a complex attack. The option allows you to specify whether you want to log traffic from the source (host) or attack (session). You also have the ability to specify whether you want to log traffic measured on a time (seconds) or packet (packets) scale. If you select to use the session preference, then the rule will only log packets from the session of the original attack. The format to use this option is:

```
tag:<HOST/SESSION>, <HOW MANY>, <SECONDS/PACKETS>,<SRC/DES>;
```

Here, the packet tags 100 packets from any host that attempts to connect to an internal system's Telnet service:

```
alert tcp any any -> $HOME 21 (tag:host, 100, packets; msg:" Tagging Telnet
to Gain Authentication Credentials and Executed Commands";)
```

Dsize

The *dsize* option allows you to specify the length or length range for a packet's payload. You can use greater than and less than signs to specify ranges for payload length, and the <> sign means "in between." For example, <100 is for packets with payload size smaller than 100 bytes, while 1<>99 specifies packets with a payload range of 1 to 99 bytes. The format for the option is:

```
dsize: (<,>, or nothing) length (<> length);
```

Oink!

The *dsize* option is ineffective in measuring the payload size of reconstructed packets. Snort 1.9 and later automatically does not alert on rules with dsize when examining reconstructed packets.

RPC

The *rpc* option allows you to determine RPC services that are accessed remotely. For this option to be properly implemented, you need to ensure that the rule uses the UDP protocol in coordination with a destination port of 111, also known as the Portmapper port. The *rpc* option takes three parameters: the application number, the procedure, and the RPC version

The asterisk is available as a wildcard to use in replacement for the procedure and version fields in the case that you do not require a specific value. The official format for the command is:

```
rpc: <APPLICATION>, <PROCEDURE>, <VERSION>;.
alert udp $EXT any -> $HOME 111 (rpc: 100023, *, *; msg:" RPC Statmon
Connection";)
```

Real-Time Countermeasures

Snort allows you to configure your sensor in such a way that you can dynamically kill specific connections and block Web sites. For these features to add the most value, the sensor should both analyze traffic and be a hop in the transmission route as if your sensor was on a firewall. Snort will send the responses on the wire based on the source and destination of the system even if you are not one of the hops; however, there is no guarantee that the connection will be killed if your system is slow.

The active response option, *resp*, allows Snort to automatically kill protocol connections based on rules that are triggered. It is the most powerful protocol-based body option currently implemented in Snort. The format to use the active response modifier is *resp: MODIFIER, MODIFIER2, MODIFIER3, etc;.*

The following TCP-based modifiers are the current options that you can specify in the Snort response strings:

- ■ *rst_all*   Resets both transmitting and receiving TCP connections

- ■ *rst_rcv*   Resets receiving TCP connections

- ■ *rst_send*   Resets transmitting TCP connections

The following ICMP-based modifiers are the current options that you can specify in the Snort response:

- ■ *strings:icmp_all*   Resets both transmitting and receiving ICMP connections

- ■ *icmp_host*   Transmit ICMP host unreachable to transmitting client

- ■ *icmp_net*   Transmit ICMP network unreachable to transmitting client

- ■ *icmp_port*   Transmit ICMP port unreachable to transmitting client

It is important to use the proper corresponding protocol modifier along with the protocol of the defined rule. Adverse network effects might occur if these options are used inappropriately, such as network and client DoS loops. The following has a rule to send an ICMP Host Unreachable response to the initiating client:

```
alert icmp $EXT any -> $DMZ any ( resp: icmp_host;msg:" In-Bound ICMP";)
```

Components of a Good Rule

If you put 10 programmers in a room and ask them all to solve the same problem, it is almost certain that each solution will be different and vary in degrees of efficiency and accurateness. Creating Snort rules is no different. Numerous methods might exist for identifying malicious attacks, yet far fewer methods exist for efficiently and precisely identifying the attacks. To minimize false positives and false negatives, it is essential to review the body of your Snort rules; specifically, reviewing the content attack signatures within the rules is key.

Even though content bugs are a headache, manually parsing and reviewing critical events can be even more of a hassle and extreme resource strain. Therefore, it is pertinent to configure your rules with the appropriate action event. Too many high-risk or critical events decrease the effectiveness of an alert. In addition to the rule content, it is also important to tweak the rules for efficiency purposes. First-rate rules should be effective, quick, and manageable.

Action Events

Configuring your sensor rules is extremely important. As subsets of configuring your rules, it is just as important to ensure proper rule content as it is to define the proper action events for your rules. Defining action events might be another difficult task for configuring the sensor because you only have two main choices: logging and alerting. The first step in determining the appropriate action event is to see into which category the rule fits. The following questions will help you define the category:

- Does the attack effect mission-critical systems?
- Does the attack provide unauthorized access to mission-critical data?
- Does the attack directly compromise a system?

If the answer to any of these questions is yes, then in most cases you would classify the rule action as Alert. If the answer is not yes, then it might only be necessary to log the data and parse through it later. The two general instances when data logging should be used are:

- The logs provide evidentiary data that can be used for identifying or prosecuting an intruder.
- The logs provide additional medium to high-risk attack information.

Defining action events requires some thought initially, but the answers should quickly become second nature.

Ensuring Proper Content

Snort's IDS is only as good as the quality of the rules that are implemented within the product during runtime. Systems with inaccurate rules, or rules that are prone to false positives and false negatives do very little in the realm of enterprise network management. Inaccurate rules mean that human resources are going to be spent on incident analysis instead of meaningful or productive rulesets.

There are numerous ways to write and test rules, but the most helpful tool to aid in the creation of Snort rules is a packet sniffer. Our personal favorite, Ethereal, is free to download and use. In addition, multiple versions of Ethereal are available from www.ethereal.org; Win32 and UNIX/Linux versions are available.

Ethereal can be used to capture and identify the exact packets sent across the wire during a network-based attack. In the case that you want to create a Snort rule for a particular type of attack, you would want to recreate the sequence in a test or controlled environment and ensure that the sniffer has proper access to packets. Then, capture the packets sent to the target from the attacking system and the corresponding packets sent back to the attacker from a successfully compromised system. Capturing both packet streams would potentially allow the Snort sensor to use an activate rule to determine when an attack attempted and, better yet, when an attack was successful.

The Ethereal Network Analyzer Win32 interface is pictured in Figure 5.2; the UNIX interface is similar. The top window displays the IP packet headers; specifically, the source and destination IP addresses, timestamp, payload protocol (if any), and info or the payload portion of the captured packet.

Figure 5.2 The Ethereal Sniffer

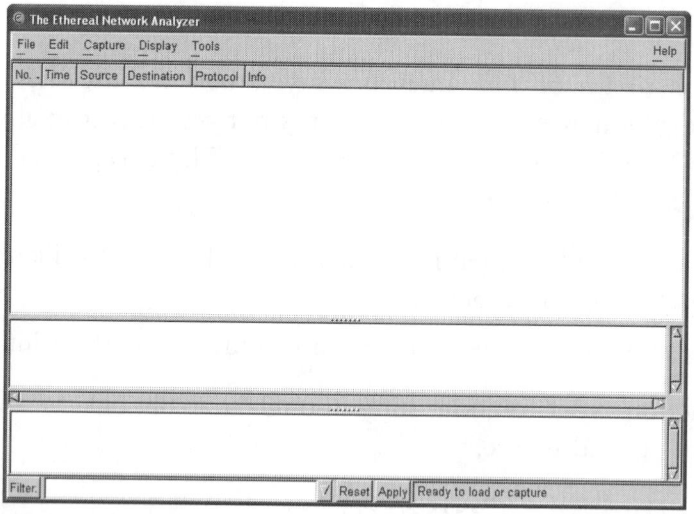

As an example in analyzing packets with Ethereal, we have included the packets for a Google search and response in Figure 5.3. The highlighted packet in the top window shows the headers for our Google search, while the middle window has more detail for specific packet fields. In addition, in the middle window we highlighted the Google HTTP GET request, and subsequently, Ethereal automatically highlighted the corresponding binary information in the bottom window. The information captured should be plenty to create a Snort rule. In this case, let's imagine that you want to create a rule to trigger when your employees search Google's site given the provided information. You could simply use the "GET /search?" string as the content, as seen in the bottom middle and bottom window of Figure 5.3. Source, destination, and any other rule instructions can be used at your discretion. The following rule is an example that would trigger if an internal system sent a Google search on port 80:

```
alert tcp $INTERNAL any -> any 80 (msg:"Google Search Query";
flow:from_client; content:"GET /search?";)
```

Figure 5.3 Analyzing a Google Search

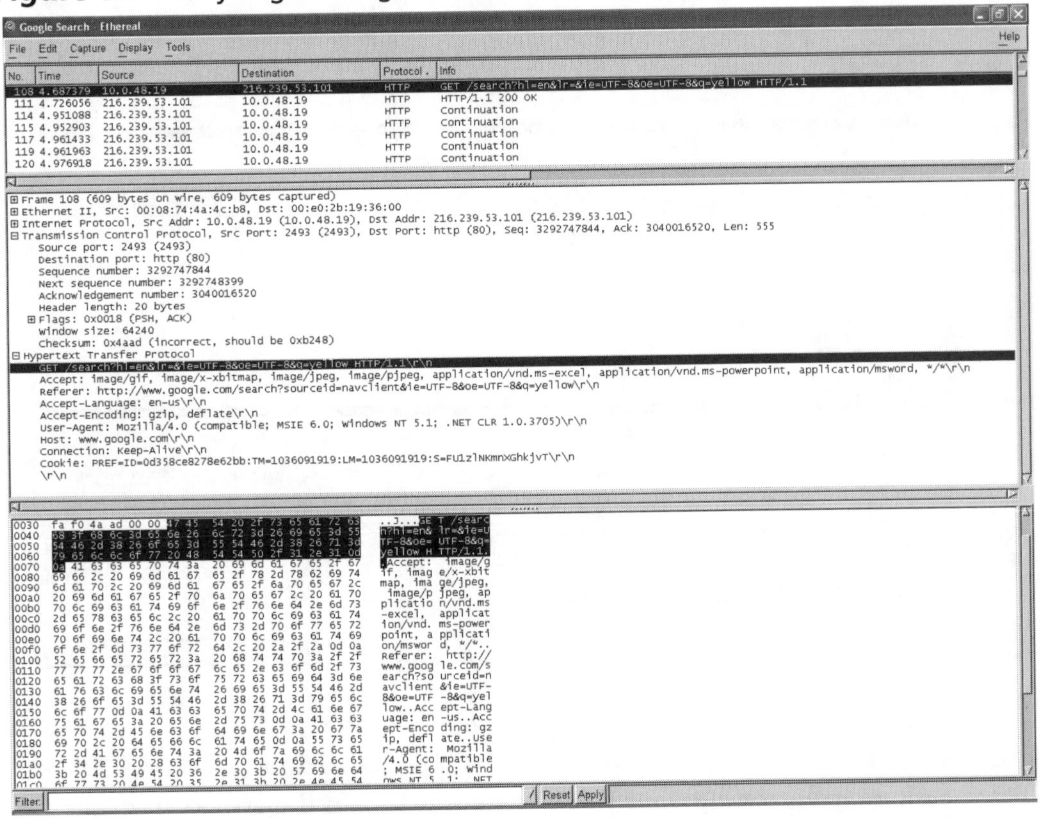

You should now feel somewhat comfortable using and analyzing packets with Ethereal. We realize that packet analysis is a very complicated task, and time and experience is the only way to improve your skills. The attack in Figure 5.4 is a popular %3F Web Directory Traversal attack. Similar to the previous example, the attack packet is highlighted in the top window, and the payload portion of the attack is highlighted in the middle and bottom windows. The %3F is not a critical attack, but does serve as an example for analyzing an attack and including content. The following is an example of a Snort rule that can be written to trigger such an attack. The rule uses the *uricontent* instruction instead of the *content* instruction, since the entire attack can be identified within the URI; this also helps to increase the accuracy of the rule.

```
alert tcp $EXTERNAL any -> $DMZ 80 (msg:"%3F Directory Traversal Attack";
flow:to_server; uricontent:"%3F";)
```

Figure 5.4 Analyzing a Web-Based Attack

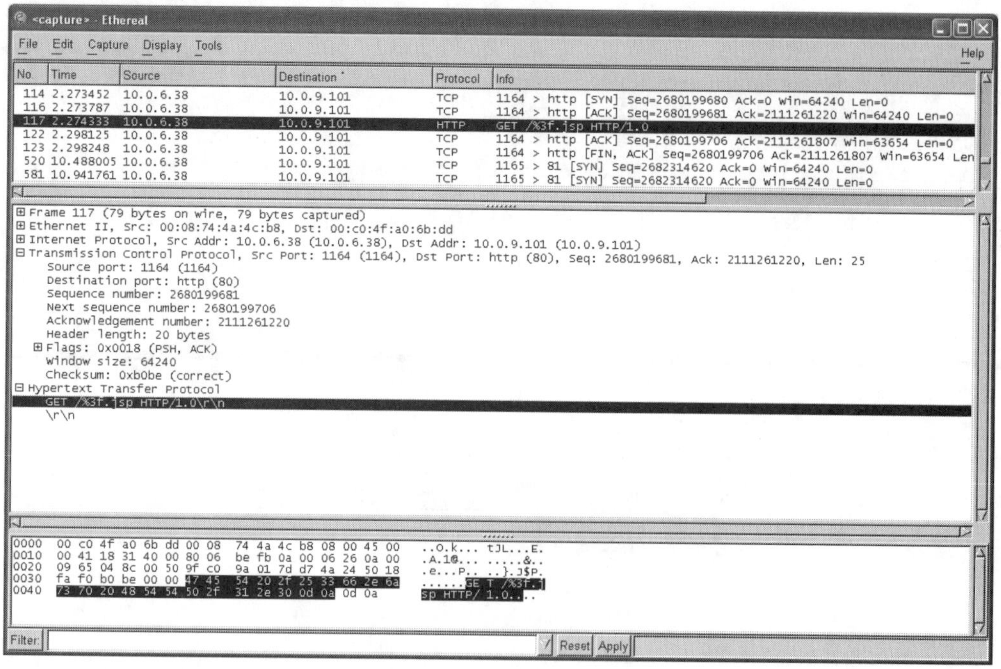

After the Snort rules have been written and verified with a test interpretation, it is highly recommended that you test your rules against real-world attacks. The best solution for testing your rule's content is to run the attacks from the perspective of an external attacker to verify that the rules are correctly identifying the attacks. Unfortunately, running the individual attacks for each exploit is not a scalable solution in and of itself. Chapter 10, "Optimizing Snort," has details on tools that can be used to help with testing your Network-based Intrusion Detection System (NIDS) setup, but beware that no currently available tool has mock attacks for all "critical" network-based attacks.

Merging Subnet Masks

Declaring subnets via subnet masks in variable declarations and rule definitions has the potential to consume unnecessary CPU resources. One quick method of maximizing Snort's potential to ensure efficient multinetwork usage is to merge subnet masks. In general, merging subnet masks are a manual task because they must be predefined and declared outside of the Snort program. Additionally, a good amount of human thought needs to go into the definition process of deciding what networks should be included within any given rule or set of rules.

Table 5.9 lists examples of single networks and addresses with the proper corresponding CIDR addresses along with the one merged subnet. Previously in the section "Assigning Source and Destination IP Addresses to Rules", Table 5.1 detailed examples of using CIDR addresses instead of the corresponding subnet masks. Table 5.9 has examples of the corresponding network addresses and subnet masks that go along with each CIDR address. The first three examples are examples of merging network subnet masks, while the last two examples merge individual IP addresses with CIDR addresses.

Table 5.9 Combining Subnet Masks (Good Examples)

Merged Subnet Mask	Subnets to Be Merged
10.1.0.0/22	10.1.0.0/24, 10.1.1.0/24, 10.1.2.0/24, 10.1.3.0/24
10.1.0.0/21	10.1.0.0/24, 10.1.1.0/24, 10.1.2.0/24, 10.1.3.0/24, 10.1.4.0/24, 10.1.5.0/24, 10.1.6.0/24, 10.1.7.0/24
10.1.8.0/22	10.1.8.0/24, 10.1.9.0/24, 10.1.10.0/24, 10.1.11.0/24
198.30.1.0/30	198.30.1.1/32, 198.30.1.2/32, 198.30.1.3/32 (single IP addresses)
198.30.1.0/29	198.30.1.1/32, 198.30.1.2/32, 198.30.1.3/32, 198.30.1.4/32, 198.30.1.5/32, 198.30.1.6/32, 198.30.1.7/32 (single IP addresses)

Fortunately, there is a tremendous amount of information on MAC and IP addresses. If you are interested in learning more about defining and referencing network addresses, Steven's *TCP/IP Illustrated* is the godfather of the books on the TCP/IP stacks.

The examples in Table 5.10 represent merged or combined subnet masks that are incorrectly defined. The first row shows a common example that users make. Namely, the subnets that you are looking to merge must be numerically sequential to one another. Notice that the four subnets that are "Subnets to Be Merged" define only class C address spaces. The second example might be the trickiest of them all. At first glance, it might appear that nothing is wrong, but the merged subnet mask 198.0.0.0/20 if redefined with the /21 CIDR address would read

198.0.0.0/21 and 198.1.0.0/21. The first class B address would be 198.0 instead of 198.1. The error in the last example should be obvious by the fact that the two IP addresses that are to be merged are random and separated by 100 other addresses—a blatant error.

Table 5.10 Combining Subnet Masks (Bad Examples)

Merged Subnet Mask	Subnets to Be Merged
10.1.0.0/22	10.1.0.0/24, 10.1.2.0/24, 10.1.4.0/24, 10.1.6.0/24
198.0.0.0/20	198.1.0.0/21, 198.2.0.0/21
10.100.80.0/31	10.100.80.1/32, 10.100.80.101/32

Merging subnet masks can save CPU resources and enhance the performance of Snort's traffic parsing engine. As a rule of thumb, you should always combine or merge subnet masks when possible, but it is imperative that only the correct addresses be included in the defined ranges.

Oink!

If you want to remove specific addresses from a merged subnet mask, you can always implement a BPF to pass on desired addresses and ranges, since the BPF engine analyzes packets before the Snort rule parsing engine.

Tools & Traps…

Automating Aggregating with Aggregate

Aggregate is a straightforward tool that can be used on most UNIX and Linux platforms to help merge or "aggregate" multiple subnets. The program receives subnets that you want to merge via standard input (STDIN) and will pump the merged subnet to standard out (STDOUT.) There are numerous small or less popular versions of the tool, but the most popular and stable version can be downloaded from *http://http.us.debian.org/*. At the Debian site, you will be able to download and read the detailed usage README.

Testing Your Rules

It is extremely important to test each and every rule that is included within your rule definition files. Improperly defined rules and rulesets can kill your system performance and flood your alert and log files. In general, there are three methods for testing your rules. The first and more difficult is conducting stress tests against your ruleset and system hardware; whereas the second merely tests the rule syntax. Stress tests are conducted by running numerous tools simultaneously to determine how many packets are dropped or missed by the NIDS. Testing rule syntax can be achieved by parsing individual rules into the Snort and TCPDump engines. The third method and by far the most difficult is to test the content of the rule by sending the attack string. In most cases, this test method is too time intense and cannot be carried out.

An effective quality assurance process is second to none when implementing a corporate NIDS into your environment. Managing IDSs requires quite a bit of network administration and area expertise when compared to other network devices such as routers and wireless access points, or other network security products such as firewalls and e-mail scanners. A sound process includes analyzing your software configuration before it enters your production environment.

Stress Tests

Vulnerability, attack, and packet stress tests are some of the most useful tests that can be performed against your Snort sensors. The goal of any stress test is to identify thresholds. In the case of NIDS, a stress test should identify the amount of data that can be processed and parsed through the Snort engine. Dropping packets due to inadequate hardware can be difficult to identify, yet identifying rules that consume large amounts of CPU cycles and decrease system performance are more difficult.

You can find free vulnerability assessment and stress test tool links:

- **NTOMax and FScan** www.foundstone.com
- **Nessus** www.nessus.org
- **Whisker** www.wiretrip.net/~rfp
- **NMAP** www.insecure.org
- **Paketto Keiretsu** www.doxpara.com
- **Nikto** www.cirt.net/nikto

The preceding free vulnerability assessment and stress test tools can be used to help design and execute system stress and benchmark tests. For example, launching three tools simultaneously from three different systems might generate a large amount of potentially malicious traffic. The stress test you create should chain together multiple tools generating large amounts of traffic. Benchmarking the tests is easier than running the actual tests. After each test, you will want to record the number of packets captured and analyzed, the number of alerts generated, and the exact size and number of entries logged. As long as you run the same tools with the same configuration and usage, the only recorded statistic that could potentially change is the size of the log. Otherwise, any inconsistencies could probably be caused from dropped packets or poor rulesets.

Individual Snort Rule Tests

You have a couple of methods for testing rules, but in general, one of the best and most accurate methods of testing for proper rule syntax is interpreting each rule individually. This might seem like a cumbersome task, but a quick Perl script that extracts individual rules from a rules file, or the reverse where you specify a directory and it opens each individual rule file and appends it to a master rules file, would be easy enough to create.

The syntax for parsing a file follows, but the more rules you have, the harder it will be to debug the scripts. The *−i* flag specifies the interface, while the *−n* flag tells Snort to exit after one packet is received. This allows you to ensure that the rule is in the proper format.

```
Test Syntax: snort -i  eth0 -n 1 -c /Snort/rules/example.rule
```

Berkeley Packet Filter Tests

Similar to testing individual Snort syntax rules, you have the ability to individually test BPF rules with the TCPDump utility. Since TCPDump is merely an interpreter for the rules, very little debugging functionality is built into the program. The easiest way to identify potential errors is to test the rule for proper syntax. The following command will individually parse the rule to ensure that it uses the correct syntax. The *−i* flag is used to define the appropriate network interface that the rule should be applied to, but in this case any valid interface is sufficient.

```
Test Syntax: tcpdump -i eth0 -n -F /Snort/bpf/example.filter
```

Tuning Your Rules

Snort provides you the ability to fine-tune your rules in a variety of methods. Fine-tuning your scripts could range from disabling nonessential rules, to modifying common rule variables to adequately map to your environment, to including BPF rulesets. We cover these three major categories for modifying your Snort sensor installation in detail throughout this section.

In addition to the major modifications that you can make, there are several small modifications as well. Small modifications include configuring Snort to run on a different interface, changing the output modes from verbose to quiet, or vice versa, modifying the file system or directory structure for rule files, and upgrading to a later version of Snort. There's one more change you might like to add to your list, defining new log and alert files.

Configuring Rule Variables

Depending on your setup and sensor, reconfiguring your environment variables can be a tedious job. If done properly, it might be as easy as opening your Snort configuration file and ensuring that the proper network and system IP addresses correspond to the proper variables. Now, if all of your variables are not defined and declared in one configuration file, you might want to consider redesigning your sensor installation. The variables in Table 5.11 can be used as generic names to implement throughout your entire ruleset in place of static addresses. Even if your configuration file becomes longer because of the number of variable definitions, it is worth the extra bit of effort to gain that added flexibility.

Table 5.11 System Variable Names

Variable Name	Functional Overview
$INTERNAL_NET	For use to declare your internal IP address range.
$DMZ	Declare your DMZ and public system addresses.
$EXTERNAL_NET	This should be the negation of your internal address range.
$DNS	Set your public DNS or DNS servers to this variable.
$WEBS	For use with your public Web servers.
$FTP	For use with your public file and FTP servers.
$FINANCIAL	You could use this to define your financial systems in case you would like to set additional rules for extra protection.

Continued

Table 5.11 System Variable Names

Variable Name	Functional Overview
$DEVELOPMENT	Development systems.
$PRODUCTION	Production systems.
$SENSITIVE	Just in case you would like to classify additional sensitive systems.

OINK**!**

All rules should contain dynamic variables that are defined in the configuration file; static IP addresses and networks are chronic problem areas for IDS administrators.

In addition to configuring your system variables, you might want to consider configuring your content list files. At the very minimum, you should create a directory to contain all of the content lists, simply for categorization and ease of use. In addition, you might find it unnecessary to block all of these sites via the response, *resp*, command. Of course, all of these depend on the business functionality and requirements of the organization. The following are some common categories frequently used throughout enterprise organizations:

- Adult site links and keywords
- Hacker, cracker, and serial Web sites and keywords
- Job posting Web sites
- Third party and Web-based e-mail sites
- Personals and matchmaker sites
- Media download Web sites
- Web-based proxy services or sites

Disabling Rules

Disabling rules in many cases is just as important as enabling and implementing particular rules or sets of rules. In most cases, ineffective rules or configurations might unnecessarily cause system logs and alerts to be generated based on non-pertinent data. As you can imagine, larger log and alert files require more energy and resources for parsing and analyzing the data. In addition to packet storage, unnecessary rules consume valuable system resources such as CPU cycles and memory during packet analysis that could have otherwise been used for analyzing other packets. Case in point, it is important to implement the rules that make sense for your environment. For example, if you are monitoring an IIS Web server, in most cases it only makes sense to enable rules that trigger on Microsoft or Web-related attacks.

There are two chief methods for disabling rules within the overall implementation and configuration for your sensor. The first and easiest if you have entire categories of rules that should no longer be included is to remove the specific include file references within the Snort configuration files.

```
#log tcp any any -> any 10 (msg:"Example Rule 1";)
```

The second method can be somewhat more tedious for large rule files, yet is significantly more effective in disabling individual rules. You can merely comment out the line containing the rule definition instead of deleting the line. This ensures that the rule is not enabled, yet is quickly available if you want to enable it in the future.

```
#log tcp any any -> any 20 (msg:"Example Rule 2";)
```

In this next rule, the previous two examples are disabled, while three will be included in the engine.

```
log tcp any any -> any 30 (msg:"Example Rule 3";)
```

Berkeley Packet Filters

The BPF schema is implemented within Snort so that you can write and leverage BPF rule files on your sensors. The BPF schema was designed to enable users to write quick packet analysis rules that are defined based on source, destination, protocol, and other pertinent header information. The BPF schema is widely used by the Win32 and UNIX-based versions of the TCPDump application. TCPDump is a program that sniffs, a.k.a. captures, network traffic off the wire. Network sniffing in combination with BPF allows you to only capture desired traffic, thereby potentially alleviating large amounts of useless data.

The BPF schema is very easy to understand, and you can use it to analyze the TCP, UDP, IP, and ICMP protocols. The rule syntax is very similar to spoken word; it uses "and" and "or" as rule operands, and uses "not" for negation. In addition to the spoken word instructions, you can use parentheses to inform the engine that a set of data should be read as one entity instead of multiple items.

The Example IMAP Filter will log all TCP traffic with the destination port set to 143; a common scenario to log IMAP destined requests. The Example 143 Traffic Rule will log all traffic with the source or destination of port 143 for protocols IP, TCP, and UDP. One obvious difference between the two rules is the protocol differences, but it is important to note that the general 143 rule does not differentiate between source and destination headers.

```
Example IMAP Filter   tcp and dst port 143
Example 143 Traffic Rule   ip and tcp and udp port 143
```

Now that you understand the basics behind BPF rules, we will cover some of the more advanced features within BPF. The previous examples should provide a basic understanding of rule syntax concerning protocol and port usage. The next two examples display rules that use parentheses to encapsulate packet entities such as a port definition or network address. The Example Cleartext Filter logs all TCP traffic destined to either port 21 or 23, Telnet and FTP, respectively. This rule is not uncommon, since it can be used to log authentication credentials traveling across the wire. The Example Network Filter logs IP traffic with a source from the 10.1.2.0/24 network destined to the 192.168.0.0/16 network.

```
Example Cleartext Filter   tcp and (dst port 21) or (dst port 23)
Example Network Filter   ip and (src net 10.1.2) and (dst net 192.168)
```

Using the negation instruction "not" is straightforward. It is an excellent way to filter out items that you do not want to log. The Example Negation Filter logs TCP destined to port 22 as long as it does not have a network address of 10.100.5.0/24. The Example Multiple Negation Filter was included to reinforce the "not" instruction, along with using parentheses inside a BPF rule. It logs all UDP traffic destined for port 111, the default UNIX and Linux port for the portmapper service, provided that it did not initiate nor is destined to either 10.9.1.4 or 10.9.1.5.

```
Example Negation Filter   tcp and (dst port 22) and not (net 10.100.5)
Example Multiple Negation Filter   udp and (dst port 111) and not (10.9.1.4
and 10.9.1.5)
```

BPF rules can be implemented within Snort via the command-line option −F or a reference in the configuration file. In either case, you must have previously created a local BPF rules file to be read into the sensor as configuration-related input. The file should be stored as ASCII text with an individual rule defined on its own line. If you want to modify the configuration file, you only need to include a single instruction: *config BPF_RULES_FILE: BPF_FILE.bpf*. Ensure that the *BPF_FILE.bpf* file has the proper permissions so that Snort can open and read in the file's data. As a side comment, BPF rules files differ from Snort rules files, and BPF rules should never be included within a Snort rules file.

You can find more information about the UNIX and Win32-based versions of the TCPDump utility at:

- **TCPDump** www.tcpdump.org
- **WinDUMP** http://windump.polito.it/

Summary

Snort, simple and flexible with a relatively small disk footprint minus the captured packet logs, when configured properly with an efficient set of rules will prove to be an irreplaceable enterprise and local application. As you might have gleaned, a couple key issues have been reinforced when it comes to designing rules: efficiency, comprehensive, and proper action. When you follow these few simple guidelines, you will find that your ruleset will be better handled for enterprise-class networks with a large number of hosts or networks demanding high transmission rates.

Throughout the chapter, we discussed rule development schematics, proper methods for testing your rules, techniques for enhancing your rules so that they perform at an optimal speed, and a couple of tips when it comes to using BPFs and subnet masks within a rule. The knowledge gained will be invaluable in the oncoming chapters and your future use of Snort. Two excellent locations for additional information on Snort and IDSs are www.snort.org and www.sourcefire.com.

Solutions Fast Track

Understanding Configuration Files

- ☑ Snort can currently parse through four protocols: IP, TCP, UDP, and ICMP.

- ☑ Simple source and destination rules do not necessarily require a body field, yet the body provides you with the important value-add features such as reporting enhancements, payload analysis, and service analysis specifics such as the *rpc* option.

- ☑ Each body option must be terminated by a semicolon, even if it is the last option before the parenthesis.

- ☑ Several freeware features within Snort enhance the commercial Sourcefire version, including activate and dynamic rules, the classtype rule option, IP options, RPC analysis, and multiple categorization and logging preferences.

The Rule Header

- ☑ Snort rule headers should be considered the main portion of the signature, since the header identifies what should be done when the rule is flagged, what protocol to use, and source and destination information including ports, IP address, and networks.

- ☑ The rule header can be divided into four main categories: rule action, protocol, source information, and destination information.

- ☑ When determining what rule action should be specified for your rule, you must ask yourself, "what is the goal of the rule and what is the level of importance if it were to occur?" There are five options for rule actions. These actions are: pass, log, alert, dynamic and activate.

- ☑ The current free version of Snort was designed to support the analysis of four different protocols: ICMP, TCP, IP, and UDP. However, additional minimal support is available for 802.11, HTTP, and ARP.

The Rule Body

- ☑ Each body option must be terminated by a semicolon, even if it is the last option before the parenthesis.

- ☑ Snort rules do not require the body field to be complete rule definitions. The body of the rule is an excellent addition that extends the breadth of rule definition beyond simply logging or alerting based on packet source and destination.

- ☑ There are a variety of options that can be used in the rule body. These options can be categorized into five categories: rule content, IP, TCP, ICMP, identifier, and miscellaneous.

- ☑ When writing Snort rules, the most powerful and important set of options that you can include within the body of the rule revolves around analyzing the payload of the packet. You can analyze payloads via binary and ASCII values in addition to specifying multiple other types of options that assist in identifying potentially malicious packet content.

Components of a Good Rule

☑ Content analysis strings should be written in binary format, and subnet masks should be merged when possible to save CPU cycles.

☑ Alerting events should be used for high-risk and time-critical events, while logging events can be more prevalent.

Testing Your Rules

☑ In general, rules should be tested in four metrics: efficiency, usefulness, accuracy, and uniqueness. An efficient rule might create duplicate logs, while an unnecessary rule might log insignificant packets. Inaccurate rules will flood your alert files and logs with false positives and, more importantly, you might not even know about false negatives. Rule uniqueness is another key factor, because in many large sets of rules it is common to find rules that are exact subsets of larger rules.

☑ It is just as important to test your system to ensure that packets are not being dropped and that you have access to the proper network packets.

☑ BPF rules can be individually tested using TCPDump or WinDUMP.

Tuning Your Rules

☑ BPF rules serve as an excellent mechanism for leveraging rules across multiple platforms and applications.

☑ You have the ability to comment out rules, remove categorized rule files, or delete instances of rules to ensure that you have the most efficient set of rules. Inefficient or unnecessary rules decrease your sensor's performance.

☑ Use the depth option to minimize the amount of information that has to be parsed during content analysis.

Frequently Asked Questions

The following Frequently Asked Questions, answered by the authors of this book, are designed to both measure your understanding of the concepts presented in this chapter and to assist you with real-life implementation of these concepts. To have your questions about this chapter answered by the author, browse to **www.syngress.com/solutions** and click on the **"Ask the Author"** form.

Q: Can I write plug-ins to manage my network(s) Snort rule alerts? I simply have too many scripts to manage without additional technology.

A: One of the inherent setbacks to IDSs is the potential number of alerts that can be generated. Consider this: You are monitoring for numerous types of attacks to your internal network from a partner network including direct port connections to any system outside your DMZ. If one system were to launch a vulnerable scan searching for open ports and vulnerabilities on 10 of your systems, it is feasible to have thousands of alerts generated within minutes. One way to administer these alerts is to have scripts that aid in correlation and analysis. Numerous helpful scripts are available, and a quick Google.com search could quickly solve some of your problems.

Q: Are there any disadvantages to using publicly available Snort rules? As an administrator, should I trust the rule content on snort.org?

A: Snort rules can obtain code to execute on your local system when a snort rule is activated, so it is advised that you quickly look at each rule you implement on your systems. This is not an uncommon recommendation when using freely available code, and falls within an administrator's realm of responsibilities.

Q: How does Snort compare to commercially developed IDSs?

A: Numerous hybrid versions of Snort are currently used in commercial applications and services globally. They range from managed security service providers using Snort hybrids internally for IDS monitoring, to companies reselling Snort appliances, to the fast-paced privatized Snort vendor Sourcefire. Due to its simplicity, Snort is at top of the list for performance, especially with the enhancements in version 2.0. However, if you seek up-to-date documentation, support, enterprise management features, and a commercial-grade GUI, you're probably suited for Sourcefire's version of Snort, or even another IDS product such as RealSecure or Dragon.

Q: Can I use Snort rules to log encrypted VPN data?

A: The simple answer is yes. It would not be difficult to log encrypted data between two points; however, the stored payload or data would still be encrypted. Note that if you want to log encrypted data, it is best to flag data based solely on headers, since in most cases the data fields within the packet will not properly reflect the actual payload.

Q: Where does Snort fit in my vulnerability assessment arsenal?

A: A good amount of security professionals do not use Snort to its fullest potential with reference to application- and network-based vulnerability assessments. Snort is extremely flexible and can be incorporated into numerous scripts and programs by configuring specialized alerts, logging mechanisms, and pre-processor plug-ins. This can allow you to log on specific types of data; for example, if you were conducting an application assessment and using whisker to request a Web site's cookie numerous times, you could potentially log those cookies and then analyze them and their similarities for content and number sequence.

Q: Should I worry about Snort being acquired and not publicly supported?

A: It is not uncommon to worry that a freely available tool will suddenly become unsupported or restricted from public use, especially if you are using it in a commercial environment. The simply fact is that Snort has been around awhile and does not appear to be going anywhere, especially with the success and emerged Sourcefire commitment to the freeware version of the product. However, none of us knows the future of the product, so as the saying goes, "use it at your own risk."

## Chapter 6

Preprocessors

Solutions in this chapter:

- **What Is a Preprocessor?**
- **Preprocessor Options for Reassembling Packets**
- **Preprocessor Options for Decoding and Normalizing Protocols**
- **Preprocessor Options for Nonrule or Anomaly-Based Detection**
- **Experimental Preprocessors**
- **Writing Your Own Preprocessor**

- ☑ **Summary**
- ☑ **Solutions Fast Track**
- ☑ **Frequently Asked Questions**

Introduction

Snort's detection capabilities originated with, and have evolved around, detecting attacks by matching packet data against well-defined patterns. Those well-defined patterns, or rules, are an evolution of signatures. Signatures are basically specifications of attacks via number and string matching against particular parts of the packet. For example, a packet directed to port 80 containing cmd.exe is generally a good sign of a hacker attacking a Windows-based Web server. An intrusion detection system (IDS) can detect this attack fairly well by checking destination port number, TCP flags (look for the ACK flag set, with the SYN flag off), and doing a simple string match against the data portion of the TCP segment. Rules are much like this, but bring an added flexibility and intelligence, allowing things such as compound statements, as in "trigger if you match this and don't match that," rules activated by a match on another rule, and finer specification of how to search for a pattern. This pattern-matching core might seem overly simple, but it is this simplicity that makes Snort one of the fastest Network-based IDSs (NIDSs) available. Snort can keep up with fast and heavily loaded networks because it generally has a well-defined amount of work to do for each packet that it must examine.

There was great demand for Snort to move beyond its rule-matching design. For example, one requested feature was protocol anomaly detection, where Snort could detect that a packet's data doesn't obey the rules of the protocol to which it belongs. This is generally not a capability possible within a straight signature/rule-based NIDS. Snort implements features such as protocol anomaly checking via preprocessors. Preprocessors handle packet data after Snort's decoder has parsed the packet into fields, but before the detection mechanism starts doing rule comparison. They can add a tremendous amount of functionality on top of Snort's rule-matching core.

Oink!

Actually, Snort does do some anomaly detection in its packet decoders as well, but we leave this for other chapters.

Now, there is a cost to adding preprocessors. Snort's extreme speed is derived from its simple rule-matching base—it will definitely lose some capability to keep up with fast or loaded networks each time a preprocessor is added. The degree of loss might or might not be perceptible, depending on the nature of the preprocessor. Due to a forward-thinking design decision by creator Marty Roesch to implement preprocessors as modular "plug-ins," one can decide exactly which preprocessors are active on a host-by-host basis. Each preprocessor is activated only by its specification in the snort.conf configuration file—if you leave it out it doesn't impact performance. One can even leave a preprocessor out of the codebase—that's much of the point of implementing preprocessors as plug-ins. Each plug-in is implemented as a separate code chunk in its own independent source file. This has added benefits in addition to speed. First, it allows Marty and the rest of Snort's developers to be less conservative about accepting new preprocessor code—if a new preprocessor plug-in is too slow or not stable as the time approaches for a release, the code can be easily deactivated by default so that people who want the preprocessor's feature anyway can have it, without requiring all other Snort users to take the same plunge. Further, it allows multiple developers to work on preprocessing and detection code simultaneously much more easily, without stepping on each other's toes.

In this chapter, we'll examine what role preprocessors have in relation to rules, how you can use and tune Snort's existing preprocessors, and how you can build a preprocessor of your own. We'll accomplish the latter by reading through the Telnet negotiation preprocessor code together, carefully discussing how it functions and how it connects into Snort, with an eye toward showing you how to build your own preprocessor.

What Is a Preprocessor?

Signature/rule-matching IDSs are extremely popular for their speed. If we're just inspecting each packet and performing number and string matches against simple patterns, we have a nimble program capable of keeping up with fast, fairly loaded networks. This form of IDS does have weaknesses, though. If its attack patterns are too general, you'll spend too much time analyzing *false positives*. If those patterns are too specific, you'll miss attacks—these misses are called *false negatives*. Much of the trouble in getting traditional rules right stems from too little expressibility in the signature language, or the inability of the IDS to understand protocols more fully. Some IDSs counter these weaknesses by using a completely different model. They might use protocol anomaly detection, where they alert on packets that don't fit normal use of the packet's protocols. Some signature/rule-based IDSs might also keep additional state on a connection. For example, we don't want our cmd.exe rule from earlier to flag on packets that aren't part of an established TCP session. Preprocessors let Snort do things such as anomaly detection and state keeping on a user-configurable basis.

You'll find preprocessors extremely useful. They make rules easier to write, lower false positive/negative counts, and give a rule-matching IDS the capability to exceed its traditionally simple detection model while maintaining performance. In the next section, we'll examine each of the major purposes for which preprocessors are used, including:

- Reassembling packets

- Decoding protocols

- Nonrule or anomaly-based detection

One thing to take note of in each preprocessor is how the rest of Snort benefits from the preprocessor's work. For example, the stream4 preprocessor doesn't modify any of the packets it examines; instead, it builds an "uber packet" of all the data in the stream, and passes that through the other preprocessors and detection engine separately. Conversely, the rpc_decode preprocessor modifies packets individually, destroying their original form and replacing them with packets free of multifragmented RPC messages. It's not important to fully understand these functions yet—we'll explore these later in the chapter. Just pay attention to what the preprocessors do with their data!

Preprocessor Options for Reassembling Packets

Snort has two preprocessor plug-ins that assist rule matching by combining data spread across multiple packets:

- stream4

- frag2

Both stream4 and frag2 are covered in additional detail in the sections that follow.

The stream4 Preprocessor

stream4, contained in spp_stream4.c, was announced in 2001 by Marty Roesch to improve Snort's handling of TCP sessions for selected traffic.

OINK!

Snort's own FAQ discusses stream4 by quoting Marty Roesch's introductory announcement—that announcement is not just historically useful, it gives hard detail on what the plug-in does.

At the time, as quoted in www.snort.org/docs/faq.html#3.14, Martin wrote:

"…I implemented stream4 out of the desire to have more robust stream reassembly capabilities and the desire to defeat the latest "stateless attacks" that have been coming out against Snort (c.f. stick and snot). stream4 is written with the intent to let Snort be able to handle performing stream reassembly for "enterprise class" users, people who need to track and reassemble more than 256 streams simultaneously. I've optimized the code fairly extensively to be robust, stable, and fast. The testing and calculations I've performed lead me to be fairly confident that stream4 can provide full stream reassembly for several thousand simultaneous connections and stateful inspection for upwards of 64,000 simultaneous sessions…".

stream4 has two goals, which we'll now explore:

- TCP statefulness
- Session reassembly

TCP Statefulness

To understand what statefulness is, we need to review the TCP protocol. TCP introduces the concept of a "session" to Internet communications. A session has a clear beginning and end, with a good deal of error correction introduced in between. The two sides of the session, the client and server to keep things simple, set things up with a series of three packets, before anyone sends any data. This series of packets is shown in Figure 6.1.

Figure 6.1 TCP Session Initiation

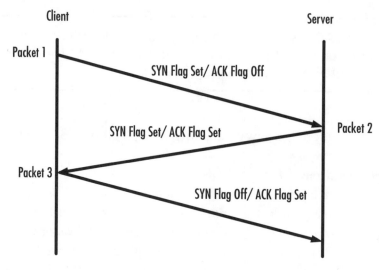

All further data packets have just the ACK flag set. While SYN is short for "synchronize," you can think of it as a request to start one of the directions of dataflow. Ack is short for "acknowledge," as it acknowledges the packets that a side has received so far. Each of these flag settings comes with a "sequence number," which serves to identify the packets sent and received. For a more thorough discussion of TCP, which you should definitely be familiar with if you're doing intrusion detection, refer to Chapters 18 and 19 (at the least) of W. Richard Stevens' *TCP/IP Illustrated, Volume 1*.

When the parties are finished communicating, they tear down the session with the sequence of packets shown in Figure 6.2.

Figure 6.2 TCP Session Termination

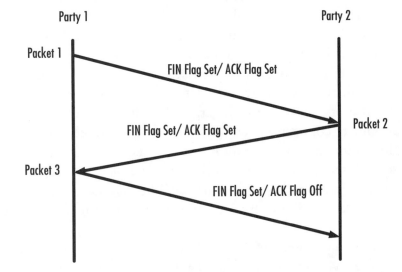

The reason we've switched from client/server descriptions to Party1/Party2 descriptions is because either party to the connection can initiate the disconnection. For example, the server usually sends that first packet with the FIN flag set to close down a Telnet session—it generally does this in response to a normal user "logout." FIN is actually short for "finish" and notifies the other party that the sender has no more data to send in that direction.

Stateless devices only look at one packet at a time—they have no memory of the previous packets. This means that their only way of gauging the status of a session is to look at the combination of flags. For example, they assume that any packet with the SYN flag unset and the ACK flag set is part of an existing connection. This is a huge weakness for a firewall! A number of port-scanning tools take advantage of this particular weakness in stateless firewalls by sending probe packets with only the ACK flag set to port-scan a machine, instead of the normal connection-initiating packets with the SYN flag on and the ACK flag off. The tools do this because a probe packet with only the ACK flag set looks like part of an existing connection that the firewall previously allowed through. Since the firewall has no memory of whether there actually was a connection that this could be a part of, it often must let the probe packets pass. Stateful devices, on the other hand, remember what handshaking packets have been sent and can thus keep track of the state of the connection.

While statelessness is a major weakness in firewalls, it carries nowhere near the same severity in IDSs. Most often, stateless IDSs simply spend unnecessary resources checking rules against invalid packets. They also generate more false-positives. Generally, this hasn't been an extreme problem. In fact, Snort's developers didn't add stateful monitoring until Coretez Giovanni released the stick tool. stick attempts to overwhelm stateless IDSs with a large number of false alert packets. By constructing these alert packets from the IDSs own ruleset, it attempts to guarantee that every packet will trigger an alert on a default ruleset. stick doesn't try to initiate connections with the normal TCP three-way handshake; this would slow things down tremendously and make it a much less effective tool. Because of this, a stateful device, which knows that each of the false alert packets is falsely claiming to be part of an established connection, can quickly disregard those packets and not spend computational or human resources on their response.

Snort is stateless in general. In 2001, Marty Roesch wrote the stream4 preprocessor, spp_stream4.c, to add optional statefulness to Snort. stream4 brings flexibility, too, allowing Snort to maintain state only on user-defined ports. This provides fine control over the additional resource drag. This statefulness allows Snort to alert on packets that falsely masquerade as part of an established connection, including those produced by tools like stick. The *-z est* flag tells Snort to not perform resource-intensive rule matching on any packets that aren't part of an established connection.

stream4 also gives Snort the ability to accurately alert on traffic based on what part of the connection it's in, using the *flow* keyword. As of Snort 1.9, you can use the *flow* keyword in a Snort rule to indicate state of the connection and direction of the traffic. For example, you might only want to alert when a packet is actually part of a server response to a previous client request. The *flow* keyword actually brings a great deal of functionality to bear, as you saw in Chapter 5, "Playing by the Rules."

Configuring stream4 for Stateful Inspection

The stream4 preprocessor is activated simply by keeping/adding a line to snort.conf like this:

```
preprocessor stream4
```

This activates stream4 and configures it as if you'd specified *timeout 30, memcap 8388608*. You might want to configure the preprocessor, though, in which case you'd add a colon ":" to the end of the line and list parameters to the right, delimited by commas. For example:

```
preprocessor stream4: detect_scans, disable_evasion_alerts
```

stream4's stateful inspection component takes the following parameters, which we'll explore together in turn:

- **detect_scans** The *detect_scans* parameter, which defaults to off if not present, tells stream4 to alert on portscans that don't use the normal TCP handshake that we reviewed earlier in this chapter. Attackers use these scan types to avoid having their scans logged by some network devices or hosts. For example, while Linux's xinetd or UNIX's TCP Wrappers will log any full connections (those that make it through the initial three-way handshake) that violate its access control lists, neither of these log incoming packets with only the FIN flag set. Conversely, a TCP-aware host must respond to a FIN-packet with an RST (reset) if the port probed is closed, and with nothing if the port probed is open. Tools such as nmap send these "stealth" scans to scan machines while avoiding having their activities logged by the target operating system. Snort will alert on these packets if you include this parameter.

- **detect_state_problems** The *detect_state_problems* parameter, which defaults to off if not present, tells stream4 to alert on problems in how TCP is keeping state. This might catch attacks or probes that Snort doesn't otherwise look for, by watching for anomalies or abuses of the state mechanisms in TCP. Snort's developers note that this option tends to create a great deal of noise because there are a number of operating systems or products that implement TCP badly. Unfortunately, as noted in the code at the time of this book's publication, Microsoft's operating systems tend to trigger these alerts normally (they frequently write data outside of the negotiated TCP Window size). You'll have to be careful with this option on a Microsoft-based or highly heterogeneous network. This option also causes Snort to alert when one side resends data that has already been ACK'd, or data with an ACK number that's smaller than one of our previous ACKs for the connection.

Tools & Traps…

False Positives

In network intrusion detection, noise, generally in the form of false positives, is something that experienced practitioners avoid at all costs in most environments. When you first start out, you might be eager to get all the information available about every packet entering, leaving, or running through your network. This is a lofty goal, but it requires so much labor in chasing down every alert that you either end up ignoring the IDS or tuning the IDS to alert less often. Unfortunately, it might feel like you're choosing the lesser of two evils.

In choosing the parameters for preprocessors, you might choose to deactivate protocol-anomaly alerting like *detect_state_problems* from the start, to avoid the false positives. If you have more time to set things up, you'll probably benefit more in the long run by turning options like this on and then deactivating the ones that produce too much nonattack-related noise. This "operator learning period" is somewhat like the learning period that statistical IDSs have—these types of IDSs spend time first analyzing what type of network traffic you normally send and then alert on the deviations. (In the case of you and Snort, there's a human being, who doesn't have the same memory for protocol details, but has much more intelligence.) Don't underestimate the importance of this learning period: tuning your IDS for your environment will make it a much more accurate tool that alerts when you're being attacked, without wasting nearly as much of your time with false positives.

- **disable_evasion_alerts** The *disable_evasion_alerts* setting, which also defaults to off, disables alerts written into stream4 to handle particular situations where the attacker tries to fake out stream reassembly. For example, he might send a packet and a slightly different "retransmission" of the packet, hoping that the stream reassembly engine will throw away the first and keep the second, while the destination host keeps the second and drops the first. In another case, an attacker might send a broken RST packet that the host will ignore, hoping that the IDS would wrongly interpret the packet and stop watching the stream. Finally, he might send data in the SYN packet (the first in the connection), hoping that the IDS would not log this unexpected data. You generally should leave this option off (thus keeping evasion alerts active) unless you get too many false positives. One example where you'd get a copious amount of false positives would be if you have some device on your network that actually *does* regularly send data in the SYN packet! Take care to thoroughly investigate these false positives before disabling these types of alerts, though—they might be the only warning you have that an attacker is playing games with your IDS.

- *ttl_limit* The *ttl_limit* parameter sets a maximum difference that will be tolerated between packets in the same session. Packets in the same session should generally have about the same number of routers to traverse on their way between the two hosts. Even when they take different paths, they should intuitively have about the same number of hops to go through. If the number of hops changes too drastically, it might be a sign of someone trying to evade detection. For example, an attacker might insert packets into the stream that will make it to the IDS, but will expire before they reach the destination. This causes the IDS to see a different picture of the reassembled stream than the destination host does. It's difficult to choose a safe value for this parameter, although 10 is probably a safe bet. Much of this will depend on how dynamic your ISP's routing is, and how dynamic the routing is to your standard destinations.

- *keepstats* The *keepstats* option keeps statistics on each session, which it can then log in either *machine* format, which is a simple flat text file, or in *binary* format, which is a unified binary output easily readable by tools such as Barnyard. This option defaults to off—you can activate it by listing *keepstats* and following it with either *machine* or *binary* as follows:

```
preprocessor stream4: min_ttl 28, keepstats binary
```

- *noinspect* The *noinspect* option, which obviously defaults to off, tells the preprocessor to deactivate stateful inspection on all ports except those on which you're doing active reassembly. Setting this option basically tells stream4's stateful inspection function to limit itself to the ports that are listed in stream4_reassemble's ports option. We'll look at that option soon.

- **timeout** The *timeout* option, which defaults to 30 seconds even if not present, sets an idle time after which stream4 can stop watching the session. If Snort doesn't receive a packet belonging to a particular session for a full timeout period, it prunes the session from its table and frees up the memory in use. This is especially necessary for sessions in which the two communicating hosts do not complete the normal three-way teardown we looked at earlier in this chapter. We don't want those sessions continuing to consume resources well after the hosts have stopped communicating. Thirty seconds is aggressively low for many organizations— it was chosen as a default to make sure that Snort could still function on minimal hardware.

- **log_flushed_streams** The *log_flushed_streams* option, which defaults to off, tells stream4 to log the "uber-packet" that it builds from the stream out to disk whenever that uber-packet causes an alert. This is good data to have, but it leads to some strange-looking packet logs.

- **memcap** The *memcap* option is described in more detail in the section that follows.

The *memcap* option, which defaults to 8,388,608 bytes even if not present, sets a maximum number of memory (in bytes) that stream4 will consume to do state-keeping and session reassembly. If stream4 runs out of memory, it prunes inactive sessions. Again, this is probably an over-aggressive default value intended to keep Snort working on minimal hardware. Systems with over 64MB of RAM could definitely increase this number easily. In an enterprise environment with capable hardware, one would probably set this to 512MB, or 536,870,912. If you want to fine-tune this number, try a setting and send a signal a USR1 signal to Snort, like this:

```
# ps -ef | grep snort
# killall -USR1 <PID>
```

Snort's output looks like this:

```
====================================================================
Snort analyzed 3 out of 3 packets, dropping 0(0.000%) packets

Breakdown by protocol:            Action Stats:
    TCP: 3          (100.000%)       ALERTS: 0
    UDP: 0          (0.000%)         LOGGED: 0
```

```
      ICMP:  0              (0.000%)          PASSED:  0

       ARP:  0              (0.000%)

     EAPOL:  0              (0.000%)

      IPv6:  0              (0.000%)

       IPX:  0              (0.000%)

     OTHER:  0              (0.000%)

   DISCARD:  0              (0.000%)

===================================================================
Wireless Stats:

Breakdown by type:

    Management Packets:  0              (0.000%)

    Control Packets:     0              (0.000%)

    Data Packets:        0              (0.000%)

===================================================================
Fragmentation Stats:

Fragmented IP Packets:   0              (0.000%)

    Fragment Trackers:   0

   Rebuilt IP Packets:   0

   Frag elements used:   0

Discarded(incomplete):   0

   Discarded(timeout):   0

  Frag2 memory faults:   0

===================================================================
TCP Stream Reassembly Stats:

      TCP Packets Used:  3              (100.000%)

      Stream Trackers:   1

       Stream flushes:   0

        Segments used:   0

  Stream4 Memory Faults:  0

===================================================================
```

Look at the final line of output that reads *Stream4 Memory Faults: 0.* A memory fault is a situation where the plug-in ran out of allocated memory and had to start pruning inactive or less-active streams. If this number is consistently greater than zero, you'll want to increase its allotment of memory. If the system itself is too low on memory, you might want to increase the physical RAM on the system. You can use a tool such as *top* to check the system's general memory usage, including its use of *swap*, or virtual memory. *Swapping* refers to the system emulating additional RAM by using a portion of the hard disk as a second memory medium, writing less-used data out to hard disk to free up memory. You don't want Snort's data being written out to disk this way because it takes the operating system a very long time to read that data back in, relatively speaking. RAM chips are much faster than hard disks! Be careful to configure this parameter carefully to avoid much swapping.

The stream4 preprocessor's session reassembly is configured through the *preprocessor stream4_reassemble* directive. Programmers will note that this is strange, since most preprocessor directives seem to correspond directly to a unique spp_preprocessor-name.c file. This is easily explained: preprocessor directives correspond to unique preprocessor functions, which usually come one to a file (these directives correspond directly to a unique preprocessor initialization function). stream4, being an extremely long and complex preprocessor, easily breaks the one-function-to-a-file convention without causing complaints.

Session Reassembly

Keeping a memory of the past packets in a TCP connection also allows Snort to catch attacks that span multiple packets. While UDP requires that all data in a message be contained in a single packet, TCP has no such requirement. TCP is used for, among other applications, highly interactive applications such as Telnet, rlogin, and SSH, each of which allows a user to interact with a remote host. As a result, a user's input might easily be spread across several packets—which is the case with Telnet. As we can see from the following few packets in a Telnet session, each keypress gets its own packet. This is a partial packet capture of a user typing the word *jay*.

```
03/13-17:58:02.520000 xxx.xxx.xxx.xxx:36922 -> xxx.xxx.xxx.xxx:23
TCP TTL:64 TOS:0x10 ID:62253 IpLen:20 DgmLen:53 DF
***AP*** Seq: 0x15807E79  Ack: 0x695B2295   Win: 0x1920   TcpLen: 32
TCP Options (3) => NOP NOP TS: 25008200 557061363
6A                                                          j
=+=+=+=+=+=+=+=+=+=+=+=+=+=+=+=+=+=+=+=+=+=+=+=+=+=+=+=+=+=+=+=+
03/13-17:58:02.530000 xxx.xxx.xxx.xxx:23 -> xxx.xxx.xxx.xxx:36922
TCP TTL:237 TOS:0x0 ID:53311 IpLen:20 DgmLen:53 DF
***AP*** Seq: 0x695B2295  Ack: 0x15807E7A  Win: 0x2798  TcpLen: 32
TCP Options (3) => NOP NOP TS: 557064184 25008200
6A                                                          j
```

```
=+=+=+=+=+=+=+=+=+=+=+=+=+=+=+=+=+=+=+=+=+=+=+=+=+=+=+=+=+=+=+=+
03/13-17:58:02.530000 xxx.xxx.xxx.xxx:36922 -> xxx.xxx.xxx.xxx:23
TCP TTL:64 TOS:0x10 ID:62254 IpLen:20 DgmLen:52 DF
***A**** Seq: 0x15807E7A  Ack: 0x695B2296  Win: 0x1920   TcpLen: 32
TCP Options (3) => NOP NOP TS: 25008201 557064184
=+=+=+=+=+=+=+=+=+=+=+=+=+=+=+=+=+=+=+=+=+=+=+=+=+=+=+=+=+=+=+=+
03/13-17:58:06.390000 xxx.xxx.xxx.xxx:36922 -> xxx.xxx.xxx.xxx:23
TCP TTL:64 TOS:0x10 ID:62255 IpLen:20 DgmLen:53 DF
***AP*** Seq: 0x15807E7A  Ack: 0x695B2296  Win: 0x1920   TcpLen: 32
TCP Options (3) => NOP NOP TS: 25008587 557064184
61                                                              a
=+=+=+=+=+=+=+=+=+=+=+=+=+=+=+=+=+=+=+=+=+=+=+=+=+=+=+=+=+=+=+=+
03/13-17:58:06.410000 xxx.xxx.xxx.xxx:23 -> xxx.xxx.xxx.xxx:36922
TCP TTL:237 TOS:0x0 ID:53312 IpLen:20 DgmLen:53 DF
***AP*** Seq: 0x695B2296  Ack: 0x15807E7B  Win: 0x2798   TcpLen: 32
TCP Options (3) => NOP NOP TS: 557064572 25008587
61                                                              a
=+=+=+=+=+=+=+=+=+=+=+=+=+=+=+=+=+=+=+=+=+=+=+=+=+=+=+=+=+=+=+=+
03/13-17:58:06.410000 xxx.xxx.xxx.xxx:36922 -> xxx.xxx.xxx.xxx:23
TCP TTL:64 TOS:0x10 ID:62256 IpLen:20 DgmLen:52 DF
***A**** Seq: 0x15807E7B  Ack: 0x695B2297  Win: 0x1920   TcpLen: 32
TCP Options (3) => NOP NOP TS: 25008589 557064572
=+=+=+=+=+=+=+=+=+=+=+=+=+=+=+=+=+=+=+=+=+=+=+=+=+=+=+=+=+=+=+=+
```

Many attacks will definitely be spread across several packets and will thus be undetectable to a nonsession-reassembling rule-matching IDS—that's the whole reason for stream reassembly. The user could type "company going broke sell stocks now," and if you are looking for "sell stocks" but the packets come across as "s", "e", "l", "l", " ", "s", "t", "o", "c", "k", "s" (one letter per packet), then without reassembly of the stream, you wouldn't catch that. The stream4 preprocessor reassembles the TCP stream so that Snort can try rule matches against the whole of the flowing data. Although this is over-simplifying somewhat, it does this by combining all the data in a stream into a large uber-packet that can then be passed through the other preprocessors and then the detection engine.

Notes from the Underground...

stream4—A Reaction to stick

Marty Roesch created stream4 at least partly in response to the stick tool. stick attempted to confuse IDS operators by sending a huge number of false positives to the IDS, in order to hide the actual attack among the noise. stick's creator, Coretez Giovanni, even designed it to construct the false positive packets from the patterns in Snort's own ruleset—in essence, stick is a simple rule-to-packet converter. It can quickly construct packets and doesn't need to understand much about them. On the other hand, almost every packet that it generates will not be a correct part of a proper TCP connection. This weakness allows a stateful device to easily ignore all of stick's false positives.

Specifically, Snort's *-z* command-line option, which, when given as *-z est*, instructs Snort to keep state on all TCP traffic and alert only on traffic where the connection is either fully established by a three-way handshake, or at least where the server side has sent something back other than an RST or FIN. This defeats stick-style attacks by allowing Snort to ignore traffic that looks like part of a connection but isn't in its state table.

Configuring stream4 for Session Reassembly

The stream4 preprocessor's other major function is session reassembly. Remember, Snort uses this to match rules across the many packets making up a session. You configure this part of stream4 by using a directive such as:

```
preprocessor stream4_reassemble: both ports 21 23 25 53 80 143 110 111 513
```

We'll examine the following options, which are set after the colon on the preprocessor directive line:

- *clientonly / serveronly* / or both The first option tells stream4 how much of the stream it should reassemble. It can simply do reassembly on the client side (traffic going to *HOME_NET*), when you set the *clientonly* option, reassembly only on the server side (traffic coming from *HOME_NET*), when you set the *serveronly* option, or *all traffic*, when you set both.

- **noalerts** This option instructs stream4 not to alert on anomalous/problem events in reassembly, such as traffic insertion. For example, the reassembly code in Snort might alert if someone uses a traffic interception/insertion tool such as hunt to insert traffic into Telnet sessions. This option is often necessary on heterogeneous networks with particular versions of Windows.

- **ports** This option indicates exactly which ports stream4 should perform reassembly on. Reassembly is resource-expensive, especially on memory—you might not choose to do this on most ports. You can set this parameter to a space-delimited set of port numbers; *all* to reassemble on all ports, or *default* to listen on the default port list of "21 23 25 53 80 143 110 111 513."

If you don't specify any arguments for *stream4_reassemble*, this signifies "clientonly ports default."

stream4's Output

stream4's stream reassembly watches the entire session and assembles an uber-packet, built from all the data in the TCP session that it's following. When the session ends, it flushes that data back into the other preprocessor functions and thus into the detection engine. This means that you might see an alert twice—the first alert would be from the original packet, and the second would be for the uber-packet built from that packet's TCP session. stream4 also flushes the current stream if it's forced by memory exhaustion to prune the stream—this is configured via the *memcap* parameter discussed previously. Finally, stream4 also flushes the stream when it has collected a particular amount of data. This amount is chosen randomly on a stream-by-stream basis—if it wasn't a random amount, an attacker could use Snort's reassembly against it by placing the attack data just far enough into the stream to make sure that part of it was flushed into one uber-packet while the remainder was pushed into the next uber-packet.

frag2—Fragment Reassembly and Attack Detection

A number of attacks use fragmentation to thwart rule-matching. Let's review fragmentation so we can understand more fully what this preprocessor accomplishes.

Fragmentation is a normal part of the Internet Protocol (IP). In essence, each type of networking hardware has a different Maximum Transfer Unit (MTU), a number that quantifies how much data can be transferred in a single "chunk" on the medium. For example, Ethernet's MTU is 1,500 bytes, and it calls its data chunks "frames." The sending IP stack in a communication generally puts as much data in a packet as it can, basically using the MTU of the outgoing network as a maximum size for the outgoing chunk. If the IP packet, as it goes through a router from one network to the next, is too large for the MTU of the next network, it gets broken into fragments. These fragments basically look like IP packets in their own right and can traverse the network. They are reassembled when they reach their destination.

Unfortunately, fragmented packets pose a difficulty to NIDSs. Remember, IDSs based on signature-matching work by matching individual packets, not collections of them, against attack patterns. An attacker can use a tool such as Dug Song's fragroute (http://naughty.monkey.org/~dugsong/fragroute) to break a packet into multiple fragment packets in the hope that no single fragment packet will match the pattern for his attack. Snort's frag2 preprocessor, in spp_frag2.c, addresses this type of attack, by reassembling fragmented packets before they go through the detection engine. In essence, it rebuilds each packet from the pieces and passes the full packet through for detection once the process is done.

frag2 is also useful in detecting fragment-based denial-of-service (DoS) attacks. These attacks will often send a series of well-designed fragments to take advantage of a host's particular IP stack vulnerabilities. For example, some machines will reboot, halt, or otherwise react negatively when they receive a fragment that has its offset configured to overwrite a previous fragment's data. Remember, fragments are supposed to be nonoverlapping parts of the packet—overlapping fragments is just the type of seemingly impossible condition that causes a host to hang.

Configuring frag2

You can configure frag2 by adding parameters after a colon on the preprocessor frag2 directive:

```
preprocessor frag2: timeout 60, memcap 4194304
```

Let's review the parameters that frag2 accepts. You'll notice that some of the parameters listed here are also in stream4 and have basically the same meaning.

- **timeout** The timeout parameter instructs frag2 to stop trying to rebuild a fragmented packet if it hasn't received a fragment in the set number of seconds. The default 30 seconds is almost certainly overly aggressive. A better default is probably 60 to 90 seconds. Sites that expect an attacker might either use high-latency links or intentionally slow down his attack should consider setting a number even a bit higher.

- **memcap** The *memcap* parameter limits the amount of memory that Snort can use to store partially rebuilt packets. When frag2 has used all of this memory, it will begin to aggressively prune partially rebuilt packets out of its fragment table. The 4MB default might be overly aggressive, especially on a heavily loaded external network interface. It's probably extremely over-aggressive for a host on the other end of a low-MTU link. You can determine a good setting for this as you did when setting memcap on the stream4 preprocessor. Send Snort a SIGUSR1 signal and read the number of "frag2 memory faults" under the "Fragmentation Stats" heading.

- **min_ttl** The *min_ttl* parameter sets a minimal IP Time-To-Live (TTL) that packets must have in order to be reassembled by Snort. If the TTL of a packet is too low to make it to its destination, you generally don't have to worry about it carrying a payload-based attack. The destination host won't receive the packet; thus, a payload-based attack won't harm that host. That's not to say that packets that don't reach the host can't have a negative effect! If an attacker sends a huge number of packets that die on the router just before the destination host, that destination host will almost certainly find the associated network connection over-saturated and thus useless. Attackers have often used fragment-based attacks to perform DoS attacks. The *min_ttl* parameter simply prevents frag2 from devoting resources to packets that won't reach their destination. You should set this parameter to the minimum number of hops between the IDS's network and the hosts you're monitoring.

- **ttl_limit** The *ttl_limit* parameter sets a maximum difference that will be tolerated between fragments of the same packet. Fragments of the same packet should generally have about the same number of routers to traverse on their way between the two hosts. Even when they take different paths, they should intuitively have about the same number of hops to go through. If the number of hops changes too drastically, it might be a sign of someone trying to evade detection. For example, an attacker might insert fragments into the stream that will make it to the IDS, but will expire before they reach the destination. This causes the IDS to see a different picture of the rebuilt packet than the destination host does. It's

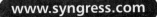

difficult to choose a safe value for this parameter, although 10 is probably a safe bet. Much of this will depend on how dynamic your ISP's routing is and how dynamic the routing is to your standard destinations.

■   ***detect_state_problems*** The *detect_state_problems* parameter activates alerting on anomalies detected in reassembling fragments. This will trigger on several conditions. If a packet has more than one fragment identifying itself as the first fragment (via a fragment offset of zero and the more fragments flag set), this will trigger. It will also trigger if fragments overlap or if a fragment arrives for a packet that is already fully rebuilt. Finally, it will trigger if a nonfirst fragment has IP options set. IP options should only be set in the first fragment. As of Snort 1.9.1, this option does not control whether frag2 alerts on rebuilt packets that are too large, as in the Ping of Death—this alerting is always active.

frag2 Output

frag2 rebuilds a packet from all the fragments it receives and then pushes the rebuilt packet through the normal path taken by a packet that has just left the decoder. The packet is logged and/or run through the preprocessor and detection mechanisms. As with the stream4 preprocessor, it's possible that a Snort rule will alert both on a fragment and on that fragment's rebuilt packet.

Preprocessor Options for Decoding and Normalizing Protocols

Rule-based pattern matching can often fail on protocols for which data can be represented in many different ways. For example, Web servers accept many different ways of writing a URL. IIS, for example, will accept backslash "\" characters in place of forward-slash "/" characters in URLs. Another example is Telnet, where an inline protocol negotiation can interrupt data that might be matched. Two characters in a pattern might be separated in the datastream by 4 bytes of Telnet negotiation codes. In each of these cases, you can define a single "right," or canonical, way to write the data that you're matching. We can change all of the URLs to match the way that rule writers expect to see them. We can remove all negotiation codes from Telnet data. These types of preprocessors might even be used to convert binary protocols into text-based representations or some other form that makes them easier to run through the detection engine. At the time of this book's publication, there exist decoding/normalization plug-ins for only the Telnet, HTTP, and RPC protocols.

Telnet Negotiation

The Telnet protocol features an inline negotiation protocol to signal what features the client and server can offer each other. The client and server intersperse this negotiation data with the normal payload data. Unfortunately, it's usually the payload data that we want to match our rules against. Snort solves the resulting problem with the telnet_negotiation preprocessor, in spp_telnet_negotiation.c, which removes all Telnet negotiation codes, leaving the detection engine to simply perform matches against the remaining session data. Later in this chapter, we'll examine the implementation of the Telnet negotiation preprocessor, to better understand how preprocessors work and how you can build your own preprocessor.

Configuring the telnet_negotiation Preprocessor

You can activate the telnet_negotiation preprocessor with a *preprocessor telnet_decode* line in snort.conf. While at the time of this book's publication, Snort's documentation and configuration file don't mention it, the telnet_negotiation preprocessor does allow you to specify a set of ports that should be filtered for Telnet negotiation codes. To accept the defaults, which are "21 23 25 119," simply activate the preprocessor in the Snort configuration file with a line like this:

```
preprocessor telnet_decode
```

To specify an alternate set of ports, add a colon and a space-delimited list of ports:

```
preprocessor telnet_decode: 23 25
```

telnet_negotiation Output

The telnet_negotiation preprocessor does not modify the original packet, as you might think it would. This is specifically because some rules will want to detect attacks or problems in the raw Telnet protocol, including the negotiation codes. Snort allows you to do this by specifying "rawbytes" after the content option you would like to set to look at the original packet. You might do this if an attack used a particular negotiation code sequence, say, to attack a buffer overflow in option subnegotiation. This preprocessor instead outputs the normalized Telnet data into a separate data structure associated with the packet, and then flags that packet as having an alternate decoding of the data. Rules that don't use rawbytes match against the alternate data, while rules using rawbytes match against the unaltered original data. (By the way, this mechanism is currently only used by the Telnet negotiation plug-in.) The other two protocol-decoding plug-ins that we'll discuss, which do HTTP and RPC normalization, (as of Snort 1.9.1) do not use the rawbytes mechanism to ensure that a rule can reference the nondecoded version of the packet. As you'll see, the HTTP normalization plug-in leaves the packet alone and simply writes the URIs it discovers into a separate data structure that Snort can read, while the RPC plug-in destructively modifies Snort's only copy of the packet.

HTTP Normalization

HTTP has become one of the most widely and diversely used protocols on the Internet. Over time, researchers have found that Web servers will often take a number of different expressions of the same URL as equivalent. For example, an IIS Web server will see these two URLs as the same:

```
http://www.example.com/foo/bar/iis.html
http://www.example.com/foo\bar\iis.html
```

Unfortunately, a pattern-matcher such as Snort will only match the pattern "foo/bar" against the first of these two. An attacker can use this "flexibility" in the Web server to attempt to hide his probes and attacks from the NIDS. Unfortunately, there are at least a few more IDS evasion techniques available to an attacker. These all work by abusing the ambiguity of the Uniform Resource Indicator (URI) portion of the URL, which is the part after the server name. For example, IIS accepts Unicode (UTF-8) encoding for the URI, as well as straight hexadecimal encoding. Using normal alphanumeric characters, hexadecimal representations, and various Unicode encoding of characters, an attacker can write his URL in many different ways. If you were to perform a "back of the envelope" estimate, there's at least four possible ways to encode each character, thus at least 4^n different ways to write an n-character URI. Practical rule-matching is not possible unless we can canonicalize the URIs. This situation screams out for a preprocessor!

Damage & Defense…

How Many Ways Can I Write a URI?

There are many ways to write a URI. For example, we could insert "../foo/" immediately after the "/foo" in our previous example, to yield an equivalent file specification. You can actually insert as many of those as you want, producing an infinite number of equivalent URI's. You'll note that handling "../"'s is not among the functions of the http_decode preprocessor. Snort catches this particular trick with a rule matching "../".

Luckily, the Snort developers have answered this scream with http_decode, normalization preprocessor, in http_decode.c. This preprocessor can be granularly configured to account for several tricks, rewriting the HTTP data it examines to a canonical form that the detection engine can match simply. Let's look at each of the tricks that it can account for and, in doing so, examine how this plug-in is configured. To activate this preprocessor, just add the following line to the Snort configuration file:

```
preprocessor http_decode
```

Configuring the HTTP Normalization Preprocessor

The HTTP normalization preprocessor will act on all traffic directed to port 80. We can change this port by adding a port list to the preprocessor directive:

```
preprocessor http_decode: 80 8080 8000
```

We'll now look at further options that can be added to the end of this list:

```
preprocessor http_decode: 80 8080 8000 unicode iis_alt_unicode
double_encode iis_flip_slash
```

- The *unicode* option tells the preprocessor to normalize Unicode, converting it to ASCII. Unicode, or UTF-8, provides a platform-independent numeric encoding for characters, in the same way that ASCII does. The difference is that Unicode provides up to 32 bits of numbers to represent those characters, unlike ASCII's 7 bits. This allows Unicode to express all the alphabets and symbols necessary for international communication. By using this option, you give Snort the capability to preprocess Unicode so string matching will still work against it.

- The *iis_alt_unicode* option tells the preprocessor to handle IIS's alternative Unicode representation, where %AB%CD is represented as %uABCD. If you have any IIS servers at your site, it's important to activate this option.

- The *double_encode* option tells the http_decode preprocessor to handle the situation where an attacker passes a URL with the percent sign, the normal signal for hexadecimal encoding, itself encoded in hexadecimal. For example, an attacker wants to hide the "/" symbol, so he sends %255c. The "%25" in %255c translates to "%," so that %255c translates to %5c. %5c translates to "/." This isn't intentional behavior, though. This was a bug in IIS 3, 4, and 5, prior to Microsoft IIS patch MS01-44. If your site's IIS servers are all patched (or new enough to not require the patch), you don't need to enable this option. Otherwise, enable *double_encode*.

- The *iis_flip_slash* option tells http_decode to flip all \s to /s in its normalization routines. This is important because attackers can replace /s with \s to avoid detection, as noted earlier in this discussion. Again, while IIS makes this translation automatically, Snort can only do so through the *http_decode* preprocessor.

- The *full_whitespace* option tells http_decode to translate tab characters into normal space characters. Apache servers, in this case, create this need; they automatically translate tab characters to space characters. An attacker can defeat normal string matching by simply exchanging space characters for tab characters. Turn this option on if you have any Apache servers.

The next three options weren't documented in either the Snort configuration file or documentation at the time of this book's publication:

- *abort_invalid_hex*
- *drop_url_param*
- *internal_alerts*

The *abort_invalid_hex* option tells the http_decode preprocessor to halt its normalization efforts if it finds an invalid hexadecimal character; for example, %0J. Apache Web servers halt processing of a request if that request contains invalid hexadecimal characters. If your site uses only Apache Web servers, it should be safe to activate this option if you don't want to hear about unsuccessful attacks using invalid hexadecimal characters.

The *drop_url_param* option tells the http_decode preprocessor to drop the parameters from the URL string. Parameters are the data items after the "?" characters in a URL, the part usually called the *query string*. They're usually supplied by browsers submitting forms using the *GET* method. In some situations, it might be wise to strip off the query string—the *drop_url_param* option instructs http_decode to do just that with every request.

The *internal_alerts* option tells http_decode to alert when it encounters certain strange conditions while normalizing the HTTP request. For example, it alerts if an HTTP request is longer than 10 characters. Valid HTTP methods include only *CONNECT, DELETE, GET, HEAD, OPTIONS, POST, PUT,* and *TRACE*. None of these is over 10 characters! It's extremely reasonable to suspect that a user submitting HTTP requests with a method longer than any of these is probably up to no good. For example, he might be hoping to exploit a buffer overflow vulnerability in the Web server. Here are some other conditions that *internal_alerts* causes this preprocessor to alert on:

- No resource was requested (the request only had a method).
- Double-encoded strings.
- The attacker submitted an illegal hexadecimal character (for example, %0J).
- The attacker supplied an overly long (illegal) Unicode encoding.

It's generally a good idea to activate *internal_alerts*, unless you get too many false positives. They should help you determine when an attacker is up to no good, even when his attacks haven't yet matched a rule.

http_decode's Output

The http_decode preprocessor writes normalized URLs into a global data structure that can be read by Snort's detection engine. The original packet is not altered by this process. This global data structure is checked against the uricontent rule directive.

rpc_decode

Applications such as Network File Sharing (NFS) and Network Information System (NIS) ride on Sun's Remote Procedure Call (RPC) protocol. RPC isn't a transport-layer protocol; in fact, it rides on top of TCP or UDP. Instead, it's an abstraction mechanism that allows a program on one host to call a program on another host. You can learn more about RPC by reading RFC 1831, "RPC: Remote Procedure Call Protocol Specification Version 2," available at www.ietf.org/rfc/rfc1831.txt.

Since RPC is intended to carry single messages, but can ride over the stream-based TCP protocol that doesn't distinguish between messages the way UDP does, Sun designed a "record" structure such that each RPC message is encapsulated in a "record." As the RFC describes, a record is made up of one or more "record fragments." These fragments aren't IP fragments—two record fragments can easily be in the same packet. They bring a simple structure. Each record is made up of one or more fragments, where each fragment starts with a bit indicating whether the record is continued into the next fragment, and a 31-bit number describing the size of the data in the fragment.

An attacker can easily break a record into fragments by manipulating the stream, so that a critical bit of data is spread across several record fragments. This would cause a 32-bit fragment header to interrupt the critical data, thereby foiling straight pattern matching. The rpc_decode preprocessor, in spp_rpc_decode.c, can defeat these attacks just as simply by consolidating records broken into more than one record fragment into a single record fragment. The only real difficulty with this process is knowing which TCP streams to send through the preprocessor. Snort uses a static list of ports, performing this process on every TCP stream destined for these ports.

Configuring rpc_decode

There's good news and bad news when it comes to configuring rpc_decode. The good news is that rpc_decode takes only a list of ports as a parameter. The bad news is that determining which ports should be in this list is difficult.

Normal client-server applications work by having the server listen on a well-defined port, such that the client knows what port to contact. For example, Telnet servers usually listen on port 23, while FTP servers listen on port 21. Server administrators can override these ports, but generally don't—when they do, they must communicate the nonstandard port to all users.

RPC works differently. RPC-based servers on a host start listening on an unreserved port, which they then register with a local *portmapper*. The portmapper, called *rpcbind* on most versions of UNIX and *portmap* on Linux, listens on a static port (TCP and UDP 111), which clients contact to learn the port numbers of the servers they seek. This nonstatic nature of server port assignments makes it difficult to configure the rpc_decode preprocessor properly. We'd like the preprocessor to act on all RPC-based traffic, but we don't know which ports our RPC-based servers are using. We could be conservative and simply choose the portmapper's listening ports. This is actually Snort's default—it listens on ports 111 and 32771. While 111 is the standard portmapper port, versions of Solaris prior to 2.6 listened on port 32771 as well. Now, we do have other options.

How might we choose more ports for rpc_decode to translate? Well, first you might notice that most of a machine's RPC-servers that start on boot seem to always show up with the same port numbers. If your network is fairly homogeneous, these should be about the same from machine to machine. You can add these port numbers to the list. Second, if you have any applications at your site that use RPC, you might add whatever port number they tend to communicate with most often. You can try to find or confirm patterns in your site's use of RPC by sniffing headers on traffic for a few days, tracking down the protocols in use on your network. Setting this list too inclusively could be dangerous, though. The rpc_decode preprocessor modifies Snort's internal representation of any packets passing through it—if it acts on non-RPC traffic, it might wrongly modify packet data.

You can activate the rpc_decode preprocessor by including the following line in Snort's configuration file:

```
preprocessor rpc_decode
```

If you want to specify ports outside of the default, simply add a colon to the end of this, followed by your space-delimited port list:

```
preprocessor rpc_decode: 111 32771 1024
```

You can also activate or deactivate RPC anomaly detection in this preprocessor with the following four directives:

- *alert_fragments* The *alert_fragments* parameter, which is off by default, instructs the RPC decode preprocessor to alert whenever it sees RPC messages broken up into multiple fragments. As this could be a sign of IDS evasion by an attacker on some networks, this might be prudent.

- ***no_alert_multiple_requests*** This parameter modifies the RPC decode preprocessor's normal behavior, so that it doesn't alert when more than one RPC query (message) is in a single packet. Especially if stream4 is doing stream reassembly on an RPC port, this setting could save you from a number of false alerts.

- ***no_alert_large_fragments*** This parameter modifies the RPC decode preprocessor's normal behavior, so that it doesn't alert when the RPC fragments might cause integer overflows and end up being too large.

- ***no_alert_incomplete*** This parameter modifies the RPC decode preprocessor's normal behavior, so that it doesn't alert when a single RPC message is larger than the packet containing it. This alert will false often when there are large RPC messages that get fragmented—since RPC messages can be 2^{31} bytes, they can exceed the MTU of the medium their packets travel on.

rpc_decode Output

The rpc_decode preprocessor actually does modify the packet that it's examining. This is one of the few preprocessors that currently overwrite the original packet data, as of Snort 1.9.1.

Preprocessor Options for Nonrule or Anomaly-Based Detection

A third class of preprocessor performs attack detection that cannot be performed using regular rules or protocol anomaly detection. The preprocessors that we examine here show how Snort can be extended easily to detect attacks in about any way a developer can imagine. Although it hasn't been done yet, one might even give Snort the capability to do statistical measurement and learning of normal network traffic, alerting on deviations from normal behavior. This is simply a wild example of how preprocessors allow a developer to add nearly any IDS functionality conceivable to Snort, giving it the capability to straddle all boundaries between types of NIDS. Before you get too excited, let's look at the two preprocessors that have been declared Enterprise-ready code at the time of this book's publication, portscan and bo (Back Orifice).

As an additional note, this class of preprocessors is more concerned with alerting than with rewriting packets. As a result, this section will not include a discussion of how each of these preprocessors place a packet back into the detection engine—this doesn't apply to them.

portscan

Some attacks just can't be detected by rule-matching or protocol anomaly detection. For example, how does one reliably detect a portscan from a single packet or connection? A portscan generally involves several probes, generally to more than one port or more than one machine. If it does not, it's extremely difficult to distinguish from an ordinary valid connection attempt. A single incoming port-80-destined packet to your non-Web server workstation could be the Internet equivalent of a "wrong number." A user could have entered a name or IP address incorrectly, or your organization's DNS entries might have an error. On the other hand, 200 port-80-destined packets addressed to each of your IP addresses, arriving in numerical order by IP address, are almost certainly a curious party's portscan. What distinguishes one from the other is a subtle combination of at least the following factors:

- Number of destination hosts
- Number of destination ports
- Time over which the packets were sent

There's no real way to take all these factors into account with straight rule-matching, even with stream reassembly. Remember, the multiple packets that we're looking for would each be seen as belonging to their own separate connection. Snort's portscan preprocessor, in spp_portscan.c, detects portscans by watching for a specific number of probe packets sent within a certain time period of each other. These probe packets can be directed entirely at one host or spread across a network of machines—all that matters is that the number of packets crosses a preset threshold in a preset period of time. Once this happens, the portscan preprocessor alerts.

This preprocessor also sounds an alert whenever it receives one of the well-known "stealth scan" packets, such as those sent by *nmap*. These include the odd/illegal packets shown in Table 6.1.

Table 6.1 Snort-Detected Stealth Packets

NULL	All TCP flags are deactivated.
FIN	Only the FIN flag is on.
SYN-FIN	Only the SYN and FIN flags are on.
XMAS	Only the FIN, URG, and PSH flags are on.

You should never encounter one of these packets on your network if it corresponds perfectly to the TCP specifications. For example, NULL packets should never happen—these correspond to a total lack of state information in a stateful protocol!

One warning is in order: the portscan preprocessor's code itself warns that, "…the connection information reported at the end of scan is wildly inaccurate." In essence, the preprocessor is fairly good at telling you that someone is scanning your network, but it's not very good at counting exactly how many probes the scanning party sent. The basic reason for this failure is that the portscan preprocessor is not building and consulting a database of all traffic sent by a scanning system. It's just not designed to maintain this much historical information. It maintains some simple counts of how many connections each host has tried to open and how many connections each host has received. It removes information on hosts often, as the user-configured expiration time is reached without a given host having initiated the threshold number of connections.

This is easier to understand with an example. Say that we're watching for five probes within 15 minutes. If a host scans four ports on our network in five seconds, then waits an hour, and then scans six ports, we won't get an alert until the second set of scans is almost complete. That's expected and normal. However, the alert won't tell us about the initial four ports that were scanned, because the preprocessor will already have forgotten about those four probes when it gets the new probes. This is part of why tuning a portscan detector is so difficult. On the one hand, you're eager to make sure that an attacker can't bypass detection by sending his probe packets very slowly. On the other hand, you can't alert on every SYN packet that enters your network unexpectedly!

Anyway, this lack of accurate reporting doesn't make the preprocessor useless. It's still decent at detecting scans—it's just not going to give you hyper-accurate data on how many probes a particular attacker sent you.

Configuring the portscan Preprocessor

You can activate the portscan preprocessor by adding the following line to your Snort configuration file:

```
preprocessor portscan:
<monitor network> <number of ports> <detection period> <file path>
```

You must replace *<monitor network>* with the target network you'd like the preprocessor to watch for scans against, listed in CIDR notation. The *<number of ports>* and *<detection period>* parameters denote a number of ports scanned within a period in seconds, specifying a time-limited threshold. Finally, the *<file path>* parameter denotes the fully qualified pathname of the file to which you'd like portscans logged. For example, to alert whenever 5 ports are scanned within a 60-second period on the 10.0.0.0/8 network, you'd add this line:

```
preprocessor portscan: 10.0.0.0/8 5 60 /var/log/portscan.log
```

The portscan preprocessor also comes with a function that allows you to specify source hosts that should be ignored. You can use this by specifying a space-delimited list of IP addresses, in CIDR notation, on a preprocessor portscan-ignorehosts line:

```
preprocessor portscan-ignorehosts: 192.168.1.1/32 192.168.2.0/24
```

Back Orifice

The Cult of the Dead Cow wrote Back Orifice in 1998 as a remote control mechanism, often used by attackers to maintain control of their compromised systems. The remote control mechanism does not use a reserved port, and it does use encryption, making it less than trivial to detect on a network. Luckily, it uses an overly simple encryption scheme to both hide and authenticate access to the target system. In this scheme, the attacker picks a password, which is then hashed into a 16-bit number. Sixteen bits is a relatively small keyspace, presenting only 65,536 possibilities. All traffic is encrypted by XOR'ing it with this hash. All requests made from the client to the server begin with the magic string "*!*QWTY?" before encryption—this "known plaintext" vulnerability makes it easy to brute-force the password. In essence, we can try XOR'ing "*!*QWTY?" with every hash value until we find one that matches one of the packets we see on the wire. Since the encryption scheme is so simple, one can easily write a program to brute-force the encryption, giving a security analyst a clear picture of what the attacker orders the machine to do.

Snort's bo (Back Orifice) preprocessor, in spp_bo.c, detects Back Orifice by examining every UDP packet of size at least 18 bytes and checking its first eight characters of payload against a precomputed table of enciphered versions of the magic string. (Actually, to save resources, it checks only the first two characters and the last two characters of this string.) The Back Orifice preprocessor computes this table when Snort first starts up, during the preprocessor's initialization phase. We'll examine the preprocessor initialization phase in the last section of this chapter, when we examine the telnet_negotiation preprocessor in-depth.

Configuring the Back Orifice Preprocessor

The Back Orifice preprocessor takes no arguments—it cannot be configured at all. In the current release of Snort, version 2.0, the configuration file passes the -*nobrute* parameter to the preprocessor, like so:

```
preprocessor bo:   -nobrute
```

This has absolutely no effect—*nobrute* has been deprecated. Originally, the preprocessor worked differently—it performed the brute-force attack on every packet, instead of implementing a lookup table. This was obviously much slower.

General Nonrule-Based Detection

As you can see, one major purpose for Snort preprocessors is to detect attacks that can't be easily caught via straight rule-matching. These represent a strong method of adding more intelligence to Snort without sacrificing the speed of straight pattern-matching. Nicely, a Snort box deployed to simply capture traffic will not have to run packets through these preprocessors, as the analyzer box(es) can perform that function well. Again, the Snort developers have worked very hard to maintain performance.

You should note that most of the preprocessors offered alerting modes that could be deactivated. These alerting modes form the basis for Snort's protocol-anomaly detection and might catch sneakier attackers. On the other hand, they might prove too noisy on some networks, depending on what operating systems are deployed. For example, stream4 tends to alert on protocol problems too often on networks with particular versions of Windows. If you have time to observe and tune your preprocessors, it's wise to leave these alerting options active initially, backing off on noisy ones. If you don't have the time or resources to tune, you can just configure each preprocessor for its primary functionality. Actually, as of Snort 1.9.1, most of the default settings assume that you prefer the latter strategy.

Experimental Preprocessors

The preprocessors listed in the following sections are all experimental or not-yet-Enterprise-grade. They're either under development, not yet finished or generally experimental; consequently, they're generally not enabled by default. However, you might want to try them out if you're either looking for the particular functionality that they offer, or you're interested in helping to develop or test new

Snort code. For example, you might want to detect ARP spoofing attacks, perhaps to see if any attackers are performing active-sniffing attacks against your switched networks. This might lead you to the arpspoof detection preprocessor, described next.

arpspoof

The arpspoof preprocessor detects Address Resolution Protocol (ARP) spoofing attacks, like those available via dsniff's arpspoof (http://naughty.monkey.org/~dugsong/dsniff/). An attacker uses ARP spoofing on a local network to trick hosts into sending him traffic intended for another host. A host that wants to send an IP packet to another host on the same LAN doesn't generally just send the packet on the LAN—it has to know the physical hardware, or Media Access Control (MAC), address of the destination host. This address looks something like AA:BB:CC:DD:11:22, as it is a six-octet number. To learn the MAC address that it needs, it broadcasts an ARP request, along the lines of "who has IP address 10.0.0.1? Tell AA:BB:CC:DD:11:22?" The destination host responds with its own MAC address, which the sender then caches and uses for all traffic it sends to that host for a set period of time, called the cache entry Time-To-Live (TTL). In an ARP spoof attack, a hostile host on the network sends out a false ARP reply, claiming its hardware address as the intended destination. The attacker wants the recipient host to cache this incorrect data and send packets to his hostile host instead of the correct destination. He'll usually configure this hostile host to forward the packets on to the correct host, to preserve the stream.

Among other things, this type of trick helps an attacker redirect traffic and eavesdrop on a switched network. Given good tools, it can even let him transparently modify the data stream, possibly injecting traffic. You can learn more about this by examining the *ettercap* tool included on this book's CD-ROM.

The arpspoof preprocessor detects this type of trickery by checking ARP traffic against a user-supplied table of IP addresses and hardware MAC addresses. You supply this table in the Snort configuration file, using the *arpspoof_detect_host* preprocessor directive:

```
preprocessor arpspoof
preprocessor arpspoof_detect_host: 192.168.1.1 f0:a1:b1:c1:d1:91
preprocessor arpspoof_detect_host: 192.168.1.2 f0:a2:b3:c4:d5:96
```

This preprocessor, in spp_arpspoof.c, can also detect unicast (nonbroadcast) ARP queries. Remember, ARP queries are supposed to be broadcast to the entire LAN. You can activate alerting on unicast ARP queries by using the *-uni-cast* option on the preprocessor activation line in Snort's configuration file:

```
preprocessor arpspoof: -unicast
```

asn1_decode

The asn1_decode preprocessor, in spp_asn1.c, detects abuses of the ASN.1 protocol that other protocols use, including SSL, SNMP, and X.509. In the current 2.0 release of Snort, this preprocessor only examines SNMP—it doesn't look at any packets other than UDP packets destined for port 161 or 162. This preprocessor is being deprecated in Snort 2.0, so it is doubtful that code will be added to examine other protocols. Currently in Snort 2.0, you can activate this preprocessor with the following line in the Snort configuration file:

```
preprocessor asn1_decode
```

fnord

One way that Snort detects previously unknown attacks is by looking for known shellcode or NOP sleds. These are critical components of buffer overflow exploits and other related exploit types. If you're not familiar with this type of exploit, consider reading Aleph1's whitepaper, "Smashing the Stack for Fun and Profit," available at www.insecure.org/stf/smashstack.txt or www.phrack.com/phrack/49/P49-14. In the year 2001, researchers, including K2 (www.ktwo.ca), began publicizing "polymorphic shellcode." K2 released a tool in March of 2001 called ADMmutate, which takes in a bit of shellcode and outputs different, but functionally equivalent, shellcode. This makes rule-based detection of shellcode much more difficult. While there are normally only a few well-publicized pieces of working shellcode for each operating system on each architecture, ADMmutate increases the number dramatically. This increases an otherwise short shellcode-detection ruleset dramatically, creating both a resource and maintenance problem.

fnord, written by Dragos Ruiu, addresses this problem by detecting the shellcode programmatically, instead of through simple pattern matches. Contained in spp_fnord.c, it's still experimental code. Further, it's being deprecated in Snort 2.0. Until then, you can try out its functionality by adding the following line to your Snort configuration file:

```
preprocessor fnord
```

portscan2 and conversation

portscan2 is a successor to the portscan preprocessor. Combined with the conversation preprocessor, this is a stateful portscan detection preprocessor. The Snort team does not yet consider this preprocessor enterprise ready, so this chapter doesn't devote much coverage to it.

portscan2 does require the conversation preprocessor. In essence, conversation provides a state engine that keeps state on TCP, UDP, and ICMP—it compiles information on which hosts have contacted which and on which ports. conversation isn't really used for its own sake—it simply provides a data compilation mechanism for portscan2.

Configuring the portscan2 Preprocessor

To understand how portscan2 is configured, you will need to understand how it operates. portscan2 keeps detailed short-term records of all session-initiating packets (potential probes) that cross Snort, from any single host to any other single host. Although in certain situations portscan2 can be configured to ignore hosts and ports; basically, it watches for to see if any one host sends too many probes and then issues alerts if it does. portscan2 accomplishes this by maintaining counts and waiting to see if thresholds are crossed. The critera for crossed thresholds is based on either too many different destination ports or hosts. portscan2 maintains this information for a short period of time, which means that it won't necessarily detect a slow (and thus stealthy) scan.

portscan2 is activated by adding a *preprocessor portscan2* line in Snort's configuration file (snort.conf). Optionally, you can add a colon after *portscan2* and add a comma-delimited set of parameters settings, like so:

```
preprocessor portscan2: targets_max 1000, scanners_max 1000, port_limit 20
```

As we'll discuss, some of this preprocessor's defaults are almost certainly too low. Let's examine the parameters that you can set:

- *targets_max* Defaulting to 1,000, this resource-control parameter controls how many targets that portscan2 will keep track of at maximum.

- *scanners_max* Defaulting to 1000, this resource-control parameter controls how many different scanning IP's portscan2 will track at maximum.

- *target_limit* Defaulting to 5, this parameter controls the target host threshold. Once any particular scanner has sent a probe to this many hosts within the timeout period, the preprocessor raises an alert.

- ■ **port_limit** Defaulting to 20, this parameter controls the port threshold. Once any particular host has sent a probe to this many ports within the timeout period, the preprocessor raises an alert.

- ■ **timeout** Defaulting to 60, this parameters sets a time in seconds that any scanning data will last. If this time is exceeded without any activity from a host, data may be pruned.

- ■ **log** Defaulting to "/scan.log," this parameter controls the pathname of the preprocessor's log-file, relative to Snort's current working directory.

The default values here are decent for catching fast portscans on small networks. If you want to catch slow scans, you'll most definitely need to increase some of these values. If an attacker configures between a 10 and twenty second delay between his probe packets, the timeout value will probably fail you. If an attacker uses a number of decoy IP addresses (as some have been known to do when they scan sniff an entire class C for replies) the default *scanners_max* value will fail you as well. As always, it's best to try a set of values out and tune them based on your experiences.

Similar to the portscan preprocessor, you can define hosts to ignore activity from. You accomplish this via a space-delimited list of host and network IPs on a *preprocessor portscan2-ignorehosts* line.

```
preprocessor portscan2-ignorehosts: 192.168.1.1 192.168.2.0/24
```

Further, you can define a port that the portscan preprocessor should ignore for each host/network, by appending an @ sign and a port number to the end of an IP address, like this:

```
preprocessor portscan2-ignorehosts: 192.168.1.1@25 192.168.2.0/24@80
```

It is also possible to pass multiple ports for an IP address by listing that IP address multiple times, like so:

```
preprocessor portscan2-ignorehosts: 192.168.1.1@25 192.168.1.1@80
```

As with other options using IP addresses in the Snort configuration file, you can definitely use the *!* character for negation.

Now, remember that the portscan2 preprocessor requires that you first run the conversation preprocessor. Let's explore how this is configured.

Configuring the conversation Preprocessor

The conversation preprocessor keeps records of each communication between two hosts, organizing it into "conversations" even for the non–session-based protocols like UDP. The conversation preprocessor does not perform reassembly, this preprocessor solely supports the portscan2 preprocessor, essentially allowing the portscan2 preprocessor to only keep track of, and potentially alert on, the first packet in a conversation. It can also alert when any packet comes through with an IP-based protocol that is not allowed on your network. You can activate the conversation preprocessor by simply including a *preprocessor conversation* line in your Snort configuration file, snort.conf. On the other hand, you may want to add parameters by placing a colon at the end of this line and then adding a comma-delimited list of parameters to the right of it, like so:

```
preprocessor conversation: timeout 120, max_conversations 65335
```

Let's look at the parameters available:

- **timeout** Defaulting to 120, this defines the time in seconds for which the conversation preprocessor maintains information. After timeout seconds of inactivity, a conversation may be pruned to save resources.

- **max_conversations** Defaulting to 65335, this resource-control parameter sets the maximum number of conversations that the conversation preprocessor will keep track of at a time.

- **allowed_ip_protocols** Defaulting to "all," this parameter allows you to define a list of allowed IP protocols, by number. For instance, TCP is 6, UDP is 17, and ICMP is 1, so you could set this to "1 6 17" to get alerts whenever non-TCP/UDP/ICMP traffic passed the sensor.

- **alert_odd_protocols** Defaulting to off, this parameter defines whether your receive alerts when a protocol not set in *allowed_ip_protocols* is detected. To activate this parameter, simply include it on the preprocessor line — it doesn't require any setting.

So, if you wanted to monitor up to 12,000 conversations, keeping data on a conversation until it had been inactive for 5 minutes (300 seconds), and receiving alerts whenever any protocols besides TCP, UDP and ICMP crossed the sensor, you'd put this in our Snort configuration file:

```
preprocessor conversation: max_conversations 12000, timeout 300,
allowed_ip_protocols 1 6 17, alert_odd_protocols
```

Just like all other preprocessors, the best way to find the best settings for your site is to pick a reasonable set and then pay attention to Snort's alerting and overall behavior, tuning as necessary.

perfmonitor

The perfmonitor preprocessor, in spp_perfmonitor.c, provides experimental performance statistics via the console or a log file. The Snort 1.9.1 configuration file describes this with the warning, "No docs. Highly subject to change." As such, it doesn't make much sense to document this preprocessor in a book.

Writing Your Own Preprocessor

In this section, we'll explore why and how you might write your own preprocessor plug-in. We'll accomplish the former by exploring the *spp_telnet_negotiation.c* preprocessor. We'll see the necessary components in a preprocessor, how it's plugged in to the Snort source code, and how it accomplishes its function. After this discussion, you'll be well on your way to writing your own preprocessor.

Over the course of this chapter, we've explored the following reasons to write your own preprocessor:

- Reassembling packets
- Decoding protocols
- Nonrule or anomaly-based detection

In essence, you write your own preprocessor whenever you want to do something that straight rule-based detection can't do without help. Let's explore each of the previously listed reasons, to understand why they needed a preprocessor to fulfill the function.

Reassembling Packets

Signature-based detection matches well-defined patterns against the data in each packet, one at a time. It can't look at data across packets without help. By reassembling fragments into full packets with frag2, you can make sure that an attack doesn't successfully use fragmentation to evade detection. By reassembling each stream into one or more pseudo-packets with stream4, you attempt to ensure that the single-packet signature mechanism is able to match patterns across multiple packets in a TCP session. Finally, by adding state-keeping with stream4, you give this signature-matching some intelligence about which packets can be ignored and where a packet is in the connection. Packet reassembly preprocessors help to ensure that Snort detects attacks, even when the data to be matched is split across several packets.

Decoding Protocols

Rule-based detection generally gives you simple string/byte-matching against the data within a packet. It can't handle all the different versions of a URL in HTTP data without help, or at least without countably infinite rulesets. The http_decode preprocessor gives Snort the ability to canonicalize URLs before trying to match patterns against them. Straight rule-matching can also be foiled by protocol-based data inserted in the middle of data that would otherwise match a pattern. Both the rpc_decode and telnet_negotiation preprocessors remove data that could be extraneous to the pattern-matcher. The rpc_decode preprocessor consolidates all of the message fragments of a single RPC message into one fragment. The telnet_negotiation preprocessor removes Telnet negotiation sequences. Protocol-decoding preprocessors make string-matching possible primarily by forcing packet data into something less ambiguous, so that it can be more easily matched.

Nonrule or Anomaly-Based Detection

Rule-based detection performs well because of its simplicity. It's very deterministic, making it easy to tune for fewer false positives. It's also easy to optimize. However, there are functions that just can't be achieved under that model. Snort has gained protocol anomaly detection, but even this isn't enough to detect some types of attack. The portscan preprocessor allows Snort to keep track of the number of scan-style packets that it has received over a set time period, alerting when this number exceeds a threshold. The Back Orifice preprocessor allows Snort to detect encrypted Back Orifice traffic without creating a huge ruleset.

This third class of preprocessors expands Snort's detection model without completely redesigning it—Snort can gain any detection method flexibly. Preprocessors specifically, and plug-ins in general, give Snort the capability to be more than an IDS. They give it the capability to be an extensible intrusion detection framework onto which most any detection method can be built. Less spectacularly, they give Snort the capability to detect things for which there isn't yet a rule directive. For example, if you needed to have a rule that detected the word *Marty* being present in a packet between three and eight times (no more, no less), you'd probably need a preprocessor—Snort's rules language is flexible, but not quite that flexible. More usefully, what if you needed to detect a backdoor mechanism only identifiable by the fact that a single host sends your host/network UDP packets whose source and destination port consistently sum to the fixed number 777? (Note: this is a real tool.)

Without going quite that far, let's explore how a preprocessor is built.

Setting Up My Preprocessor

Every preprocessor is built from a common template, found in the Snort source code's templates/ directory. As you consider the Snort code, you should consider the following filename convention. We'll talk about the snort/ directory—this is the main directory you get when you expand the Snort source tarball or zipfile. Its contents look like this:

```
[jay@localhost snort]$ ls
acconfig.h       config.h.in     contrib    install-sh  missing         src
aclocal.m4       config.sub      COPYING    LICENSE     mkinstalldirs   stamp-h.in
ChangeLog        configure       doc        Makefile.am rules           templates
config.guess     configure.in    etc        Makefile.in snort.8
```

The templates directory contains two sets of plug-in templates—to build a preprocessor plug-in, we want the spp_template.c and spp_template.h files.

```
[jay@localhost snort]$ ls templates/
Makefile.am  spp_template.c  sp_template.c
Makefile.in  spp_template.h  sp_template.h
```

You should take a look at these template files as you consider the Telnet negotiation preprocessor. This preprocessor is with the others in the snort/src/preprocessors directory.

```
[jay@localhost preprocessors]$ ls
Makefile.am          spp_fnord.c          spp_portscan2.h
Makefile.in          spp_fnord.h          spp_portscan.c
spp_arpspoof.c       spp_frag2.c          spp_portscan.h
spp_arpspoof.h       spp_frag2.h          spp_rpc_decode.c
spp_asn1.c           #spp_http_decode.c#  spp_rpc_decode.h
spp_asn1.h           spp_http_decode.c    spp_stream4.c
spp_bo.c             spp_http_decode.h    spp_stream4.h
spp_bo.h             spp_perfmonitor.c    spp_telnet_negotiation.c
spp_conversation.c   spp_perfmonitor.h    spp_telnet_negotiation.h
spp_conversation.h   spp_portscan2.c
```

In the rest of this section, we'll explore the code in the file spp_telnet_nego-tiation.c, making references to the matching spp_telnet_negotiation.h header file as necessary. Remember, this book refers to the production Snort 2.0.0 code, which you can find on the CD accompanying this book. Let's start looking at this code:

```
/* Snort Preprocessor for Telnet Negotiation Normalization*/
/* $Id: spp_telnet_negotiation.c,v 1.14.2.1 2002/11/02 21:46:14 chrisgreen
Exp $ */


/* spp_telnet_negotiation.c
 *
 * Purpose:  Telnet and FTP sessions can contain telnet negotiation strings
 *           that can disrupt pattern matching.  This plugin detects
 *           negotiation strings in stream and "normalizes" them much like
 *           the http_decode preprocessor normalizes encoded URLs
 *
 * Arguments:  None
 *
 * Effect:  The telnet nogiation data is removed from the payload
 *
 * Comments:
 *
 */
```

The preprocessor starts out simply describing what its purpose is and how it can be called. You'll notice as we read through the code that the "Arguments" description in the previous comments is inaccurate—the code takes a space-delimited list of ports as an argument.

Before we continue reading code, we should talk about this preprocessor's purpose, so you understand what the code is doing. The best way to understand this thoroughly is to read the Requests for Comments (RFC) document describing the Telnet protocol.

> **OINK!**
>
> The Telnet protocol is described in detail in RFC 854, available via www.faqs.org/rfcs/rfc854.html. For even more comprehensive and easier-to-follow coverage, consider W Richard Stevens' *TCP/IP Illustrated Volume 1*. This is an essential and standard reference for understanding TCP/IP protocol implementations.

Telnet's creators knew that it would need to function between many devices, potentially with somewhat different levels of intelligence and flexibility. To this end, the Telnet protocol defines a Network Virtual Terminal (NVT), a "minimal" concept to which Telnet implementers could tailor their code. The protocol allows two NVTs to communicate to each other what options (extra features) they might or might not support. They communicate with escape sequences, which start with a special Interpret as Command (IAC) character. Following this character is a single-byte number, which codes a command. The command sent is usually a request that the other side activate/deactivate an option, if available, a request for permission to use an option, or an answer to a previous request from the other side. Most of these sequences, then, are three characters long, like this fictional one:

```
IAC     DON'T   SING
255     254     53
```

The protocol also allows for deleting the previous character sent via the *Erase Character* (*EC*) command and erasing the last line sent via the *Erase Line* (*EL*) command, both of which need to be accounted for in the preprocessor. It also allows for a *No Operation* (*NOP*) command, which tells it to do nothing—it's not clear why this is included in the protocol. Finally, it allows for complex negotiation of parameters of the options via a "subnegotiation" stream of characters, initiated with a *Subnegotiation Begin* (SB) character, followed by the option that it references, and terminated by a *Subnegotiation End* (SE) character. Such a sequence might look like this:

```
IAC     SB    SING      HUMPTY-DUMPTY      SE
255     250   53        1                  240
```

There's more to Telnet than this, but this is enough to read and understand the preprocessor code. Let's get into that code now.

What Am I Given by Snort?

We'll now take an in-depth look at the preprocessor's code, exploring what each line of the code does. Commentary follows the lines of code lines that it references. If your C skills are rusty, don't worry—you'll probably find this discussion quite understandable. The Telnet negotiation preprocessor is one of the simplest preprocessors. Let's take a look at it together.

```
/* your preprocessor header file goes here */
```

```
#include <sys/types.h>

#ifdef HAVE_STRINGS_H
#include <strings.h>
#endif
```

The preceding lines just import standard C header files.

```
#include "decode.h"
#include "plugbase.h"
#include "parser.h"
#include "log.h"
#include "debug.h"
#include "util.h"
#include "mstring.h"
#include "snort.h"
```

The preceding lines import Snort's function prototypes, constants, and data structures, so that this plug-in can reference them. The plugbase.h header file, in particular, contains prototypes for the important functions that every preprocessor plug-in must call. Table 6.2 lists the other header files with their corresponding functions.

Table 6.2 Header Files and Their Corresponding Functions

Header File	Function
sdecode.h	Parses packets into data structures
parser.h	Performs all input parsing (for example, snort.conf)
log.h	Logs all packet-data, printing/ formatting headers and data
debug.h	Performs Snort's debugging, with enforcing granular levels of detail
util.h	Miscellaneous utilitarian functions
mstring.h	Provides string functions not pro vided by C standard libraries
snort.h	Provides major data structures and Snort's primary functions

While not all of the header file listed in Table 6.2 are necessary, they've probably been included to keep things simple and maintainable for the programmer.

```
/* external globals from rules.c */
extern char *file_name;
extern int file_line;
```

The previous three lines are also standard—they allow the preprocessor to describe where its configuration directives came from. An example would be "line 43 of the snort.conf file."

```
extern u_int8_t DecodeBuffer[DECODE_BLEN]; /* decode.c */
```

As of Snort 1.9.1, this function is specific to the telnet_negotiation preprocessor. The preprocessor prunes negotiation code by copying all non-negotiation data from the packet it's examining into a globally available *DecodeBuffer*. It then signals that the packet has an alternate form, allowing the detection engine to look at either form of the packet data, based on whether the rules it evaluates specify "rawbytes." Oddly, even though rawbytes sounds like a more general option, it's implemented strictly for the benefit of Telnet.

OINK!

Rawbytes signals that the rule should look at the non-negotiation-modified version of the Telnet packet.

```
/* define the telnet negotiation codes (TNC) that we're interested in */
#define TNC_IAC   0xFF
#define TNC_EAC   0xF7
#define TNC_SB    0xFA
#define TNC_NOP   0xF1
#define TNC_SE    0xF0


#define TNC_STD_LENGTH   3
```

The first five constants define the numerical versions of the codes that we explored earlier. The last constant simply codifies the fact that any negotiation sequences are at least three characters long.

```
/* list of function prototypes for this preprocessor */
```

```
extern void TelNegInit(u_char *);
```

As we'll explore soon, the *TelNegInit()* function initializes the preprocessor when Snort first starts. It calls a function to parse the preprocessors arguments from the snort.conf file and adds the main work function (*NormalizeTelnet()*) to the list of preprocessors called to examine every packet. Every preprocessor must have one of these functions to perform these two tasks. It must also have a Setup function to link this one to the Snort codebase—we'll explore *SetupTelNeg()* soon.

```
extern void NormalizeTelnet(Packet *);
```

As we'll explore later, this function performs the real task of the preprocessor. The previously discussed *Init* function will register this with Snort's main preprocessor engine.

```
static void SetTelnetPorts(char *portlist);
```

This function parses the Telnet negotiation preprocessor's arguments and is called by *TelNegInit()*. It parses a simple port list into a data structure that *NormalizeTelnet()* can reference before trying to work on a packet.

```
/* array containing info about which ports we care about */
static char TelnetDecodePorts[65536/8];
```

This array stores the TCP ports that the preprocessor will be paying attention to. Notice that it stores this via a single *bit* for every port between 0 and 65,536, not a *byte*.

```
/*
 * Function: SetupTelNeg()
 *
 * Purpose: Registers the preprocessor keyword and initialization
 *          function into the preprocessor list.
 *
 * Arguments: None.
 *
 * Returns: void function
 *
 */
void SetupTelNeg()
{
```

```
    /* Telnet negotiation has many names, but we only implement this
     * plugin for Bob Graham's benefit...
     */
    RegisterPreprocessor("telnet_decode", TelNegInit);


    DEBUG_WRAP(DebugMessage(DEBUG_PLUGIN, "Preprocessor: Telnet Decode
Decode is setup...\n"););
}
```

Setup TelNeg() links this preprocessor to the Snort code by registering its rules file keyword *telnet_decode* with its initiation function, *TelNegInit()*. The obvious reason for this registration is so that the initialization code isn't called if the keyword referring to the preprocessor isn't present in Snort's configuration file. This registration takes place via the *RegisterPreprocessor()* function from plugbase.c.

This is the first function in the preprocessor that Snort calls. It is called from plugbase.c, to which we must add it by hand. This process, which we'll describe after explaining this code, is also outlined in snort/doc/README.PLUGINS.

```
/*
 * Function: TelNegInit(u_char *)
 *
 * Purpose: Calls the argument parsing function, performs
 * final setup on data structs, links the preproc function
 * into the function list.
 *
 * Arguments: args => ptr to argument string
 *
 * Returns: void function
 *
 */
void TelNegInit(u_char *args)
{
    DEBUG_WRAP(DebugMessage(DEBUG_PLUGIN, "Preprocessor: TelNeg
Initialized\n"););


    SetTelnetPorts(args);
    /* Set the preprocessor function into the function list */
    AddFuncToPreprocList(NormalizeTelnet);
}
```

This function is called by Snort early in its run, as it parses the Snort rules file. It is a standard preprocessor *Init()* function, which is always registered by the preprocessor's *Setup()* function. The purpose of this function is to call an argument-parser and to add the preprocessor's main function to the preprocessor function list. Remember, a packet entering Snort goes through the decoder to be parsed, then each of the preprocessors in order, and then finally goes to the detection engine. *AddFuncToPreprocList()*, from plugbase.c, adds our preprocessor's main function to the linked list of preprocessor functions.

```
/*
 * Function: PreprocFunction(Packet *)
 *
 * Purpose: Perform the preprocessor's intended function.  This can be
 *          simple (statistics collection) or complex (IP defragmentation)
 *          as you like.  Try not to destroy the performance of the whole
 *          system by trying to do too much....
 *
 * Arguments: p => pointer to the current packet data struct
 *
 * Returns: void function
 *
 */
void NormalizeTelnet(Packet *p)
{
```

This is the real workhorse of the preprocessor. In essence, this is the function for which *SetupTelNeg()* and *InitTelNeg()* exist to provide to Snort. This structure of functions is standard, as you'll note when reading the other preprocessors and the preprocessor template.

The function starts out receiving a simple pointer to the packet currently being considered. (You can find the structure definition for *Packet* in snort/src/decode.h.) Let's look at the variables that it defines.

```
char *read_ptr;
    char *start = (char *) DecodeBuffer; /* decode.c */
    char *write_ptr;
    char *end;
    int normalization_required = 0;
```

- *read_ptr* points to the current byte being considered in the incoming packet data.

- *start* points to the beginning of the destination buffer (DecodeBuffer).

- *write_ptr* points to the current position to which we're writing in DecodeBuffer.

- *end* points to the end of the incoming packet data.

- *normalization_required* tells us whether we need to normalize this packet.

```
/* check for TCP traffic that's part of an established session */
if(!PacketIsTCP(p))
{
     return;
}
```

Like every preprocessor function, this one must decide whether it should even be looking at this packet. If the packet isn't a TCP packet, the preprocessor needs to exit.

```
/* check the port list */
    if(!(TelnetDecodePorts[(p->dp/8)] & (1<<(p->dp%8)))) ·
    {
         return;
    }
```

p->dp is the packet's destination port. If this port was not among those that this preprocessor should affect, we need to exit.

Again, note that the port is being checked in this array using a bitwise check. For example, if dp=14, then *p->dp/8* will be 1, thus referring to the second byte in the array. *1<<(p->dp%8)* means "shift the binary number 00000001 by the remainder of dp/8." 14%8 is 6, so *1<<(p->dp%8)* is, in binary, 0100 0000. By AND-ing the second byte in the array with this number, we get the status of the sixth byte.

```
/* negotiation strings are at least 3 bytes long */
if(p->dsize < TNC_STD_LENGTH)
{
     return;
}
```

Finally, we're looking at something specific to the Telnet protocol. This *if* statement just says that, since any Telnet negotiation sequence must be at least 3 bytes long, it doesn't need to see any packet whose data is less than 3 bytes.

```
/* setup the pointers */
read_ptr = p->data;
end = p->data + p->dsize;
```

This sets our start and end points on the incoming packet data:

```
/* look to see if we have any telnet negotiaion codes in the payload */
while(!normalization_required && (read_ptr++ < end))
{
    /* look for the start of a negotiation string */
    if(*read_ptr == (char) TNC_IAC)
    {
        /* set a flag for stage 2 normalization */
        normalization_required = 1;
    }
}
```

This code runs through the incoming packet data looking for the start of a Telnet negotiation code sequence. This code doesn't perform any modifications—it's just here to *quickly* determine if the packet will need normalization. As soon as it finds a single IAC character, it flags that normalization is required and halts.

```
/*
 * if we found telnet negotiation strings OR backspace characters,
 * we're going to have to normalize the data
 *
 * Note that this is always ( now: 2002-08-12 ) done to a
 * alternative data buffer.
 */

if(normalization_required)
{
```

If we found an IAC character, then this routine normalizes the data:

```
    /* rewind the data stream to p->data */
    read_ptr = p->data;
```

```
/* setup for overwriting the negotaiation strings with
 * the follow-on data
 */
write_ptr = (char *) DecodeBuffer;
```

We set the *read_ptr* to the beginning of the incoming packet data, and the *write_ptr* to the start of the output buffer. Remember, *DecodeBuffer* is a global variable that the detection engine will look in for our alternative version of the packet.

```
/* walk thru the remainder of the packet */
while((read_ptr < end) && (write_ptr < ((char *) DecodeBuffer) +
DECODE_BLEN))
    {
```

DECODE_BLEN is the constant length of the *DecodeBuffer*. The *while* loop allows us to copy data from the packet data to the *DecodeBuffer*, skipping negotiation sequences.

```
        /* if the following byte isn't a subnegotiation initialization
*/
        if(((read_ptr + 1) < end) &&
            (*read_ptr == (char) TNC_IAC) &&
            (*(read_ptr + 1) != (char) TNC_SB))
        {
```

This code looks for negotiation sequences (initiated by IAC) and skips the *read_ptr* forward the appropriate number of bytes. Remember, skipping *read_ptr* forward without doing a copy ensures that the skipped data doesn't make it into *DecodeBuffer*. Note that this code doesn't want to handle the suboption negotiation case; hence, its decision not to branch if the second byte in the sequence is a *Subnegotiation Begin* (TNC_SB) character.

```
/* NOPs are two bytes long */
            switch(* ((unsigned char *)(read_ptr + 1)))
            {
            case TNC_NOP:
                read_ptr += 2;
                break;
```

If the sequence is just an IAC, NOP, then it's only two characters long.

```
            case TNC_EAC:
                read_ptr += 2;
```

```
        /* wind it back a character */
        if(write_ptr > start)
        {
             write_ptr-;
        }
        break;
```

EAC is a backspace. When we see one, we skip the two characters of negotiation (IAC, EAC), but also decrement *write_ptr*, so that the byte that was at *write_ptr* is overwritten on our next character write.

```
    default:
        /* move the read ptr up 3 bytes */
        read_ptr += TNC_STD_LENGTH;

}
```

In all other non-subnegotiation cases, we need to skip exactly three characters.

```
}
/* check for subnegotiation */
else if(*(read_ptr+1) == (char) TNC_SB)
{
    /* move to the end of the subneg */
    do
    {
        read_ptr++;
    } while((*read_ptr != (char) TNC_SE) && (read_ptr < end));
```

Remember that our last *if* branch refused to handle subnegotiation. This one handles them—it simply moves the *read_ptr* forward until it gets past the terminating *Subnegotiation End* (SE) character, thus omitting the entire sequence from *DecodeBuffer*.

```
}
else
{
    DEBUG_WRAP(DebugMessage(DEBUG_PLUGIN, "overwriting %2X(%c)
with %2X(%c)\n",

            (char)(*write_ptr&0xFF), *write_ptr,
            (char)(*read_ptr & 0xFF), *read_ptr););
```

```
                    /* overwrite the negotiation bytes with the follow-on
bytes */

                    *write_ptr++ = *read_ptr++;

            }
```

This is the case where we weren't at the start of a negotiation code. We just copy another character from the packet data to *DecodeBuffer*.

```
    }


    p->packet_flags |= PKT_ALT_DECODE;


    p->alt_dsize = write_ptr - start;
```

The code now sets two variables on the original packet's data structure. The first tells the detection engine that the telnet_negotiation preprocessor has created a second, altered version of the packet data by using a bitwise-OR to set a Snort internal packet flag. Don't worry; this is changing data that Snort keeps on the packet, not in the original data collected from the packet. The second variable stores the length of the data placed in *DecodeBuffer*.

```
        DEBUG_WRAP(DebugMessage(DEBUG_PLUGIN,
                "Converted buffer after telnet normalization:\n");
            PrintNetData(stdout, (char *) DecodeBuffer, p->alt_dsize););
```

DebugMessage() now logs the results of the telnet_negotiation preprocessor's handiwork. If Snort is at the appropriate level of debug, this will come out.

```
    }
}
```

Now, for the sake of brevity, we're not going to explain the argument-parsing function much. This function, as is standard with most of the preprocessors, is a mostly optional routine called by the preprocessor *Init()* function, which is *InitTelNeg()* in this case.

```
/*
 * Function: SetTelnetPorts(char *)
 *
 * Purpose: Reads the list of port numbers from the argument string and
 *          parses them into the port list data struct
 *
 *
```

```
 * Arguments: portlist => argument list
 *
 * Returns: void function
 *
 */
static void SetTelnetPorts(char *portlist)
{
    char portstr[STD_BUF];
    char **toks;
    int is_reset = 0;
    int num_toks = 0;
    int num = 0;

    if(portlist == NULL || *portlist == '\0')
    {
        portlist = "21 23 25 119";
    }
```

If this function does not get a list of ports in the Snort configuration file, it chooses ports 21, 23, 25, and 119.

```
    /* tokenize the argument list */
    toks = mSplit(portlist, " ", 31, &num_toks, '\\');
```

mSplit is one of the functions in mstring.c, Snort's string-handling functions.

```
    LogMessage("telnet_decode arguments:\n");

    /* convert the tokens and place them into the port list */
    for(num = 0; num < num_toks; num++)
    {
        if(isdigit((int)toks[num][0]))
        {
            char *num_p = NULL; /* used to determine last position in
string */
            long t_num;

            t_num = strtol(toks[num], &num_p, 10);

            if(*num_p != '\0')
```

```
        {

FatalError("ERROR => Port Number invalid format: %s\n", toks[num]);

        }

        else if(t_num < 0 || t_num > 65335)

        {

        FatalError("ERROR => Port Number out of range: %ld\n", t_num);

        }


    /* user specified a legal port number and it should override the
        default */
        port list, so reset it unless already done */
        if(!is_reset)
        {

            bzero(&TelnetDecodePorts, sizeof(TelnetDecodePorts));
            portstr[0] = '\0';
            is_reset = 1;

        }


    /* mark this port as being interesting using some
        portscan2-type voodoo, and also add it to the port
        list string while we're at it so we can later
        print out all the ports with a single LogMessage() */
        TelnetDecodePorts[(t_num/8)] |= 1<<(t_num%8);
        strlcat(portstr, toks[num], STD_BUF - 1);
        strlcat(portstr, " ", STD_BUF - 1);
    }
    else
    {

        FatalError("ERROR %s(%d) => Unknown argument to telnet_decode

                "preprocessor: \"%s\"\n",
                file_name, file_line, toks[num]);

    }

    }
```

```
      /* print out final port list */
      LogMessage("     Ports to decode telnet on: %s\n", portstr);
}
```

As promised, this function was fairly simple.

Examining the Argument Parsing Code

Let's look at *SetTelnetPorts()*, the only function in this preprocessor that we haven't examined yet. This simple function just takes a port list from Snort and parses it into a data structure usable by the main preprocessor function that we just explored.

```
/*
 * Function: SetTelnetPorts(char *)
 *
 * Purpose: Reads the list of port numbers from the argument string and
 *          parses them into the port list data struct
 *
 * Arguments: portlist => argument list
 *
 * Returns: void function
 *
 */


static void SetTelnetPorts(char *portlist)
{
```

The *SetTelnetPorts()* function takes a pointer to a string as an argument, this string is the space delimited list of ports that Snort determines from the *preprocessor telnet_decode* line its configuration file. More specifically, Snort passes everything after the colon (:) on that line as a string to *TelNegInit()*, which passed it to the *SetTelnetPorts()* function. *TelNegInit()* receives that pointer as its only argument (the initiation functions of all preprocessor plug-ins receive that same one argument), a pointer to the string of text that followed the colon in their preprocessor directive lines in Snort.conf.

```
      char portstr[STD_BUF];
      char **toks;
      int is_reset = 0;
```

```
int num_toks = 0;
int num = 0;
```

Let's detail what each of these variables do.

- **portstr** This is a string that the function constructs specifically so that it can report a list of ports that it found in the log.

- ****toks** This is a two-dimensional character array (an array of pointers to strings) that will point to the tokenized (separated) strings, which each encode a port.

- **is_reset** A flag describing whether the default port list has been replaced by a user-supplied one.

- **num_toks** The number of ports parsed by the function.

- **num** A simple integer counter used in a *for* loop.

```
if(portlist == NULL || *portlist == '\0')
{
        portlist = "21 23 25 119";
}
```

In the default Snort 1.9.1 configuration file, there's no port list specified. This is accomplished with the line:

```
preprocessor telnet_decode
```

You'll note that this line does not contain a colon, and thus contains no arguments. In this case, the preprocessor (and thus this function) will receive a string pointer with *NULL* as its contents. This may seem equivalent to the situation where you include a colon in the syntax, but do not add any text after the colon, like this:

```
preprocessor telnet_decode:
```

In this case, the preprocessor receives a pointer to a string of zero length as an argument, which is basically the string *\0*. This is the case even if you added some spaces after the colon, because Snort strips terminating whitespace off the end of the lines in snort.conf. Basically, this *if {}* construct tells the preprocessor to use its default port list of "21 23 25 119" if it receives no input.

The preprocessor calls the Snort function *mSplit()*, from mstring.c, which can be thought of as the "Marty String" library.

```
/* tokenize the argument list */
toks = mSplit(portlist, " ", 31, &num_toks, '\\');
```

Here is the definition of *mSplit* and the comments that describe it:

```
char **mSplit(char *str, char *sep, int max_strs, int *toks, char meta)
  *      char *str => the string to be split
  *      char *sep => a string of token seperaters
  *      int max_strs => how many tokens should be returned
  *      int *toks => place to store the number of tokens found in str
  *      char meta => the "escape metacharacter", treat the character
  *                   after this character as a literal and "escape" a
  *                   seperator
  *
  *   Returns:
  *      2D char array with one token per "row" of the returned
  *      array.
```

This function parses the string portlist into 0–31 shorter strings, called *tokens*, using space as the separator and allowing that separator to be *escaped* by preceding it with \\. Each one of these strings should be an ASCII representation of a port number.

LogMessage, another Snort function, writes information by default to the console via or to a log facility, if configured to do so. You'll see this output at the end of this subsection, when we're done exploring the code.

```
LogMessage("telnet_decode arguments:\n");
```

Now the code loops through each of the strings (tokens) that *mSplit()* created, converting them to long integers storing them.

```
/* convert the tokens and place them into the port list */
for(num = 0; num < num_toks; num++)
{
```

First, it checks to see if the first character in our string is an ASCII representation of a digit (0-9) with the *isdigit()* C library function:

```
if(isdigit((int)toks[num][0]))
{
```

This following lines are where things begin to get a bit more tricky.

```
char *num_p = NULL; /* used to determine last position in string */

    long t_num;
```

This defines two new variables:

- **num_p** This is a pointer to terminating, non-decimal part of the port string

- **t_num** This is a long integer which stores the port number that gets pulled out of the string.

```
t_num = strtol(toks[num], &num_p, 10);
```

This converts the num[th] token (string) into a long integer using the C standard library *strtol()* function. *strtol()*, which converts strings to long *ints*, takes a pointer to the string, a pointer to store a result in, and a numerical base as its arguments. Normal decimal numbers are base 10, while binary numbers are base 2 (the Snort configuration file uses base 10 port numbers). *strtol()* returns the integer form of the number that it finds and sets *num_p* to point to the part of the string that is after the decimal number. If our string is, as Snort expects, simply a string of ASCII digits between zero and nine, terminated by a \0, this pointer should just point to the terminating \0 character.

The *if* statement checks to see if the first character pointed to by *num_p* is a \0. If it is not, then this particular string was not made up strictly of ASCII characters between zero and nine, and an error occurs. It calls *FatalError()*, which prints the message *ERROR => Port Number invalid format*, along with the particular string that it was parsing, and then causes Snort to exit. The error message is either printed to the console or to the system log. The output is similar to what you will see here:

```
if(*num_p != '\0')

{

    FatalError("ERROR => Port Number invalid format: %s\n",
toks[num]);

}
```

If our string is fine, but the number to which it converts is either negative or too large to be a valid TCP port, it causes Snort to exit, printing *ERROR => Port Number out of range:* and the port number to the console or system log:

```
else if(t_num < 0 || t_num > 65335)

{

    FatalError("ERROR => Port Number out of range: %ld\n", t_num);

}
```

Now, if neither of these error conditions comes up, the string is fine and the function can store it in the list of ports.

```
/* user specified a legal port number and it should override the default
        port list, so reset it unless already done */
    if(!is_reset)
```

Contrary to the comment and to the *is_reset* structure, this block of code runs both when the user has input a specific port list on the *preprocessor telnet_negotiation* snort.conf directive and when the user has left one off. If you're very interested in how this particular function works, it's important that you understand this misrepresentation, if you're not so interested, don't worry, because this doesn't really generalize to the other preprocessors.

For the most part, the *is_reset* variable keeps track of whether the function has initialized its two important output data structures yet.

First, it zeroes out the *TelnetDecodePorts* data structure. This structure is a 65,536/8 byte array that stores the ports the preprocessor should examine in a bit-wise true/false fashion. This was described earlier, when we were examining the *NormalizeTelnet()* function:

```
    {
        bzero(&TelnetDecodePorts, sizeof(TelnetDecodePorts));
```

It also blanks the *portstr* string by setting its first character to the \0 string terminator character:

```
        portstr[0] = '\0';
```

Finally, it sets *is_reset* so that it doesn't re-initialize these values now that it's populating them with data:

```
        is_reset = 1;

    }
```

Now, whether or not the data structures just got initialized, the function now has to store the port number that got translated from the string that it's currently handling.

First, it activates the t_numth bit in the *TelnetDecodePorts* array. Remember from the *NormalizeTelnet()* function that this activates the $(t\_num\%8+1)^{th}$ bit of the $(t\_num/8+1)^{th}$ byte. To make this more concrete, think of the example where t_num is 14. Then *t_num/8* will be 1 and *t_num%8* will be 6. Therefore, this will activate the seventh bit of the second byte in the array. If this is confusing, you might want to reread the explanation for the code walkthrough of *NormalizeTelnet()*

```
/* mark this port as being interesting using some portscan2-type voodoo,
   and also add it to the port list string while we're at it so we can
   later print out all the ports with a single LogMessage() */
        TelnetDecodePorts[(t_num/8)] |= 1<<(t_num%8);
```

Finally, the function adds the string representation of the port number to its *portstr* string, which gets logged at the end of this function.

```
        strlcat(portstr, toks[num], STD_BUF - 1);
        strlcat(portstr, " ", STD_BUF - 1);
    }
```

This next *else* block corresponds to the *if(isdigit((int)toks[num][0]))* test at the beginning of this loop. The code internal to the block gets executed if the first character of the string it is evaluating is not a numerical digit (between zero and nine).

```
    else
    {
        FatalError("ERROR %s(%d) => Unknown argument to telnet_decode "
                   "preprocessor: \"%s\"\n",
                   file_name, file_line, toks[num]);
    }
```

The loop ends here and logs the list of ports that it parsed (stored in *portstr*) out to the console or the system logs.

```
    }


    /* print out final port list */
    LogMessage("    Ports to decode telnet on: %s\n", portstr);
}
```

In default detection mode, Snort will display this message and the upcoming one with its portlist on the screen at start-up, before its version announcement, similar to the following:

```
telnet_decode arguments:
     Ports to decode telnet on: 21 23 25 119


1310 Snort rules read...
1310 Option Chains linked into 139 Chain Headers
0 Dynamic rules

+++++++++++++++++++++++++++++++++++++++++++++++++++++

Rule application order: ->activation->dynamic->alert->pass->log



        -== Initialization Complete ==-


-*> Snort! <*-
Version 1.9.1 (Build 231)
By Martin Roesch (roesch@sourcefire.com, www.snort.org)
```

This is all of the preprocessor code that we'll need to look at. In the next section, you'll learn how preprocessor code is placed into Snort. Now, since Marty designed the preprocessor architecture to be simple and modular through plug-ins, this is a pretty easy process.

Getting the Preprocessor's Data Back into Snort

The telnet_negotiation preprocessor works much like other preprocessors, with the exception of its unique method of getting data back to the detection engine. Different preprocessors do this in different ways. For example, frag2 sends the packet it just reconstructed back through the same detection engine that gave it all the fragments of the packet. It avoids an infinite loop by setting a flag on the packet noting that said packet is a rebuilt fragment packet. Another example is http_decode, which creates a canonical URL from the data in an HTTP packet and then passes that URL by itself into a separate variable. You can perform this process in whatever way makes the most sense, unless the Snort developers create a standard and required API for passing back preprocessed data.

Adding the Preprocessor into Snort

Snort's plug-ins are linked into it in a fairly static way. In essence, you need to do the following to link in a new plug-in:

1. Insert an *include* directive in plugbase.c for your plug-ins header file.

2. Insert a call to your plug-ins *Setup()* function in plugbase.c's *InitPreprocessors()*.

3. Add your plug-ins code and header file to the preprocessors/Makefile.am.

Let's practice doing this for the telnet_negotiation preprocessor, as if it hadn't been done yet. First, we need to add our telnet_negotiation.h header file into plugbase.c. Here's the relevant portion of plugbase.c:

```
#include "detect.h"


/* built-in preprocessors */
#include "preprocessors/spp_http_decode.h"
#include "preprocessors/spp_portscan.h"
#include "preprocessors/spp_rpc_decode.h"
#include "preprocessors/spp_bo.h"
#include "preprocessors/spp_stream4.h"
#include "preprocessors/spp_frag2.h"
#include "preprocessors/spp_arpspoof.h"
#include "preprocessors/spp_asn1.h"
#include "preprocessors/spp_fnord.h"
#include "preprocessors/spp_conversation.h"
#include "preprocessors/spp_portscan2.h"
```

We can just add a single line to the end of this list:

```
#include "preprocessors/spp_telnet_negotiation.h"
```

Second, let's insert our *Setup()* function into plugbase.c, so that our plug-in has a chance to register itself. We're adding this call to *InitPreprocessors()*:

```
void InitPreprocessors()
{
    if(!pv.quiet_flag)
    {
        printf("Initializing Preprocessors!\n");
    }
    SetupHttpDecode();
    SetupPortscan();
```

```
        SetupPortscanIgnoreHosts();

        SetupRpcDecode();

        SetupBo();

        SetupStream4();

        SetupFrag2();

        SetupARPspoof();

        SetupASN1Decode();

        SetupFnord();

        SetupConv();

        SetupScan2();

}
```

Now we can add the Telnet negotiation plug-ins *Setup()* function, called *Setup TelNeg()*:

```
        SetupTelNeg();
```

Finally, we need only add our preprocessor's source files to:

`snort/src/preprocessors/Makefile.am:`

```
libspp_a_SOURCES = spp_arpspoof.c spp_arpspoof.h spp_bo.c spp_bo.h \
spp_frag2.c spp_frag2.h spp_http_decode.c spp_http_decode.h \
spp_portscan.c spp_portscan.h spp_rpc_decode.c spp_rpc_decode.h  \
spp_stream4.c spp_stream4.h spp asn1.c spp_asn1.h spp_fnord.c spp_\
fnord.h spp_conversation.c spp_conversation.h spp_portscan2.c spp_\
portscan2.h spp_perfmonitor.c spp_perfmonitor.h
```

We can add our Telnet negotiation preprocessor like so:

```
libspp_a_SOURCES = spp_arpspoof.c spp_arpspoof.h spp_bo.c spp_bo.h \
spp_frag2.c spp_frag2.h spp_http_decode.c spp_http_decode.h \
spp_portscan.c spp_portscan.h spp_rpc_decode.c spp_rpc_decode.h  \
spp_stream4.c spp_stream4.h spp asn1.c spp_asn1.h spp_fnord.c spp_\
fnord.h spp_conversation.c spp_conversation.h spp_portscan2.c spp_\
portscan2.h spp_perfmonitor.c spp_perfmonitor.h spp_telnet_negotiation.c \
spp_telnet_negotiation.h
```

That's all there is to it—adding a Snort preprocessor is pretty easy!

Summary

Preprocessors add significant power to Snort. Snort's existing preprocessors give it the capability to reassemble packets, do protocol-specific decoding and normalization, do significant protocol anomaly detection, and add functionality outside of rule-checking and anomaly detection.

The stream4 and frag2 preprocessors enhance Snort's original rule-based pattern-matching model by allowing it to match patterns across several packets with TCP stream reassembly, TCP state-keeping, and IP defragmentation. Data carried by TCP is generally contained in several packets—stream reassembly can build a single packet out of an entire stream so that data broken across several packets can still match attack rules. As packets are carried across networks, they often must be broken into fragments. frag2 rebuilds these fragments into packets that can then be run through Snort's detection engine.

The telnet_negotiation, http_decode, and rpc_decode preprocessors all serve the primary purpose of data normalization. The Telnet negotiation preprocessor removes Telnet's inline feature-negotiation codes from the protocol, allowing more deterministic content matching. It accomplishes this while still leaving the original data intact, so that rules with the *rawbytes* keyword can access the original application data for unhindered pattern matching. The http_decode preprocessor deals with the problem created by Web servers that accept many forms of the same URL by creating a "canonical" form of the URL to which rule-maintainers can write their URLs. This preprocessor does not do data replacement either—the canonicalization can be accessed by using the *uricontent* keyword in a HTTP rule. RPC, when carried over TCP, must still be separated into discrete messages. The protocol makes this separation by defining a formal message as built of one or more message fragments. The fragment mechanism creates ambiguity in rule creation, since fragment headers can occur anywhere within the application data. The rpc_decode preprocessor normalizes the RPC protocol by converting all multiple-fragment RPC messages into single-fragment messages. It makes these adjustments inline, and thus destructively, in the original decoded packed data.

The first two types of preprocessors enhance Snort's rules-checking and add substantial protocol anomaly detection. They allow Snort to perform rule-checking across packets and within non-trivial protocols. Finally, by using greater understanding and memory of the protocols involved, they perform protocol anomaly detection to catch attacks that don't necessarily match an existing signature.

The third type of preprocessor we discussed allows Snort to move beyond the rules-based and protocol anomaly detection models for a particular purpose.

portscan counts probe packets from each given source and attempts to detect portscans. Back Orifice watches UDP packets for stored encrypted values of a plaintext string known to be the header for a popular hacker remote control tool. Each of these functions cannot be easily accomplished with Snort's existing rules or protocol-anomaly detection engines.

You can build your own preprocessors fairly readily, starting with Marty Roesch's template. Your preprocessor will need a Setup function to link its snort.conf keyword to its initialization function. It will need an initialization function to parse options, set up data structures, and add the main preprocessor function to Snort's list of preprocessors. Finally, it will need a main function to take in a packet and perform some task. That task might involve rewriting the data in the packet, parsing a particular part of the packet into a new global data structure accessible to the detection engine, or alerting on a condition not expressible via rules. Once you've coded these functions, the preprocessor can be linked into Snort via the plugbase.c file by following the instructions in snort/doc/README.PLUGINS. It can be easily compiled into Snort via the snort/src/preprocessors/Makefile.am file. We examined this process by exploring the Snort Telnet negotiation preprocessor, an existing plug-in that's simple enough to understand but still useful.

Solutions Fast Track

What Is a Preprocessor?

☑ Preprocessors are written as "plug-ins" to allow them to give Snort flexible extensibility, configurable on a host-by-host basis.

☑ Preprocessors give Snort the ability to handle data stretched over multiple packets.

☑ Snort uses preprocessors to canonicalize data in protocols where data can be represented in multiple ways.

☑ Snort uses preprocessors to do detection that doesn't fit its model of flexible pattern matching.

☑ Preprocessors provide Snort with much of its anomaly detection capabilities, which can detect some attacks that might not yet have rules.

Preprocessor Options for Reassembling Packets

☑ stream4 adds statefulness to Snort, so that it can ignore packets that will be ignored by the target host.

☑ stream4 adds stream reassembly to Snort, so that it can detect attacks broken across several packets in a TCP stream.

☑ frag2 reassembles packets from their associated fragments, allowing it to detect attacks broken across multiple fragments.

Preprocessor Options for Decoding and Normalizing Protocols

☑ telnet_negotiation normalizes Telnet traffic, removing the inline feature-negotiation codes that are part of the Telnet protocol.

☑ http_decode normalizes URLs in HTTP requests, making pattern-matching possible even when attacks obfuscate URLs with Web server-specific alternative encodings.

☑ rpc_decode normalizes RPC traffic, forcing all RPC messages into single-fragment messages.

Preprocessor Options for Nonrule or Anomaly-Based Detection

☑ Preprocessors can also allow you to add nearly any detection model to Snort.

☑ portscan detects portscan attacks by watching for the number of incoming packets from each source to exceed a packet-per-time-period threshold. It also watches for NMAP "stealth" packets.

☑ The Back Orifice preprocessor detects a host on your network being controlled via Back Orifice by watching UDP traffic for 2^{16} possible versions of the encrypted Back Orifice "magic string" application header.

Experimental Preprocessors

☑ arpspoof detects ARP spoofing attacks by checking ARP responses against a static table of ARP-to-IP addresses.

☑ asn1_decode detects abuses of the ASN.1 protocol, used by SSL, SNMP, and X.509.

☑ fnord detects polymorphic shellcode by looking for shellcode programmatically, instead of via straight pattern matches.

☑ perfmonitor outputs performance statistics for Snort, but has no goal of consistency of output over its development cycle.

☑ portscan2 is the successor to portscan, but is not yet in Enterprise-ready condition. This preprocessor is the sole user of the conversation preprocessor.

Writing Your Own Preprocessor

☑ Preprocessor development begins with the spp_template.c file in Snort's templates directory.

☑ A preprocessor requires a *setup* function to link its snort.conf keyword to its initialization function, and an initialization function to parse arguments, set up data structures, and register the preprocessor function into Snort's preprocessor function list.

☑ Each new preprocessor must be linked into Snort via two insertions into plugbase.c and an addition to the preprocessor/Makefile.am file.

Frequently Asked Questions

The following Frequently Asked Questions, answered by the authors of this book, are designed to both measure your understanding of the concepts presented in this chapter and to assist you with real-life implementation of these concepts. To have your questions about this chapter answered by the author, browse to **www.syngress.com/solutions** and click on the **"Ask the Author"** form.

Q: If Snort is rules-based, why is there anomaly detection in the preprocessors? How do you classify Snort?

A: According to Marty Roesch, Snort is an extensible intrusion detection framework with a rules-based detection engine and a number of anomaly-detection features encompassed in its packet decoders and preprocessors subsystems.

Q: What is the difference between a signature and a rule?

A: Signatures are generally very static and inflexible, consisting primarily of a single positive pattern match statement and one or more numerical equality checks on header fields in the packet. Rules are much more intelligent and flexible. For example, Snort allows you to look for one string match in the packet data while simultaneously requiring that another string not match the packet data. Other features of the rules language allow you to define additional context for these comparisons. Finally, state-keeping features that allow you to accurately and precisely express whether the client or server is sending the communication and where in the session said communication is generally aren't part of straight signature-checking.

Q: Why does Snort send the individual packets of a stream under reassembly to the detection engine when the entire stream will go through the detection engine as a whole?

A: Snort sends the individual packets in a stream through the detection engine partly because the packets themselves might match attack rules that the stream will not. For example, the TCP/IP flags the packets will not be preserved, but might match an attack rule.

Q: Why does Snort contain both a stream reassembly and state-keeping prepro-cessor (stream4) and another state-keeping preprocessor (conversation)?

A: stream4 and conversation have quite different purposes. stream4 exists specifi-cally to add TCP state-keeping, keeping track of where we are in a TCP ses-sion, and TCP stream reassembly, reassembling an entire TCP stream into one or more large packets, allowing rules to match against data that's split across several TCP segments/packets. Conversation, on the other hand, keeps track of all IP protocols, including the non-stateful UDP and ICMP protocols. It maintains a limited set of state information specifically so that it can help portscan2 intelligently tell the difference between a conversation-starting probe packets and a reply packet.

Q: What is protocol normalization and why do I need it?

A: Protocol normalization attempts to put a protocol into a *canonical* format so that rules can more easily match attack data. This is needed, otherwise an attacker can make one or more small changes in the attack data that will not cause the target system to interpret it differently, but will cause the minutely altered data to get past a rule that would have normally have matched. One simple example of this is that Microsoft IIS Web Servers allow the client to send a URI with /'s changed into \'s and will handle them as equivalent, this change will evade a normal rules or signatures-based IDS unless it supports HTTP normalization. Snort does include HTTP normalization, implemented in its http_decode preprocessor.

## Chapter 7

Implementing Snort Output Plug-Ins

Solutions in this chapter:

- **What Is an Output Plug-In?**
- **Exploring Output Plug-In Options**
- **Writing Your Own Output Plug-In**

☑ **Summary**

☑ **Solutions Fast Track**

☑ **Frequently Asked Questions**

Introduction

Have you ever wondered how weak technology companies stay in business? Why some companies decide to go with inferior products, especially those that are purchased to protect an organization's data? Or how substandard new products gain market share? The answers are abundant, but time and time again a common theme surfaces. Reporting has always been a key component to deal makers and breakers. Gathering and correlating data is only half of the technology product equation, with the other half being comprised of data presentation and reporting. Manually categorizing and analyzing data can be an extremely time-consuming and resource-intense process; therefore, any technology that enables the user and lessens the resource requirement is beneficial.

The Snort development team realized this business driver with the creation of an open Output Plug-In API. Snort output plug-ins, also referred to as Snort output modules, were first introduced in version 1.6. The introduction of output plug-ins officially completed Snort's inauguration to the elite group of enterprise-class intrusion detection systems (IDSs). Output plug-ins provide administrators the ability to configure logs and alerts in a manner that is easy to understand, read, and use in their organization's environment. For example, if Acme Widgets uses MySQL databases to store all corporate and client information, it can be assumed that there is a good amount of in-house knowledge on MySQL. Therefore, it would make sense that Acme would also want their Network IDS (NIDS) logs and alerts to be stored in a MySQL database or even in a different table of a current database.

Snort currently has a wide range of output plug-ins to support different types of technologies, products, and formats to include databases, packet dump text files, header dump files, and XML to name a few. The source code for each of the plug-ins is included within the Snort source distribution. By the conclusion of this chapter, you should understand Snort plug-ins, the role in which they play in formatting data, and the overall schema and API that the plug-ins implement. Depending on your programming experience and level of skill, you might also be able to write your own output plug-ins.

What Is an Output Plug-In?

Output plug-ins were introduced in version 1.6. These plug-ins allow for a more flexible formatting and presentation of Snort output to the administrator. These output modules are executed whenever Snort's alert or logging subsystems are called, following the execution of preprocessors and the packet capture engine. Packet, or traffic, analysis would be pointless without the output plug-ins to process, format, and store the data. The plug-ins define aspects pertaining to data storage, format, and transportation media. They live within the product and have an open API so that individuals and organizations outside the Snort development team can write customized methods to allow Snort to better interface within their environment.

In general, output plug-ins can be considered product add-ons since they can be written by anyone and included within Snort during compile time. After the plug-ins have been built within the Snort application, you will be capable of referring to it via Snort configuration files, the command line, and from within defined Snort rules. The packet capture engine within Snort retrieves packets off the wire and "sends" them to the analysis module. If the packet or packets trigger an alert or log event, the data is passed to the corresponding output module. Figure 7.1 depicts the logical flow of information at a high level within Snort. The flexible architecture of Snort will continue to allow future additions such as the output plug-ins to be included within the product.

Figure 7.1 Snort Output Plug-In Architecture

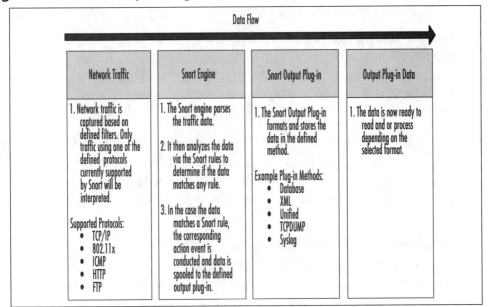

Output plug-ins can seem somewhat complex, especially if you are not an avid or skilled programmer; however, this should not limit your ability to understand exactly how the plug-ins work. For the most part, each plug-in is very different in the realm of formatting and storing the Snort data. Function and code development for data handling is usually a direct reflection of the skill level of the plug-in author or author team. The main functionality tasks can be quite technically and algorithmically different, since most of the time it is completely original code. There are some commonalities within plug-ins that range in architecture and design to function calls and structure definitions.

Key Components of an Output Plug-In

Snort output plug-in functionality can be divided into seven main categories: copyright and header information; include files, dependencies and global variables; keyword registration; argument parsing and function list linking; data formatting, processing, and storage; preprocessor processing; and application cleanup and exiting. The following list details each aspect of the plug-ins.

- **Copyright and header information** Each of the existing Snort output plug-ins has a distinct copyright notice that can be added at the discretion of the developer. There is also a header that details the purpose of the plug-in, any arguments that the plug-in requires, the effect, and any additional comments.

- **Include files, dependencies, and global files** Files and file dependencies, as with most applications, are a critical aspect of the program and are self-explanatory. Global variables, or variables that are used throughout the master application, are also key characteristics of plug-ins.

- **Keyword registration** Output plug-ins are referenced and called from the configuration file and from the command line. As a part of the plug-in, you must define and link the keyword to the Snort application so that it knows that something "special" should occur when it parses the word.

- **Argument parsing and function list linking** Since most of the plug-ins require arguments to be passed along during the declaration process, it is necessary to write code that handles such data. For example, if you were using a logging function, you would probably need to specify the name of the log that you wanted to use for data storage. In addition to parsing the arguments, output plug-ins must also cross link functions with the main Snort engine.

- **Data formatting, processing, and storage** Unique aspects of plug-ins, these tasks are the "meat" of the plug-in and as such must be included. Simply stated, if there were no functions to process, format, and store the data, the output plug-in would be incomplete and useless.

- **Process preprocessor arguments** In the case that any preprocessor arguments exist, sufficient data handling code must be written for these so that Snort and the output plug-ins can distinguish preprocessor elements before parsing commences.

- **Cleanups** In most cases, functions to clean up memory, application connections, and open sockets are included within output plug-ins to ensure that Snort executes in the most efficient manner possible.

OINK!

Understanding how a plug-in works is not as complicated as writing actual Snort output plug-ins. More information and in-depth techniques on writing output plug-ins can be found later in the chapter.

Exploring Output Plug-In Options

Snort output plug-ins have numerous commonalities and dissimilarities. Besides the customized plug-ins that can be created, there are multiple built-in methods that can modify and store data. Initially covered in Chapter 5, "Playing by the Rules," Snort permits users to log to text files and databases in numerous fashions. While the output plug-ins are most often defined in a configuration file, they are created as stand-alone C programs, and called upon from triggered Snort rules. Throughout this section, you will become deeply familiar with the technologies and formats that are currently built into the Snort application.

More information on how to use and pass data to these output plug-ins can be found in Chapters 4, 5, and 8.

Default Logging

Snort provides some simple ways to log both generated alerts and alert-related packet data. In most cases, this packet data is network traffic that has been collected with Snort's packet capture engine. These logs provide users, administrators, and engineers with a bit of flexibility as to how Snort data should be stored. For example, you might want Snort to store its logs according to source IP address, so that you don't have to sort them manually. The simplest method to log packets is using the *−l* flag via the command line.

```
cloud@host:/root# snort -l ./log
```

The following two examples are log entries generated by Snort. Figure 7.2 displays a packet log of an ICMP echo, and Figure 7.3 is the corresponding ICMP echo response. As you might glean, the examples are not complete PCAP packet dumps, merely header information.

Figure 7.2 Example ICMP Echo Request

```
cloud@host:/root# cat ./log/192.168.1.123/ICMP_ECHO
02/12-08:56:11.252959 192.168.1.123 -> 192.168.1.10
ICMP TTL:64 TOS:0x0 ID:0 IpLen:20 DgmLen:84 DF
Type:8  Code:0  ID:42240    Seq:0   ECHO
```

Figure 7.3 Example ICMP Echo Reply

```
cloud@host:/root# cat ./log/192.168.1.10/ICMP_ECHO_REPLY
02/12-09:54:05.820069 192.168.1.10 -> 192.168.1.123
ICMP TTL:255 TOS:0x0 ID:64527 IpLen:20 DgmLen:84
Type:0  Code:0  ID:61952  Seq:0   ECHO REPLY
```

The Snort *-d* and *-e* flags display packet headers and application data in a descriptive manner. In Figure7.4, it is important to ensure sure that the directory *log* exists. In the case that no log exists, Snort will exit with an error message. In the following example, Snort logs all packets to the master *log* directory in a directory hierarchy based on the source address within each IP datagram (in this case, any IP address that does not fall into our home network 19.168.1.0/24). The *−h* flag declares the hierarchy-based logging schema. As a quick reminder, the *−l* flag defines the logging directory to store the saved packet logs. Assume that the following 192.168.1.0/24 address space is the organization's internal address range; if you are not versed in CIDR addressing, 192.168.1.0/24 is equal to the 192.168.1.0 class C network.

Figure 7.4 Logging Internal Network Traffic with Snort

```
gabe@host:/root# snort -d -e -l ./log -h 192.168.1.0/24
//       ICMP Echo
gabe@host:/root# cat ./log/192.168.1.123/ICMP_ECHO
02/12-09:56:26.737220 0:E0:29:9E:5D:6E -> 0:A0:24:D1:75:6A type:0x800
len:0x62
192.168.1.123 -> 192.168.1.10 ICMP TTL:64 TOS:0x0 ID:0 IpLen:20 DgmLen:84
DF
Type:8  Code:0  ID:62208    Seq:0    ECHO
87 F1 49 3E 5E 9A 04 00 08 09 0A 0B 0C 0D 0E 0F    ..I>^..........
10 11 12 13 14 15 16 17 18 19 1A 1B 1C 1D 1E 1F    ...............
20 21 22 23 24 25 26 27 28 29 2A 2B 2C 2D 2E 2F    !"#$%&'()*+,-./
30 31 32 33 34 35 36 37                            01234567


//       ICMP Echo Reply
gabe@host:/root# cat ./log/192.168.1.10/ICMP_ECHO_REPLY
02/12-09:56:26.737257 0:A0:24:D1:75:6A -> 0:E0:29:9E:5D:6E type:0x800
len:0x62
192.168.1.10 -> 192.168.1.123 ICMP TTL:255 TOS:0x0 ID:64528 IpLen:20
DgmLen:84
Type:0  Code:0  ID:62208    Seq:0    ECHO REPLY
87 F1 49 3E 5E 9A 04 00 08 09 0A 0B 0C 0D 0E 0F    ..I>^...........
10 11 12 13 14 15 16 17 18 19 1A 1B 1C 1D 1E 1F    ...............
20 21 22 23 24 25 26 27 28 29 2A 2B 2C 2D 2E 2F    !"#$%&'()*+,-./
30 31 32 33 34 35 36 37                            01234567
```

Binary logging was originally introduced into Snort to minimize the CPU cycles that had to be dedicated to data reporting, and not traffic capturing and analysis. Most sensors that have heavy loads of traffic to analyze or have weaker hardware use some type of binary logging. Binary logging also helps to minimize log size, not that log size should ever be an issue. If size becomes an issue, it is probably because your sensor is poorly configured or you are under extremely heavy attack. The following informs Snort to log all packet data to the *./log* directory in the binary format.

```
gabe@host:/root# snort -l ./log -b
```

Using the straight log-to-binary instruction eliminates the need to create robust directory hierarchies, since all packet data is logged in one potentially very large binary-formatted file. The binary files can be read back with any TCPDump-compatible packet sniffer or analyzer, such as Ethereal, TCPDump, or Iris. Snort also has the built-in ability to read back this data by making use of the −*r* flag, for playback mode. Playback mode must be run on an instance of Snort that is not already running, capturing packets. Figure 7.5 is a screen dump of the Snort playback mode being executed on a binary packet log. The example payload consists of two ICMP packets stored in binary format. Figure 7.5 illustrates the packet's source and destination information, packet header, and payload.

Oink!

eEye's Win32 packet capture program Iris can be downloaded from www.eeye.com.

Figure 7.5 Snort Playback Mode

```
gabe@host:/root# snort -vd -r ./log/snort-0212@0931.log
*HEADER INFORMATION WAS REMOVED FOR SPACE PURPOSES


        --== Initializing Snort ==--
Decoding Ethernet on interface \INTERFACE_REMOVED


        --== Initialization Complete ==--


02/12-09:31:05.744958 192.168.1.123 -> 192.168.1.10
ICMP TTL:64 TOS:0x0 ID:0 IpLen:20 DgmLen:84 DF
Type:8  Code:0  ID:55808   Seq:0  ECHO
96 EB 49 3E 02 C1 00 00 08 09 0A 0B 0C 0D 0E 0F     ..I>............
10 11 12 13 14 15 16 17 18 19 1A 1B 1C 1D 1E 1F     ................
20 21 22 23 24 25 26 27 28 29 2A 2B 2C 2D 2E 2F     !"#$%&'()*+,-./
30 31 32 33 34 35 36 37                              01234567
```

Continued

Figure 7.5 Snort Playback Mode Continued

```
=+=+=+=+=+=+=+=+=+=+=+=+=+=+=+=+=+=+=+=+=+=+=+=+=+=+=+=+=+=+


02/12-09:31:05.744988 192.168.1.10 -> 192.168.1.123

ICMP TTL:255 TOS:0x0 ID:38079 IpLen:20 DgmLen:84

Type:0  Code:0   ID:55808   Seq:0   ECHO REPLY

96 EB 49 3E 02 C1 00 00 08 09 0A 0B 0C 0D 0E 0F       ..I>............

10 11 12 13 14 15 16 17 18 19 1A 1B 1C 1D 1E 1F       ................

20 21 22 23 24 25 26 27 28 29 2A 2B 2C 2D 2E 2F       !"#$%&'()*+,-./

30 31 32 33 34 35 36 37                                 01234567


=+=+=+=+=+=+=+=+=+=+=+=+=+=+=+=+=+=+=+=+=+=+=+=+=+=+=+=+=+=+

Run time for packet processing was 0.12402 seconds



===================================================================

Snort analyzed 2 out of 2 packets, .

Breakdown by protocol:                    Action Stats:

     TCP: 0              (0.000%)          ALERTS: 0

     UDP: 0              (0.000%)          LOGGED: 0

    ICMP: 2              (100.000%)        PASSED: 0

     ARP: 0              (0.000%)

   EAPOL: 0              (0.000%)

    IPv6: 0              (0.000%)

     IPX: 0              (0.000%)

   OTHER: 0              (0.000%)

 DISCARD: 0              (0.000%)

===================================================================

Wireless Stats:

Breakdown by type:

    Management Packets: 0          (0.000%)

    Control Packets:    0          (0.000%)

    Data Packets:       0          (0.000%)
```

Continued

Figure 7.5 Snort Playback Mode Continued

```
================================================================
Fragmentation Stats:
Fragmented IP Packets: 0              (0.000%)
     Fragment Trackers: 0
     Rebuilt IP Packets: 0
     Frag elements used: 0
Discarded(incomplete): 0
     Discarded(timeout): 0
  Frag2 memory faults: 0

================================================================
TCP Stream Reassembly Stats:
       TCP Packets Used: 0              (0.000%)
         Stream Trackers: 0
          Stream flushes: 0
           Segments used: 0
   Stream4 Memory Faults: 0

================================================================
```

An advanced method for logging binary data can be implemented via the Unified plug-in, which we cover later in this section.

In addition to standard and binary logging, Snort's Berkeley Packet Filter (BPF) interface is also available at the command line. Snort BPF provides such options as navigation filters, and several methods of manipulating binary log data. More details on BPF are available within Chapter 5. Chapter 5 also covers the details of logging only attack-relevant packets, also referred to as enabling NIDS mode. Just as a refresher, Snort officially becomes a NIDS instead of merely a packet logger when the -c flag is used in conjunction with a Snort rules configuration file.

```
gabe@host:/root# snort -de -l ./log -h 192.168.1.0/24 -c snort.conf
```

The Snort.conf configuration file should contain a set of Snort rules in addition to any other configuration-related instructions, which are applied to every packet that Snort captures and analyzes. Only packets that match a rule within your rule file generate a Snort alert. With NIDS mode, packets can be logged in ASCII or in binary format and stored via a variety of output modules.

Syslog

Snort provides a mechanism for sending sensor alerts to the UNIX syslog facility. This can be accomplished by running Snort via the command line with the *–s* flag, or by making use of *alert_syslog* configuration instruction in the Snort configuration file. As you have learned, maintaining consistent Snort configurations is mandatory for enterprise-level intrusion detection.

Syslog provides a standard method for logging system messages, kernel traps, and other important messages. Syslog supports UNIX domain sockets, and is capable of local and remote logging. Syslogd is the traditional UNIX syslog daemon, although syslog–ng, also known as syslog next generation, is another popular version of the daemon. The *alert_syslog* output plug-in allows Snort users to define priorities within the rules and provide enhanced flexibility in logging alerts through a set of instruction parameters, keywords. The keywords are used to inform Snort of the actions that should be executed upon particular traffic and rule configuration anomalies.

- **Options** LOG_CONS, LOG_NDELAY, LOG_PERROR, LOG_PID
- **Facilities** LOG_AUTH, LOG_AUTHPRV, LOG_DAEMON, LOG_LOCAL(0–7), LOG_USER

The following is an excerpt from a Snort configuration file where the *alert_syslog* output module has been enabled. As defined in the excerpt, the output plug-in schema defines one or more facilities in addition to any options that are also declared within the configuration file.

```
output alert_syslog: LOG_AUTH LOG_ALERT
```

Tools & Traps…

Not Just a Fruit!

Kiwi Software created a successful and fully functional Win32 port of the popular UNIX-based syslog application, ironically referred to as Kiwi Syslog. It resides as a local application on most Microsoft-based platforms to include the commercial powers Windows NT, 2000, and XP. Kiwi Syslog can be used in place of the UNIX syslog application to log and store the inputted system messages. Detailed and current information on downloading and configuring Kiwi Syslog can be found at their Web site (www.kiwisyslog.com).

PCAP Logging

The Packet Capture Library (PCAP) is defined as a portable framework for low-level network monitoring that uses the standard PCAP format. There are multiple applications within the PCAP library, including network statistics collection, security monitoring, and network debugging. The libpcap interface within Snort supports a filtering mechanism called BPF (described in detail in Chapter 5). Snort's network monitoring architecture is based on the PCAP library. Because of this and the Win32 ports of PCAP, WinPCAP, Snort has proved quite portable across numerous platforms to include Solaris, Linux, multiple flavors of BSD, and numerous versions of Microsoft's Windows. Since Snort is capable of generating PCAP logs, it is possible to make use of the many available PCAP-compatible packet sniffers and analyzers, such as the ever popular Ethereal and Iris… and to be completely honest, just about every other network traffic analyzer out there.

The *log_tcpdump* Snort output plug-in logs and stores traffic packets in a PCAP formatted file. In view of the fact that this is such a widely accepted format, it has allowed for increased flexibility when working with such log files. As mentioned, there is an array of software available for examining PCAP formatted files. Figure 7.6 is a partial dump of a *log_tcpdump* Snort plug-in generated log file.

Figure 7.6 Replaying a TCPDump Formatted File

```
gabe@host:/root# tcpdump -r snort_tcpdump.log

21:16:55.333580 192.168.1.123 > vault.nonexistent.net: icmp: echo request

21:16:55.333617 vault.nonexistent.net > 192.168.1.123: icmp: echo reply

21:16:56.350427 192.168.1.123.3619 > vault.nonexistent.net.8080: S
129548898:129548898(0) win 5840 <mss 1460,sackOK,timestamp 694489
0,nop,wscale 0> (DF)

21:16:56.384452 192.168.1.123.3643 > vault.nonexistent.net.3128: S
129280222:129280222(0) win 5840 <mss 1460,sackOK,timestamp 694491
0,nop,wscale 0> (DF)

21:16:56.438479 vault.nonexistent.net.6001 > 192.168.1.123.3652: R 0:0(0)
ack 138480606 win 0 (DF)

21:16:57.040513 vault.nonexistent.net.x11 > 192.168.1.123.3866: R 0:0(0) ack
140201788 win 0 (DF)

21:16:57.198293 192.168.1.123.3922 > vault.nonexistent.net.socks: S
133341313:133341313(0) win 5840 <mss 1460,sackOK,timestamp 694572
0,nop,wscale 0> (DF)
```

Continued

Figure 7.6 Replaying a TCPDump Formatted File Continued

```
21:16:58.373683 192.168.1.123.4353 > vault.nonexistent.net.snmp: S
141096774:141096774(0) win 5840 <mss 1460,sackOK,timestamp 694690
0,nop,wscale 0> (DF)

21:16:58.523514 192.168.1.123.4396 > vault.nonexistent.net.705: S
137958228:137958228(0) win 5840 <mss 1460,sackOK,timestamp 694706
0,nop,wscale 0> (DF)

21:16:58.622938 192.168.1.123.4445 > vault.nonexistent.net.snmptrap: S
133972684:133972684(0) win 5840 <mss 1460,sackOK,timestamp 694715
0,nop,wscale 0> (DF)
```

More information on libpcap and TCPDump can be found at www.tcpdump.org/release. You can find more information on the Win32 port of libpcap, WinPCAP, at http://netgroup-serv.polito.it/winpcap.

Snortdb

Snort is capable of logging alerts and packets to several different types of databases, including MySQL, PostgreSQL, SQL Server, Oracle, and any UNIX ODBC-compliant database. The database output plug-in, and the general ability to log to databases, added Snort to the short list of commercial-grade robust and flexible NIDS. Database output allows data to be stored, viewed in real time, in addition to the plethora of other categorization and querying benefits that come with selecting a database plug-in.

The snippet in Figure 7.7 was taken from a default Snort configuration file for the *output database* output plug-in. Within the instructions in the configuration file, you can define the action event (*log* or *alert*), database type, username, password, database name in case there are multiple databases or database needs, and host.

Figure 7.7 Database Plug-Ins

```
# database: log to a variety of databases
# -------------------------------------
# See the README.database file for more information about configuring
# and using this plugin.
#
# output database: log, mysql, user=root password=test dbname=db
host=localhost
# output database: alert, postgresql, user=snort dbname=snort
```

Continued

Figure 7.7 Database Plug-Ins Continued

```
# output database: log, unixodbc, user=snort dbname=snort
# output database: log, mssql, dbname=snort user=snort password=test
```

OINK!

You must choose the appropriate action for this plug-in, log or alert. If *log* is selected, then the corresponding plug-in will run on the log output chain; however, if *alert* is selected, the corresponding plug-in will run on the alert output chain to process and output data.

A series of scripts are included within the "contrib" directory within the Snort source tree. In Figure 7.8, assume that we have created a MySQL database called "snort," into which we placed our Snort logs. It is also important to note that we compiled Snort with the *-with-mysql=<dir>* option. Using the *create_mysql* script that is bundled with Snort, it is feasible to quickly create the necessary tables for the Snort data repository. Figure 7.8 illustrates a MySQL database being created and the *create_mysql* script being executed.

Figure 7.8 Creating the Snort Database

```
//      Manually Creating the Snort DB
mysql> create database snort;
Query OK, 1 row affected (0.00 sec)
//      Executing the Create_MySQL Script
mysql> source create_mysql;
Query OK, 0 rows affected (0.00 sec)
Query OK, 1 row affected (0.00 sec)
Query OK, 0 rows affected (0.00 sec)
Query OK, 0 rows affected (0.00 sec)
Query OK, 0 rows affected (0.00 sec)
Query OK, 0 rows affected (0.01 sec)
Query OK, 0 rows affected (0.00 sec)
Query OK, 0 rows affected (0.00 sec)
Query OK, 0 rows affected (0.00 sec)
Query OK, 0 rows affected (0.00 sec)
```

Continued

Figure 7.8 Creating the Snort Database Continued

```
Query OK, 0 rows affected (0.00 sec)

Query OK, 0 rows affected (0.01 sec)

Query OK, 0 rows affected (0.00 sec)

Query OK, 0 rows affected (0.00 sec)

Query OK, 0 rows affected (0.00 sec)

Query OK, 0 rows affected (0.00 sec)

Query OK, 1 row affected (0.00 sec)

Query OK, 1 row affected (0.00 sec)

Query OK, 1 row affected (0.00 sec)

Query OK, 0 rows affected (0.01 sec)

Query OK, 1 row affected (0.00 sec)

Query OK, 1 row affected (0.00 sec)
```

After the database has been created and the script executed, you can verify the installation and configuration by running the SQL *show tables* command. The *show tables* command ironically displays all of the tables within the database. Figure 7.9 shows what tables should have been created when the *create_mysql* script was executed.

Figure 7.9 Snort's Created Tables

```
mysql> show tables;
+------------------------------+
| Tables_in_snort              |
+------------------------------+
| data                         |
| detail                       |
| encoding                     |
| event                        |
| icmphdr                      |
| iphdr                        |
| opt                          |
| reference                    |
| reference_system             |
| schema                       |
```

Continued

Figure 7.9 Snort's Created Tables Continued

```
| sensor                  |
| sig_class               |
| sig_reference           |
| signature               |
| tcphdr                  |
| udphdr                  |
+------------------------====--+
16 rows in set (0.00 sec)
```

Storing our Snort logs within a relational database is much more efficient than storing them in flat files. They will be far more manageable in this form. There are several tools available for extracting and formatting Snort database logs. The output in Table 7.1 is from a script written by Yen-Ming Chen of Foundstone Inc. Mr. Chen's script retrieves Snort logs from a specified database and outputs high-level information. The HTML links were removed from this report due to formatting issues. Yen-Ming Chen's script can be downloaded from http://packetstormsecurity.org/sniffers/snort/snort_stat.pl.

```
Total events: 40
Timestamp begins at: 2003-02-12 22:42:20
Timestamp ends at: 2003-02-12 22:52:44
Total signatures: 10
Total Destination IP observed: 1
 Total Source IP observed: 1
```

Table 7.1 Snort_Stat Log Retrieval

Number of Reports on Each Signature

Numbers	Signature	Latest Timestamp
12	4	2003-02-12 22:52:37
8	2	2003-02-12 22:52:44
6	10	2003-02-12 22:52:44
2	5	2003-02-12 22:52:38
2	6	2003-02-12 22:52:35
2	7	2003-02-12 22:52:35

Continued

Table 7.1 Snort_Stat Log Retrieval

Numbers	Signature	Latest Timestamp
2	8	2003-02-12 22:52:38
2	1	2003-02-12 22:52:33
2	9	2003-02-12 22:52:36
2	3	2003-02-12 22:52:35

Tools & Traps...

Sorry ... We're Not Talking about the Microsoft SAM File

The Snort Alert Monitor (SAM) is a program that you can use in conjunction with Snort to provide a bit of real-time analysis on potential threats and realized attacks. SAM is available at www.lookandfeel.com. The most valuable aspect of SAM is that it can report and present alerts in an executive manner, graphically. SAM intends to complement, not replace, Snort or any other mainstream additional Snort add-ons. According to Look and Feel Software, "Snort was great for identifying suspicious traffic, and ACID was great for digging in to the details, but we needed something that was a little higher overview and able to sound alarms if certain conditions were met." Unfortunately, at the time of printing, the only database that was supported by SAM was MySQL. The Database Login dialog box in Figure 7.10 is the interface for configuring SAM and its ODBC connections. It is important to note that SAM does not encrypt any part of the authentication schema.

Figure 7.10 SAM Database Configuration

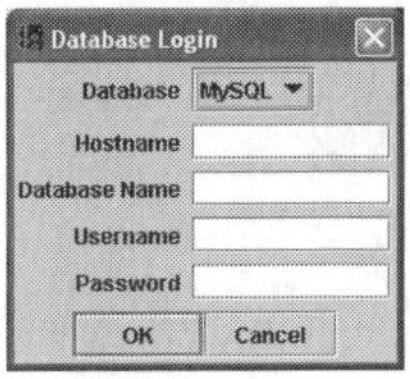

The SAM interface allows you to view the top attacks as defined by rule ID, top attackers as defined by IP address, and up-to-date information on attacks broken down by specific time allocations. You can also drill down to specific tidbits of information by clicking on IP address and attack ID links. In addition to the graphs at the bottom and quick link columns on the right, a noticeable stoplight on the left provides a "kindergarten-grade" alert status—red being the undesired color. Figure 7.11 is the SAM interface without a database connection.

Figure 7.11 SAM Interface

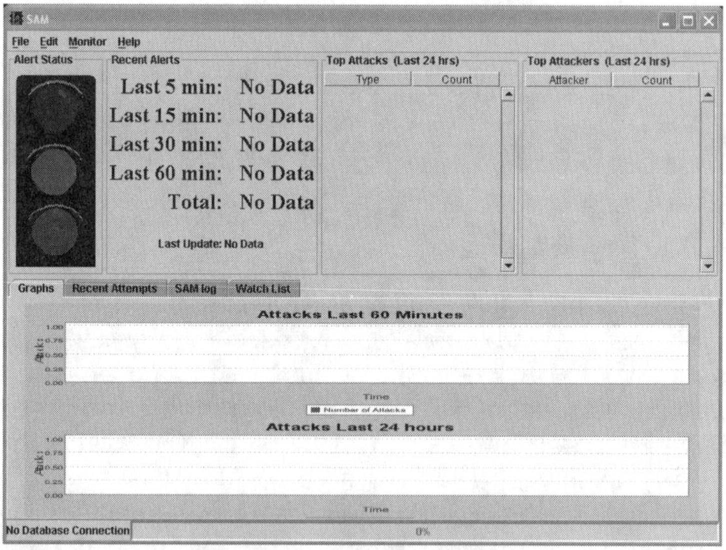

When SAM is running in conjunction with Snort, it maintains an ODBC connection to the MySQL database server. Depending on the amount of traffic, sensor placement, triggered rules, and bandwidth limitations, it is possible to notice a network slowdown because of SAM. If feasible, you might want to consider placing your SAM application on the same system that houses your database.

Unified Logs

Unified logs are the future of Snort reporting, logging, and output. The increased speed and efficiency is completely driving this initiative. The unified plug-ins decrease the number of processes that the Snort engine must use on noncapture or analysis functions, thereby "hopefully" increasing the likelihood that packets are not dropped.

Snort's unified output plug-in is designed to be fast and efficient, logging output in straight binary format. Many administrators prefer this method of logging, as it is acceptable for use with Snort's most popular reporting tools, Barnyard and Cerebus. The unified logging output plug-in supports two arguments: the name and size of the file that you want to store the logs to. The path to these files should be included along with the name if they do not reside locally in reference to the Snort binary. Figure 7.12 is an example unified log instruction from the Snort configuration file. Notice how there are two entries, one for alerts and another for logs. Each instruction has a 128MB file limit as defined by the *limit 128* declaration.

Figure 7.12 Unified Output Plug-In Configuration Excerpt

```
# output alert_unified: filename snort.alert, limit 128
# output log_unified: filename snort.log, limit 128
```

Why Should I Use Unified Logs?

We are not sure that we can stress this enough, but unified logs significantly increase the efficiency of the Snort sensor. As previously stated, unified logs are currently the "best-of-breed" solution for outputting Snort-gathered data. The only major modification that we see coming down the pipeline is the potential to send Snort unified data directly to a database. This type of solution would allow for real-time data storage outside of Snort, without decreasing the ability to efficiently categorize and sort through the data, functions provided within databases.

If you are thinking, "Isn't unified logging just cheap threading?" you are correct. It frees up the Snort engine so that its resources can be directed to the vital processes of capturing and analyzing packets. CPU cycles are redirected from the main Snort binary and passed on to the future interpreting application. In simple terms, it takes the weight and stress off the Snort engine for payload translation. With all of this said, unified logging provides a bit more than simply threading processes. It allows for an application-wide enhancement without modifying the main engine. Moreover, developing portable threads is no easy task, especially considering the complexity of creating a parser to format data output.

OINK!

It is not uncommon to see commercial environments using unified logs for long-term forensic data storage.

What Do I Do with These Unified Files?

Unified files can be viewed and analyzed in a number of different ways, and as you know, the benefits of using the unified log plug-in are speed, speed, and might we say, speed. Currently, Barnyard is the tool of choice for unified log processing, and two of the three modes of operation allow for continual, or streaming, analysis. The *continual* and *continual with checkpoints* modes will process *spo_unified* formatted data will continue to process unified file logs. Barnyard can receive input in one of two ways, via its input processors or from an output plug-in. In either case, the bulk of the data processing is still taken away from the Snort process. The other major difference for the plug-in is that it requires another application to interpret the data.

Notes from the Barnyard...

Ensuring Quality within Barnyard

Barnyard comes with a –R option that allows users to execute test runs of the application during development or configuration time. It will parse all of the configuration options, both from configuration files and via the command line, and output any errors to *STDOUT*. It proves to be a valuable feature for testing and debugging systems and should be included in any automated quality assurance or system test.

Dry Run Mode is an excellent feature; unfortunately, other freeware and commercial tools lack this type of functionality.

Unified logs are often stored in a manner that does not follow a typical naming schema. The following is a sample listing of a snort log directory. The unified log is snort.log.1045599382.

```
-rw-------    1 root    root              0 Feb 18 15:16 alert
-rw-------    1 root    root              0 Feb 18 15:16 portscan.log
-rw-------    1 root    root              0 Feb 18 15:16 scan.log
-rw-------    1 root    root   24 Feb 18 15:16 snort.log.1045599382
```

Since the information logged by this plug-in is stored as binary data, many programs supporting TCPDump formatted logs can be used to navigate through its contents. As we stated, the more popular programs are Cerebus and Barnyard. While Barnyard is quickly becoming the standard, Cerebus is still holding strong.

Cerebus

Cerebus is described by the Cerebus development team as "a text-based full-screen alert analysis system for Snort unified alert output." It allows for multiple alert files to be loaded into its embedded database system, as well as real-time queries, and is geared for enterprise organizations. The Cerebus database technology uses statically linked binaries and does not require any additional database software. Realizing that you use it on single databases, the real value of the product comes through when you analyze and interpret large volumes of Snort alert and packet data from multiple databases. Another valuable feature of Cerebus is that it supports retrieving and analysis of remote data over a network. You can download Cerebus and more information at (www.dragos.com/cerebus).

OINK!

Cerebus Lite is freely available, while a commercial version that supports a greater number of alert files is available with an associated price tag. At the time of printing, Cerebus Lite was free for personal use, or free for 14 days if used in a commercial environment.

Barnyard

Barnyard has the ability to gather data from Snort's unified output plug-in and send it to an alternate location, such as a database. It decouples the output stage from Snort and gives a boost in performance and reliability. Barnyard is distributed under QPLed. Figure7.13 is an example of Barnyard processing two unified Snort logs.

Figure 7.13 Barnyard Processing Two Unified Snort Logs

```
//       Analyzing with Barnyard
gabe@host:/root# barnyard -o -f /var/log/snort/snort.log.1045099117
//       Barnyard Log Dump
[**] [1:366:4] ICMP PING *NIX [**]
[Classification: Web Application Attack] [Priority: 3]
Event ID: 1      Event Reference: 1
02/13/03-01:18:39.069619 192.168.1.123 -> 192.168.1.10
ICMP TTL:64 TOS:0x0 ID:0 IpLen:20 DgmLen:84 DF
Type:8  Code:0  ID:197    Seq:0    ECHO
5F 83 4A 3E 5B 68 03 00 08 09 0A 0B 0C 0D 0E 0F     _.J>[h.........
10 11 12 13 14 15 16 17 18 19 1A 1B 1C 1D 1E 1F     ...............
20 21 22 23 24 25 26 27 28 29 2A 2B 2C 2D 2E 2F     !"#$%&'()*+,-./
30 31 32 33 34 35 36 37                                 01234567


[**] [1:408:4] ICMP Echo Reply [**]
[Classification: Web Application Attack] [Priority: 3]
Event ID: 2      Event Reference: 2
02/13/03-01:18:39.069653 192.168.1.10 -> 192.168.1.123
ICMP TTL:255 TOS:0x0 ID:61629 IpLen:20 DgmLen:84
Type:0  Code:0  ID:197    Seq:0    ECHO REPLY
5F 83 4A 3E 5B 68 03 00 08 09 0A 0B 0C 0D 0E 0F     _.J>[h.........
10 11 12 13 14 15 16 17 18 19 1A 1B 1C 1D 1E 1F     ...............
20 21 22 23 24 25 26 27 28 29 2A 2B 2C 2D 2E 2F     !"#$%&'()*+,-./
30 31 32 33 34 35 36 37                                 01234567


//       Analyzing with Barnyard
gabe@host:/root# barnyard -o -f /var/log/snort/snort.alert.1045099117
//       Barnyard Alert Dump
02/13/03-01:18:39.069619 {ICMP} 192.168.1.123 -> 192.168.1.10
[**] [1:366:4] ICMP PING *NIX [**]
[Classification: Web Application Attack] [Priority: 3]

02/13/03-01:18:39.069653 {ICMP} 192.168.1.10 -> 192.168.1.123
 [**] [1:408:4] ICMP Echo Reply [**]
```

Continued

Figure 7.13 Barnyard Processing Two Unified Snort Logs

```
[Classification: Web Application Attack] [Priority: 3]
```

Barnyard is capable of outputting reports as CSV, HTML, and common delimited, to mention a few. More information on the details for installing, configuring, maintaining, and tweaking Barnyard can be found in Chapter 11, "Mucking Around with Barnyard."

Writing Your Own Output Plug-In

Writing a customized output plug-in can be one of the best investments that an organization can make in reference to maintaining intrusion detection networks and systems. Yes, it is an investment. Whether it be monetary, time, or a combination of the two, creating an output plug-in has the potential to be extremely resource intensive. Before you consider writing an output plug-in, think about the requirements and reasoning for doing so. Does it need to be real-time data storage and processing, or can a parser or script be used to modify the data alerts and log? If possible, a post storage data modifier or analyzer should be used to save system resources during the traffic analysis phase. Whether a post storage script or output plug-in, identifying in-house talent and resources are also musts before even considering to travel "down the development path."

An uncommon yet legitimate and professional method for creating an output plug-in is to hire an outside party. We know of a few firms that chose to go this route. In general, the creation of the plug-in should not be too expensive, and the total price should fall somewhere between $2,000 and $7,000. Besides Sourcefire and Silicon Defense, security consulting boutiques such as Foundstone, @Stake, and Guardent might be good places to start looking for help.

Why Should I Write an Output Plug-In?

Simply put, you might want to write your own plug-in if one in existence does not meet your current organizational or technical requirements. As an organization, implementing and maintaining an IDS can and should be a major investment when done correctly. Monitoring potential and realized threats is a complicated, ongoing process, and as such should be implemented in a way that has minimal impact on network management and administrators.

Determining the return on investment (ROI) for writing an output plug-in is one of the initial steps that should be conducted during the initial conversations.

Some initial research should be conducted to get an idea or estimate on the amount of time that it will take to create a functional plug-in. The following are some questions that can help determine the estimated development time:

- Does a similar plug-in already exist? If so, can you grab some logic or code from it?

- Are test systems required? If so, do you have tests systems readily available to aid in creating the plug-in?

- How complicated is the task you are looking to accomplish? Is it simply modifying data. or is there a new type of storage mechanism that should be taken into consideration?

If example code or logic exists, or if you already have test systems, then you might already have an advantage. However, that still doesn't mean it is easy. Here are some of our best guesses that can be of some assistance in determining the time requirement for developing a new output plug-in. Table 7.3 lists the skill level and an estimated development time for developing a Snort output plug-in.

Table 7.3 Estimated Snort Output Development Time

Skill Level	Estimated Development Time
Snort and programmer expert—Persons with excellent structured programming skills, who not only understand but would feel comfortable modifying current Snort output plug-ins, and understand the technology requirements for the new plug-in.	One to two days
Programming expert—An excellent structured-language programmer with experience in structures, links, memory allocation, (potentially) sockets and data transfer, and data modification as mentioned under "Moderate programming skills," but might not have any "real" experience in using or implementing Snort-specific features.	Two to four days
Moderate programming skills—Programmers with general structured programming skills as mentioned	Two to four weeks

Continued

Table 7.3 Estimated Snort Output Development Time

Skill Level	Estimated Development Time
under "Low programming skills," plus abilities to modify data in respect to separation, searching, and queuing.	
Low programming skills— Programmers with general structured programming experience. General structured programming experience includes knowledge of input, output, multifile applications, argument processing, and external file and variable usage.	In excess of three weeks
Don't even consider it— If you do not minimally possess low programming skills, then you or your organization should probably look for another solution.	Appropriate only for ambitious persons without defined deadlines.

OINK!

Table 7.3 was designed for an easy to moderate technology and data storage schema. Obviously, the development time would increase along with the increase in the output plug-in level of difficulty.

Setting Up My Output Plug-In

Setting up, designing, coding, and implementing a new Snort output plug-in can have similarities across all platforms. In this section, we will cover the major aspects of the *spo_alert_full* output plug-in and draw conclusions on analogous characteristics of this particular plug-in to that of developing a new Snort-enabled technology output plug-in.

Most of the Snort output plug-in headers follow a standard format that strictly defines the purpose, arguments, effect, and the name of the output plug-in. The header provides technical information, quickly, so that users and administrators can understand the plug-in requirements and overall motivation and mission of the output plug-in Figure7.14.

Figure 7.14 The Snort Full Alert Output Plug-In Header

```
/* spo_alert_full
 *
 * Purpose:  output plugin for full alerting
 *
 * Arguments:  alert file (eventually)
 *
 * Effect:
 *
 * Alerts are written to a file in the snort full alert format
 *
 * Comments:   Allows use of full alerts with other output plugin types
 *
 */
```

All output plug-ins must define the appropriate header and include files. These files can include anything from network protocol APIs to groupings of other source header file declarations.

```
#Header Files
```

It is common practice and a requirement in nearly all structured programming language applications to declare all function prototypes. The prototypes are generally listed at the top of the program, but this is coincidently due to learned best practices.

```
void AlertFullInit(u_char *);
SpoAlertFullData *ParseAlertFullArgs(char *);
void AlertFull(Packet *, char *, void *, Event *);
void AlertFullCleanExit(int, void *);
void AlertFullRestart(int, void *);
```

Global variable definitions are another common characteristic for enterprise applications. These variables can be used throughout the program and within other additional built-in modules to include Snort output plug-ins.

```
/* external globals from rules.c */
extern char *file_name;
extern int file_line;
```

Initially setting up and configuring your output plug-in involves a few key steps, including globally registering the output plug-in keyword and initializing the function in the Snort output plug-in list (Figure 7.15). In most cases, this function would not need to return any values and does not accept any parameters or additional information.

Figure 7.15 Setting Up the Plug-In

```
/*
 * Function: SetupAlertFull()
 *
 * Purpose: Registers the output plugin keyword and initialization
 *          function into the output plugin list.  This is the function
 *          that gets called from InitOutputPlugins() in plugbase.c.
 *
 * Arguments: None.
 *
 * Returns: void function
 *
 */
void AlertFullSetup()
{
}
```

Initializing the function in reference to argument parsing and performing the final setup of data in regard to data input should be conducted here (Figure 7.16). By now, the program should have prepared all of the rudimentary plug-in preparation tasks.

Figure 7.16 Alert Initialization

```
/*
 * Function: AlertFullInit(u_char *)
```

Continued

Figure 7.16 Alert Initialization

```
 *

 * Purpose: Calls the argument parsing function, performs final setup on
data
 *            structs, links the preproc function into the function list.
 *
 * Arguments: args => ptr to argument string
 *
 * Returns: void function
 *
 */
void AlertFullInit(u_char *args)
{
}
```

Obviously, creating and formatting the output is the most important function within the output plug-in. In a function similar to this, you would gather the captured data, analyze said data, and conduct all of the formatting for the plug-in (Figure7.17).

Figure 7.17 Formatting and Report Generation

```
void AlertFull(Packet *p, char *msg, void *arg, Event *event)
{
    *Here lies the bulk of the program
}
```

Similar to the subsequent restarting function, the Cleanup and Closing the Loose Ends function can handle memory management issues, session management anomalies, and anything else that needs to be cleaned up or reallocated.

```
void AlertFullCleanExit(int signal, void *arg)
{
}
```

In some cases, proper output plug-in execution requires the restart of certain functions, communication sessions, and other module-specific technologies.

```
void AlertFullRestart(int signal, void *arg)
{
}
```

This overview was provided for a very specific instance of one current Snort output plug-in. The goal was not to define every line of code or even provide insight into program-specific algorithms or logic; it was to provide an overview of the core functions and functionality found within most output plug-ins.

Dealing with Snort Output

Sometimes, you might find that it is easier to work with what Snort gives you instead of creating a new output plug-in. Considering the current varying options and formats, in most cases you might simply want to go the down the path of least resistance and deal with post-Snort data modification.

One of the easiest and certainly the most popular method for creating a customized Snort data interface is creating some type of database interface. The current relational database plug-ins update the databases in real time when new threats are identified, rule triggered, and data logged. The data accessed from the databases can still be considered real time. These databases provide an excellent medium for accessing up-to-the minute data without having to "reinvent the wheel." As you now know, there are multiple database output selections you can select, ranging from the enterprise choice of Oracle to the freeware version of MySQL.

Perl with Tcl/Tk, Java, Visual Basic, PHP, and even Visual C++ are suitable languages to code Snort database interfaces. While there are many others, PHP and Perl are two of the most popular due to the easy language syntax, Web-based nature, and rapid development characteristics. Table 7.4 details a few of the vital pros and cons that should be weighed when considering a database solution.

Table 7.4 The Pros and Cons of Using Snort Database Information

Pros	Cons
Real-time information.	In comparison to the other options, databases have the potential to be bandwidth intense.
Some of the data correlation can be achieved inside of the relational databases.	Databases alone are enterprise applications in themselves, and as such might require maintenance in regard to user management, patching, and system configuration.
Relational databases allow you to create multiple tables and relations to potentially access subsets of data from multiple Snort sensors.	Costs might be associated with implementing the database option if a non-freeware option is selected.

Continued

Table 7.4 The Pros and Cons of Using Snort Database Information

Pros	Cons
Storing the data in the databases might be a more flexible solution going forward.	For the most part, accessing the data in a secure manner is left up to the user.
	Network databases are popular "hacker targets." Application security should not an option; it should be mandatory.
	Heavy development time.

Another option that is available if you do not want to use a database to store Snort logs is to go the flat file route. Using flat files poses an interesting situation in that these files are usually stored on the Snort sensor. Some of the more popular flat file plug-ins are *Alert_fast*, *Alert_full*, *Alert_CSV*, and *Log_TCPDump*. It is possible to retrieve these files remotely, but the logistics and time delta between the event and event notification might prove to be unacceptable. Flat file analysis really hits its full value proposition when a single data element or type of data element is desired. It is a poor enterprise solution. Table 7.5 highlights a few of the pros and cons of using a file flat analysis schema.

Table 7.5 The Pros and Cons of Using Snort Flat File Information

Pros	Cons
Decent speed on small to medium-sized networks.	Flat files must be parsed and interpreted before data modification can begin.
Simplicity, in general accessing flat files to retrieve data is not an overly complicated task.	Depending on the size of the file and the amount of available system memory, parsing the file might bring your system to a screeching halt (same with XML).
There shouldn't be any additional costs associated with going this route.	Inflexible.
The "time-to-market" or development time should be minimal.	Post-real-time speeds.
	In general, flat files are stored on the Snort sensors.

XML has hit the market like a gigantic red dump truck. Everyone seems to be drawn into the perceived benefits and mystic of the technology, while the gratuitous Microsoft "endorsement" doesn't seem to be hurting anything either. XML has several of the same issues as flat files do, since in most cases these files would be stored locally on the sensors. The only notable advantage over a flat file plug-in is that XML-formatted output is easier to extend and more flexible in the case that it should be used in future applications. Table 7.6 lists XML technology pros and cons in reference to Snort sensor databases.

Table 7.6 The Pros and Cons of Using Snort XML-Formatted Information

Pros	Cons
Immerging technologies that support XML-formatted data feeds.	XML files must be parsed and interpreted before data modification can begin.
To date, XML has been a relatively secure technology.	Depending on the size of the file and the amount of available system memory, parsing the file might bring your system to a screeching halt (same with flat files).
Storing the data in XML might be a more flexible solution going forward.	Post-real-time speeds.
In general, XML files are stored on the Snort sensors.	

An excellent new feature in Snort is the ability to store unified or binary data, or to provide such data as an input stream to another program using such information. Using binary data and unified data streams threads processes away from the Snort executable, thus allowing Snort to focus on the more critical processes such as data collection and storage. Chapter 11 addresses all of the intricacies of unified data and processing such data. Table 7.7 lists the pros and cons of using spooling streams.

Table 7.7 The Pros and Cons of Using Snort Unified and Binary Information

Pros	Cons
Unmatched speed.	Extremely complicated development or plug-in modification.
Unmatched Snort plug-in and sensor performance.	Additional applications are required to process the data streams.
Snort's Barnyard application is maintained by the Snort development and is quickly becoming an integral part of the product.	Data selection and categorization is not on par with data inputted into the database.
Flexible and scalable.	

All things considered,. our recommendation is twofold. If you are looking for a quick fix to a problem, or to merely create a "hack job" that gets the issue resolved, then by all means go with a script that pulls relevant information out of a PCAP or header infused alert file. Such a solution would be adequate if your goal was to determine what attacks were generated from a particular source. Now, if the goal is to create an enterprise-grade or purely a more sustainable application, then the choice should be obvious, relational databases or unified data streams. Once the code to access and retrieve the data is flushed out, data selection and modification will seem trivial. Moreover, using a Snort database might prove beneficial down the road when future NIDS projects arise.

Summary

The Snort application has gone through many different architectural, algorithm-specific, and implementation modifications. With just about all of these changes have come direct, positive product and feature enhancements. One of the most beneficial features built into Snort with reference to reporting and data presentation is Snort's ability to use output plug-ins. These plug-ins enable network and security administrators, engineers, and managers alike to optimize the product for their environment and to ensure that minimal resources are spent maintaining the technology. Minimizing resources will also have a direct impact on the mean-time-to-data-analysis, which defines *how fast your company can react to any incident.*

Currently, there are several different options that you have when using the output plug-ins. Various options allow data to be formatted in PCAP, straight text headers with packet destination and source information along with rule messages, XML text databases, and multiple relational databases to include MySQL, Oracle, and MS SQL. Along with the format of the data, Snort provides the ability to store and transmit the formatted data in numerous methods. Storing alerts and logs locally, transmitting data to UNIX sockets, and pushing data to local and remote databases are all potential methods. It is not necessary to use plug-ins for everything, given that complementing utilities are available. Log parsers, graphical interfaces, and correlation engines allow the user to further format data with application wrappers and scripts. Barnyard, ACID, and Cerebus are three of the most popular complementary Snort applications.

The existing output plug-ins are nice, but the real value-add comes with Snort's ability to create customized plug-ins. Because the Snort development team has implemented an open API structure for the use of output plug-ins, both private organizations and professional security teams can design in-house plug-ins. These in-house plug-ins can be driven by technology or customers, but the common goal should always remain: to minimize manual data compilation tasks. These plug-ins access a highly technical subset of functions and application calls that reference configuration instructions and the corresponding parameters defined during Snort runtime. The bulk of the plug-in resides in formatting the input data while also handling the technologies used during the output phase.

We found that just about any technological executive or manager freely voices the fact that data is useless unless it can be quickly analyzed and used to make decisions. Part of Snort's answer to inherent technology issue is output plug-ins. Our recommendation: If freeware Snort is a valuable asset within your organization, it is essential that you have an engineer or scientist who completely understands output plug-ins.

Solutions Fast Track

What Is an Output Plug-In?

☑ Output plug-ins, a.k.a. Output Modules, were introduced in Snort version 1.6 and are an excellent mechanism for storing information in a customizable formats and locations. It was the first major movement into creating an open reporting API.

Exploring Output Plug-in Options

☑ Currently, Snort has plug-ins that support multiple reporting formats to include straight text headers, PCAP, UNIX syslog, XML text databases, and numerous other types of relational databases.

☑ Captured and defined data can be stored in local alert and packet logs and local and remote databases, in addition to blindly transmitting the data to a UNIX socket.

☑ Additional programs such as Acid, Barnyard, and Cerebus are an irreplaceable asset in analyzing and modifying data reports.

Writing Your Own Output Plug-In

☑ Writing Snort output plug-ins is no easy task if you have little to no C programming experience. It is much more complex when compared to Snort rule authoring, since to date all of the output plug-ins are written in C.

☑ A potentially quicker alternative to writing an output plug-in is writing a plug-in wrapper. For example, if the goal is to format data instead of modifying real-time data formatting and storage, then it might be faster and more economical to write a Perl script that automatically runs against the payload and outputs the desired information.

☑ The output plug-ins have some common similarities to include global variable definitions and prototyping, keyword registration, argument and preprocessor argument processing, plug-in and function cleanup and exiting, and data formatting and transmission.

Frequently Asked Questions

The following Frequently Asked Questions, answered by the authors of this book, are designed to both measure your understanding of the concepts presented in this chapter and to assist you with real-life implementation of these concepts. To have your questions about this chapter answered by the author, browse to **www.syngress.com/solutions** and click on the **"Ask the Author"** form.

Q: Do you have any recommendation on what type of output module to use on a mobile workstation?

A: Let's presuppose that as a traveling computer, security is an essential requirement, CPU and memory are valuable commodities, and that it is being monitored and used the majority of the time. It is probably in your best interest to only use alerts with minimal information, since we can assume that if you were attacked, immediate action would be taken. Packet headers and rule content messages should suffice. Specifically, fast alerts would be our UNIX recommendation, while the SMB client (a.k.a. Windows PopUp), would be the choice for Windows users.

Q: What kind of bandwidth hit will I take if I choose to log alerts to a remote database?

A: Bandwidth consumption is completely derived from two factors; the first is the amount of data that is transmitted across the sensor network, and the second is the ruleset that is implemented on the sensor. We recommend keeping the primary log database on the Snort sensor to minimize network impact if you can afford the hardware, because running a database will impact system performance. If you do not have this option and your network uses under 20 percent of its available bandwidth on a common workday, then it is probably okay to go ahead and use a remote database plug-in. To test and prototype the options, you can monitor local logs and sizes to determine whether the data load would be too great if imposed on the network.

Q: Can I log to multiple databases even if they are different types of databases?

A: The short answer is yes; now for the real answer, since there are multiple ways to reach the end goal. Snort provides users with the ability to log to multiple instantiations of the same database plug-in, log data to multiple identical and different databases, and log data to miscellaneous other data types. The following are examples of output instructions that can be defined in a configuration file.

Example: Multiple formats including a database:

```
output mydatabase: oracle, dbname=security host=securitydb.poc2.com user=joe
output log_tcpdump: /logs/snort/tcpdump/current.log
```

Example: Multiple databases:

```
output mydatabase: mysql, dbname=dmzsnort host=10.1.1.7 user=dbadmin
password=badidea

output mydatabase: oracle, dbname=security host=securitydb.poc2.com user=joe
password=badidea
```

Example: Multiple instances of the same database

```
output mydatabase: oracle, dbname=sensor host=sensor.poc2.com port=10302
user=admin password=bads

output mydatabase: oracle, dbname=sensor host=backup.poc2.com port=10302
user=admin password=bads
```

## Chapter 8

Exploring the Data Analysis Tools

Solutions in this chapter:

- Using Swatch
- Using ACID
- Using SnortSnarf
- Using IDScenter

☑ Summary

☑ Solutions Fast Track

☑ Frequently Asked Questions

Introduction

So you have Snort up and running. If you think the work stops here, you're wrong. The purpose of setting up the IDS is not only to obtain data about network traffic (intrusion attempts, specifically), but to analyze this data and take action based on the results. Tuning of rules (described in Chapter 5, "Playing by the Rules") is done best when based on the live data from the current ruleset.

Try this as an exercise: Set up Snort on a rather busy network with the original set of signatures from the distribution package, and leave it to run as is for a while—a week, for example. You will be surprised at how many alerts it will generate—most probably hundreds, if not thousands. This enormous volume of alerts implies that you will not be able to obtain any general overview of what is going on in your network by simply browsing log files.

The important side of intrusion detection is that you probably want to not only register events, but also react to the intrusion attempts somehow in real time (more or less). Are you going to sit and scroll through ever-growing logs all day? Realistically, no. Better to have some application notify you of ongoing intrusion.

In this chapter, we look at four popular tools that can help you in both aspects of using Snort data—consolidating/analyzing, and alerting people who deal with incident response tasks. These tools are:

- Swatch
- ACID
- SnortSnarf
- IDScenter

 For your convenience, the current versions of these tools (at the time of printing) are included on this book's companion CD-ROM. You can find these tools in the Chapter 8 directory.

Using Swatch

The "Simple log WATCHer and filter," more commonly referred to as Swatch, is a Perl program developed by Todd Atkins (www.oit.ucsb.edu/~eta/swatch). It is probably one of the simplest, yet still very powerful tools that can be used in automation of responses to Snort alerts. Swatch monitors your log files for specific triggers, and when any of these triggers are matched, performs a certain action, such as sending a system administrator an e-mail about this event.

Performing a Swatch Installation

Swatch installation is not overly difficult. The package is written in Perl and can be downloaded from www.stanford.edu/~atkins/swatch, or can be accessed from the accompanying CD-ROM. Swatch requires the following Perl modules for proper functioning:

- Date::Calc
- Date::Parse
- File::Tail
- Time::HiRes

If you do not have these modules, you can download them from CPAN (http://search.cpan.org), either via Web or by using the CPAN Perl utility. Its usage is described in the corresponding man page—simply run **man CPAN** at the Linux command prompt to read the documentation. The CPAN utility is easy to use. Just type at the command prompt:

```
#perl -MCPAN -e shell
```

You will get a *cpan>* prompt. To install a package (for example, *Date::Calc*), type the following:

```
cpan> install Date::Calc
```

This command will produce a lot of output describing each step performed. An abbreviated portion of the output (namely the beginning and the end) is shown here:

```
Running make for S/ST/STBEY/Date-Calc-5.3.tar.gz
CPAN: LWP::UserAgent loaded ok
Fetching with LWP:
  ftp://ftp.perl.org/pub/CPAN/authors/id/S/ST/STBEY/Date-Calc-5.3.tar.gz
... skipped...
Writing /usr/lib/perl5/site_perl/5.6.0/i386-linux/auto/TimeDate/.packlist
Appending installation info to /usr/lib/perl5/5.6.0/i386-linux/perllocal.pod
  /usr/bin/make install  -- OK
cpan>
```

The *OK* message on the next to last line means that the package was successfully installed. If CPAN detects that some dependencies are missing from the

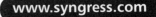

system, it will attempt to download and install the missing packages without any input from you, which means that you will not have to worry about missing packages.

If you prefer to download the installation package (the distribution package contains installation instructions and an install script) for any of the modules listed previously (or Swatch itself) and then install it manually, you need to unpack the package into /usr/local/src and run the following commands (these commands are generic for most Perl packages):

- perl Makefile.PL

- make

- make test

- make install

- make realclean

If there are no error messages displayed during this process, the package is properly installed. Swatch is installed in the same way. If you miss some of the prerequisites, you will see messages like this:

```
[root@snort swatch-3.0.4]# perl Makefile.PL
Warning: prerequisite Date::Calc failed to load: Can't locate Date/Calc.pm
in @INC (@INC contains: /usr/lib/perl5/5.6.0/i386-linux /usr/lib/perl5/5.6.0
/usr/lib/perl5/site_perl/5.6.0/i386-linux /usr/lib/perl5/site_perl/5.6.0
/usr/lib/perl5/site_perl .) at (eval 4) line 3.
Warning: prerequisite Date::Parse failed to load: Can't locate
Date/Parse.pm in @INC (@INC contains: /usr/lib/perl5/5.6.0/i386-linux
/usr/lib/perl5/5.6.0 /usr/lib/perl5/site_perl/5.6.0/i386-linux
/usr/lib/perl5/site_perl/5.6.0 /usr/lib/perl5/site_perl .) at (eval 5)
line 3.
```

These messages mean that *Date::Calc* and *Date::Parse* are missing on the system.

Configuring Swatch

After Swatch is successfully installed, you will need to configure it. The configuration is stored in one file, commonly named *swatchrc*, although you can use any name you like. It is always a good idea to keep the default configuration file-name, so as not to confuse any other administrators of the systems with which you are working. This file contains the list of rules, patterns, and corresponding actions. Each Swatch rule can contain several fields. Consider the following rule:

```
watchfor /spp_stream4/
bell
echo normal
mail addresses=abuse@yourcompany.net,subject=--- Snort Alert! ---
throttle 00:00:10
```

The first mandatory line, *watchfor*, contains a pattern in the form of a regular expression. The syntax of regular expressions is described, for example, in the *man grep* UNIX documentation page. In our case, this pattern describes that Swatch has to look for a string *spp_stream4* in a log file and then perform a set of described actions. This line may also contain the *ignore* keyword instead of *watchfor*, which means that the matched entry must be ignored.

The next lines specify the actions that must be performed when the regular expression in *watchfor* line is matched. *Bell* causes the system to produce a sound; *echo* prints the matched entry to the standard output stream (stdout). The *Mail* action is the most useful in our case—it will mail a matched entry to the specified address (abuse@ourcompany.net) with the subject "---Snort Alert!---". Of course, it is possible to specify any other e-mail addresses and subjects. Multiple *mail* actions are also supported.

OINK!

The *Mail* action of Swatch uses sendmail, so you must have it installed to use this feature. For those of you who use postfix or another MTA, as long as you have enabled sendmail replacement (using the *postfix-enable* command with postfix), you should not have a problem.

The *throttle* action means that for the stated period of time, matching of this rule is suspended. This action is useful when you are receiving many similar alerts and do not want your mailbox filled with Swatch reports. In our example, the *throttle* action means that for the next 10 seconds, this matched rule will be ignored—even if the same pattern appears in the monitored log file, no action will be performed by Swatch.

There is one more action—*exec*. It runs the command specified as a parameter of the action. For example, you can run a script that will alert you via pager in a way similar to the following:

```
exec "call_pager 123456 $0"
```

This line assumes that your script for sending messages to the pager is *call_pager*, and it takes as a parameter a pager number and a message. *$0* here will be substituted by a matched log entry.

Using Swatch

Using Swatch after you have created the configuration file is simple. Swatch can be started in a variety of ways:

- Via a Snort initialization script
- Used separately as part of *init* set of scripts
- Manually

The following is a command line used for starting Swatch:

```
/usr/local/bin/swatch -c /var/log/.swatchrc -t /var/log/snort/alert &
```

This line assumes that Swatch is installed in /usr/local/bin directory, the configuration file .swatchrc is located in the /var/log directory, and the Snort alert file is in the /var/log/snort directory. Note that the *-c* option defines the location of the configuration file, and the *-t* option tells Swatch which log file to monitor. The *&* sign at the end of the line means that this command is started in the background. Background processes cannot communicate with the terminal or *stdin/ stdout* streams, so you cannot use *echo* actions in the Swatch configuration file if you want to start it in the background.

You can also set up Snort logging to syslog in addition to its standard log files using the output option (in snort.conf):

```
output alert_syslog: LOG_AUTH LOG_ALERT
```

Then, each alert will appear in /var/log/messages (the default location on Red Hat) in the following way (lines are wrapped in this example):

```
Feb 12 19:19:00 witt snort: [117:1:1] (spp_portscan2) Portscan detected
from 10.1.1.34: 1 targets 21 ports in 24 seconds {TCP} 10.1.1.34:33531 ->
10.1.1.30:1439

Feb 12 19:19:01 witt snort: [1:1418:2] SNMP request tcp [Classification:
Attempted Information Leak] [Priority: 2]: {TCP} 10.1.1.34:33531 ->
10.1.1.30:161
```

```
Feb 12 19:19:01 witt snort: [1:615:3] SCAN SOCKS Proxy attempt
[Classification: Attempted Information Leak] [Priority: 2]: {TCP}
10.1.1.34:33531 -> 10.1.1.30:1080
Feb 12 19:19:01 witt snort: [111:12:1] (spp_stream4) NMAP FINGERPRINT
(stateful) detection {TCP} 10.1.1.34:33541 -> 10.1.1.30:21
Feb 12 19:19:01 witt snort: [1:628:1] SCAN nmap TCP [Classification:
Attempted Information Leak] [Priority: 2]: {TCP} 10.1.1.34:33543 ->
10.1.1.30:1
Feb 12 19:19:01 witt snort: [111:10:1] (spp_stream4) STEALTH ACTIVITY (XMAS
scan) detection {TCP} 10.1.1.34:33544 -> 10.1.1.30:1
Feb 12 19:19:02 witt snort: [111:9:1] (spp_stream4) STEALTH ACTIVITY (NULL
scan) detection {TCP} 10.1.1.34:33539 -> 10.1.1.30:21
```

Each alert generated by Snort starts with *snort:* prefix, so you might set up an action in the Swatch configuration file to react to all syslog messages with this string:

```
watchfor /snort:/
mail addresses=abuse@yourcompany.net,subject=--- Snort Alert! ---
throttle 00:00:10
```

Alternatively, if you want to receive e-mail alerts on IIS-related attacks, you can use something like this in your *.swatchrc*:

```
watchfor /IIS/
mail addresses=abuse@yourcompany.net,subject=--- Snort Alert, IIS attack! --
throttle 00:00:5
```

Figure 8.1 shows a more complicated example of a Swatch configuration file.

Figure 8.1 Swatch Configuration File for Monitoring Snort syslog Alerts

```
watchfor /MS-SQL/
     echo bold
     mail addressess=root,subject=--- Snort MS-SQL Attack Alert ---
     exec echo $0 >> /var/log/MSSQL
     throttle 00:10

watchfor /Portscan detected/
     echo bold
     mail addresses=root,subject=--- Snort Port Scan Alert ---
     exec echo $0 >> /var/log/portscans
```

Continued

Figure 8.1 Swatch Configuration File for Monitoring Snort syslog Alerts

```
watchfor /approved AXFR/
    echo bold
    mail addresses=root,subject=--- Snort Zone Transfer Alert ---
    exec echo $0 >> /var/log/zonetransfers
```

When this configuration is used, alerts related to MS-SQL exploits will be e-mailed to the "root" user and also stored in a file /var/log/MSSQL. Port scanning alerts and zone transfers will also cause Swatch to send an e-mail to the same user, but with a different subject line, and store the e-mails in different files. The following action is useful for producing separated log files for different types of alerts. It adds a matched log line to the specified file:

```
exec echo $0 >> file
```

Swatch can also be used in monitoring syslog files for other events that are not generated by Snort. For example, the following rule will alert the "root" user about failed authentication events:

```
watchfor   /failed/
echo bold
mail addressess=root,subject=Failed Authentication
```

OINK!

It is more convenient to monitor syslog events than, for example, Snort alert files, because syslog messages are always one line, while in alert files, each alert produces several line of text, which is not always useful for pattern matching.

To conclude, Swatch is a simple but powerful tool for real-time monitoring and alerting.

Using ACID

While the main use of Swatch is for alerting, Analysis Console for Intrusion Databases (ACID) is a tool for data browsing and analyzing. ACID is basically a set of PHP scripts that provide interface between a Web browser and the database where Snort data is stored. This tool has been in development for about three years as of the time of this writing, but is still described as a Beta release. ACID has grown into a very powerful consolidation and analysis tool.

ACID is maintained by its creator, Roman Danyliw, as part of a larger project called AirCERT (www.cert.org/kb/aircert). At the time of writing, the current version of ACID is 0.9.6b22. Originally designed for solely processing Snort data, ACID is now independent of the Snort database structure and can work with various data produced by various other engines (provided that they are imported into ACID database in some way); for example, Linux IP filter firewall or Cisco access-list related messages. A script *logsnorter* is included in Snort distribution and is designed to import logs with alerts from these engines into Snort database, so this data becomes available to ACID, too.

At this time, ACID provides the following features:

- An interface for database searching and query building. Searches can be performed by network-specific parameters such as attacker's IP address, or by meta parameters such as time/date of an event or by triggered rule.

- A packet browser that can decode and display Layer 3 and Layer 4 information from logged packets.

- Data management capabilities, including grouping of alerts (so that it is possible to group all events related to an intrusion incident), alert deletion, or archiving and exporting to e-mail messages.

- Generation of various graphical charts and statistics based on specified parameters.

The rest of this section describes the installation of ACID and its prerequisites, Snort configuration, and the ways in which ACID can be used for intrusion detection and analysis. You can download ACID from www.cert.org/kb/acid, or install it from the accompanying CD-ROM.

Installing ACID

The structure of ACID is multitiered and scalable. You can use it on just one computer, or you can have an up to three-tiered architecture. Figure 8.2 shows logical parts of the system.

Figure 8.2 Multitiered Architecture of an IDS and ACID Console

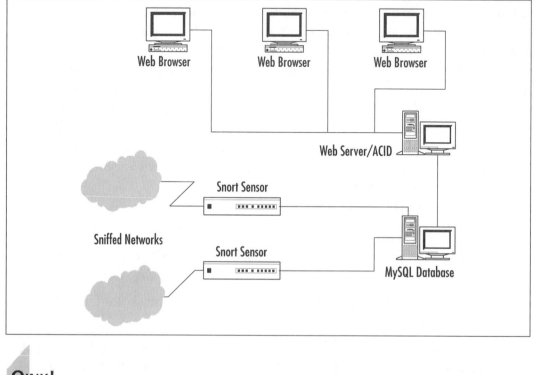

> **OINK!**
>
> ACID is included on the accompanying CD-ROM.

As you can see, ACID works with alerts stored in a database by sensors. A set of PHP scripts is used for creating queries and browsing the results. Currently, ACID officially supports PostgreSQL and MySQL, but it is possible to modify it to work with other SQL-based DBMS supported by PHP. You can use any Web server as long as it supports PHP4 (although you might run into difficulties with the optional graphing functionality of ACID, because the libraries it uses are mainly designed for Linux and Apache).

Prerequisites for Installing ACID

We will assume that a Web server and a database are installed on the same host. Your Snort sensor is probably located on another machine, although it is not important for us—ACID does not work with the sensor directly, only with database data. If you would like to separate a Web server (front end) from the database (back end), almost nothing changes in the ACID configuration—only some IP addresses in configuration files. It is even possible to have many Web servers working with one database. Moreover, of course, the number of Web clients is not limited even for one Web server.

Operating System on ACID Host

In this section, we will mainly use Linux—Red Hat 7.2 or higher. The operating system used is not overly crucial; all of the ACID components can be installed (with minimal modifications) on any UNIX operating systems or even Microsoft Windows (although the latter requires more tweaking). If you plan to use the ACID host only as a server, you can install a minimal set of packages—the only crucial parts are networking and software development tools. If you also want to use a graphical Web browser on the same host (for testing purposes, for example), you will need to install X-Windows related packages too (including Gnome or KDE) and the browser itself. Actual selection of packages depends on your choice—it is easy to add any missing dependencies when needed.

We will set an IP address of 10.1.1.30 for our ACID server.

Tools & Traps...

When Size Matters

As was already noted, running Snort on a busy network can produce a significant number of alerts. With a standard set of rules it can generate tens of megabytes of data per day on a network with just a couple of busy Web sites. In addition, nothing stops you from writing configuration files for logging all more or less interesting data to store as a reference for future investigations. This data can quickly fill a hard drive.

Continued

www.syngress.com

If you have only one partition (on Linux)—root—that holds the entire file system, filling it up might cause the machine to stop functioning. It is considered good practice to have the log and database partitions separated from the / (root) and /boot partitions. In case of Red Hat distribution, one way to separate logs and databases from the root partition is to create a separate large partition for /var directory—all MySQL data and various logs are usually stored under this directory entry.

The Web Server

We will use the Apache 1.3 Web server on Linux, because it is a native environment for ACID. You can either download it from www.apache.org and compile manually, or use a package that comes with the Red Hat distribution. For example, to install Apache from an RPM package, use the following (x-x here is a minor version number, which may vary):

```
# rpm -ivh apache-1.3.x-x.i386.rpm
# chkconfig --level 2345 httpd on
# /etc/rc.d/init.d/httpd start
```

These commands install the package, add an httpd daemon to the set of daemons automatically started on run levels 2 to 5, and start the Web server. In Red Hat distributions it is assumed that the Web site root is located in /var/www/html directory on the host.

PHP

ACID scripts are written in PHP language, so naturally we need to add PHP4 support to our Web server. There are many different ways to set it up. For example, it can be set up as an Apache module or run as an external CGI application. The important features for us are:

- **Database support** MySQL or PostgreSQL. We will use MySQL throughout this section.

- **GD support** This is a graphing library used for producing graphs.

- **Socket support** This is used only for performing native "whois" queries.

You can either build PHP from source or use Red Hat packages. When building from source, you need to use at least the following options in PHP configuration:

```
./configure [your config options] --with-mysql --with-gd --enable-sockets
```

For MySQL support:

```
./configure [your config options] --with-pgsql --with-gd --enable-sockets
```

For PostgreSQL support, an option -- *with-apache* makes PHP work as an Apache Web server module, which speeds script execution significantly. If you do not want to deal with compiling the source, it is possible to use Red Hat packages that are already included in the distribution. Their names vary from distribution to distribution. In Red Hat 7.2, a package for PHP is called php-4.0.6-7.rpm, and MySQL support for PHP is provided via the php-mysql-4.0.6-7.rpm package. They are installed as follows:

```
#rpm -ivh php-4.0.6-7.rpm php-mysql-4.0.6-7.rpm
```

After installation, it is recommended to modify a configuration file /etc/php.ini as follows:

1. Disable display of inline PHP error messages in generated HTML files by setting *display_errors=off* in production environment, or at least set *error_reporting = E_ALL & ~E_NOTICE*, which will limit the number of reported error messages.

2. Configure SMTP on the server. On Windows you need to set the *SMTP* variable to the path of your SMTP server executable module. On UNIX, set the *sendmail_path* to the path of sendmail executable (for example, *sendmail_path=/usr/sbin/sendmail*).

3. On Windows platforms you will also need to set the *session.save_path* variable to a temporary directory writable by the Web server (for example, c:\temp). Windows-related configuration and installation issues are documented at www.php.net/manual/en/install-windows.php.

Support Libraries

The following libraries need to be installed. Not all of them are critical for ACID functionality—the only important one is ADODB; others can be omitted if you are ready to sacrifice graphing features of ACID.

We already mentioned the GD library. This is a library for raw image manipulation and supports GIF/JPEG/PNG formats. It is available at www.boutell.com/gd. The minimum version that can be used with ACID is 1.8. Red Hat, again, provides an RPM package with this library—in 7.2, it is called gd-1.8.4-4.rpm. GD depends on some other libraries (usually installed as a part of system setup, but just in case we will list them here):

- libpng, available at www.libpng.org/pub/png

- libjpeg-6b, available at www.ijg.org

- zlib, available at www.gzip.org/zlib

Another set of scripts (it is called a library too, but it is not a binary code distribution, only PHP scripts) provides an interface from PHP to GD. This is a PHPlot library, which can be downloaded from www.phplot.com. The distribution simply needs to be unpacked to a directory where PHP can access the scripts, usually something like /var/www/html/phplot.

```
$ cp phplot-4.4.6.tar.gz /var/www/html
$ cd /var/www/html
$ tar xvfz phplot-4.4.6.tar.gz
$ mv phplot-4.4.6 phplot
```

Beginning with version v.0.9.6b22, ACID uses another graphing library— JPGraph instead of PHPlot. It is available from www.aditus.nu/jpgraph and can be installed in the same way:

```
$ cp jpgraph1.8.tar.gz /var/www/html
$ cd /var/www/html
$ tar xvfz jpgraph1.8.tar.gz
$ mv jpgraph1.8/src jpgraph
```

You can check to see if the PHPlot library was successfully installed by trying to view an /phplot/examples/test_setup.php URL on your Web server. If the installation was successful, you will see something similar to Figure 8.3.

Finally, you will need to install ADODB—an abstraction layer for PHP interaction with the database. This library is available at http://php.weblogs.com/adodb and is installed in the same way as previously described:

```
$ cp adodb122.tgz /var/www/html
$ cd /var/www/html
$ tar xvfz adodb122.tgz
$ mv adodb122 adodb
```

Figure 8.3 PHPlot Is Successfully Installed on a Web Server

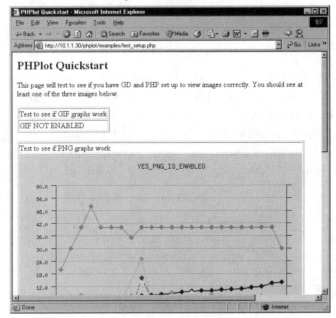

MySQL or PostgreSQL

The underlying database probably is already installed—you simply need to follow general recommendations for setting up database logging with Snort. If it is not installed, you can use Red Hat packages from distribution or download some from www.mysql.com .The setup of database logging is described in Chapter 7, "Understanding the Output Options," in the section *Snortdb*. We will assume that Snort is set up to log in to MySQL database called snort_db, which is located on the same host as the Web server. MySQL user used for logging is "snort," and the password is "password."You can use other values; just make sure that you set up proper permissions for database users. The Snort configuration file snort.conf must have the following line to log in to our database:

```
output database: log, mysql, user=snort password=password dbname=snort_db
host=10.1.1.30
```

Database tables need to be set up properly. There is a script *create_mysql* included in the Snort distribution (in /contrib subdirectory, also there is one for PostgreSQL setup) that when run creates all necessary tables. Scripts can also be downloaded from http://cvs.sourceforge.net/cgi-bin/viewcvs.cgi/snort/snort/ contrib. It can be run as follows:

```
# mysqladmin -u root -p create snort_db
# mysql -u root -p
mysql> connect snort_db
mysql> source create_mysql
```

Next, create two users ("snort" for allowing Snort sensor to log in to database, and "acid" for ACID console to manipulate the data in the same database) and set passwords for them. You can omit the *DELETE* privilege here so the corresponding user will not be able to delete records from the database. For example, you can create a copy of the ACID console that will work under the user account that can browse events, but not delete them.

```
mysql>grant INSERT, SELECT on snort_db.* to snort;
mysql>grant INSERT, SELECT on snort_db.* to snort@%;
mysql> grant CREATE, INSERT, SELECT, DELETE, UPDATE on snort.* to acid;
mysql>grant CREATE, INSERT, SELECT, DELETE, UPDATE on snort.* to acid@%;
```

Finally, set passwords for these users:

```
mysql>connect mysql
mysql> set password for 'snort'@'localhost' = password('password');
mysql> set password for 'snort'@'%' = password('password');
mysql> set password for 'acid'@'localhost' = password('acidpassword');
mysql> set password for 'acid'@'%' = password('acidpassword');
mysql> flush privileges;
mysql> exit
```

Please note that without the *flush privileges* command, no changes in password and privilege settings will become effective.

Activating ACID

ACID installation is also simple—you need to pack the set of scripts in a location under Web server root directory, for example:

```
$ cp acid-0.9.6.tar.gz /var/www/html
$ cd /var/www/html
$ tar xvfz acid-0.9.6.tar.gz
```

It is also possible to install several copies of ACID under different locations and configure them for working with other databases, other database users/ passwords, protect access to those directories with different Web server passwords, and so forth. These copies will be entirely independent.

Now that we are finished installing packages, let's proceed to ACID configuration.

Configuring ACID

First we need to set up some parameters for ACID to work with the database. The main configuration file for ACID is an acid_conf.php file located in the ACID directory on a Web server. Table 8.1 lists the most important parameters.

Table 8.1 ACID Database Configuration Parameters

Command	Description
$DBlib_path	Full path to the ADODB installation (Note: do not include a trailing "\" character in any of the path variables)
$Dbtype	Type of the database used ("mysql", "postgres")
$alert_dbname	Alert database name
$alert_host	Alert database server
$alert_port	Port on which MySQL or PostgreSQL server is listening (no need to change it if the default port is used)
$alert_user	Username for the alert database
$alert_password	Password for the username

In our case, they are configured as follows:

```
$DBlib_path = "/var/www/html/adodb"
$DBtype = "mysql"
$alert_dbname = "snort_db"
$alert_host ="10.1.1.30"
$alert_user ="acid"
$alert_password ="acidpassword"
```

Another set of database parameters can be used for archiving alerts (moving them from the active database to a backup one):

- **$archive_dbname** Archive/backup database name
- **$archive_host** Archive database server
- **$archive_port** Port number for archive database server
- **$archive_user** Username for archive database
- **$archive_password** Password for this username

They are similar to the previous ones. The following parameters might need to be set up:

- **$ChartLib_path** This creates a full path to the PHPlot install (/in our case, var/www/phplot).

- **$chart_file_format** The file format options are *gif*, *png*, or *jpeg*. We will be using *png*.

- **$portscan_file** This creates a full path to a Snort portscan log file. This allows processing of portscan data generated by Snort *portscan* preprocessor. Usually this data is not logged to a database.

It is always a good idea to protect access to the ACID pages by a Web server password. As an example, we will require a user name "admin" and password "adminpassword" from a user trying to access the location /acid on a Web server via the Web browser.

```
# mkdir /usr/lib/apache/passwords
# htpasswd -c /usr/lib/apache/passwords/.htpasswd admin
(enter "adminpassword" at the prompt)
```

Then the following lines need to be added to httpd.conf file—a configuration file for httpd daemon. In Red Hat, this file is located in the /etc/httpd/conf directory.

```
<Directory "/var/www/html/acid">
AuthType Basic
AuthName "ACID console"
AuthUserFile /usr/lib/apache/passwords/.htpasswd
Require user admin
AllowOverride None
</Directory>
```

After making these changes, you need to restart httpd daemon:

```
/etc/init.d/httpd restart
```

Now we are ready to connect to the console for the first time. Accessing the URL http://10.1.1.30/acid first brings up a request for a password, and then the page shown in Figure 8.4 appears.

This means that there are some tables missing. ACID adds extra tables to the database. Clicking on the link **Setup page** runs a script that updates the database with the required tables (Figure 8.5).

Figure 8.4 Initial Setup for ACID-Specific Tables

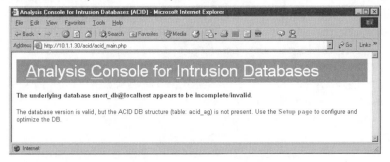

Figure 8.5 Setting Up ACID Tables

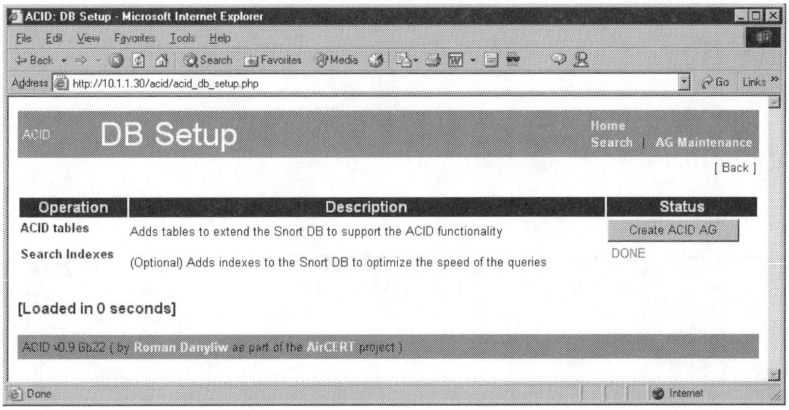

After clicking the **Create ACID AG** button, we are ready to start using ACID.

Damage & Defense…

ACID Security

As you probably noticed, there are no security features embedded in ACID itself; therefore, to ensure security of its setup you will need to do additional tweaking. Your requirements will determine which tools you will use.

For one, you might be interested in using SSL (HTTPS connections) or TLS instead of plaintext communications between the browser and the server. In Apache, this is achieved by using the mod_ssl module (www.modssl.org).

Continued

As you have previously seen, access to the ACID console can be restricted by using native Web server authentication mechanisms—passwords or certificates. As was also previously mentioned, it might be useful to create at least two separate copies of ACID and configure one of them with only read database permissions. To restrict permissions for a specific copy of ACID, simply revoke the *DELETE* privilege from the database user configured in this copy.

The most important security issue is that all database passwords are hardcoded in the PHP scripts in cleartext, so extreme caution needs to be applied to the host configuration. Any exposure of source code for PHP scripts will expose the password to an attacker.

Using ACID

Using ACID is rather simple. Its screens are self-explanatory most of the time. Let's look at the main screen (Figure 8.6).

Figure 8.6 ACID Main Screen

![Screenshot of the Analysis Console for Intrusion Databases (ACID) main screen in Microsoft Internet Explorer. Address bar shows http://10.1.1.30/acid/acid_main.php. The page header reads "Analysis Console for Intrusion Databases". Text shows: Added 0 alert(s) to the Alert cache. Queried on: Mon February 10, 2003 21:07:43. Database: snortdb@localhost (schema version: 106). Time window: [2003-01-28 19:06:31] - [2003-01-28 19:12:51]. Sensors: 1, Unique Alerts: 46 (7 categories), Total Number of Alerts: 230. Source IP addresses: 3, Dest. IP addresses: 2, Unique IP links 4. Source Ports: 80, TCP (78) UDP (2), Dest. Ports: 78, TCP (77) UDP (2). Traffic Profile by Protocol: TCP (65%), UDP (34%), ICMP (< 1%), Portscan Traffic (0%).]

This screen shows the general statistics for ACID; namely, the number of alerts divided by protocol, the counts of source and destination ports for triggered

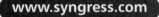

rules, and so forth. Clicking on a link provides additional details about the particular category. Figure 8.7 provides an example listing of all of the unique alerts (alerts grouped by the triggered rule).

Figure 8.7 Unique Alerts

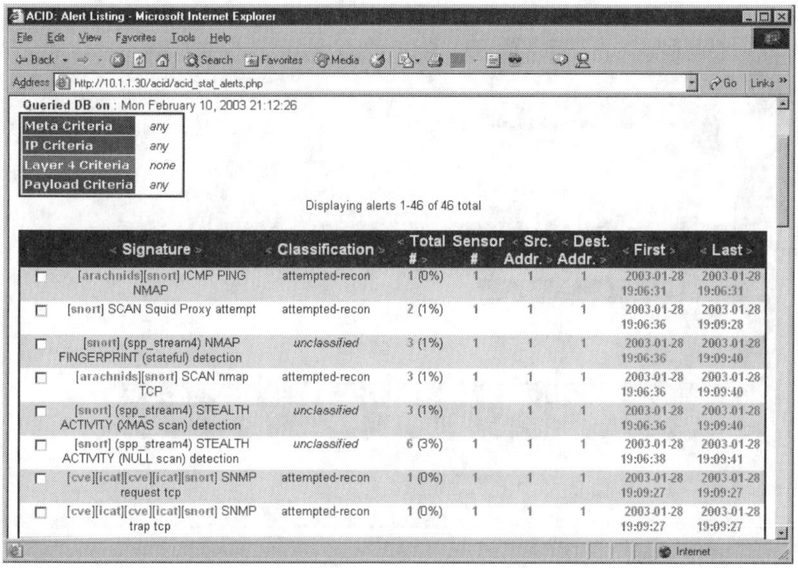

Each line (alert) has several clickable fields; the most interesting of these are probably the classification field and the references to various attack databases links (for example, lArachnids or CVE). This data is taken from rules when Snort logs an alert to the database. If you click on the **cve** link in the line that has such a link in the *Signature* field, you will be taken to the description of this attack in CVE (a database of vulnerabilities). The Snort link leads to the similar description on the www.snort.org site. Classification helps group attacks by their type, which is also set up in Snort rules file.

Each individual packet logged can be displayed in a decoded format, showing various flags, options, and packet contents (Figure 8.8).

The unique alert display can be used for checking any "noisy" signatures and tuning them. You can sort the listing in ascending or descending order of number of alerts, and then select the ones that are triggered more often. Sorting is done by clicking on a corresponding arrow (> or <) in the header of the relevant column (Figure 8.7).

Figure 8.8 Displaying a Single Alert

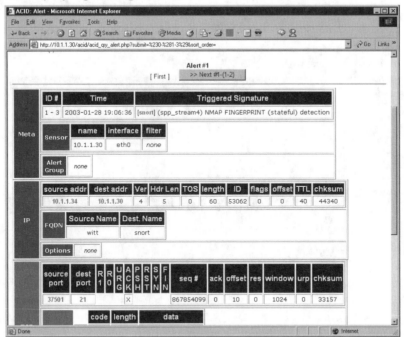

Querying the Database

One of the most important features of ACID is its searching tools. It is possible to create database queries with many parameters—from signature type to packet payload contents (provided that this information has been logged in the database). The main search screen is shown in Figure 8.9.

As you can see, in the Meta Criteria section it is possible to specify different Snort sensors (in a case when you have many sensors storing data in the same database), search in a specific alert group only (more about alert groups in the next section), and match signatures (exactly or by a substring in their name), classification, and time periods. It is also possible to search only for packets with specific Layer 3 and Layer 4 information, plus perform a context search inside captured packets' payload. For example, let's find all alerts triggered by signatures related to Nmap scanner. This can be achieved by specifying the *signature* field in *meta criteria* as *roughly = NMAP* and clicking the **Query DB** button. The result of this query is shown in Figure 8.10.

Figure 8.9 Search Parameters

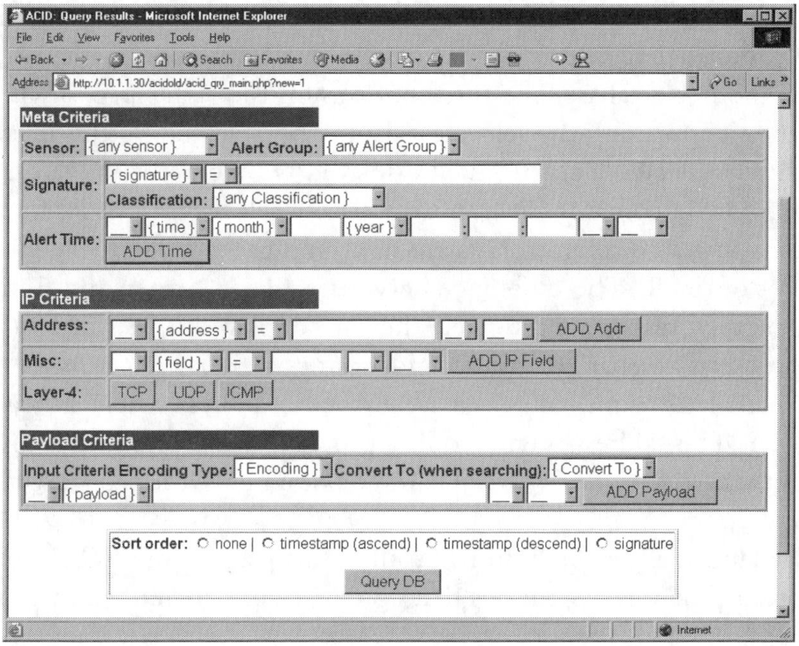

Figure 8.10 All NMAP-Related Alerts from the Database

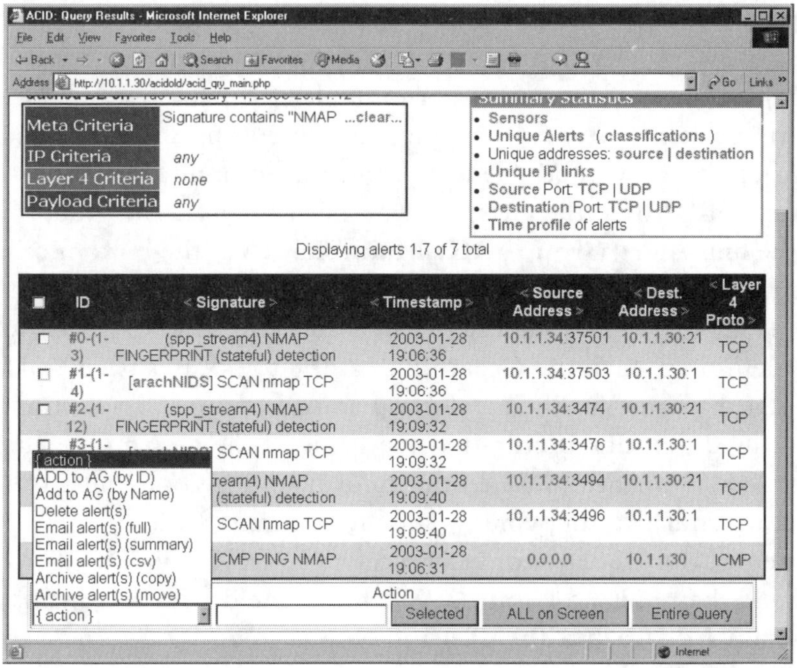

In the bottom-left corner is an *action* field, which specifies possible actions that can be done with the results of the query. The displayed alerts can be added to an alert group, deleted from the database, e-mailed in various formats, or archived to another database. The three buttons on the right specify which alerts are used when performing the selected action. The Selected button means that only specifically selected alerts from all displayed will be used (the leftmost column of the table contains check boxes for row selection). The ALL on Screen button means that all displayed alerts are used, and the Entire Query button uses the entire set of results. The difference between ALL on Screen and Entire Query is that when many results are returned, they are displayed in sets of 50 (by default, which can be changed in the acid_conf.php file).

The Email alerts action takes as a parameter an address where the results should be sent. This address is entered in a provided field. The Add to AG action also takes a parameter—an *alert group* name or number. Other actions do not need parameters.

Actually, almost all of the buttons on the front page of the ACID console are simply shortcuts for various queries that could be constructed via main search interface.

Alert Groups

Alert groups are entities used to logically group various alerts and attach annotations to sets of events (alerts). An alert group has a number, a text name, and an optional annotation or commentary. For example, if you are researching a particular intrusion incident, you might be interested in putting all of the related alerts into one group, so you will be able to reference it in running queries, e-mailing results, and so forth. To do the grouping, you need to create the group first. When you click the link **Alert Group (AG) Maintenance** at the bottom of the ACID main screen, you are presented with the window shown in Figure 8.11.

In our example, we are using the ID of **1** and the name **first group**. To create another group, click the **Create** link at the top of this page. You will be asked to enter the name for the new group and an optional description. For our example we used **grinder incident** as the name of the new group. The group ID is generated automatically. When this information is saved, the list of the groups appears similar to the window shown in Figure 8.12.

Now we can run a query (for example, let's search for all SNMP-related alerts) and add the results to Group 2. When presented with the query results, select an action **Add to AG (by ID)** and enter **2** as an ID. Alternatively, you can use **ADD to AG (by Name)** and enter the name given to our group. After clicking **Entire Query**, all search results will be added to the specified group. Figure 8.13 shows how the parameters are entered in the Query Results screen, and Figure 8.14 displays the resulting listing of the groups.

Figure 8.11 Listing of Alert Groups

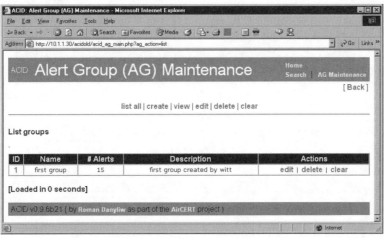

Figure 8.12 Creating a New Group

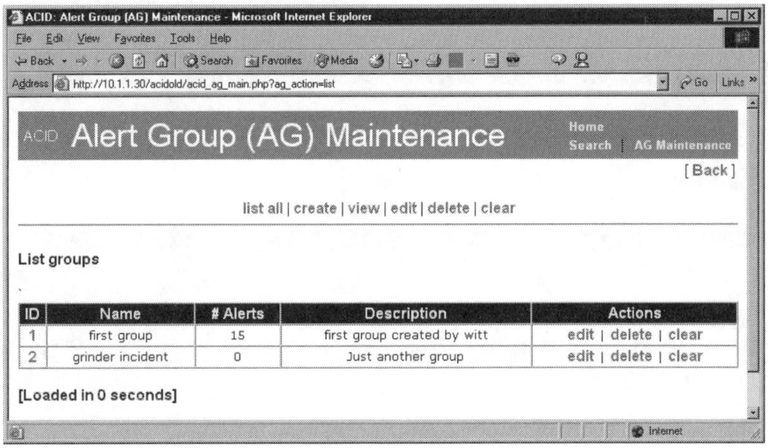

Figure 8.13 Adding Search Results to an Alert Group

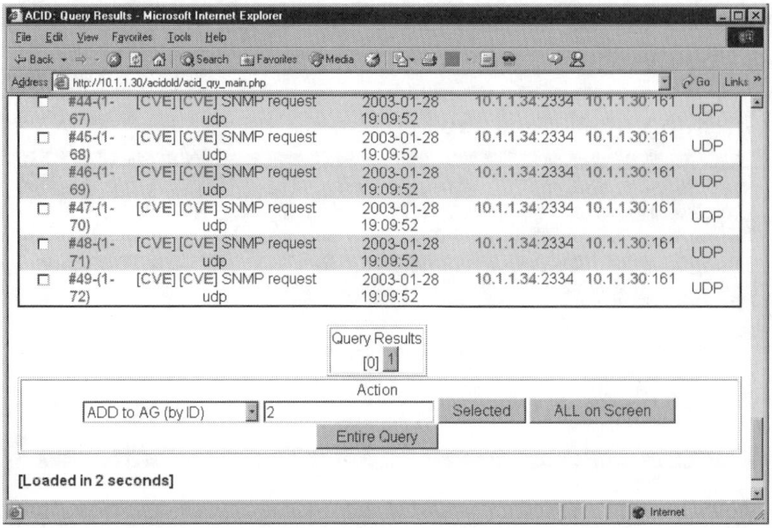

Figure 8.14 Result of Alert Grouping

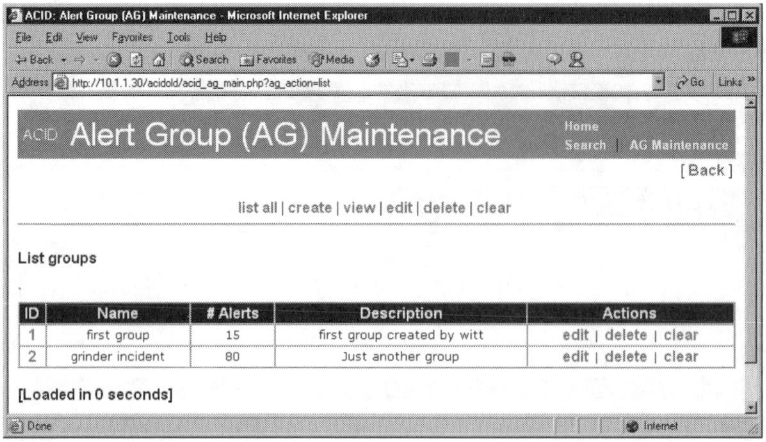

Each group can be modified:

- The Edit link presents you with the screen for modifying the group's name and description.

- The Delete link deletes the group. It does not delete the alerts, only the group as a logical entity.

- The Clear link clears a group's contents by ungrouping all alerts from it; it does not delete the alerts from the database.

Database maintenance is described in the section *Managing Alert Databases*.

OINK!

An alert can be part of multiple groups simultaneously.

Graphical Features of ACID

ACID has a tool that can produce a graphical summary of alerts based on date periods, alert group membership, source and destination ports, and IP addresses. An interface for the graph generation is shown in Figure 8.15.

Figure 8.15 Alert Graphing

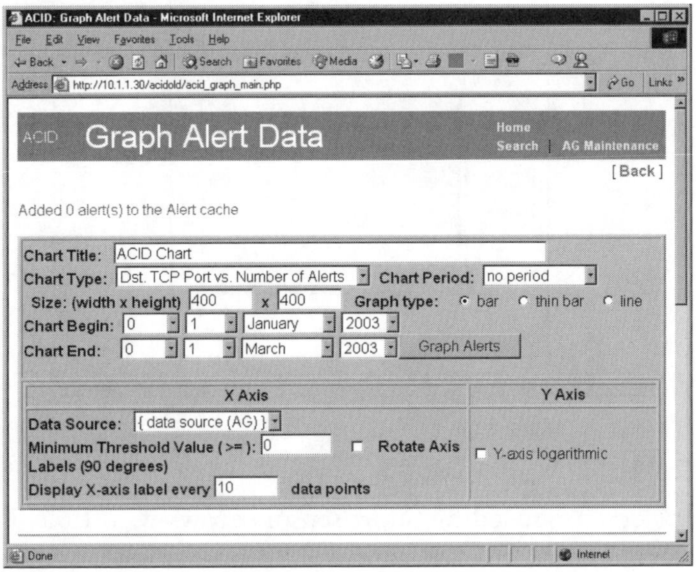

Many of the features within the graph parameters are relatively self-explanatory.

- The Chart Type parameter allows for the selection of a specific type of graph to be generated.

- The Data Source parameter allows limiting alerts by date, specified by the Chart Begin and Chart End parameters, and by alert group. If you select an alert group in this drop-down box, only alerts from this group will be used as a source data set.

Another interesting feature is the Chart Period parameter. If nothing is selected here, the X-axis will list either all dates or all ports/IPs depending on the chart type. If you select a period such as a week or a day, all alerts are grouped by day of the week or hour of the day. This allows creation of statistics such as daily distribution of alerts depending on a day of the week or time of day. Try it, and you will see that most attacks usually happen during the night and/or on weekends (at least the script-kiddies attacks, which amount to the biggest part of intrusion traffic). Figure 8.16 shows a sample ACID chart.

Figure 8.16 A Sample ACID Chart

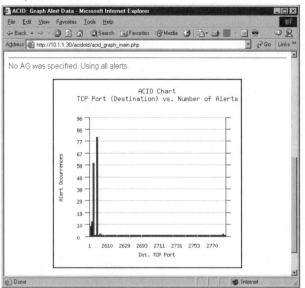

Managing Alert Databases

The database of alerts produced by Snort sensors grows with time. If a significant number of alerts are logged, the database will become quite large, resulting in slow searches. To keep the alert database to a manageable size, there are various methods you can employ.

The simplest management technique is referred to as *trimming*. Simply put, trimming translates to deleting the uninteresting, and older alerts triggered by false positives. If you want to delete an alert or a set of alerts, run a query that includes the alert as one of the results, choose **Delete Alerts** action in the Results screen, and press the corresponding button:

- Click **Selected** if you want to delete only part of alerts displayed.

- Click **All on Screen** to delete all displayed alerts.
- Click **Entire Query** to delete all results of the current query.

Another management technique is *archiving*. Archiving is the process in which you move the undesired alerts to another database. To use this feature, you need to create a second database in exactly the same way that the main one was created. This is accomplished by using the *create_mysql* or *create_postgresql* scripts (for information on how to use these scripts, please review the section *Installing ACID Prerequisites* in this chapter). Let's assume that this database is called *snort_archive*. After that, you need to specify parameters of this database in *acid_conf.php* file; for example:

```
$archive_dbname = "snort_db"
$archive_host ="10.1.1.30"
$archive_user ="acid"
$archive_password ="acidpassword"
```

Now after running a query it is possible to select an action **Archive alerts (move)** or **Archive alerts (copy)**. After one of the buttons **Selected**, **ALL on Screen**, or **Entire Query** is pressed, corresponding alerts are moved (or copied) in the archive database (Figure 8.17 shows the successful results of copying). You can set up a second copy of ACID in another Web server directory and specify this archive database as active for this copy. After that, you will be able to browse the archive as well.

Figure 8.17 Successful Copying of One Alert to the Archive Database

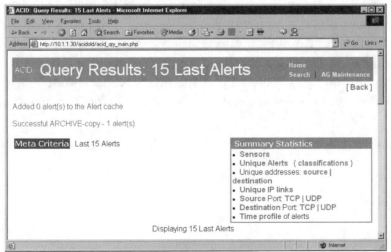

To sum up, ACID is currently probably the best open-source GUI tool for interactive Snort event analysis.

Using SnortSnarf

SnortSnarf is a Perl script, which takes Snort log files (it also has a plug-in for accessing MySQL databases), parses them, and produces a set of static Web pages with the results, grouping Snort alerts by signatures, IP addresses, and providing Web links to additional informational resources for detected attacks. Its distribution package also includes CGI scripts for creating incidents reports based on groups of alerts. SnortSnarf can be run as a cron job at regular intervals or run manually from time to time. The following formats of log files are supported (in addition to MySQL databases):

- Snort alerts files (either standard or –A fast type)
- syslog files containing some Snort entries
- spp_portscan log files
- spp_portscan2 log files

It is also possible to have SnortSnarf reference rules definition files and extract detailed information about attacks, linking it with individual alerts.

Installing SnortSnarf

SnortSnarf can be found at www.silicondefense.com/software/snortsnarf/ SnortSnarf-052301.1.tar.gz, and on the accompanying CD-ROM. Basic installation of SnortSnarf is not overly complicated. If you have Perl 5 installed on your host and a Web server running, the installation can be completed with the addition of single Perl module, specifically *Time::JulianDay*. This module is included in the distribution in the Time-modules subdirectory. This module is installed as many other Perl modules—you need to run the following commands in the subdirectory:

```
perl Makefile.PL
make
make test
make install
```

It may also be useful to copy the contents of the /include subdirectory of SnortSnarf distribution package to a place where the Perl interpreter will be able to find them; For example, *site_perl* or a directory where SnortSnarf will be run.

To produce a set of Web pages from alert files, you need to execute the following command:

```
./snortsnarf.pl -rulesfile rules-file -rulesdir rules-subdirectory -d
destination-folder source-file1 ... source-fileN
```

For example (the line is wrapped):

```
./snortsnarf.pl -rulesfile /etc/snort/snort.conf -rulesdir /etc/snort -d
/var/web/www/snarf /var/log/snort/alert
```

This command will run SnortSnarf on a /var/log/snort/alert file, place the results in /var/web/www/snarf directory, and in the process make reference to rules descriptions from the /etc/snort/snort.conf configuration file. If you point your Web browser to the corresponding location, you will see a page similar to Figure 8.18.

Figure 8.18 SnortSnarf Results

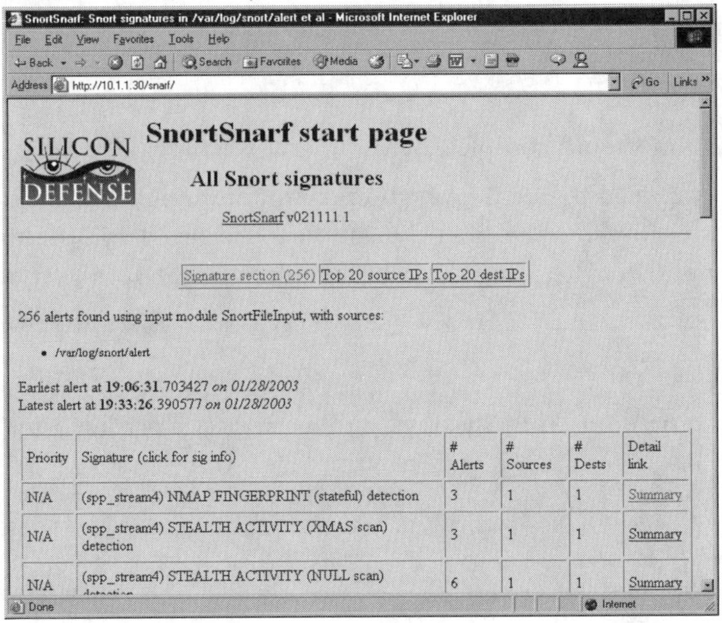

Provided links allow further exploration of displayed alerts.

Configuring Snort to Work with SnortSnarf

Now that you have seen the basic functionality of SnortSnarf, let's see a full example of its configuration. Assume that we already unpacked SnortSnarf in the /usr/local/src/snortsnarf directory. You should now complete the following steps:

1. Copy SnortSnarf script to the /etc directory and put the corresponding include files in the subdirectory site-perl.

```
#>cd /usr/local/src/snortsnarf/Time-modules
#>perl Makefile.pl
#>make
#>make test
#>make install
#>cp /usr/local/src/snortsnarf/include/SnortSnarf /usr/lib/perl5/site-perl/5.6.0
#>cp /usr/local/src/snortsnarf/snortsnarf.pl /etc
```

2. Perform a test run of SnortSnarf (provided that Snort is already running and logging to /var/log/snort/alert file, the default setting) using the command:

```
#>perl /etc/snortsnarf.pl -d /var/www/html/snortsnarf /var/log/snort/alert
```

This action should complete without any warnings or errors.

3. Now we need to add a crontab entry for running SnortSnarf regularly; in this example, we will set the action to occur every 30 minutes. This is accomplished by adding the following line to the root's crontab:

```
30 * * * * perl /etc/snortsnarf.pl -d /var/www/html/snortsnarf -refresh=30 /var/log/snort/alert
```

This can be done in many ways, either via editing crontab manually using the *crontab -e* command, or, for example:

```
#>cd /etc/cron.d
#>cat > SnortSnarf
30 * * * * perl /etc/snortsnarf.pl -d /var/www/html/snortsnarf -refresh=30 /var/log/snort/alert
<Ctrl>d
#>crontab -u root SnortSnarf
```

The *refresh=30* option will make SnortSnarf generate Web pages and force the browser to refresh them every 30 minutes.

Basic Usage of SnortSnarf

Now that the SnortSnarf process has been automated, let's browse through some of the pages it provides. The main page (Figure 8.18) shows the total number of alerts, the date range of the alerts, the source of the alerts, and a summary screen of the various alerts. For each signature, the summary listing includes the signature name, total number of alerts, number of sources, number of destinations, and a Summary link for all signatures of that type. On the Summary screen are links pointing for further information (Figure 8.19). This information is taken from the rules description, so you will need to run SnortSnarf with the *-rulesfile option* if you want to use this feature.

Figure 8.19 Summary for "WEB-CGI uploader.exe access" Signature

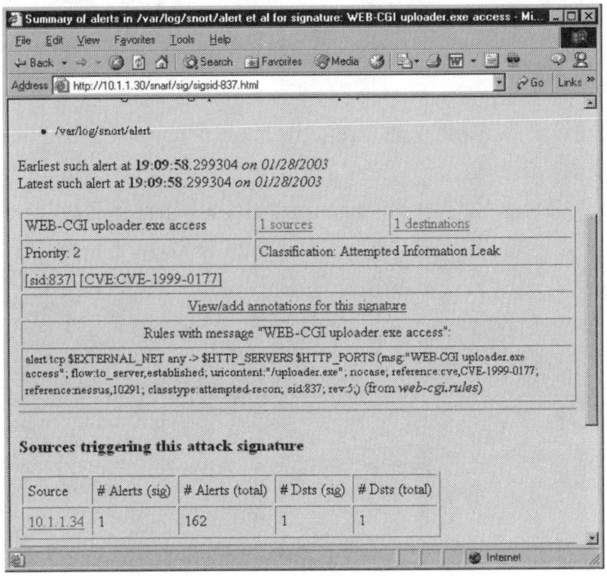

Clicking on the links **[sid:837]** or **[CVE:CVE-1999-0177]** will take you to either the snort.org site or the Common Vulnerabilities and Events (CVE) database, respectively, where more detailed explanation of this signature can be found.

The Top 20 source IPs link will display a summary of the 20 IP addresses that regularly appear as an attack source (Figure 8.20).

The IP links present in the Source IP column will take you to a page displaying a summary of signatures triggered by the traffic from this particular source. This summary page also contains links that will help you discover to whom this IP address belongs—whois lookups, DNS lookups, and so forth.

Figure 8.20 Top 20 Attacking IPs

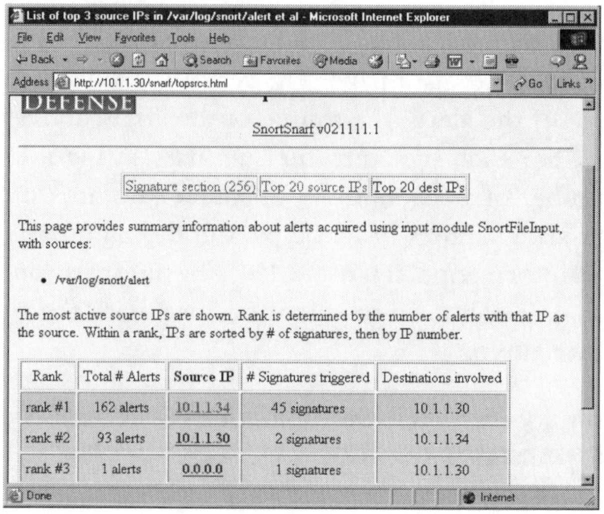

Optional features of SnortSnarf include a tool for creating incidents reports. This feature resembles the ACID alert grouping and e-mailing. Its install is described in README.SISR in SnortSnarf distribution package.

The SnortSnarf script has many options other than those described in this section. It is possible to specify various filters by:

- Sensor ID
- Alert priority
- Date
- Time

The main difference with ACID is that you need to specify everything on the command line and not interactively. To sum up, SnortSnarf (similarly to ACID) helps you to bring data together. The format is such that potential problems can be easily analyzed and researched. This analysis will verify if there was an incident, and Snort alert logs and system log files will provide data of what was possibly compromised. When a security incident occurs, the link in the SnortSnarf browser window will allow the analyst to review the incident data and start looking for ways to prevent further incursions. This further research and analysis of SnortSnarf reports will help provide enough information to make incident-related decisions. The analysis should help identify if your defense in-depth plan failed. With this knowledge of what failed, where it failed, and how it failed, plans can be made on how to prevent unauthorized access in the future.

Using IDScenter

IDScenter (www.packx.net) is a program for Windows-based Snort installations. IDScenter provides centralized rule management, Snort process monitoring, alert monitoring, reporting, and various features for blocking attacks (via plug-ins). Other goodies include an integrated XML log viewer, and Web browser capabilities for checking reference information for detected attacks.

The full set of features is available in the current version 1.1; however, RC2 also contains the following:

- Snort 1.9/1.8/1.7 support.

- Snort service mode support (IDScenter takes over control of the Snort service).

- Snort Configuration wizard, which allows setting of Snort variables, configuration of preprocessor plug-ins, output plug-ins, and specifying rulesets.

- A ruleset editor that supports all Snort 1.9.1 rule options, including import of rules from files or Web sites into existing rulesets.

- AutoBlock plug-ins that allows writing your own plug-ins (DLL) for your firewall. One plug-in for ISS NetworkICE BlackICE Defender is included (possibility to block IPs, TCP and UDP ports, ICMP packets, set block duration). It also includes a Delphi framework for writing new plug-ins for other firewalls.

- Alert notification via e-mail, alarm sound, or only visual notification. Notification features include the possibility to send the specified number of lines from the Snort log, and checking of alerts logged not only to a text file but MySQL database, too. It can be configured to add attachments for e-mails it sends, such as the current process list.

- Testing of configuration.

- Monitoring, which allows it to monitor up to 10 alert files and MySQL database.

- Log rotation capabilities for compressing and archiving log files according to the specified schedule.

- An integrated log viewer for text log files, XML logs, plus an HTML viewer.

- Ability to execute a program if an attack is detected.

As you can see, it includes most of the features that Windows-based installations lack. The same functionality can be achieved on UNIX by using the tools described earlier in this chapter—Swatch, ACID, SnortSnarf, and possibly a Webmin module for Snort configuration.

Oink!

If you are interested in Webmin, the package is available from www.webmin.com, and the Snort module for it can be downloaded from www.snort.org/dl/contrib/front_ends/webmin_plugin/snort-1.0.wbm. Webmin is also available on the accompanying CD, and details for installation can be found in Chapter 3, "Installing Snort."

Although it is nice to have all of the functionality combined into a single program instead of combining three or four of them, remember that a monolithic tool will always lack some flexibility. For example, ACID is still the best when it comes to database browsing and exploration of alert data, and Swatch is more flexible in configuring alert matching and reporting.

Installing IDScenter

Before installing IDScenter, you will need to follow the common procedure of installing Snort on a Windows machine (for more details on installing Snort, please refer to Chapter 3). Do not forget to install WinPCAP (http://winpcap.polito.it), as it is used by both Snort and IDScenter (this installation is also described in detail in Chapter 3 and should be reviewed prior to attempting to install IDScenter). The IDScenter package is available for download at www.packx.net (and on the accompanying CD-ROM) and includes a graphical installer that simplifies the installation process of IDScenter.

When the IDScenter application is started, it moves to the system tray and is displayed as a big black dot. Clicking on this icon opens the configuration window (Figure 8.21).

Figure 8.21 Main Configuration Screen of IDScenter

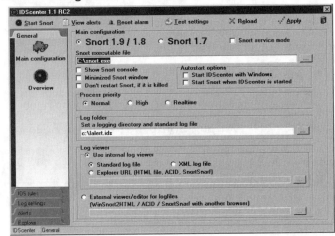

Configuring IDScenter

The simplicity of IDScenter installation process is compensated with the sheer number of configuration options that it provides. Each of five main sections contains a number of panels, and each of these panels includes many switches and entry fields. The five main sections are as follows:

- General

- IDS Rules

- Log settings

- Alerts

- Explorer

At the top of the IDScenter window are main control buttons with self-explanatory names: Stop Snort, View alerts, Reset alarm, Test settings (which basically runs Snort with the *-T* switch in order to test current configuration created by IDScenter), Reload, and Apply. Before you start using IDScenter, you have to perform some basic steps to create a minimal working configuration and then possibly change it to suit your own needs.

Minimal Configuration of IDScenter

The most basic IDScenter configuration requires that you configure a number of things.

On the General/Main configuration panel you will need to configure:

- The version of Snort you are using
- Snort process priority
- Location of Snort executable
- Log file

On the IDS Rules/Snort configuration panel, you will need to configure:

- The location of the configuration file
- External editor for rule files (such as Notepad.exe, for example)

The IDS Rules tab can be used for specifying other parameters stored in the Snort configuration file.

The Log Settings panel is used to configure the logging parameters of the various logging options of your choice.

The Alerts tab is used to configure alert detection for at least one Snort log file, which will be monitored by IDScenter for alerts.

After filling in these parameters, click **Apply**; this will generate IDScenter configuration. If you forgot something vital, the program will inform you about this problem (these messages can also be located on the General/Overview panel). See Figure 8.22 for an example report of an incomplete configuration.

Figure 8.22 Errors in IDScenter Configuration

![IDScenter 1.1 RC2 configuration window showing configuration errors including "Log settings: Snort log folder doesn't exist" and "Alert detection: Files not specified for alert detection", with Snort commandline C:\snort.exe -c "D:\rules\snort.conf" -l "c:"]

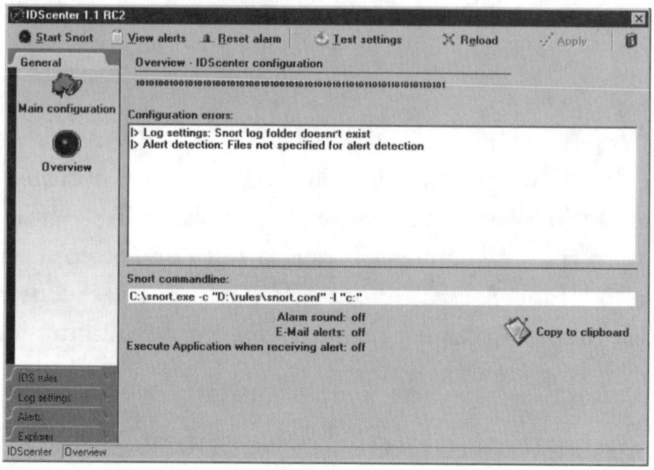

If there were no errors, IDScenter reports that the configuration script was successfully created (this message appears on the bottom line of the window).

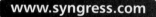

Basic Usage of IDScenter

As noted previously, the main goal of IDScenter is to simplify the process of configuring Snort. Let's walk through the screens dealing with Snort setup and see exactly how the configuration is done. The first screen is shown in Figure 8.21. Most of the options displayed there are self-explanatory. The less obvious options are as follows:

- The Show Snort console will start the Snort process with an open console window and not just as a background Windows process.

- The Minimized Snort window will minimize this window.

- The Snort Service mode starts Snort as a Windows service.

- The Process priority options are used to select the priority level for Snort process (and not for the IDScenter itself).

- The Log file input box allows for the selection of a file (full path) where the Snort logs are stored. The same file (only the filename without the directory) must be later given as a parameter to the output plug-in for the IDS Rules/Output plug-ins option.

- The IDS Rules section helps in creating and editing of Snort rules files.

- The Snort Config screen displays the selected rules file and allows hand editing of its contents. There are also some wizards provided. Specifically the Network variables, Preprocessors, Output plug-ins and Rules/ Signatures options.

Oink!

If a preprocessor plug-in is not known to IDScenter, its configuration will be lost the next time you store the configuration (by clicking **Apply**). Conversely, if there are unknown output plug-ins, IDScenter will preserve their configuration.

- The Variables wizard displays all variables found in the Snort rules file and provides tools for their editing. If you click on a variable (for example, **HOME_NET**), you will see the display shown in Figure 8.23.

Figure 8.23 Using the Variable Wizard

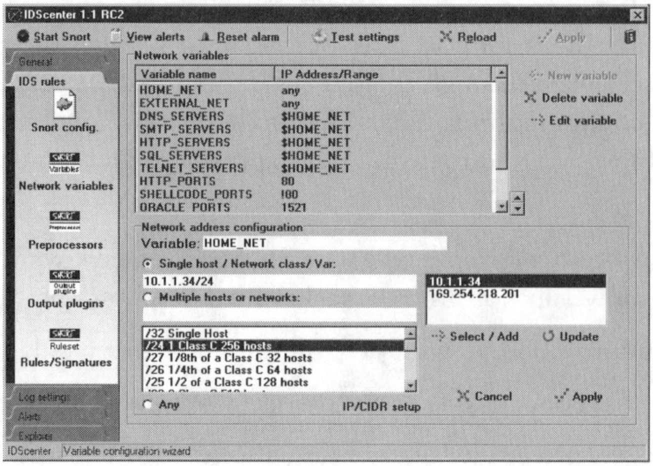

In the bottom part of this screen you can choose between various options for specifying the value of this variable:

- Single host/Network class/Var
- Multiple hosts or networks
- Any

When specifying IP address and netmasks for networks, you can use the selection from the box on the right, which lists IP addresses of all interfaces found on the host, and standard netmasks, which are displayed together with their description in the bottom-left corner. Clicking **Apply** in the bottom-right corner updates the value of selected variables.

The Preprocessors screen currently allows configuration of the following pre-processor plug-ins:

- stream4 stateful inspection and stream reassembly
- portscan/portscan2 detection
- frag2 defrag
- IP protocol conversation
- http_decode
- Telnet/FTP decode
- Back Orifice detection

- rpc_decode
- ARP spoof detection

All check boxes and entry fields that appear on this screen are translated into corresponding plug-in options and stored in the Snort configuration file (Figure 8.24).

Figure 8.24 Configuring Protocol Preprocessors

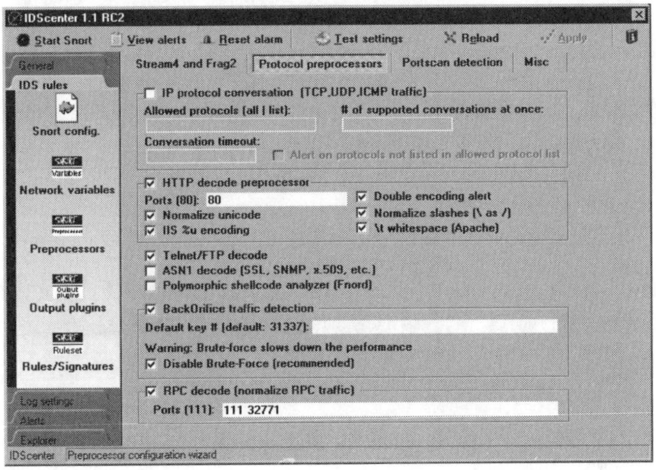

Another very useful wizard is available for the configuration of output plug-ins. This allows configuration of all types of output that Snort currently supports. You do not need to know the names for plug-in parameters and their placement—simply select which plug-in you want configured and fill in the appearing entry fields (Figure 8.25). This wizard also allows creation of custom rule types as collections of output plug-ins by clicking **Create type**.

Not available in any of other tool described in this chapter, IDScenter includes a ruleset editor (Figure 8.26).

As a first step in the ruleset editor configuration, you need to select a classification file by clicking on the **Select** option in the Classification file section located at the bottom of the screen. After that, you can use this screen for selecting which rulesets to include in your Snort configuration via the provided check boxes. It is possible to open a ruleset in the editor by selecting it and clicking **Edit ruleset**. This opens a screen similar to the ruleset listing, but with individual rules instead of whole rulesets as entries in the list. It is also possible to include/exclude specific rules, import rules from other files, and edit each rule. Figure 8.27 shows a screen for editing a specific rule.

Figure 8.25 Selecting and Configuring Output Options for Snort

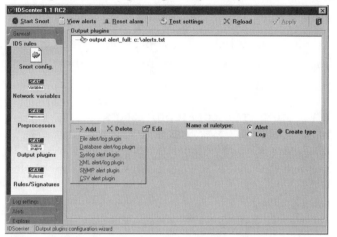

Figure 8.26 The Main Screen of the IDScenter Ruleset Editor

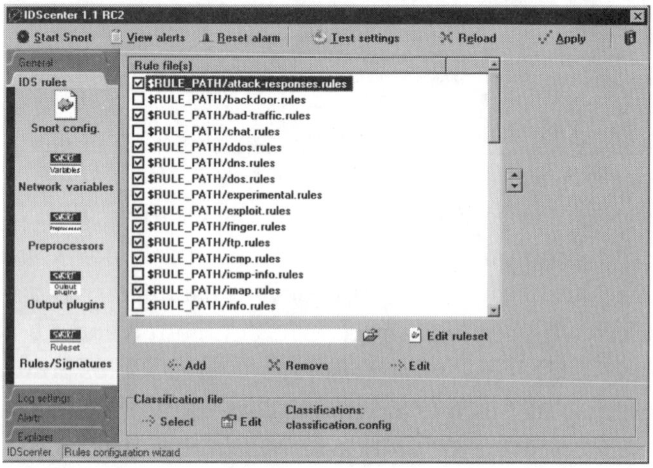

Figure 8.27 Editing "BAD TRAFFIC bad frag bits" Rule

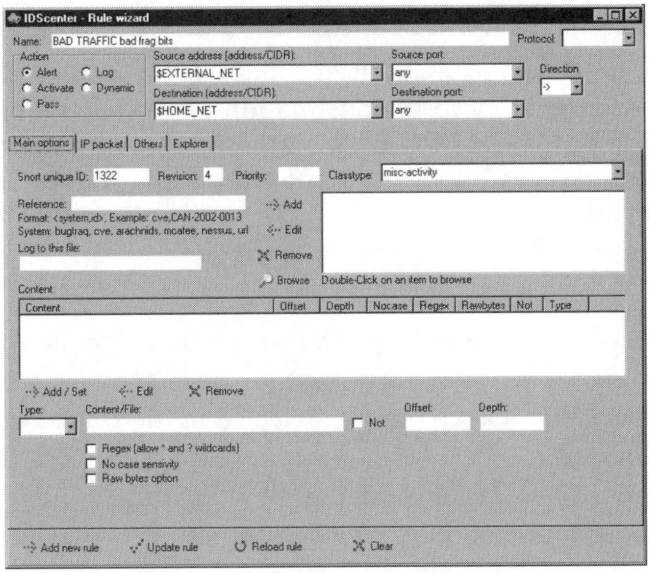

This editor supports full Snort 1.9.1 rules syntax. The Explorer tab allows browsing of information related to this rule online using references to CVS or the snort.org Web site.

The Log settings section of this window provides tools for configuring logging options (command-line parameters) of Snort and also log rotation, which is performed by IDScenter. Figure 8.28 shows the screen for log rotation configuration.

Figure 8.28 Log Rotation Settings

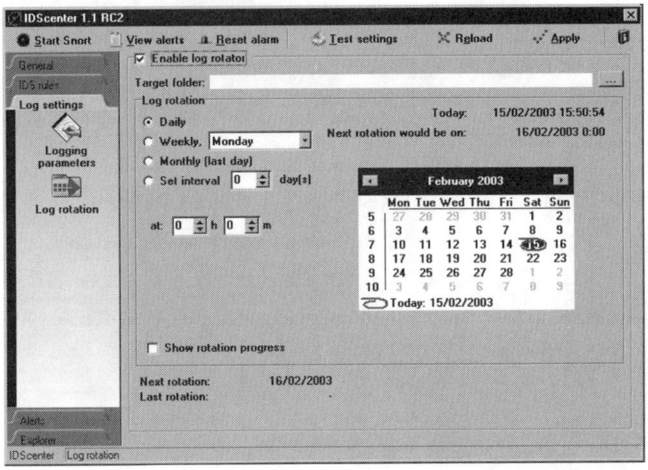

OINK!

While performing log rotation, IDScenter will move the entire contents of the source log directory to the destination where backups are stored. Therefore, do not choose for log storage the same folder that the folder Snort executable is in—it will be removed during rotation and Snort will not start again.

The Alerts section configures how IDScenter reacts when it notices a Snort alert in one of the sources it monitors—text log files, XML log files, or MySQL database. At least one data source must be selected in Alert Detection screen for this feature to work.

The Alert notification screen configures how IDScenter will react when it detects a Snort alert in one of the configured sources. It is possible to make it produce a sound (selectable), execute a command, or run a plug-in. Included are two different plug-ins for ISS/NetworkICE BlackICE firewall. The first plug-in only blocks IPs. The second plug-in can block TCP ports and UDP ports, and has also ICMP blocking support (but not all NetworkICE BlackICE versions support the ICMP rules). Figure 8.29 shows the configuration screen for ISS plug-in v2.

Figure 8.29 BlackICE AutoBlock Plug-In v2 Configuration

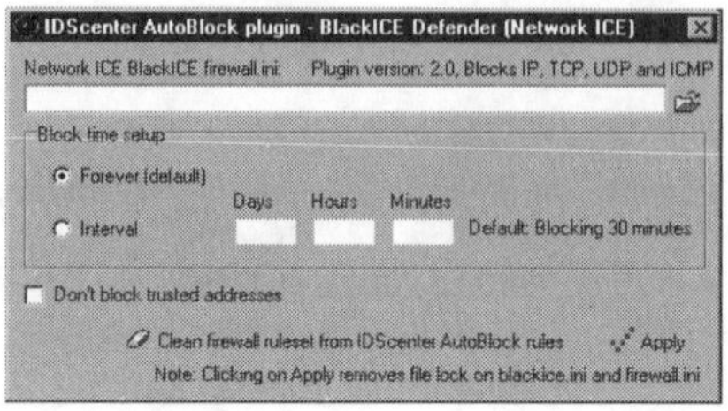

The Alertmail screen allows the user to set up an e-mail alert. This alert will be sent each time IDScenter detects a Snort event. IDScenter uses an internal e-mail client, so you only need to configure the SMTP server it should use, destination e-mail address, and optionally some messages parameters such as e-mail subject or debug logging of all SMTP sessions.

Each time IDScenter detects an alert, its icon in the system tray starts flashing. If you click on the flashing icon, an internal log viewer is opened. The internal log viewer contains the following features:

- Log search: just type a word and click **Search**. To find the next word matching the pattern, click **Search** again.

- If you select an IP address in the displayed text, this address will be displayed in the WHOIS box on the top of the Log Viewer page. The "Whois" request will give you more information about the selected IP.

- If you select something other than an IP address, the viewer sets this text in the "CVE search" field. This allows you to directly search the CVE database from viewing this log file.

- It is also possible to print a log file from this viewer.

The internal log viewer also can display Snort XML log files or Web pages (it uses Internet Explorer for Web browsing).

Altogether, IDScenter in its current state is a powerful tool for configuring Windows-based Snort installation and monitoring alerts. Its ruleset editor is the best editor available at the time of this writing. However, IDScenter lacks the ability to research and analyze alert data, which is provided by ACID and, to a certain degree, SnortSnarf.

Summary

The ultimate goal of installing and using Snort is to help a security analyst to monitor and study intrusion attempts. Currently, intrusion-related traffic on the Internet is high. If your sensor is located on a busy network, it can generate megabytes of data each day. Obviously, you need some tool to automate the process of monitoring and alerting, because it is impossible for a human to browse such a huge amount of data and come to any meaningful conclusions.

There are various tools available for this purpose. We covered four of them, each with a different functionality. Swatch is a tool for real-time log file monitoring and alerting; ACID is an interactive tool for alert database exploration and data analysis; SnortSnarf provides features for generation of static HTML reports from log files; and IDScenter is a tool for centralized management and monitoring of Snort installations on the Windows platform.

Swatch is a Perl script. It monitors your log files for specific triggers and when any of these triggers are matched, performs a certain action, such as sending a system administrator an e-mail about this event. It can monitor any text file, not just Snort alerts; for example, syslog file for brute force connection attempts. It is also useful as a tool for sorting alerts of different types into different files.

ACID is a Web-based interactive console for exploration and management of Snort alert database. It can also use data from other intrusion detection engines provided that they are somehow imported in the same database. There is a script provided in Snort distribution that is able to import some of these alerts.

ACID provides the means to perform database queries (from meta-signature level to the packet contents), and database management—trimming and archiving of selected alerts and various graphing tools. It also allows an analyst to group selected events into logical alert groups for further study or e-mail reports to specified persons.

SnortSnarf is a noninteractive tool that is supposed to be run one time or periodically as a cron job to process Snort log files and produce a set of static HTML pages with information about Snort alerts. It also allows an analyst to create alert groups and file reports, although this part of its functionality is rather cumbersome when compared to ACID.

Finally, IDScenter is a graphical tool that helps manage almost every aspect of Windows-based Snort installation. It includes a configuration file creator and a very advanced rule editor, and can monitor specified alert sources and perform actions when an alert is found.

Solutions Fast Track

Using Swatch

- ☑ Swatch is a log-monitoring tool, based on pattern matching.

- ☑ Swatch is a Perl script with a simple configuration file listing patterns and corresponding actions.

- ☑ Actions that Swatch can perform include sending e-mail and executing arbitrary commands when a specific pattern is matched.

- ☑ It is more convenient to have Swatch monitor syslog files instead of Snort alert files, because it performs matching on a line basis, and Snort logs more than one line to a standard alert file.

Using ACID

- ☑ ACID works with MySQL or PostgreSQL databases.

- ☑ To work properly, it needs a Web server with PHP 4 and a set of PHP libraries installed.

- ☑ ACID deployment can be scaled so that many different Web servers work with one database, or so that different consoles have different access rights.

- ☑ The search feature allows database exploration and correlation of events.

- ☑ Database management allows clearing of alerts or moving them into an archive database.

Using SnortSnarf

- ☑ SnortSnarf processes Snort log files and creates a set of static HTML pages with various details and correlations between data. It can process various events that are not logged to a database; for example, portscan log files.

- ☑ It is more useful to have SnortSnarf run periodically as a cron job.

☑ If you provide SnortSnarf with a reference to your rules file, it will include rule-related information in its output, such as exploit database reference links or rule descriptions.

Using IDScenter

☑ IDScenter can help you create a Snort configuration file from scratch by filling in some forms.

☑ IDScenter includes a powerful ruleset editor and can instantly point you to the Web page that describes the rule or alert.

☑ IDScenter can monitor various sources of alerts, such as plain text files, XML log files, or MySQL database. When an alert is logged, IDScenter will perform a specified action, ranging from ringing the PC bell to auto-blocking the intruder.

☑ The internal log viewer of IDScenter can instantly link alerts to "whois" databases or vulnerability descriptions on the Web.

Frequently Asked Questions

The following Frequently Asked Questions, answered by the authors of this book, are designed to both measure your understanding of the concepts presented in this chapter and to assist you with real-life implementation of these concepts. To have your questions about this chapter answered by the author, browse to **www.syngress.com/solutions** and click on the **"Ask the Author"** form.

Q: What database permissions are needed for proper ACID functioning?

A: Snort needs only "Insert" and "Select" privileges to log in to a database. ACID needs "Select" privilege for running queries, "Insert" and "Update" for alert groups support and caching, and "Delete" for alert deletion.

Q: What is the version of PHP that ACID can use?

A: PHP 4.0.4pl1.

Q: How can I add the support for portscan files processing by ACID?

A: It is a little tricky. When logging to a database, Snort only logs an occurrence of the portscan event and not all of the port's data. It is possible to force

ACID to process a text portscan log (only one file can be configured). The file to be processed is configured in the *$portscan_file* variable. ACID does not store retrieved information in a database, but processes this file on demand, so it is not possible to search by IPs occurring in a portscan file.

Q: How do I compact a MySQL database after many deletion/archiving manipulations?

A: The following shell script can be used (assuming the database is called snort_db):

```
for table in `echo show tables|mysql snort_db|tail +2` do
    echo optimize  table $table|mysql snort_db done
```

Q: When I start my Swatch script in the background, it stops very soon—what's wrong?

A: You possibly have *echo* actions used in a configuration file. Background processes are not allowed to communicate with the console, so when an alert is triggered with this action, the Swatch process is stopped by the system.

Q: Is it possible to browse the contents of a packet that triggered an alert in SnortSnarf?

A: To a certain degree, yes. There is an option *-ldir*, which forces SnortSnarf to include in its output links to specific log files in which the alert was stored. When you click on such link, the corresponding log file will be opened in a browser. Of course, these files have to be located in a directory accessible by the Web server.

## Chapter 9

Keeping Everything Up to Date

Introduction

As with many other open-source projects, the Snort Intrusion Detection System (IDS) is evolving all the time. To keep up with its development and use additional features that appear in new releases, you need to be able to update your installation periodically. The update process is usually simple—versions of Snort are backward compatible—so all you need to do is recompile the source (if you prefer building Snort yourself) or reinstall a package; for example, a Red Hat .RPM module, which is available from the distribution site.

As with all open-source projects, it is possible that someone has coded some extra functionality into his Snort package that is not in the distributed version, and you want to try it out. In this case, you can patch your Snort source code with the changes distributed by that person and see the results.

The most important updates are the rule updates that should be applied to the Snort sensors. Rule updates are created by other people in response to emergencies, such as new, overwhelming attacks—similar to CodeRed and the recent MS SQL Slammer worms. Several rule databases are updated on a regular basis and available at various Web sites; for example, www.snort.org and www.whitehats.com If you plan to stay current with new attack detection (and you probably will), you need to continuously monitor one or more sources for new rules and regularly update your rule files. Several tools exist for performing this task, and this chapter describes their uses.

Applying Patches

If you are using Snort as a production-level Network Intrusion Detection System (NIDS), you will probably never need to patch it. Throughout the development of Snort, each major change or bug fix is distributed as part of both the new minor and major releases. Updating Snort usually consists of downloading the new package and installing it over the existing one. The basic backward compatibility with previous versions of Snort is rarely broken, and during the last year, the most significant compatibility issues arose only with database schema changes (used by the snortdb database logging plug-in).

If you are interested in bleeding-edge functionality, then you probably downloaded and installed Snort via a CVS (for more information, please refer to the section *Installing from Source* in Chapter 3, "Installing Snort").

Oink!

It's a bad idea to apply inter-release patches to a production system unless there is an emergency such as a serious vulnerability. As previously noted, Snort developers react quickly when a problem arises in a released version of the package.

Downloading Snort source via CVS is simple. You can download it from an anonymous CVS server:

```
cvs -d:pserver:anonymous@cvs.snort.sourceforge.net:/cvsroot/snort login
cvs -z3 -d:pserver:anonymous@cvs.snort.sourceforge.net:/cvsroot/snort co
snort
```

After that, updating takes only one command (from the root of your Snort source directory or, for example, from the "rules" folder to get updates only for the rules):

```
cvs -z3 update
```

If you still need to apply a specific patch to a module that is not in the CVS, you can obtain a .DIFF file, which actually contains patch information for one or many source files, and then run a standard UNIX patch program to apply the patch. Usually, the command will look similar to the following:

```
patch -p0 originalfile < patchfile
```

In the previous syntax, *originalfile* is the file to be modified, and *patchfile* is the file with the patch information inside it (.DIFF file).

After applying the patch, you will need to rebuild Snort.

Updating Rules

The most important updates for an IDS are changes in its rules. These can be new rules or modifications of old rules; for example, an updated rule will generate less false positives and/or false negatives. Rules can also be updated in their classification ("classtype") or external references ("reference") parts.

How Are the Rules Maintained?

There are several sources of rules for Snort, the main one being www.snort.org. You can find a current set of rules in the www.snort.org/dl/rules directory. The other place to find Snort rules is the www.whitehats.com Web site. Its set of rules is somewhat different from www.snort.org. In the past, this site was more popular because it was updated almost daily, but these days, the Snort site keeps up, and as far as we've noticed, it has a very comprehensive rule base that is also constantly updated. Rules on the Snort site are added or modified by Snort developers or are submitted to a special "snort-sigs" mailing list by users. Everyone can contribute to the rule base. If you are interest in submitting your own rules, you should refer to www.snort.org/snort-db/help.html for information about the submission process. Each rule submitted to the Snort Web site has to be described and formatted as per Figure 9.1, taken from www.snort.org/snort-db/snort-sid-template.txt).

Figure 9.1 Template for Rule Submission

```
# This is a template for submitting snort signature descriptions to

# the snort.org website

#

# Ensure that your descriptions are your own

# and not the work of others.  References in the rules themselves

# should be used for linking to other's work.

#

# If you are unsure of some part of a rule, use that as a commentary

# and someone else perhaps will be able to fix it.

#

# $Id$

#

#

Rule:

--

Sid:

--

Summary:

--

Impact:

--
```

Continued

Figure 9.1 Template for Rule Submission

```
Detailed Information:

--

Attack Scenarios:

--

Ease of Attack:

--

False Positives:

--

False Negatives:

--

Corrective Action:

--

Contributors:

--

Additional References:
```

Attacks, for which signatures are needed most, are listed at www.snort.org/cgi-bin/needed.cgi. Newest rules can also be found in the HEAD (development) branch of the CVS repository for Snort.

Damage & Defense…

Change Management in Snort Rule Maintenance

Apart from technical issues, there are other topics concerning rules management. Upgrading a production system is similar to making changes in software products. This involves change management as a core process, which ensures that any change is tested, approved, and implemented in a consistent manner and there is always a rollback plan in case anything goes wrong.

When applied to rule maintenance, this process might involve the following steps:

1. Obtain new rules or changes to the existing ones.

Continued

2. Test new or modified rulesets on a separate (nonproduction) system to find out if the ruleset is correct (see the section *Testing Rule Updates* later in this chapter).

3. Run Snort with this ruleset for a predefined period on a test system, and watch for any alerts—are there too many false positives/false negatives, and so forth?

4. Decide when this ruleset will be applied to a production system, and get this change approved by the relevant person (for example, system owner).

5. Implement the change.

6. If there is anything wrong with the implementation, carry out the rollback plan and investigate the cause of the error.

How Do I Get Updates to the Rules?

The method for receiving rule updates depends on your choice of your main source of information regarding rules. As noted previously, there are many options, including the Snort.org Web site, the Whitehats.com Web site, several mailing lists, the CVS repository, and other people's research. In contrast to the many sources of information for rule updates, there are only two choices when it comes to implementing updates to your ruleset:

- Doing everything manually, which would entail downloading or creating files with new signatures and adding them to your rulesets.

- Partially or fully automating your update process.

If your system uses a minimal number of rules, then you most likely will have enough time to use the manual update method. It is really the best way to updating your rule base, because you will be able to review and examine each rule and its usability for your setup. If there are many rules in your rule database and you would like to somehow automate the process, several tools exist for doing so:

- For UNIX platforms, one is oinkmaster, which can also be used on any Perl-capable Windows machine.

- For Windows, it is also possible to use IDScenter (see Chapter 8, "Exploring the Data Analysis Tools") to make editing and merging rulesets easier. Note that IDScenter will not help you in downloading rules.

Oinkmaster

Oinkmaster is a Perl script created to automate the process of downloading and merging Snort rules. Its homepage is http://nitzer.dhs.org/oinkmaster/. It is also distributed on Snort site in the downloads/contributions section. Besides a Perl interpreter, oinkmaster requires Perl, tar, gzip, and wget available on the machine where it will run.

Oinkmaster fetches Snort rules from the archive address specified in oinkmaster.conf, comments out the unwanted rules, and prints what rules have been changed since the last update. Unwanted rules are specified in the file oinkmaster.conf—this helps to specify that some rules should never be included in the updated rulesets. In this file, you can also tell oinkmaster to skip entire files that you do not want to update or check for changes (for example, in the snort.org distribution of rules, all ICMP rules are placed in the icmp-info.rules file—if you are sure you do not need those, you can specify this file as unwanted). The following files in the archive are updated and checked for changes (or added if missing on your system):

- ★.RULES
- ★.CONF
- ★.CONFIG
- ★.TXT
- ★.MAP

This script can be run manually or as a cron job, but we again stress that fully automated updating of rules is not recommended; for example, a typo in a downloaded archive could wreak havoc on your entire rule base. It is always recommended to at least test a new ruleset before implementing it on a live system (see the section *Testing Rule Updates* later in this chapter.)

The following are the most important configuration directives in an oinkmaster.conf file:

```
url = http://www.snort.org/dl/signatures/snortrules.tar.gz
```

This directive specifies where to download the updates. If you used Whitehats.com rules, then this line would look like this:

```
url = http://www.whitehats.org/ids/vision18.tar.gz
```

The following directive instructs oinkmaster to skip updating of the file local.rules.

```
skipfile local.rules
```

You definitely will need the following line in oinkmaster.conf file, because file snort.conf contains your own settings and there is no use in replacing it with the downloaded one.

```
skipfile snort.conf
```

In addition, if you do not use Barnyard, then you do not need to update the SID map file:

```
skipfile sid-msg.map
```

The following lines, or lines similar to these, will disable updating signatures with the specified numbers, namely 1, 2, and 3:

```
disablesid 1
disablesid 2
disablesid 3
```

The oinkmaster script as follows, where *rulesdirectory* is the directory where the old rules are located and where at the end of the run the updated rulesets are placed:

```
./oinkmaster.pl -o rulesdirectory
```

Some useful command-line options are:

- *-c* Instructs oinkmaster to only print information about changes that have occurred since the previous download and not actually change rule files.
- *-b* Specifies a backup directory for the old rule files.

Oinkmaster can be run as a cron job similar to the following:

```
30 2 * * * cd /usr/local/oinkmaster; ./oinkmaster.pl -o /snort/rules/ -b
/snort/backup 2>&1
```

After each run, the script prints information about what was changed (added, enabled, disabled, and so forth) in the rulesets. The types of information it produces include:

- **Added** This is a new rule; its SID did not exist in the old rules file.

- **Enabled** The rule with this SID was commented out in the old rules file, but is now activated (uncommented) (this might be caused by removing the rule's SID from oinkmaster.conf).

- **Enabled and modified** The rule with this SID was commented out in the old rules file, but is now activated and sad been modified.

- **Removed** The rule with this SID does not exist in the new rules file.

- **Disabled** The rule with this SID still exists, but has now been commented out (either because it is now commented out in the downloaded file, or because its SID was added to oinkmaster.conf).

- **Disabled and modified** The rule with this SID still exists, but has now been commented out. The actual rule had also been modified.

- **Modified active** The rule with this SID has been modified and remains an active rule.

- **Modified inactive** The rule with this SID has been modified, but remains an inactive (commented out) rule.

Figure 9.2 shows sample output from oinkmaster.pl.

Figure 9.2 Changes in the Rule Files Reported by oinkmaster

```
[***] Results from Oinkmaster started Tue Dec 25 23:36:07 2002 [***]


[*] Rules added/removed/modified: [*]


  [---]           Removed:         [---]
 -> File: web-cgi.rules:
    alert tcp $EXTERNAL_NET any -> $HTTP_SERVERS 80 (msg:"WEB-CGI
infosearch fname"; flags: A+; uricontent:
"fname=|7c|";reference:arachnids,290;classtype:attempted-recon; sid:822;
rev:1;)


  [///]           Modified active:        [///]
 -> File: dos.rules:
    Old: alert tcp $EXTERNAL_NET any -> $HOME_NET 7070 (msg:"DOS Real
Server template.html"; flags: A+;
content:"/viewsource/template.html?"; nocase;reference:bugtraq,1288;
classtype:attempted-dos; sid:277; rev:1;)
```

Continued

Figure 9.2 Changes in the Rule Files Reported by oinkmaster

```
    New: alert tcp $EXTERNAL_NET any -> $HOME_NET 7070 (msg:"DOS Real
Server template.html"; flags: A+;
content:"/viewsource/template.html?"; nocase; reference:cve,CVE-2000-0474;
reference:bugtraq,1288;
classtype:attempted-dos; sid:277; rev:2;)


[*] Non-rule lines added/removed/modified: [*]
    None.


[*] Added files: [*]
    None.
```

As you can see, one rule from web–cgi.rules was removed, and two rules were modified in the dos.rules file.

> **NOTE**
>
> If you want to be careful with rules updates, then probably the best way to use oinkmaster is to run it with the -c switch, which will only produce the change report and will not modify the rules. Then, you need to check this report for updated or added rules and consider including/modifying these rules in your configuration.

How Do I Merge These Changes?

Sometimes you might need to put together several rule files downloaded from different sources. Fortunately, there exist a universal numbering system for the rules (SID numbers), which is respected by all rule maintainers. Furthermore, each rule has (since Snort 1.8) a "revision" number, which allows automated comparing of two version of a rule. This revision number is specified in a *rev* section of rule definition; for example:

```
alert tcp $EXTERNAL_NET any -> $HTTP_SERVERS $HTTP_PORTS (msg:"WEB-MISC
cross site scripting attempt"; flow:to_server,established;
content:"<SCRIPT>"; nocase; classtype:web-application-attack; sid:1497;
rev:6;)
```

The preceding definition is for a sixth revision of a rule with the SID 1497. Snort distribution includes a C program snortpp.c, which allows merging of many rules files while considering their SID numbers and revisions. If two or more input files have definitions of the same rule, only the definition with the highest revision number will be included in the output file.

It is run as follows:

```
snortpp –o outputfile rulesfile1 rulesfile2 ... rulesfileN
```

If the -o option is not specified, the results are printed on standard output (stdout).

Using IDScenter to Merge Rules

Using Windows, it is possible to use the rules editor included in the IDScenter program. This editor is able to merge rules files and enable/disable rules inside files individually. On the Rules/Signatures screen of the IDS Rules section, you can select a file with rules and open it in the Editor window. The Editor window has a button labeled Import, which allows you to select any text file. This file will be merged with the one being edited. After this, it is possible to enable, disable, or edit specific rules in the resulting file. Figure 9.3 shows the rule import dialog. After reviewing, the result can be saved or discarded.

Figure 9.3 Merging Rules Files in IDScenter

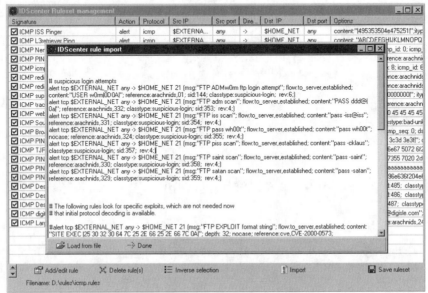

Testing Rule Updates

You should test each change in the rule base. Simple typographical errors in a rule or in the configuration line could lead to the unsuccessful start of Snort, or the rule being ignored or doing not what it is supposed to do. One of the arguments against fully automated rule update (for example, running oinkmaster as a cron job and then restarting Snort after the update is finished) is that if something goes wrong during the update, Snort will not start. If this occurs, and you do not have any type of Snort monitoring processes set up, it could be some time until you realize that your Snort IDS is inoperative. For a production environment, this is bad—we maintain that it is better to have an IDS with a slightly (but not very) outdated ruleset, than to run a network with an IDS that doesn't work at all.

Tools & Traps…

Keeping Snort Alive

You can check to see if the Snort process is running in several ways. For example, you can create a simple script similar to this:

```
#!/bin/sh
#
#check-snort script - if snort process is not running, it sends an
email alert to the root user
if [ `pgrep snort` = "" ] ; then
        echo "Snort is dead!" | mail root
        exit 0
    fi
```

and run it as a cron job with the following entry:

```
15 * * * * /usr/local/bin/snort-check
```

It is possible to change the script action so that it restarts Snort with correct parameters it is not running. Another possibility would be to use a "daemontools" package for monitoring the Snort process. This tool is located at http://cr.yp.to/daemontools.html.

The simplest way to check new rulesets is to run the new Snort configuration with the -*T* option (and without the -*D* option, which will move Snort process into background—we do not need that at the test stage). Doing so will check the configuration and report any discrepancies. The sample output is shown in Figure 9.4.

Figure 9.4 Snort -*T* Command Output

```
[root@snort root]# snort -c /etc/snort/snort.conf -T
Initializing Output Plugins!
Log directory = /var/log/snort


Initializing Network Interface eth0


        --== Initializing Snort ==--
Decoding Ethernet on interface eth0
Initializing Preprocessors!
Initializing Plug-ins!
Parsing Rules file /etc/snort/snort.conf


+++++++++++++++++++++++++++++++++++++++++++++++++++++
Initializing rule chains...
No arguments to frag2 directive, setting defaults to:
    Fragment timeout: 60 seconds
    Fragment memory cap: 4194304 bytes
    Fragment min_ttl:    0
    Fragment ttl_limit: 5
    Fragment Problems: 0
Stream4 config:
    Stateful inspection: ACTIVE
    Session statistics: INACTIVE
    Session timeout: 30 seconds
    Session memory cap: 8388608 bytes
    State alerts: INACTIVE
    Evasion alerts: INACTIVE
    Scan alerts: ACTIVE
    Log Flushed Streams: INACTIVE
    MinTTL: 1
```

Continued

Figure 9.4 Snort -*T* Command Output

```
        TTL Limit: 5
        Async Link: 0
No arguments to stream4_reassemble, setting defaults:
        Reassemble client: ACTIVE
        Reassemble server: INACTIVE
        Reassemble ports: 21 23 25 53 80 143 110 111 513
        Reassembly alerts: ACTIVE
        Reassembly method: FAVOR_OLD
http_decode arguments:
        Unicode decoding
        IIS alternate Unicode decoding
        IIS double encoding vuln
        Flip backslash to slash
        Include additional whitespace separators
        Ports to decode http on: 80
rpc_decode arguments:
        Ports to decode RPC on: 111 32771
telnet_decode arguments:
        Ports to decode telnet on: 21 23 25 119
Conversation Config:
        KeepStats: 0
        Conv Count: 32000
        Timeout    : 60
        Alert Odd?: 0
        Allowed IP Protocols:   All

Portscan2 config:
        log: /var/log/snort/scan.log
        scanners_max: 3200
        targets_max: 5000
        target_limit: 5
        port_limit: 20
        timeout: 60
database: compiled support for ( mysql )
database: configured to use mysql
```

Continued

Figure 9.4 Snort *-T* Command Output

```
database:               user = root
database: password is set
database: database name = snortdb
database:               host = localhost
database:    sensor name = 10.1.1.30
database:        sensor id = 1
database: schema version = 106
database: using the "log" facility
1276 Snort rules read...
1276 Option Chains linked into 131 Chain Headers
0 Dynamic rules

+++++++++++++++++++++++++++++++++++++++++++++++++++++

Rule application order: ->activation->dynamic->alert->pass->log


        --== Initialization Complete ==--


-*> Snort! <*-
Snort sucessfully loaded all rules and checked all rule chains!
database: Closing connection to database "snortdb"
```

The output consists of several parts. The first part is the output plug-in initialization, and then Snort starts loading configuration for preprocessors and rule-sets from the configuration file. It reports preprocessor plug-ins parameters and output formats enabled. The phrase in bold—**Snort successfully loaded all rules and checked all rule chains!**—states that our configuration is accepted. If we made a typographical error in one of the rules—for example, missed a space—then the end of the output would look like the following:

```
database:    sensor name = 10.1.1.30
database:        sensor id = 1
database: schema version = 106
database: using the "log" facility
```

```
ERROR /etc/snort/smtp.rules (9) => Invalid port: 25(msg
Fatal Error, Quitting..
```

Here, the error was detected on line 9 of the smtp.rules file. Snort will not start until this rule is fixed or commented out.

On Windows platforms, when using IDScenter 1.1 it is possible to test settings by clicking on the **Test settings** button in the upper part of the screen, which basically does the same thing—starts Snort with an extra −*T* option (see Figure 9.5).

Figure 9.5 Testing the New Snort Configuration in IDScenter

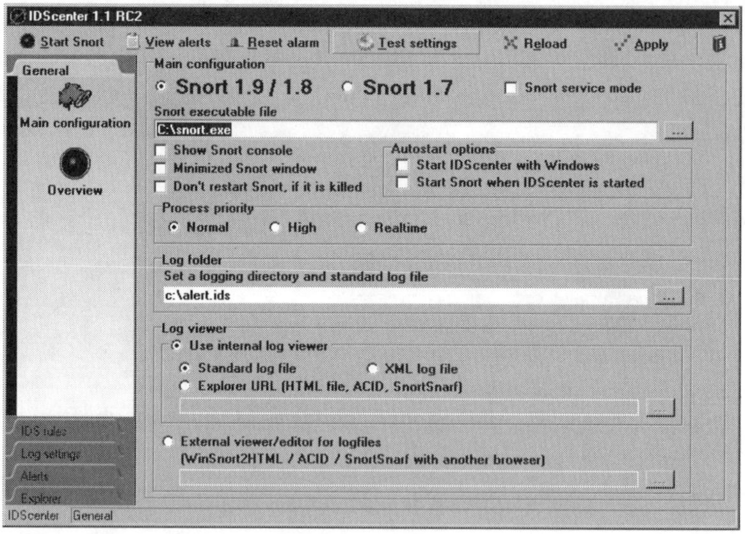

Testing the New Rules

You can test Snort recognition of new rules in several ways. The best way is to try to use the related exploits on the network monitored by Snort. There are also some tools that allow testing of specific rules based on their description. The most popular ones are:

- Snot, which is available at www,stolenshoes.net/sniph/index.html
- Sneeze, which is available at http://snort.sourceforge.net/sneeze-1.0.tar

Both are similar in that they take a set of Snort rules and generate exactly the traffic that these rules are supposed to be triggered by. For example, you can place rules you want to test into a file inside the Snot directory (for example, "test.rules") and run Snot as follows:

```
snot -r test.rules -d destination_host -s source_host -n number_of_packets
```

Snort should detect *number_of_packets* alerts with source IP address of *source_host* and destination of *destination_host*. This might not work with the signatures that are watching for established TCP connections, but it does provides a rough overview of its detection capabilities. "Sneeze" is a Perl script of the same functionality.

Watching for Updates

There are several sources for new rules information:

- Security mailing lists, especially ones maintained by Snort developers, www.snort.org database (www.snort.org/snort-db).

- Snort CVS repository, especially its development branch (it can be also browsed on the Web at http://cvs.sourceforge.net/cgi-bin/ viewcvs.cgi/snort/snort/doc/signatures/?only_with_tag=HEAD).

- You can also develop your own signatures based on the information about exploits on the Bugtraq mailing list or similar ones (see Chapter 5, "Playing by the Rules," for information about writing rules).

Mailing Lists and News Services to Watch

The main mailing list dedicated to Snort signature development is the "snort-sigs" list. You can subscribe to it at https://lists.sourceforge.net/mailman/listinfo/ snort-sigs. Information on this list includes new rule submissions and discussion of improvements to existing rules. Occasionally, some tips on rule management are also discussed there. For rules from the Snort CVS, it is also useful to watch the "snort-cvsinfo" list (https://lists.sourceforge.net/mailman/listinfo/ snort-cvsinfo), although information about rule changes in CVS is usually doubled in the "snort-sigs" list.

General security lists rarely post Snort signatures, but it is always possible to obtain some information from them for creating new rules, and it will be also useful if you submit your new rules to the "snort-sigs" list. Do not forget to use the submission template shown in Figure 9.1. The list of "most wanted" or incomplete signatures is located at www.snort.org/cgi-bin/needed.cgi.

The Whitehats Web site contains a regularly updated set of rules. There are also some rulesets created by exporting rules from other IDSs such as Dragon or Defenseworx (www.whitehats.com/ids/). It also features a forum for information exchange on new signatures (www.whitehats.com/cgi/forum/messages.cgi ?bbs=forum&f=2), although it does not have much traffic compared to the traffic on the "snort-sigs" mailing list.

Summary

Snort is an open-source IDS, and as such, is under constant development. New minor and major releases appear regularly. To maintain an up-to-date IDS, you will need to update your installation periodically. The update of executables does not need to be done each time a new release is issued, especially for production systems. Each upgrade has to be carefully considered.

The process of upgrading executables is rather simple, as backward compatibility is usually preserved. It is usually possible to simply install a new executable over the old one while preserving configuration information.

Much more important are updates to the rules. They need to be watched regularly. There are semi-automated tools for rule management, oinkmaster being the most convenient at the time. This tool allows downloading and comparing of new rulesets with old ones with or without performing on-the-fly changes to the rules. It is better, though, to manually review new and changed rules before putting them into Snort configuration files. There are also tools for merging rule files, both for UNIX and Windows. The keywords *sid* and *rev* in rule definitions allow you to uniquely identify rules and their versions during the update or merge process.

Each new configuration of Snort has to be tested. The simplest way to do so is by starting Snort with the *-T* option, which makes it check the configuration and report on any errors. The Snot and Sneeze tools allow simulating traffic described by Snort rules to check their detection. Both take rules from the specified file and produce IP packets that will trigger these signatures.

The main source of information about new rules is the www.snort.org Web site. There is also a "snort-sigs" mailing list that is dedicated to signatures submission and discussion of rules development. Another worthy resource is the www.whitehats.com Web site, which contains several rulesets, including rules imported from other IDSs. It also hosts a Web forum where Snort rules are discussed. Rules can be also downloaded from the Snort CVS repository.

Solutions Fast Track

Applying Patches

☑ Snort can be updated by installing a new distribution package over the old one, preserving its configuration.

☑ It can also be updated by checking out and recompiling source code from the CVS repository.

☑ It is possible to apply specific patches by usual UNIX means using the *patch* command.

Updating Rules

☑ Rules need to be updated regularly—the more often, the better. However, this should not interfere with Snort availability as an IDS— the more time it is online, the better.

☑ Rules can be updated manually (the best, but most time-consuming way), or in a semi (or fully) automated way.

☑ The best tool for automating rules updates at this time is the oinkmaster Perl script. It can download and compare new rules files to your existing ones, and (if required) make changes in your configuration. oinkmaster is highly configurable—it is possible to disable updating of specific rules or skip whole rules files altogether.

☑ Snort distribution includes a program snortpp.c, which can merge several rules files into one, while checking rule revision numbers and leaving in the resulting file only definitions with the highest version.

Testing Rule Updates

☑ Running Snort in a test mode using the *-T* option can test each new configuration of Snort.

☑ It is possible to use tools such as Snot and Sneeze to generate traffic that will trigger specific rules in order to check to see how Snort detects them.

Watching for Updates

☑ The main sources for new rules information are the www.snort.org Web site and a "snort-sig" mailing list.

☑ Submission of new rules are always welcome on the "snort-sigs" mailing list, and there exists a unified template for such submissions.

☑ The www.whitehats.com Web site contains several other rulesets, including some that are created based on rulesets from other IDSs.

Frequently Asked Questions

The following Frequently Asked Questions, answered by the authors of this book, are designed to both measure your understanding of the concepts presented in this chapter and to assist you with real-life implementation of these concepts. To have your questions about this chapter answered by the author, browse to **www.syngress.com/solutions** and click on the **"Ask the Author"** form.

Q: Are there other tools for managing rules other than those described in this chapter?

A: Of course, because Snort is very popular, there are several other tools created for this purpose, including:

- A Webmin module for Snort configuration and rule management (www.webmin.com and http://msbnetworks.net/snort)

- Snorticus (http://snorticus.baysoft.net)

- SRRAM (http://sourceforge.net/projects/srram)

Q: After Snort upgrade, there is something wrong with database logging.

A: Sometimes the schema for database storage is changed with new releases (there were approximately five changes during the past three years). Sometimes after this change you need to recreate all tables using the corresponding script from /contrib subdirectory of the distribution package. Usually, it is not possible to upgrade the old database, only to start anew.

Q: After Snort upgrade, I cannot see some IP addresses of events in the ACID console.

A: This issue is similar to the previous one. The database schema might have changed with the upgrade, so you need to upgrade ACID as well so it will be able to work with the new database.

Q: Which commands can I use to update Snort rules from CVS?

A: After you checked out the Snort source tree, use the following for updating rules only:

```
cvs -d :pserver:anonymous@cvs.snort.sourceforge.net:/cvsroot/snort
update *.rules
cvs -d :pserver:anonymous@cvs.snort.sourceforge.net:/cvsroot/snort
update sid*
cvs -d :pserver:anonymous@cvs.snort.sourceforge.net:/cvsroot/snort
update class*
```

Q: After merging rules files with my old ones, I am receiving many error messages and/or false positives, what can be wrong?

A: You have probably changed your configuration file (snort.conf) in the process of merging new rules, so parts of the configuration are lost—variables, plug-in parameters, and so forth. This often happens when there is a single file with rules and configuration in it. It is recommended to keep all configuration data in a separate main configuration file, and include rules files into it with *#include* directive. This will allow you to exclude main snort.conf from the update process.

## Chapter 10

Optimizing Snort

Solutions in this chapter:

- **How Do I Choose What Hardware to Use?**
- **How Do I Choose What Operating System to Use?**
- **Speeding Up Your Snort Installation**
- **Benchmarking the Deployment**

- ☑ **Summary**
- ☑ **Solutions Fast Track**
- ☑ **Frequently Asked Questions**

Introduction

So far, you have learned many of the reasons why Snort is a powerful, important tool to add to your network security toolbox. However, the hype is all for naught if Snort is not installed on a proper machine, running an operating system (OS) that meets your organizational requirements, and you have the technical capabilities to set it up properly. This chapter explains several system configurations that will attempt to optimize Snort performance for dissimilar business requirements on diverse network environments.

In the first couple of sections, we will examine the hardware necessary, as well as recommended, for running Snort on several OS platforms and network configurations. As would be expected for such vastly different OSs (Linux, BSD, Windows, or Solaris), the amount of computing power required to run Snort efficiently on one system could vary on another system. An important note to keep in mind is that the goal of building a Snort box is to limit any type of packet loss. Otherwise, you could miss an attack, or fail to log a crucial bit of evidence.

Later in the chapter, we discuss the pros and cons of the different OSs for running Snort. The choice of using Linux, BSD, Windows, or Solaris will depend most importantly on the comfort level you have with each OS. With little or no experience with a particular OS, it would be pointless to attempt a Snort installation on that OS. However, hardware deficiencies can sometimes be made up for with tweaks to the OS. With this in mind, your choice of OS can be influenced by factors such as the speed of Linux or ease of use of Windows.

How Do I Choose What Hardware to Use?

When choosing the hardware that you want to have for your sensor, you have to take a few factors into consideration. First, you must consider the size of the network you are planning to monitor. If you are only watching a relatively small (between 20 and 40 computers) network, the sensor you are building is not going to need as much power as a sensor to monitor a large, enterprise-sized network. There are also factors concerning the OS choice and what it can take advantage of on the hardware side. We detail information on this throughout the remainder of this chapter.

Obviously, cost is always a concern. One of the benefits of using Snort is that the software is open source and free. You wouldn't want to waste your savings on the software by buying more hardware than you can use. In short, buy what you need, and use what you buy. The point of having a Network Intrusion Detection System (NIDS) is to monitor all packets of interest flowing through your network, so the point of constructing your stand-alone sensor is to make sure that all of those packets are captured and logged. Building your sensor from a hardware perspective should have one goal: to not lose any packets. With this in mind, let's discuss the four pieces of hardware that are going to determine and define your sensor's performance.

- Processor speed and architecture
- Memory
- Disk space
- Network interfaces

First, processor speed and architecture will determine how quickly the packets are analyzed and catalogued. The major differing architectures with varying designs include Intel, SPARC, and MAC. You want to make sure that the processor has enough speed so as to reduce the possibility of creating a bottleneck and therefore result in packet loss.

Second, you want to have enough memory to run your OS and Snort effectively and efficiently, while also providing enough room to keep the incoming packets in the system memory before being transferred to the hard drive or other media source. On that note, you want to have a large-format media source to write the log files to. A large hard drive usually suffices, but might have to be backed up with some other form of media eventually (writing to a CD, DVD, or tape drive). This way, you can have all of your log files stored away. A large hard drive is not always necessary if you plan to back it up with some removable media at the end of the day (a good piece of advice of which to take note).

The final piece of hardware, and in many ways the most important, is your network interface card (NIC). It is imperative to have a high-quality, high-bandwidth-capable card. In most cases, it will be counterproductive to purchase and use a 10 Mbps network card, especially considering the cost of NICs. It will defeat the purpose of having a sensor if you have bandwidth spikes, or periods of heavy traffic, on your network over 10 Mbps (which might happen a lot for even smaller networks). It is mandatory to have a 100 Mbps NIC, preferably a name brand such as Intel or 3Com. If the network supports it, and you have the extra money, spring for a gigabit card. This way, you can always be sure that your NIC is not responsible for any packet drops.

What Constitutes "Good" Hardware?

The best hardware is that which doesn't allow any packet loss. Obviously, incidental packet loss might happen, and so your goal in constructing a "good" sensor system is to minimize the packet loss due to hardware limitations. The previous guidelines are reasonable standards to try and use for your system. The point to all of this, to determine the right hardware for your system, boils down to some facts about your network and decisions you have to make about how you want to administer the box. Your goals should be to:

- Limit packet loss.

- Stay within your means; don't overspend on something that is already free.

- Be sure that the system you set up completes the task that it is supposed to.

Processors

For your processor, you have to compromise between performance and price. If you have the capital to get a truly top-of-the-line processor, it won't hurt. Of particular interest is the new Intel Pentium IV 3.06 GHz processor. The special feature of this processor is Hyper-Threading technology. This aspect of the processor permits a second pipeline for applications to be opened automatically inside the chip to act similar to a multiple-processor system. Why is this important? It allows Snort to continue running in one pipeline without great loss to processing power while another set of applications can be engaged for, say, routine maintenance. The goal behind this is to limit any network monitoring downtime. This processor is obviously overkill for many systems, and the Hyper-Threading technology might not yet be fully used in a Linux system. This processor might only get its full value out of a Windows system at present. Another option that allows for similar work (multitasking processes) is a multiprocessor configuration. This could be done with several processors; both AMD and Intel make processors capable of being used in MP systems. The Intel Xeon Processor has Hyper-Threading technology, is not as expensive as a Pentium IV, can be used in MP systems, and as such is an intelligent choice for any x86 configuration. For non-x86 setups, the only real power player is the 64-bit UltraSPARC processor. It has the flexibility and the power that required for a processor. However, it will limit your operating system choice, as there are no Windows versions that are compatible with Sun hardware.

RAM Requirements

The amount of RAM required is a a sticky question. If you have RAM with a high bus speed, you will not need as much of it. Getting too much could substantially increase the cost of your NIDS. As of this writing, RAM for x86 systems is relatively inexpensive, so it's difficult to go wrong by estimating on the high side. If you're planning to use a more proprietary platform, such as an UltraSPARC, memory costs might be more of a factor. The OS you choose will give you a minimum amount recommended. For example, you are going to need more RAM for your system if you are going to run Snort off of a Windows platform as opposed to a more streamlined OS such as Linux. Generally, the size of your network and the amount of expected traffic will give you an idea of how much RAM you need. Realistically, we will say that 128MB is required for a Linux system, while 256MB is minimal for a Windows-based system.

Storage Medium

When choosing your large-format media, you must make decisions about how you are going to operate your NIDS each day. If you plan to make a library of your daily log files, then getting a smaller sized media source is a good idea. This could be a Zip drive, CD, or even something like a Smart Media card. The latter is a smaller and more easily stored option, but could be prohibitively expensive. Now, if the number of times you plan to back up your log files is not daily, but more toward weekly or monthly, then a large hard drive is needed as well as a very large removable media source. This is probably impossible if you are dealing with an enterprise-sized network, where daily backups will be needed. However, in a small network, backing up will not be as daunting a task. Over all, a 60GB hard drive should be fine for either setup. With the relative inexpensiveness of hard drives, it should be reasonably priced.

Network Interface Card

Finally, there is the NIC. As we touched on earlier, there is a definite requirement for a 100 Mbps card. If the funding is there, get the gigabit card. We cannot stress this enough. Your goal is to minimize packet loss, and this is the easiest way to do so. Now, if you have a small network, you really don't have to worry about anything greater than 100 Mbps. You should also consider the incoming bandwidth size. If your network is running off of a T1, then your Snort box is really not going to have a difficult time watching that. The bulk of its time will taken up watching the internal network (if that is how you set it up).

NOTE

We have not yet taken into account internal bus speed. Network cards can become limited if the corresponding bus speed is not high enough to matter; for example, you will never come close to using a 1GB inter-face card on an ISA bus.

How Do I Test My Hardware?

This book does not intend to be the definitive guide for purchasing and config-uring computer OSs and hardware. Instead, it should be used as a guide to assist in developing a set of platform-specific tests. In general, five categories of tests should be executed on each Snort sensor to ensure that you have the hardware properly installed and configured.

- **Network connectivity** The most important aspect of testing your hardware is to ensure that your NICs are functioning properly. In most cases, Snort sensors require that you use your card in two different methods: regular and promiscuous. In simple terms, it is important that you test to make sure that your card can send and receive packets in reg-ular mode as well as capture packets successfully while in promiscuous mode. In addition to packet sniffing, users commonly require remote access to this system for management purposes. One of the best ways to gain remote administration access is via a second NIC. The second NIC can serve as a secure link inward without compromising the other card's ability to capture packets.

- **Sensor placement** After determining that your NICs are working, sensor placement tests will ensure that you can capture the packets that you intend to capture. We realize that this is not a "real" hardware test, but it is just as important as the hardware tests. Ensure that no unin-tended network routes or filters are disallowing you to analyze poten-tially malicious traffic. This step is especially important on switched networks, where Snort monitoring might require special switch configuration to set up port mirroring.

- **CPU usage** There are multiple methods for testing your CPU usage. The goal of the CPU tests is to verify that you have the processing power to handle a heavy load of packets during a network traffic spike, or sudden increase in bandwidth consumption. The method in which you will derive the most value is multifaceted and requires a few types of tests. A good breadth of tests without consuming too much time and resources is to run the following three tests:

  - **Idling** When the sensor is idling and no packets are being analyzed, ensure that a maximum of 2 to 3 percent of your CPU is being used.

  - **25 percent** Suppose you are on a network that supports a transmission rate of 10 Mb/s. In this scenario, you should ensure that you are under 20 percent CPU utilization when the traffic hits about 2.5 Mb/s, or about 25 percent of your bandwidth capacity.

  - **50 percent** Similar to the previous case, when your bandwidth capacity is at approximately 50 percent, it is important to maintain a CPU utilization rate less than or equal to 45 percent.

- **Hard disk** A rather trivial test, but you should ensure that you have an adequate amount of space available on your hard drive after your installing and configuring your OS. Believe it or not, some installations of Windows XP Professional consume over 3GB of drive space. Add some applications and you could easily be over 5GB. On a completely irrelevant note, a Visual Studio .NET installation can take as much as 2GB. The point is to take a few seconds and check your system.

- **Logging** Snort packet and alert logs are the central point for traffic analysis, reporting, and data collection. It is essential to ensure that the logs have the proper rights and attributes for writing, and that there are no configuration anomalies that would limit the log size to something less than what you defined during configuration.

More information on creating and executing sensor stress tests and rule syntax tests can be found in Chapter 5, "Playing by the Rules."

How Do I Choose What Operating System to Use?

The choice of OS for your Snort installation depends on several factors. Ease of use, performance, and familiarity are all aspects that must be taken into account. The choice of hardware in your Snort box is also going to be a determining factor of which OS is best to use. For example, as a streamlined OS, Linux might be the best choice for a low-performance machine. However, in a high-performance machine, the choice of OS will be less dependent on hardware.

First, the most effective OS choice for any network administrator is going to be the OS with which he or she is most familiar. For example, if you are proficient with Windows software, but are completely new to Linux, the obvious choice is going to be Windows. It is difficult enough to learn a program like Snort, let alone teach yourself an OS at the same time.

Another option that will influence your OS choice is ease of use. There are going to be intricacies for each OS used for your Snort installation. As with many products, Windows-based software is going to be easy to use and set up— this includes Snort. Although there are some technical complications with the Snort product on a Windows system, such as WinPCAP issues, Microsoft kernel updates, and "cold" (requiring reboot) system fixes, the documentation is out there and easily accessible to correct any problems that might arise. The Linux-based platform has even more documentation on it and is more stable, as Snort was originally written to run on such an OS. Again, these are things to look at when choosing your OS.

Finally, for performance, you must examine the way the OS is built. Of course, the more "bulky" OS (Windows) is going to have performance drags unlike the streamlined Linux. This is expected, and hardware can help make up differences in the performance of the OS. As stated earlier, all of these factors must be taken into account; no one factor should influence your decision on which OS to use. Now let's discuss your choice of OS in greater detail.

What Makes a "Good" OS for a NIDS?

When choosing a "good" OS for Snort, you must consider integration into your network infrastructure. You don't want to run a Snort box that is going to interfere with normal operations. The goal of setting up any NIDS should be ease of installation and administration. Because of this inherent goal, this entire section can be summed up in one powerful statement, referred to as our Golden Rule for selecting a NIDS platform: "Select the platform that your organization is most familiar with and will easily integrate into your current environment administration process."

Notes from the Underground…

Leveraging Win32 IPSEC via Snort

Don't count out Windows yet! A while back, we downloaded an excellent Perl script, or at least at that time what we thought was an excellent script, for our Slackware box that monitored Snort logs and automatically updated IPTable filters. Unfortunately, we could not find anything that would do that for a Windows-based OS, so we decided to write our own. Understand that this was not an effort to modify the win32 kernel, but more or less an endeavor to get a similar technology for a Windows 2000 laptop. After two minutes of research, we decided to try to create a Snort monitoring mechanism that would somehow automatically trigger and then block attacker IP addresses via IPSec rules.

The monitoring mechanism was easy enough. It loads the stats of the alert file and checks every second to see if the file has been accessed. When it identifies that the file has been accessed, it then grabs an attacker IP address and compares it to any other previously analyzed attack IP addresses in hopes of minimizing redundant IPSec filters. Provided that it is a new IP address, the script will then pass that address as a parameter to the filter function. In this case, the function *ipfilter*() will disallow the attacker from connecting to port 135 on the local system. If you are unfamiliar with IPSec filters, they are similar to Berkeley packet filters in declaration syntax but drastically different in functionality.

For this Perl script to work, you must have the following:

- ActiveState's Perl interpreter
- Microsoft's IPSECPOL.exe utility included within the Windows 2000 Resource Kit
- Win32 Snort installed and configured

Snort usage:

```
snort -c ids.conf -A fast -N -l .
```

Continued

Just about anything can go into the configuration file, as long as your script can find and access the alert.ids file. This script can also be found on this book's companion CD-ROM.

```perl
#Proof of Concept PERL Script to Allow Win32 Snort to Leverage
Microsoft's IPSEC Engine
#By: James C. Foster
#######
#Monitor the Alert File so that you know when to activate the
 IPSEC filters
$file="alert.ids";  #This is the name and path of the alert file
@stats=stat($file);
$iat=@stats[8];  #Record alert file statistics
while(1)
{
  sleep 1;
  @stats=stat($file);
  if ($iat != @stats[8])
    {print "Something was added to the Alert.ids file\n";
      ###Call sub function to grab attack IP
      $alertip=&get_alert_ip;

      ###Call sub function to compare IP to attacker IP array and
      ignore list
      &compare_ip($alertip);

      $iat = @stats[8];
    }
  else {print "Still Waiting\n";}
}
#######
#Grab the attacker's IP address from the alert file
sub get_alert_ip{
open (ALERT, "alert.ids") or die "Cannot open or read alert file";
    while (<ALERT>)
      {
```

Continued

```perl
                next if (/^\s*$/); #skip blank lines
                  next if (/^#/); # skip comment lines
            if (/\.*\s(\d+\.\d+\.\d+\.\d+)\.*/) #Grab the IP Address
              {
                $alertip=$1;
                    print "Alert IP address is $alertip \n";
              }
         }
close (ALERT);
#Check to see if you got it!
if ($ip eq ""){ print "Could not get the IP address out of the
alert file! \n";}
$alertip;
}
#########
#Compares the new IP address to the IP address I have already
 captured
sub compare_ip{
my ($compareip) = @_;
open (COMPARE, "attackers.old") or die "Cannot read the ignore file,
$!\n";
  while (<COMPARE>) {
    chop;
    next if (/^\s*$/); #skip blank lines
    next if (/^#/); # skip comment lines
    if (/(.*)/)
    {
       $alertip=$1;
       if ("$alertip" eq "$compareip")
         {
            print "Somebody old is still attacking \n";
         }
       else
         { #Send the new IP address to the IPSEC filter subfunction
            &ipfilter($compareip);
```

Continued

```
                $tag=1;
            }

         next;

       }

   }

close (COMPARE);

if ($tag eq 1)

   {

   system ("echo $compareip >> attackers.old");

   }

}

#########

#Proof of Concept that filters all inbound protocol connections to
 my NetBIOS port (135)

sub ipfilter{

my ($attackerip) = @_;

use Win32;

use Win32::Process;

Win32::Process::Create($afilter2::Process::Create::ProcessObj,
'C:\\snort\w32\ipsecpol.exe', "ipsecpol -f $attackerip=0:135:tcp",
0, DETACHED_PROCESS, ".");

Win32::Process::Create($afilter2::Process::Create::ProcessObj,
'C:\\snort\w32\ipsecpol.exe', "ipsecpol -f $attackerip=0:135:udp",
0, DETACHED_PROCESS, ".");

Win32::Process::Create($afilter2::Process::Create::ProcessObj,
'C:\\snort\w32\ipsecpol.exe', "ipsecpol -f $attackerip=0:135:raw",
0, DETACHED_PROCESS, ".");

Win32::Process::Create($afilter2::Process::Create::ProcessObj,
'C:\\snort\w32\ipsecpol.exe', "ipsecpol -f $attackerip=0:135:icmp",
0, DETACHED_PROCESS, ".");

}

#########
```

Disclaimer: This is not meant to be used in an intrusion
prevention capacity and was included for research and educational
purposes only.

Continued

> The following are references that you might find useful in implementing, testing, or modifying the previously detailed proof-of-concept script.
>
> - **ActiveState Software** www.activestate.com
> - **IPSec** www.microsoft.com\windows2000\reskit\
> - **Perl** www.perl.org

What OS Should I Use?

The obvious answer to this is, the OS with which you or your organization is most familiar. It is nothing short of painful to attempt to set up a stable Snort box on an OS with which you have no experience. As long as you follow our Golden Rule, you will come to find that maintaining your sensor will not be a complicated task. Table 10.1 lists some environment-neutral pros and cons for selecting a base platform in case your organization has multiplatform skill sets and standards.

Table 10.1 Measuring the OS Selection

Windows		UNIX & Linux	
Pros	**Cons**	**Pros**	**Cons**
Easy installation and configuration	High CPU overhead	CPU Efficient platform	Initial installation and configuration
Windows-based system administration	Not Snort's native platform	Wide variety of additional tools available	Steep learning curve
Microsoft security features such as EFS		Can use automated filters such as Perl scripts that enable IPTable rules	

OINK!

If you are one of the 99 percent of companies that are cost conservative, you will get more for your money if you select a UNIX-based OS. The software is less expensive (if you pick a free OS), and, as discussed, you can get by with a bit less hardware.

How Do I Test My OS Choice?

Testing your OS is somewhat similar to testing your hardware configuration. There are a plethora of tests that will ensure and assess everything from network connectivity, to administration, to sensor thresholds. In general, the goal of testing your OS is to make sure that everything runs smoothly. You want to ensure that the installation and configuration of the OS, in addition to any other applications, did not adversely affect performance. The following five categories encompass the main concentrations of tests that should be included in your OS test plan.

- **Hardware tests** should be included in the test plan for your intrusion detection sensor.

- **Stress tests** should be included to identify the stress thresholds of an intrusion detection sensor. Detailed information can be found in Chapter 5, "Playing by the Rules."

- **Remote administration** is an essential feature for network security applications and tools, especially those that report real-time security incidents. Verify that all remote administration applications function in a secure and on-demand manner. In the case of an emergency, it is critical that administrators be able to collect and analyze network and attack data. Microsoft's new remote administration solutions are actually secure when connecting to trusted systems. They use the Remote Desktop Protocol (RDP) 5.5, which encompasses an authentication and encryption (encoding) schema. Other administration programs such as PCAnywhere and VNC should be configured to enable encryption, and have the latest patches.

- **Log management** is essential. It is important to test your sensor's logging capabilities. Included within the gambit of tests should be procedures to confirm that large files are handled properly, and to ensure that all of the output modules were successfully implemented. Running tests to test log files sizes is easy. Simply create a rule to monitor all data (the following example should be sufficient) so that your sensor logs fill quickly. After the logs have hit their maximum capacity, observe the following results. In addition, the following rule will log to the configured "log output module," so this method can also test the flexibility of the in-place logging mechanisms.

```
log ANY ANY -> ANY ANY (msg: Testing Log Procedures);
```

Log management is coupled and included within this gambit of testing in addition to Snort testing because here we focus on testing the platform-layer implementation; specifically, how the OS handles the defined logging modules.

■ **System administration** covers technical administration of the system, and policy and managerial administration tasks such as installing maintenance patches, maintaining user accounts, and viewing system and security logs and reports. We are quite sure that a good amount of these tests are already in place within your organization. If not, this might lengthen the road ahead. The current patches and system fixes should be ascertained from the respective vendor Web sites for the underlying platforms in addition to any other installed applications. Managing user accounts is not a complicated task because of two key data points. First, network sensors should not be installed on systems with multiple functions; and second, only administrative users should have accounts on these boxes.

Speeding Up Your Snort Installation

If you are familiar with Snort and the underlying platform, installing and configuring your sensor should only require a modest amount of effort and resources. With this said, if you are not very familiar with your OS of choice and Snort, installing and configuring your Snort sensor could require more intense amounts of organizational resources. Furthermore, installing and configuring multiple sensors might prove to be a heavy burden on time, even with the proper technical skill set.

A few common goals that might present obstacles in initially designing and implementing your intrusion detection network include collecting and analyzing all logs in a central location, implementing a manageable rule updating policy, implementing a secure method for managing all of the sensors, and all the legwork required to get all the sensors brought up to "production status."

Numerous methods to minimize resources and time during the initial setup process exist. Installation and configuration scripts can quickly help automate numerous manual tasks such as system rebooting, log analysis, and user management. In addition to automation scripts, the method in which you initially set up your sensor will play a huge role in the flexibility of and future reuse of your sensor configuration. Creating reusable configuration and variable files plays a significant role in getting the most out of your installation and development time.

Furthermore, the ability to tweak your preprocessors and output plug-ins can dramatically decrease the burden of the CPU load. Lastly, there is always the option to clone the drive; however, this only works if you want the sensors to be exactly alike, which is not always a viable option for distributed networks.

The following references serve as a quick refresher if you would like to get detailed information about any of the topics previously mentioned.

- Installation tweaks—Chapter 3 "Installing Snort"

- Creating portable configuration and variable files—Chapter 5, "Playing by the Rules"

- Flexible preprocessors—Chapter 6, "Preprocessors"

- Flexible output plug-ins—Chapter 7, "Snort Output Plug-Ins"

Deciding Which Rules to Enable

Snort's ruleset is the most critical asset of your intrusion detection sensor. In addition to being the most complex and time-intense aspect of the setting up Snort, it is also the most configurable. Because of this, it is very easy to improperly configure your system. We have seen both extremes; sensors with only 10 rules because the administrator thought he only needed rules for current vulnerabilities and threats, and sensors with over 1500 rules that created a 10- to 35-percent packet loss ratio on normal to peak traffic periods, respectively.

One of the most popular and effective methods for determining appropriate rulesets adopts two key principles.

- Identifying key protocols and services that are used on your network. If NetBIOS and HTTP services are the only services used on a particular network segment, then only rules referencing those services need to be applied. An additional general rule that defines external sources attempting to connect to a nonutilized network service should be created to log the traffic.

- Determining the level of granularity required for your evidentiary logs. For example, if the network is merely a development network, then the attack details and rules might not need to be as stringent as that of a finance or publicly facing network.

Figure 10.1 is a tool that you can use to assist in ensuring the proper categorization for Snort rules and rulesets. The tool requires a bit of subjectivity in the definition for the threat's threat level. We view critical threats as any automated exploit or tool that assists in exploiting a vulnerability.

Figure 10.1 Categorizing Rules

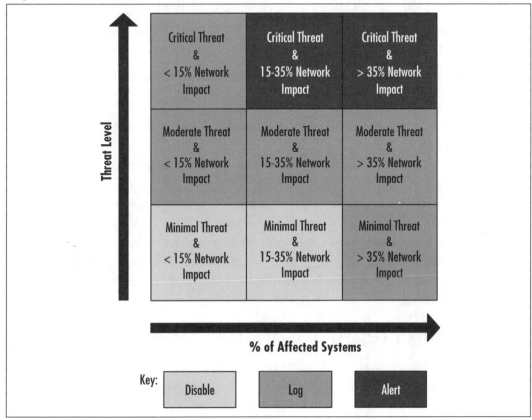

Critical threats are proliferating the Internet at a fast pace, such as most of the e-mail borne viruses, popular new exploits, and vulnerabilities that allow administrator-level access to system resources or data and in most cases are easy to leverage. As an enterprise organization, these critical threats are where you want to spend the majority of your company's time and energy. A moderate threat is one that requires more than one step to complete and usually requires an adequate amount of technical ability to exploit from a malicious user perspective. Other moderate threats include vulnerability proof-of-concept code and vulnerabilities that affect popular software products. Finally, minimal threats would be considered more difficult attacks that leverage system information or any other noncritical pieces of information. Minimal threats are those that require a considerable amount of technical "know-how," a highly specific scenario to exploit the vulnerability, or numerous manual procedures that must be sequenced together in a specific order. The following are some well-known threat examples categorized in our schema.

- **Critical threats** SQL Slammer Worm, CodeRed, IIS Unicode Attacks

- **Moderate threats** MDAC Remote Buffer Overflow, Wu-FTP Buffer Overflow, OpenSSL bugs

- **Minimal threats** Bind TSIG, "Obscure" CGI vulnerabilities, SMTP VRFY vulnerability

Network impact refers to the number of systems within your environment that are affected by the threat. A network with 500 nodes—servers, workstations, and network devices—that has 25 IIS servers would have an impact of 5 percent for a threat such as a Microsoft self-propagating Web server worm. We realize that our tool is not perfect since it does not account for percentage of private, production, or transaction systems; however, it can be used to help create your baseline. You might determine that you want to only determine the threat level pertaining to externally facing systems or production-status systems. Both are commonly analyzed scenarios and can add value if presented to "decision makers" or administrators in a timely fashion.

Configuring Preprocessors for Speed

Introduced in Snort version 1.5, preprocessors provide an API for administrators and developers to define sets of instructions to be interpreted and executed on captured traffic. The preprocessor's unique value is derived from the fact that it analyzes the data before potentially passing it to the Snort ruleset. This feature adds many technical benefits, especially in the realm of identifying more complex network attacks that are obfuscated and/or divided between multiple packets. Explicit preprocessor features within Snort include TCP packet reassembly, decoding HTTP, fragmentation alerts, portscan identification, and stateful inspection protocol support.

As with most of the features within Snort, it is recommended to ensure that the ROI exists before implementing any preprocessors. However, preprocessors present a unique problem because, if configured improperly, it is quite easy to create a potential infinite looping or denial-of-service (DoS) anomaly that would bring your sensor to a screaming halt.

The conversation preprocessor takes in a number of parameters, but most importantly, it provides a user the capability to set the timeout value and the number of simultaneous sessions that can be monitored. The preprocessor relies on human knowledge during configuration time because it allows you to monitor the entire range of 65,535 ports. A timeout value of 60 seconds could easily allow an attacker to take down the sensor by flooding packets for 30 seconds and then send an attack that would go unnoticed.

It is difficult to pinpoint recommendations for configuring your preprocessors while maintaining acceptable levels of performance. Our recommendation is to use your common sense, and hopefully that sense in combination with our previous recommendation to buy a powerful machine will ensure that your plug-ins will serve as intended. Some rules to live by include:

- Don't monitor more than 10,000 connections with any single preprocessor.

- Multiple portscan preprocessors are not needed.

- HTTP decoding is only needed for systems that receive inbound HTTP connections; in other words, your Web servers.

- Use the new Stream4 for packet reassembly and inspection.

- Similar to HTTP decoding, Telnet decoding for Telnet and FTP should only be used on systems with corresponding Telnet and FTP servers (in most cases, ports 23 and 21).

It was not our intent to scare you away from using preprocessors, since some of them were designed to be more accurate and efficient than their commercial counterparts. Learn them, consider their ROI, design them to correlate on data from pertinent and relevant systems, and implement efficiently.

OINK!

For more in-depth information on preprocessors, please refer to Chapter 6.

Using Generic Variables

Generic variables can and should be used wherever possible. Why, you ask? Well, generic variables allow users, administrators, and intrusion detection engineers to quickly pull and reuse Snort rulesets in different environments. Instead of the rules being tied to specific IP addresses, whether internal or external, the rules are tied to variable names. For example, if a Snort rule were to detect a certain type of Web-based attack, then naturally you would only want it to analyze packets destined toward internal Web servers.

Snort provides users the ability to create stand-alone configuration files or numerous smaller configuration files that are linked to one main configuration file that Snort analyzes during execution. This is a perfect method for creating reusable sets of rules, since the only areas that would require modification are the variable definitions. Consider the time savings for changing 15 to 50 variable names instead of changing 1000 or more Snort rules.

A collection of the most common generic variables declarations include internal network ranges, external networks, DMZ or transaction zone addresses, Web servers, DNS servers, mail relays, routers, client networks, and so forth. These variable names and types are seen throughout Snort documentation and current Snort rules in formats such as $HOME_NET or $DMZ.

OINK!

More detailed examples of using generic variables can be found in Chapter 5.

Choosing an Output Plug-In

Snort output plug-ins are excellent for modifying and presenting log and alert data in a customizable fashion. During the installation and configuration process of your sensor, you have the ability to enhance Snort's reporting features without using any additional add-on tools such as ACID or SnortSnarf to assist in log analysis. Just as a quick recap: Plug-ins allow you to define files to use for storage in addition to the format of the data that goes into those files.

When selecting an output plug-in, you should determine the business and technical factors of your selection. For example, the projected traffic rate should be taken into consideration when designing the sensor. In addition, you need to run through the plug-ins and do what we refer to as a *common sense test*. A common sense test is just verifying that you are not trying to output to syslog on a Windows 2000 system or write to C:\Snort\logs on an OpenBSD sensor.

There are additional factors in selecting output plug-ins that will potentially affect the overall choice and functionality of the system:

- Too many plug-ins can hinder system performance.

- Individual rules that output data to multiple files can also impede performance.

- Data format defined within the plug-ins should be streamlined; complex data formatting should be completed outside the Snort engine, such as that in a Perl parsing program.

- Only pertinent data should be included in the plug-ins.

OINK!

Output plug-in paths, locations, and references might have to modified if declared statically, especially if different platforms were used. We recommend creating a logging structure that is not only type-fully named, but also consistent across your entire intrusion detection network.

Benchmarking Your Deployment

In the business world, benchmarks serve as a tool to help an organization improve its business processes. Technically, benchmark tests can serve as an excellent resource to aid in identifying strengths and weaknesses in test subjects, systems, and cases. In our case, proper Snort benchmark testing will identify current and potential configuration-related bottlenecks due to improper configurations, lackluster hardware, or software inefficiencies. Keys to conducting a high-quality benchmark are proper comparison systems, one-off configuration modifications, repeatable results, and documentation. It might seem like a great deal of specific information and, to be honest, conducting a commercial-grade benchmark consumes a considerable amount of time and resources. Therefore, for the remainder of this section, we will refer to benchmarks in two ways. Both will be related to Snort tests, but one will be referred to as commercial-grade benchmarks (CGB) and the other as ad hoc benchmarks (AB). The first is self-explanatory, and the other simply means that you are executing a less formal test in search of one or two advantageous outcomes. An example would be implementing a new rule and seeing the impact that rule has on your sensor and if the performance impact is worth the gathered data.

If you are asking yourself, "Do I really need to conduct a benchmark test, since I only want to use Snort as an additional resource in my environment in the case of an emergency or one-off scenario?" the answer might be "no." In general, benchmarks are used in commercial organizations for commercial-grade applications; however, Snort stands apart from the crowd as a publicly available tool that has the quality of any other private product. Whatever your decision, expect to spend 40 to 80 engineer hours for system preparation and testing.

Benchmark Characteristics

Benchmarks, either good or bad, have certain distinguishing characteristics. Numerous factors can lead up to or directly contribute to the success or failure of a test. Such factors range from inadequate resources or time allocation to improper tool automation. Subsequent sections detail some of the disastrous pitfalls that should be avoided, in addition to vital elements that should be included in the benchmark.

Attributes of a Good Benchmark

Strong benchmarks result from a combination of solid documented business requirements and functional test plans. It is key to understand the business drivers for conducting the benchmarks, even if the driver is to simply "create a leaner, faster, more efficient Snort intrusion detection platform." In addition to creating the vision of a benchmark, documented goals and milestones should also be included in the requirements. For example, if your goal is to determine if it is better to place Snort on an old Linux system or relatively new Win32 system, then the milestones in achieving this goal would be: Create identical Snort configurations on production-ready test systems. The following list provides you with some generic guidelines for creating a good benchmark.

- Determine and specify a test set of intrusion detection rules to implement on both test systems.

- Identify and gather required assessment tools (for example, vulnerability scanners, port scanners, and so forth).

- Develop process and procedure automation via scripting or manual procedures.

- Develop a benchmark test plan.

- Conduct the benchmark.

- Analyze the results and determine future action items.

Snort benchmarks coincide with most other types of technical benchmark assessments in reference to test methodology. In practice, it is purely another technology-enabled management tool. As a rule of thumb, the more automation, the better!

Attributes of a Poor Benchmark

At the risk of sounding sarcastic, we must say that most of the attributes of a poor benchmark can be derived by taking the inverse of the attributes of a good benchmark in the previous section. With that said, there are a few exceptions. The most widespread flaw when conducting a benchmark is to permit uncontrolled variables and factors the ability to construe test results. For example, Snort benchmarks should be tested in controlled cells, or environments, so that only network traffic that is sent from other controlled systems is captured and analyzed by the sensor. Therefore, running your tests in a production environment is probably a very bad idea. Another common mistake is modifying more than one element between the two test cases. It would provide very little insight into the true performance differences of an OpenBSD versus Windows 2000 Snort install if both rulesets were completely different. The last aspect often overlooked is running multiple tests during the benchmark; not only running multiple types of different tests, but also multiple identical tests for verification purposes.

To recap, avoid these three common flaws:

- Conducting benchmarks in an uncontrolled environment
- Measuring and comparing dissimilar systems
- Being satisfied with the results of one test run

What Options Are Available for Benchmarking?

The options for benchmarking an IDS in today's market are few, and if you are counting viable enterprise solutions, then the answer is "none." Minus the surplus of vulnerability and port scanners, and chained exploit scripts, there are six commonly used tools to aid in benchmarking. Of the six, the only one that is close to commercial grade and has a graphical interface is IDS Informer. The remainder of the options are command-line tools and, in most cases, scripts. The technical abilities range from stateful attacks to blind CGI requests.

IDS Informer is our top recommendation for consulting and enterprise organizations that require easy installs, graphical interfaces, and good reporting. If you simply require a freeware tool or comprehensive script, then it is a toss up between IDS Wakeup and Ftester (Firewall Tester).

IDS Informer

Blade Software's (www.gui2000.com) IDS Informer is the current industry standard for testing IDS features and implementations. The graphical interface and configurable features far surpass any other available IDS testing tool or application. With offices in the United States, the United Kingdom, and India, the Blade staff also publishes application bug fixes and attack updates on a regular basis.

The GUI provides an easy to understand and use interface for configuring IDS Informer. As seen in Figure 10.2, the user can specify the source IP and MAC address for all of the attacks and define the destination IP address. If the destination IP address is unreachable, the destination MAC will be forced to use a broadcast address of FF-FF-FF-FF-FF-FF. Otherwise, the engine will use the retrieved, corresponding MAC address of the defined destination IP address. IDS Informer can also configure the transmission rate and Time-To-Live (TTL) for the attacks. Each of these provides greater flexibility in case the tool is being executed in a production environment. Informer also provides the capability to graphically select any of the network cards found on the system.

Figure 10.2 Blade IDS Informer Configuration

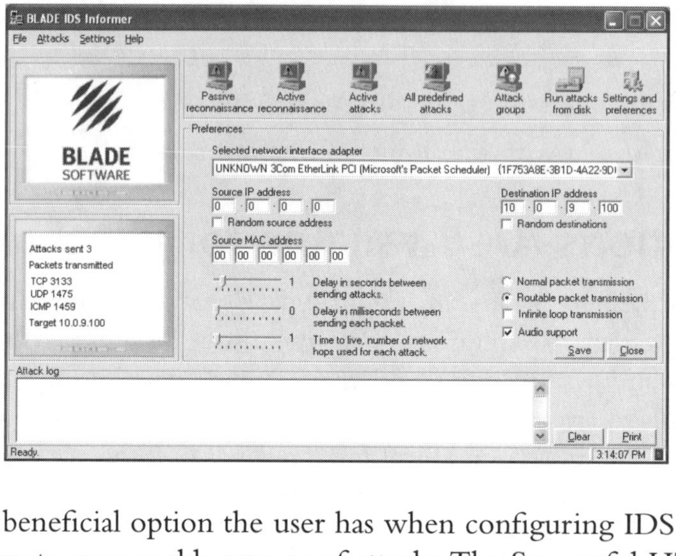

The other beneficial option the user has when configuring IDS Informer is the ability to create manageable groups of attacks. The Successful HTTP group created in Figure 10.3 contains the following three successful attack sequences: HTTP IIS .htr access, HTTP IIS Index .htw Cross-Site Scripting, and HTTP IIS

.asp showcode. Group creation allows an administrator or consultant to predefine small and manageable subsets of attacks.

Figure 10.3 IDS Informer Attack Groups

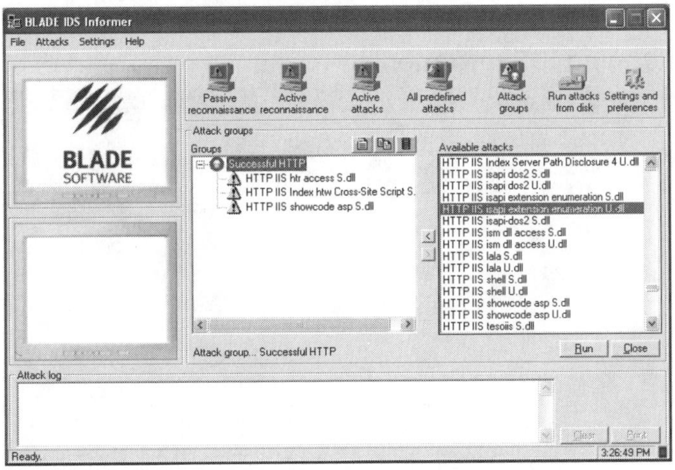

The prime disadvantage of this product is that it has a price tag; however, at the affordable price of $5,000 per license, it will prove to be a valuable addition to any consultant and developer shop. Blade Software has offered specials that allowed extended trial periods for auditors and consultants in the past. Besides the attack reports being a little weak on technical content, the only other considerable downside of the product was the inability to create custom attack simulations. Granted, the ability to quickly configure the attacks created by Blade exists, but it would be nice if an open API existed to allow end users the ability to create and run additional attacks.

After the settings and preferences have been configured for the test environment, you are one step away from running Informer. As explained previously, Informer provides the user with the flexibility to determine what attacks should and should not be executed on the network. Informer also has the capability to launch all of the attacks against the predefined target as seen in Figure 10.4. All 10 default attack groups were included in Figure 10.4 and over 7000 packets were transmitted in total.

At the bottom of Figure 10.4 is the space that is provided to view the attack log of the most recent set of tests. Each attack comes with a corresponding entry in the attack log so that the attacks can be correlated to the IDS sensor logs in search of false positives, false negatives, and other poor configurations. The following is an attack log dump after a complete test was run with All Predefined

Attacks enabled. As you can see, source and destination information is included along with protocol and transmission specifics. Unfortunately, no attack strings and content are logged. Such information would assist administrators looking to test their systems, and enhance their system with new rules.

Figure 10.4 Running IDS Informer

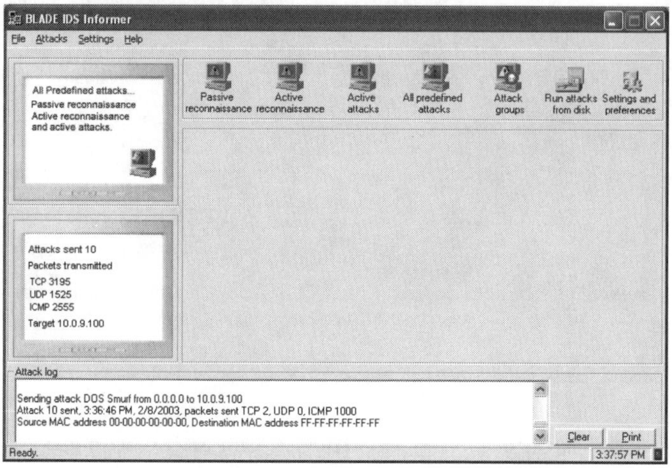

```
Sending attack Trace route ICMP from 0.0.0.0 to 10.0.9.100
Attack 1 sent, 3:19:16 PM, 2/8/2003, packets sent TCP 0, UDP 0, ICMP 96
Source MAC address 00-00-00-00-00-00, Destination MAC address FF-FF-FF-FF-FF-FF


Sending attack Finger user S from 0.0.0.0 to 10.0.9.100
Attack 2 sent, 3:19:18 PM, 2/8/2003, packets sent TCP 12, UDP 0, ICMP 0
Source MAC address 00-00-00-00-00-00, Destination MAC address FF-FF-FF-FF-FF-FF


Sending attack DNS Zone transfer S from 0.0.0.0 to 10.0.9.100
Attack 3 sent, 3:19:19 PM, 2/8/2003, packets sent TCP 16, UDP 0, ICMP 0
Source MAC address 00-00-00-00-00-00, Destination MAC address FF-FF-FF-FF-FF-FF


Sending attack Nmap UDP scan from 0.0.0.0 to 10.0.9.100
Attack 4 sent, 3:19:22 PM, 2/8/2003, packets sent TCP 2, UDP 1475, ICMP 1457
```

Source MAC address 00-00-00-00-00-00, Destination MAC address FF-FF-FF-FF-FF-FF

Sending attack Nmap TCP scan from 0.0.0.0 to 10.0.9.100

Attack 5 sent, 3:19:26 PM, 2/8/2003, packets sent TCP 3122, UDP 0, ICMP 2

Source MAC address 00-00-00-00-00-00, Destination MAC address FF-FF-FF-FF-FF-FF

Sending attack HTTP IIS unicode 1 S from 0.0.0.0 to 10.0.9.100

Attack 6 sent, 3:19:27 PM, 2/8/2003, packets sent TCP 9, UDP 0, ICMP 0

Source MAC address 00-00-00-00-00-00, Destination MAC address FF-FF-FF-FF-FF-FF

Sending attack Backdoor Back orifice S from 0.0.0.0 to 10.0.9.100

Attack 7 sent, 3:19:28 PM, 2/8/2003, packets sent TCP 0, UDP 45, ICMP 0

Source MAC address 00-00-00-00-00-00, Destination MAC address FF-FF-FF-FF-FF-FF

Sending attack RPC Linux statd overflow S from 0.0.0.0 to 10.0.9.100

Attack 8 sent, 3:19:29 PM, 2/8/2003, packets sent TCP 25, UDP 5, ICMP 0

Source MAC address 00-00-00-00-00-00, Destination MAC address FF-FF-FF-FF-FF-FF

Sending attack HTTP IIS htr overflow S from 0.0.0.0 to 10.0.9.100

Attack 9 sent, 3:19:30 PM, 2/8/2003, packets sent TCP 7, UDP 0, ICMP 0

Source MAC address 00-00-00-00-00-00, Destination MAC address FF-FF-FF-FF-FF-FF

Sending attack DOS Smurf from 0.0.0.0 to 10.0.9.100

Attack 10 sent, 3:19:33 PM, 2/8/2003, packets sent TCP 2, UDP 0, ICMP 1000

Source MAC address 00-00-00-00-00-00, Destination MAC address FF-FF-FF-FF-FF-FF

IDS Wakeup

IDS Wakeup (www.hsc.fr/ressources/outils/idswakeup) is a command-line tool that uses a collection of other tools and attack strings to test intrusion detection sensors. It is by far one of the most comprehensive freeware utilities of its kind, and is distributed by its creators, Herve` Schauer Consulting. The simulated attacks range from malicious FTP requests to protocol-based DoS sequences, to Web server buffer overflow strings. One of the key differentiators of this tool when compared to the other freeware programs is the TTL feature. Modifying the TTL field within a packet allows you to send attacks that might trigger IDS rules but not affect the production servers. This has proven to be an excellent feature for consultants and administrators who want to take advantage of this tool's capabilities during production hours without fear of disrupting business.

IDSWakeup is a UNIX-based tool that can be executed locally. It requires that you pass it a source and destination IP address. There is no need to specify a port since the attacks come with corresponding port assignments. Another useful feature of the tool is the ability to define how many cycles should be completed before exiting: IDSWakeup usage:

```
./IDSWakeup <source IP> <destination IP> <number of cycles> <TTL>.
```

The program has two dependencies. First, you must install and configure HPing2, which can be downloaded from www.kyuzz.org/antirez/hping,

The second dependency is a program released with IDSWakeup called IWU. IWU is another command-line utility created to quickly send datagrams and it requires that you install Libnet. Libnet is a set of libraries that can be used to streamline the process of developing network-based applications. The frameworks and structures for implementing and using protocols are the best. Libnet and other security projects can be downloaded from the Packet Factory Web site at www.packetfactory.net/.

The following is an example of a test that was run on an internal network with a source address of 10.1.1.1 and a destination address of 10.0.2.130. The tool will run twice before exiting and should not disturb the target system due to the defined TTL value of 1.

```
# /root/IDSW/./IDSwakeup  10.1.1.1  10.0.2.130  2  1

-=-=-=-=-=-=-=-=-=-=-=-=-=-=-=-=-=-=-=-=-=-=-=-=-

-   IDSwakeup : false positive generator

-   Stephane Aubert

-   Hervé Schauer Consultants (c) 2000

-=-=-=-=-=-=-=-=-=-=-=-=-=-=-=-=-=-=-=-=-=-=-=-=-

   src_addr:0  dst_addr:127.0.0.1  nb:1  ttl:1


   sending : teardrop ...

   sending : land ...
```

```
   sending : get_phf ...
   sending : bind_version ...
   sending : get_phf_syn_ack_get ...
   sending : ping_of_death ...
   sending : syndrop ...
   sending : newtear ...
   sending : X11 ...
   sending : SMBnegprot ...
   sending : smtp_expn_root ...
   sending : finger_redirect ...
   sending : ftp_cwd_root ...
   sending : ftp_port ...
   sending : trin00_pong ...
   sending : back_orifice ...
   sending : msadcs ...
            245.146.219.144 -> 127.0.0.1 80/tcp  GET /msadc/msadcs.dll
HTTP/1.0
   sending : www_frag ...
            225.158.207.188 -> 127.0.0.1 80/fragmented-tcp
              GET /................................ HTTP/1.0
            181.114.219.120 -> 127.0.0.1 80/fragmented-tcp
              GET /AAAAAAAAAAAAAAAAAAAAAAAAAAAAAAAAAAAAAAAAAAAAA\
              AAAAAAAAAAAAAAAAAAAAAAAAAAAAAAAAAAAAAAAAAAAAAAAA\
              AAAAAAAAAAAAAAAAAAAAAAAAAAAAAAAAAAAAAAAAAAAAAAAA\
              AAAAAAAAAAAAAAAAAAAAAAAAAAAAAAAAAAAAA/../cgi-bin/phf HTTP/1.0
(cut remaining tool dump to save page space)
```

Sneeze

Sneeze (http://snort.sourceforge.net/sneeze-1.0.tar) took a somewhat difference approach compared to the two previous IDS benchmarking tools. Written by Brian Caswell and Don Bailey, the tool was designed to parse Snort IDS rules files with the goal of generating sensor false positives, or fake attacks. Sneeze implements an ingenious tool concept that exposes potential issues that administrators face during the continuous battle of monitoring IDSs and eliminating false positive issues. A significant amount of time is spent analyzing network attacks via the alert and packet logs from Snort, as one of the underlying goals for all IDSs is to provide pertinent, accurate information. A simple attack intrusion detection signature matches malicious packets destined for a sensitive host, but the true value of an IDS is shown through complicated signatures and rules that correlate malicious attack strings and their corresponding target responses. Sneeze allows you to become familiar with the Snort rules that are prone to false positives and the intricacies in determining if indeed the attack is legitimate.

Sneeze serves as a free yet useful tool for quickly tracking and testing IDS sensors in a production environment. The latest release of the tool has been tested with Snort 1.8 and its corresponding ruleset.

Sneeze is a command-line tool written in Perl that can only be run from UNIX-based platforms. The default parameters the tool requires are the destination host and rules file. Additional options are available. We feel that each of the options is more or less self explanatory, so we only include a tool dump here:

```
Usage C:\sneeze\sneeze.pl -d <dest host> -f <rule file> [options]
-c count           Loop X times.  -1 == forever.  Default is 1.
-s ip              Spoof this IP as source.  Default is your IP.
-p port            Force use of this source port.
-i interface       Outbound interface.  Default is eth0.
-x debug           Turn on debugging information.
-h help            Duh?  This is it.
```

There are only two prerequisites to running the tool. First, you must have a good Snort rules file that you intend to use to feed data to the Sneeze engine. Varying combinations of content and destination port and IP addresses are characteristics of a good rules file. In addition, you will also need to preinstall the Net::RawIP Perl module. Sneeze uses this module to lay the groundwork for writing raw packets, spoofed packets, and general packet transmission. You can download the Net::RawIP module from www.cpan.org/modules/by-module/Net.

The biggest downside of the tool is that it can only be run in the UNIX-based environment strictly because it uses the Net::RawIP module. Unfortunately, it was not designed to be platform neutral.

Miscellaneous Options

In addition to the three options previously presented, there are a few other tools worthy of a quick mention. Stick (www.packetstormsecurity.org/distributed/ stick.tgz), quite possibly the most publicized and inappropriately hyped IDS testing tool, was released some ago to intrusion detection sensor developers. Stick has several useful features, the most notable being speed. Yet, it also has one very large downside: it does not effectively monitor and handle the packet and attack state, thereby allowing an intrusion detection engine to potentially finger the tool. A similar program, Snot, has the same problem but serves as another adequate example tool to generate attacks. For more information on Snot, visit www.stolenshoes.net/sniph/index.html.

The last tool worthy of mentioning is Ftester. Ftester is comprised of two Perl scripts, which can be downloaded from http://ftester.sourceforge.net. One script sends network attacks to remote hosts, allowing you to spoof source addresses and ports. The other script is a sniffer that is used to read in the attack packets sent to the destination system. The first can be used to test NIDS and HIDS, and the second is used in combination with the first to test network filters and firewalls. One important differentiator between Ftester and Snot/Stick is that Ftester simulates bona fide TCP connections, thereby permitting stateful attacks. Ftester requires that you configure the ftest.conf file to set up the attack packets to send to the "packet cannon engine." It also requires that you have the following Perl modules installed:

- Net::RawIP
- Net::PcapUtils
- NetPacket

Summary

It is imperative that you first decide what OS you are going to use as the underlying platform for your intrusion detection sensor. Our Golden Rule is "select the platform with which your organization is most familiar and will easily integrate within your current environment administration process." Monitoring and managing an IDS, or more realistically, network of sensors, is an extremely time-consuming job. As such, we recommend going with whatever is familiar to your organization to lessen the headaches of managing yet another nonconforming network device. Currently, the publicly available version of Snort can be configured to run in an assortment of methods on multiple platforms, including Windows NT/2000/XP/9*x*, Red Hat, Mandrake, Solaris, OpenBSD, FreeBSD, and various other Linux and UNIX-based OSs. After determining the OS of choice, you must then purchase or set up the appropriate hardware. A good rule of thumb is to always buy in excess in the following four areas: memory, CPU and motherboard processing power, NICs, and hard disk space. You might be thinking, "That's everything in a computer." Notice that we didn't say anything about graphics capabilities, audio cards, monitors, parallel drives, or multiple types of disk drives.

The next step in setting up the Snort NIDS is developing and executing a plan to create a flexible sensor so that numerous automation techniques can be used in rolling out an environment-wide grouping of sensors. Creating flexible sensor configurations could include potentially everything from creating disk clones to Snort automation scripts and installing remote server administration software. In addition to the multitude of application-generic steps you might undertake, it is also feasible to set up your Snort rules and configuration files in such a manner that allows you to easily modify Snort when porting it to another system. Generic variables such as *$INTERNAL*, *$EXTERNAL*, *$DMZ*, and *$NOT_ME* help tremendously when configuring rule files, so that instead of modifying potentially hundreds upon hundreds of Snort rules, you only need to change the dynamic variables. In addition to variable declarations, you can also tweak the installation by modifying your preprocessors and output plug-ins in hopes of increasing sensor efficiency.

The last aspect before rolling your sensor into a production environment is to double-check your work. Designing and executing a test plan for your sensors should be mandatory. Assuring a level of production-level quality is a requirement in most large commercial entities nowadays, and frankly, such plans are not used enough. Unfortunately, the list of commercially available intrusion detection testing applications and tools is short… or should we say that the list encompasses IDS Informer. Blade Software's IDS Informer is the only intrusion detection application that has a graphical interface for Win32 platforms. Informer allows users the ability to configure the source IP and MAC address and to specify attack modules to send over the wire. Freeware tools that you can use to assess your sensor implementations include IDS Wakeup, Sneeze, Ftester, Stick, and just about any other port and vulnerability scanner you can get your hands on.

Snort intrusion detection can be a highly effective and useful network application in your environment if the proper thought and resources are leveraged throughout the entire NIDS implementation lifecycle. It can prove to be a great technological advantage in fighting digital enemies or simply a neglected resource hog—the choice is yours to make.

Solutions Fast Track

How Do I Choose What Hardware to Use?

☑ Don't be cheap on hardware; performance peaks will instantly find the holes in weak hardware.

☑ Examine hardware specifications for features that cater to Snort.

☑ Buy in excess when dealing with CPU power, memory, hard disk space, and NIC speeds.

How Do I Choose What Operating System to Use?

☑ Linux and UNIX-based OSs are faster and more efficient, but if you don't know them well, it is advisable to purchase more powerful hardware and go with a Microsoft base.

☑ Use the advantages of the OS to create the most powerful Snort installation possible. Hence, leverage the efficiency, security, and administration aspects of whatever OS you decide upon.

Speeding Up Your Snort Installation

☑ Creating a more efficient and custom instance of Snort is essential to maximizing your sensor's potential. This can be accomplished by ensuring that only rules that add value in the appropriate means are implemented on your system.

☑ Defining the proper output and preprocessor plug-ins can mean the world when it comes to dropped packets because of a peak in network traffic.

☑ Disk cloning, installation scripts, remote administration, and generic variable declarations all aid in decreasing the mean time to complete the Snort installation process.

Benchmarking the Deployment

☑ Benchmarks are an excellent way to measure system capabilities and thresholds; however, they are of no use unless you use them in comparison tests. Benchmarks should be compared on business, managerial, and technical levels.

☑ Automation is key when developing sound Snort benchmarks.

Frequently Asked Questions

The following Frequently Asked Questions, answered by the authors of this book, are designed to both measure your understanding of the concepts presented in this chapter and to assist you with real-life implementation of these concepts. To have your questions about this chapter answered by the author, browse to **www.syngress.com/solutions** and click on the **"Ask the Author"** form.

Q: If I had to place an emphasis on hardware or OS choice, which is more important for having a stable Snort box up and running?

A: The more important aspect is to get the OS right. If you don't know how to use Linux, then installing Snort on a Linux box will do you no good. You can tweak your ruleset or manipulate the system load to accommodate some hardware deficiencies, but your ability to actually work the computer is most important. (There are minor exceptions: Don't try to realistically run Snort on a 286—hardware must be within reason.)

Q: Does network configuration determine which OS is chosen?

A: No. The fact that your network is a Windows network will not rule out the possibility of using Linux as the OS for your Snort box, and vice versa. With this in mind, we direct you to the previous question about OS performance as a criterion for choosing your OS.

Q: What kind of rules should be defined for mobile sensors; for example, Snort running on a consultant's Windows XP Professional laptop?

A: We recommended running a slimmed down ruleset that would include attacks pertinent to Windows XP Professional in addition to any applications running on that box. Specific rules to protect against NetBIOS user and share enumeration, Plug-in-Play attacks, registry connections, portscans, and other Microsoft XP-centric attacks should be included in the mobile ruleset.

Q: If familiarity is not an issue in choosing an OS, what is the best choice?

A: Linux. As the OS for which Snort was originally written, as well as being a powerful, portable, streamlined OS, Linux will outperform Solaris and Windows easily. As with so many things in the computing world, Windows will undoubtedly be a system hog and diminish program performance. Since Linux doesn't have the same sort of problem, you can easily make the decision.

## Chapter 11

Mucking Around with Barnyard

Solutions in this chapter:

- **What Is Barnyard?**

- **Preparation and Installation of Barnyard**

- **How Does Barnyard Work?**

- **What Are the Output Options for Barnyard?**

- **But I Want My Output Like "This"**

☑ **Summary**

☑ **Solutions Fast Track**

☑ **Frequently Asked Questions**

Introduction

With the ever-growing popularity of the Internet and the increasing numbers of technical savvy (or not so savvy) people, your local area network (LAN) is constantly bombarded by unwanted traffic. Network security is a serious issue for Internet traffic toward your network, which is usually protected by various firewall architectures. The internal threat to network resources is, sometimes surprisingly, prevalent as well. You never know who in your company just read the latest article in "The Computer Security Bugle" and is, even as you read this, e-mailing a portscanning tool to all of his friends. Snort is a remarkable tool for detecting wrongfully traversing packets on your network and responding with appropriate alerts, configured responses, and logging packet information for your review.

In today's world, no one has time to waste meticulously searching through pages of log files, especially searching for something that might not even be there. Snort's ability to use particular rules and set up specific alerts helps tremendously with this problem. With the selection of output plug-ins to choose from, Snort does a great job in allowing you to produce your output files in a pleasant format. However, a problem might arise: While Snort is busy with the resource-consuming process of writing packet captures to a human-readable database file, the network is still functioning as vigorously as usual.

As with any relentlessly run computer process, keeping up with such a fast pace creates a potential for errors, and Snort sensors might encounter problems with its real-time data collection. If the network adapter must analyze each packet on the local broadcast domain, it might have trouble collecting data as well. Writing alerts and packet logs to a database, while capturing live packets, is a resource-exhausting routine, and the potential for the Snort sensor, and the network card, to drop packets is always there. On a congested network, the database writes in particular will take resources away from the Snort sensor and could cause the loss of important network status information.

A tool needed to be developed to assist Snort with the challenges of continuously growing network traffic. This tool would need to be versatile and adapt to various databases, and allow you to configure settings to your own personal needs. Created exclusively for Snort, Barnyard (at the time of this writing, 0.1.0) is a utility for reading Snort unified output files and binary log output files, and then dispatching events to formatted, readable log and alert files as needed. In this chapter, we discuss how Barnyard allows Snort to work free of the all-consuming database writes, the ease of configuring Barnyard for integration with Snort processors, and how to create output that will best suit your needs, or the needs of your organization.

What Is Barnyard?

There are many choices when it comes to creating and displaying alerts and log file data. We know that Snort allows us to select the input and output options to correspond with these various output tools and databases. Barnyard is an output utility that takes advantage of Snort's *unified* output plug-in and the binary log output. The *unified* output plug-in accepts information from the Snort sensors and writes binary feeds to a log file, which might contain both alert files and packet log files. Because Snort doesn't need to convert the raw packet data into a readable format, the *unified* output plug-in, *spo_unified*, allows Snort to run as fast as possible. Due to its impressive speed and tools available that read the unified format, such as Barnyard, the unified output format is considered the future standard for Snort on high-traffic networks. Another choice for Snort user is the binary log output. This also works well when speed is an issue.

Snort relies on Barnyard to accept and decouple the spooled events provided by the unified output system or from binary log output, either as the output is produced continuously, or by reading previously created logs. This process allows Snort to operate at full speed and reassure us that it is using its resources for monitoring our network traffic effectively. Barnyard will take the burden of writing our logs to the database, allowing us to make them as detailed and verbose as we like with no adverse impact to the Snort sensors.

Barnyard's ability to integrate with Snort's output plug-ins allows it to acclimate itself to output files of almost any type. Using various configuration options and runtime switches, we can create output files that fit our schedule, cater to our needs, and most importantly, save us a great amount of time.

Preparation and Installation of Barnyard

The installation of Barnyard is fairly straightforward for the standard UNIX/Linux user. The first thing we will need is to have Snort running on our system. For a detailed discussion of Snort installation, please refer to Chapter 3, "Installing Snort."

You will also need to have a working database configured for Snort. For the purpose of this chapter, we will be using the MySQL database server and a database called *snort*.

NOTE

> You can obtain the documentation for installing and configuring MySQL database and download the binaries, or RPMs, at www.mysql.com/downloads, and the installation documentation can be found at www.mysql.com/doc/en/Quick_install.html The install documentation specified here is for a "binary distribution," (not packaged, which we'll find out later is our preferred method of installation). This Web site also contains methods for testing your install and links to lots of other MySQL documentation.
>
> In addition, Barnyard requires library files that come with the "client," "devel," and dynamic client libraries, also known as "shared," versions of the program. The Web site indicates that folks at MySQL recommend using the binaries and compiling your program yourself.

Now, with Snort and MySQL already installed and configured, we can start the process of installing Barnyard. Barnyard can be downloaded at www.snort.org/dl/barnyard, or can be found in the directory for Chapter 11 on the CD-ROM that accompanies this book. There aren't any RPMs available, so we will need to compile the program to our system's personal settings. For the purpose of this exercise, we have downloaded Barnyard-0.1.0.tar.gz into my /usr/local/ directory.

OINK!

> You can find updates and recent, or future, changes to Barnyard at the SourceForge Web site, http://cvs.sourceforge.net/cgi-bin/viewcvs.cgi/barnyard. Sometimes, these updates can come in very handy. This site contains a message board for Barnyard as well, and is the place to go to post questions, complaints, or "compliments," regarding Barnyard where other Barnyard users can view them and respond if needed.

Now we will unzip the following files:

- **cd /usr/local/** Move to the directory containing our downloaded file.

- **tar –zxvf Barnyard-0.1.0.tar.gz** This will create a new Barnyard-0.1.0 directory and extract the files, from the compressed file, into it. This process took close to two minutes on our system.

Next, we will need to consider the database configuration. We can choose from several Configure-time options during the installation process. These options are used to distinguish support for the type of database we will be using. By default, Barnyard does not provide database support, and we will need to select a Configure-time switch in order to do so.

The following is a list of the Barnyard Configure-time switches:

- *--enable-mysql* Provides support for the MySQL database.

- *--with-mysql-includes=DIR* Sets the include directories for MySQL database support to the directory where our MySQL includes exist.

- *--with-mysql-libraries=DIR* Sets the library directories for MySQL database support to the directory where our MySQL library files are located.

OINK!

Setting both the *—with-mysql-includes=DIR* and the *—with-mysql-libraries=DIR* Configure-time switch values enables the Postgres OP module.

- *--enable-postgres* Enables support for the PostgreSQL database.

- *--with-postgres-includes=DIR* Sets the include directories for PostgreSQL database support to the directory where our postgres includes exist.

- *--with-postgres-libraries=DIR* Sets the library directories for PostgreSQL database support to the directory where our Postgres library files are located.

OINK!

Setting both *-with-postgres-includes=DIR* and *–with-postgres-libraries=DIR* Configure-time switch values enables the Postgres output plug-in module.

We will need to add support for the MySQL database. Our current MySQL database has been built and installed into its default directories. Barnyard's *configure* script will find it without any problems. As previously described, choose the options that best suit your system.

Unless otherwise specified with the *includes* and *libraries* switches and their respective directories, Barnyard will search the default install directories for our database files. If our database's library files are in a directory other than their defaults and we do not select the appropriate options, we will receive an error and the *configure* script will quit. The following is an example of an error generated by in improperly configured script:

```
**********************************************
ERROR: unable to find mysql headers (mysql.h)
checked in the following places
          yes/mysql.h
**********************************************
```

This problem is easily fixed, because the error messages are very specific and will tell us what files Barnyard is unable to find. From this point, we should simply run the *configure* script with the correct switches in place.

- **cd /usr/local/Barnyard-0.1.0** Move into the directory containing our unzipped Barnyard files.

- **./configure --enable-mysql** This will analyze our system settings and determine the location of files needed to construct a list used when building the program. This process took less than three minutes with our particular system.

We can now build Barnyard with the following syntax:

```
make && make install
```

This will use the *configure* script we just created to build the program and, by using the *&&*,use the result of the *make* to install it on to our system. The entire process took less than one minute.

OINK!

If you have time, we encourage experimenting with different methods of Barnyard setup to get a feel for the install process of Barnyard and the files it uses (use different directories or database support, an so forth). One of the things that makes the UNIX operating systems so appealing is that there are so very many options from which to choose.

In some more advanced situations, we might have certain needs that won't be recognized by the *configure* script; for example, we might not want to use the default compiler *configure* looks for (GNU C/C++). If this is the case, we will need to edit the configure file on our system, such as the env program, to override the *configure* script and use the compiler of our choice. This will allow the *configure* script to correctly compile to the details of our system.

Another useful feature of Barnyard is the ability to simultaneously compile the package for multiple computer models. If we were running a version of *make* that supports VPATH (specifies a list of directories that *make* should search), we would place the object files for each computer architecture in their own directory and run the *configure* script in that directory. *Configure* automatically checks for the source code in the directory in which it resides and the parent directory of that residence to construct the list that *make* will use to build our program. By reading this configuration list, *make* will compile a program's binary files into an installation that is tailored to our computer system and can be installed onto our system with the *make install* command.

Using a *make* that does not support VPATH means that we will have to create the packages one architecture at a time. We would need to run the command *make distclean* before reconfiguring for another architecture. This command will remove any files that were created during a previous *configure* or *make* and assure that our new program compilation will start with only the original distribution files.

Notes from the Underground…

Personal Installation Issues

I ran into some problems with my first installation of MySQL. Running Red Hat Linux 7.2 with MySQL database 3.23.55, and the current version of Barnyard 0.1.0, I had installed the MySQL client, devel, and shared RPMs (the prepackaged versions for Red Hat). Everything seemed to be running okay and I was excited to get started with my Barnyard installation process.

While preparing my Barnyard install and using the *–enable-mysql*–with *mysql-includes*, I received an unusual error. MySQL acted as though it had installed, yet Barnyard could not find the correct directory for my lib (library) files. I looked, and could not find the directory for my lib files either. I tried to install MySQL again and received the message, "MySQL already installed." Next, I tried to uninstall MySQL and received the message, "MySQL not installed."

Frustrated and not wanting to waste any more time on the installation, I downloaded the binary form and installed it. I had no problems. I even installed it right over the mess I just told you about with no problems. Interestingly, at the binary download area of the MySQL Web page, way at the bottom, I saw a note that the Linux version of RPMs for x86 has been reported to be corrupt. Live and learn.

How Does Barnyard Work?

As discussed earlier in this chapter, Snort, when running in Network-based Intrusion Detection System (NIDS) mode, will be hard at work parsing rule files and detecting rogue packets. In some cases, Snort is jumping from one rule to the next, facilitating the best way to handle a particular situation and/or activating other dynamic rules triggered by specific events. It's easy to see how Barnyard could be beneficial to the Snort process. Barnyard can run in one of three modes of operation:

- **One-shot mode** Running in this mode, Barnyard will read the specified binary log file, process the data according to our configurations, and quit. This mode of operation can be indicated by the use of the *-o* switch.

- **Continual mode** Running in this mode, Barnyard will read the specified binary log file, process the data according to our configurations, and proceed to process new data as it is created by Snort.

- **Continual w/ checkpoint mode** Running in this mode, Barnyard will run as it does in continual mode with an added feature. Indicated with a *-w* switch, this mode of operation will use *Write-Ahead Logging*, (WAL). WAL, also known as *waldo*, maintains a transaction log to keep track of what data has been processed and what hasn't. WAL uses a *checkpoint* file to mark a specific point within the transaction log upon initialization and at predetermined intervals. If Barnyard is unexpectedly terminated, these marks will indicate where Barnyard stopped processing. When reinitialized, Barnyard can pick up where it left off and not miss any data.

OINK!

Many combinations of switches can be used. For example, if you weren't sure how Barnyard last shut down, you could use the *-w* and the *-f* switches together; the Barnyard process will start processing the file indicated with the *-f* switch. However, if there is any information in the *waldo* file, the *-w* switch will take precedence and start from the *checkpoint* location in the transaction log, thus keeping you from losing any data. The various switches used while initializing Barnyard are discussed in more detail later in the chapter.

Using the Barnyard Configuration File

Barnyard and Snort function quite similarly. Once initialized, Barnyard will look for the configuration file as indicated by the *-c = DIR* switch used. The barnyard.conf file is a basic list of instructions, or guidelines, for Barnyard to follow and is one of the most important and modifiable features. At first, the barnyard.conf file might seem a bit intimidating. If you are a beginner, you might find it easier to print the file out and parse it on your own with a highlighter in hand. After reviewing the file, you should realize that it is very straightforward and includes quite a bit of good documentation for each category.

At first, you might find the documentation very helpful; however, once you are more familiar with the application you might opt to eventually delete it, leaving only the relevant information for Barnyard to use. This makes evaluating and updating the barnyard.conf file much easier. If you choose to take this approach, we recommend creating a backup of the original file for your own reference and just in case the configuration does not work the first time. It is sometimes easier to start from a fresh configuration file than to rebuild a corrupt one. Again, in this day and age, it is hard to find any extra time, but if you do happen to find any, rebuilding a corrupted Barnyard configuration file would be a great learning experience.

Notes from the Underground...

Should You Spend the Time Reconstructing the barnyard.conf File?

I will vouch for the learning experience and the acquired intimacy you will gain with the Barnyard configuration file by trying to reconstruct a corrupt version. During my first experience with Barnyard, I had not created a backup copy of my barnyard.conf file and tried to correct the various options and database settings I manually edited with vi editor. This introduced more errors and I seemed to be digging a deeper hole for myself.

I had chosen a time in my schedule, (personal time), that allowed me the ability to figure some of the self-inflicted chaos out. Unfortunately, not quite as much time as I needed to weed out all the errant data.

In an attempt to keep my system clean, once I install any programs, I don't perceive a need to keep the binaries around. Therefore, I ended up having to download and extract another barnyard.conf file from the binary code. Editing the fresh, unadulterated version, I was able to get Barnyard going again in a matter of minutes.

I will admit I took the long way as far as problem resolution goes. I spent a lot of time experimenting with an unsound configuration file.

The good news is I can now create and reconfigure a barnyard configuration file from scratch, which will come in very handy when the need to use different databases or plug-ins presents itself. The morale of the story must be: I spent the time in a controlled test environment, (home), instead of on my live network at the office. Not to mention I could wear my pajamas.

Barnyard Innards

Internally, Barnyard is very similar to Snort. Barnyard reads a configuration file, (barnyard.conf) for instruction, reads output data from Snort and converts it to an internal format (like Snort's decoders), processes the data (like Snort's detection plug-ins), and writes the data out in user-specified formats (like Snort's output plug-ins). For this to work, we will need to declare some of our general system features, set up our DPs (input plug-ins), and configure our output plug-ins.

There are three areas with which we will need to become familiar while configuring our Barnyard configuration file: configuration declarations, data processors, and the output plug-ins. These settings will provide a foundation for Barnyard to run on our system and enable the appropriate features. We discuss these three areas in greater detail in the following sections.

Configuration Declarations

Within this configuration declaration area, we can set up our general settings which include the computer hostname and the interface Snort is monitoring. There are a few other options supplied for us as well, such as configuring Barnyard to run in *daemon* mode (background), or setting a filter. This part of the configuration file is to save time at the command prompt, and keep us from having to enter a three- or four-line *run* statement. Two of the options are listed next and are currently only used with the ACID database output plug-in.

```
config hostname: (your computer name or localhost)
config interface: (select your sniffing interface)
```

For more information on ACID, please refer to Chapter 8, "Exploring the Data Analysis Tools."

Data Processors

DPs, or input plug-ins, are the translating tools needed to pull information from Snort's unified spooler, or binary log output plug-in, and put that data into a form readable by Barnyard output plug-ins, described next. Here we will select the type of DPs we will be using with Barnyard. In most cases, it is fine to leave them as originally found in the barnyard.conf file. The syntax for all three of these options is the same and is automatically set up by default:

```
processor <processor_name>
```

The default setup includes the following DPs:

- **dp_alert** This processor has the ability to read the alert (also known as *event*) format created by Snort's unified spooler plug-in, *spo_unified*. When Snort generates an alert, it will spool the necessary data to the appropriate log file. The *dp_alert* processor will then read this data. *dp_alert* works in conjunction with Barnyard's output plug-in *alert_fast*, the output plug-in used for the alert input type. This processor takes no arguments and works in its default state.

- **dp_log** This processor contains the ability to read the log format produced by the *spo_unified* plug-in. When Snort recognizes a packet that needs to be logged, the *spo_unified* plug-in will write this data to the specified log file. The *dp_log* processor will then read this data. *dp_log* and works in conjunction with Barnyard's output plug-in *log_dump*, the output plug-in used for the log input type. This processor does not need any arguments set either and works fine in its default setup.

- **dp_stream_stat** This processor includes the ability to read the binary output from Snort's *spp_stream4* plug-in. This processor is used with output plug-ins that support stream4 technology such as the *alert_syslog* output plug-in. Again, this processor takes no arguments.

Output Plug-Ins

In this area, we will select the type of output plug-ins we would like to use with Barnyard. These output plug-ins will need to be matched up with their associated input plug-ins as previously mentioned. For example, if we are using *dp_log* to read our log files, we will need to use the *log_dump* output plug-in (described next) to create a human-readable format. Listed next are the three primary output plug-ins we will want to use with our Barnyard configuration file. They will accept the data from the processors and produce output we desire. The format for the output plug-ins has no arguments and is also set by default:

```
output <plug-in_name>
```

The following default output plug-ins are included with the initial *barnyard.conf* file:

- **alert_fast** This output plug-in will covert the data received by the *dp_alert* input plug-in to a format similar to the *fast alert* mode of Snort. This format consists of one line per specified output file. The *alert_fast* format increases the output production time significantly because it will not write all the packet header information to the output.

- *log_dump* This output plug-in will convert data received from the *dp_log* input plug-in into a format similar to the *ASCII packet dump* mode of Snort. This format will include verbose information and will be particularly useful for analyzing network traffic, as provided from the *dp_log* input plug-in, via Snort's *spo_unified* plug-in.

- *alert_syslog* This output plug-in will take data from the *dp_stream_stat* input plug-in and convert the data to a format similar to the *alert_syslog* output plug-in of Snort. This process will output alerts to the syslog service. The features of Snort's *alert_syslog* can be used within Barnyard by specifying options in the Snort rules file. The predetermined specifications (for example, *alert priority*) will make their way to the *alert_syslog* output plug-in via the *dp_stream_stat* plug-in.

The following is a barnyard.conf file used for this chapter. This configuration file will give us an idea of what the file looks like and how the previous syntax examples of the output plug-ins and DPs are listed together. As mentioned earlier, the documentation included with the default barnyard.conf file, for the most part, has been removed. Removing the documentation resulted in reducing the file from almost three pages to less than one page, making it much more readable. The edited version of the barnyard.conf file can be viewed in the following output:

```
# Step 0: Configuration declarations - set up system configurations to avoid
# excessive typing when running an instance of barnyard
config hostname: localhost
config interface: eth1


# Step 1: setup the data processors - comment out, (or delete), the
# dataprocessors we will not be using by using are indicated by the "#".
processor dp_alert
processor dp_log
# processor dp_stream_stat


# Step 2: setup the output plugins - comment out, (or delete), the
# output plug-ins we will not be using by using are indicated by the "#".
output alert_fast
output log_dump
```

```
# output alert_syslog

# Step 3: database reporting - input the configuration for our database
# needs, this is created for our mysql setup.
output database: log, mysql, dbname=snort user=root host=localhost
detail=full
output database: alert, mysql, dbname=snort user=root host=localhost
detail=full
```

OINK!

Normally, for security reasons, you would not want to keep your database user as root, and you would want to set up a strong password. While learning how to use Barnyard, using *user=root* with no password or a username with root privileges will suffice. For our learning exercises, we know that root privileges (UNIX version of administrator for Windows users) will not have any problems with file permissions.

In the real world, if a "cracker" accessed your network, he would more than likely try to find a way to cover his tracks—hence the search for your reporting database. The username "root" will probably be at the top of the list of usernames to try while running a password-cracking tool on your database. If root is your username for the database, the cracker has just won half the battle (not to mention "half the battle" to your entire system, and from there, the cracker's possibilities become bewildering).

There are other output processors we can use that are still in the experimental stage. For example, *alert_html* will output alert data to Web pages, and *alert_csv* will create comma-separated value lists. The *alert_csv* output plug-in has numerous options from which to choose for formatting output. These options are listed in the initial barnyard.conf file with brief descriptions.

Once you become accustomed to the operations of Snort and Barnyard, have fun experimenting and playing with the different output options. We can now see how easy it is to modify the barnyard.conf file and specify various, personal settings. With the open-source code, you might end up creating something useful that others users won't believe they've done without.

Oink!

A quick reminder: Have a backup copy of the original Barnyard configuration file to use as a reference or to replace the edited one if necessary.

Create and Display a Binary Log Output File

Now that we have discussed the installation process and modified the barnyard configuration file to our preferences, we will walk through a Snort capture to produce a *binary log output* file. After generating the packet capture, we will run an instance of Barnyard, with the appropriate switches enabled, and create an output file.

1. First, we are going to create our *binary log output* file. Run Snort to create a log file that combines both alert and log files together in a binary logdump format.

   ```
   Snort -b -c /usr/local/snort/snort.conf - h HOME_NET -i eth1 -L
   youropfile
   ```

2. Once Snort is running, we can run some suspicious traffic such as Nmap or another port-scanning tool of your choice. We will be running "Angry IP scanner" to set off a few alerts. After generating some mischievous traffic on our network, go ahead and press the key combination **Ctrl+C** to exit Snort.

3. Next, let's look at what we just created.

   ```
   cd /var/log/snort   Move into the default Snort logging directory.
   ```

   Notice the naming scheme of the log file: *<month><date>@<time>*. By using the *–L* switch, Snort will add this format to the end of our chosen output filename by default; in our case, the file will be Test22003@1103 (or whatever month/date/time you happen to be running your process). If we don't specify a filename, the file will simply be named with this month/date/time format. This naming scheme is useful for distinguishing various log files within one standard directory. It is also beneficial for avoiding accidental overwrites of older data. Write down the name of this file, as we will use it to tell Barnyard what file we want processed.

4. Now that we have created a Snort unified output file, we will run Barnyard to parse the log file and produce our desired output. Before we actually invoke Barnyard, let's review the assorted options we have to choose from. These options will direct Barnyard to run in a particular mode *(one-time, continual, or continual w/ checkpoint)*, and can direct Barnyard to directories for any additional files it will need to use (waldo, library files, and so forth). There are 15 different options that will allow us to run Barnyard in our specific environment. Table 11.1 lists the different options.

Table 11.1 Runtime Switches

Option	Extended Name	Action
-a (directory)	Archive	Specify directory to package files for backup after processing.
-c (conf file)	configuration file	Specify location of barnyard.conf to use.
-d (directory)	directory	Directory from which to read unified spool files. Default is "/var/log/snort".
-D	Daemon mode	Run Barnyard in the background.
-f (file)	file	Used with continual mode to set the name of the base spool file to read, or set name of the target file in "one-shot" mode.
-g (file)	generator	Location of generator names file to be read (gen-msg.map). Maps Snort DP alerts with their associated events.
-h	Help	Show list of runtime switches and usage data.
-L (directory)	Logging	Choose the directory and file to log output.
-o	one shot mode	Process the spool file and quit.
-s (file)	sid	Location of the Snort rule ID file (sid-msg.map). Maps sids with their associated alert message.
-t (time)	Time	Set the time (seconds) to be compared with the unified spool file creation time.

Continued

Table 11.1 Runtime Switches

Option	Extended Name	Action
		Of available files to process, the file with an age less than or equal to this setting will be read first.
-w (file)	waldo	Indicates the name of the checkpoint file and initializes it. If Barnyard unexpect edly stops, waldo will mark that point of the log file where Barnyard stopped processing. When Barnyard starts again, it will begin reading at that point. This process is known as Write-Ahead Logging (WAL).
-R	(Dry) Run	Used for debugging purposes, processes command-line info and displays the con figuration file as it is read.
-X (file)	-X	Running in daemon mode, indicates the pid file.
-V	Version	Display the version and exit.

Now that we have examined the different runtime options, we can run Barnyard and process our Snort unified output. For this example, the *-L* switch is being implemented. To accurately use this option as stated in the following syntax, we will need to create a new directory within the /var/log directory called *barnyard*. This is entirely optional, but it is a good way to separate our processed files from the unprocessed files. Let's create the directory here:

```
mkdir /var/log/barnyard <enter>
```

Running Barnyard

The syntax we can use to parse our newly created log file is as follows:

```
[root@localhost /local]# barnyard -o -c /etc/snort/barnyard.conf \

-f /var/log/snort/youropfile.log -L /var/log/barnyard \
-g /etc/snort/gen-msg.map -s /etc/snort/sid-msg.map
```

Let's take a closer look at the options we have selected and what they mean. To make the command syntax easier to read, we implemented the " \ " symbol at the end of each line, indicating that it is all to be included as one line. By using the *–o* switch, we indicated that we only want Barnyard to process the selected file and then quit. Using the *-c* switch, we specified that the appropriate configuration file is located at /etc/snort/barnyard.conf. This option will indicate the DPs and OPs we want to use in developing our output, and the type of database to which the output will be reported. The spool file Barnyard will process is located at the *-f* /var/log/snort directory, and the file we just created is called youropfile.log. We have used the *−L* switch to indicate that our processed output file is to be stored in the /var/log/barnyard directory. The *−g* and *−s* switches indicate the location for Barnyard to generate alerts and map to *Snort rule IDs*, respectively.

Review the output shown in the following example. Of course, the output you receive will be depend on your network settings and whatever traffic you have running on it. This output should be fairly similar in its form.

Let's review the Barnyard output, as it was reported to our MySQL database, and see what we have come up with by accessing our MySQL database:

```
mysql
mysql> connect snort
mysql> select * from event:
+---------------------------------------------------+
| sid | cid | signature      | timestamp            |
+---+----+-----------+----------------------+
|   1 |   1 |              2 | 2003-02-10   11:03:44 |
|   1 |   2 |              2 | 2003-02-10   11:03:44 |
|   1 |   3 |              2 | 2003-02-10   11:03:44 |
|   1 |   4 |              2 | 2003-02-10   11:03:44 |
|   1 |   5 |              2 | 2003-02-10   11:03:45 |
|   1 |   6 |              2 | 2003-02-10   11:03:45 |
|   1 |   7 |              2 | 2003-02-10   11:03:45 |
|   1 |   8 |              2 | 2003-02-10   11:03:45 |
|   1 |   9 |              2 | 2003-02-10   11:03:46 |
|   1 |  10 |              2 | 2003-02-10   11:03:46 |
|   1 |  11 |              2 | 2003-02-10   11:03:46 |
|   1 |  12 |              2 | 2003-02-10   11:03:47 |
|   1 |  13 |              2 | 2003-02-10   11:03:47 |
|   1 |  14 |              2 | 2003-02-10   11:03:47 |
|   1 |  15 |              2 | 2003-02-10   11:03:47 |
|   1 |  16 |              2 | 2003-02-10   11:03:48 |
|   1 |  17 |              2 | 2003-02-10   11:03:48 |
|   1 |  18 |              2 | 2003-02-10   11:03:48 |
|   1 |  19 |              2 | 2003-02-10   11:03:48 |
```

Barnyard Output Explanation

By using the *–b* switch, we created the *spo_unified binary dump*. Next, we started Barnyard using the appropriate switches to process that output file into a human-readable format. Now let's see what Barnyard actually did.

1. Barnyard initialized and registered all built-in functions and plug-ins.

2. Barnyard read the command line, which in turn lead Barnyard to read the configuration file (and the *waldo* file if one was selected).

3. The gen-msg.map, sid-msg.map, and the classification.config files were then initialized. As mentioned with the runtime switches, the gen-msg.map file maps Snort DP alerts with their associated events. The sid-msg.map file will map Snort IDs (or sids) with their associated alert messages. The classification.config file will allow Barnyard to classify alerts into categories of severity. There are defaults set for these classifications, and within this file we can change these priorities to best suit our own networks. The following is an excerpt from the classification.config file. We can see *config classification:* (initialization code) followed by a brief description (*attempted-recon*), a name for the classification (*Attempted Information Leak*), and the priority set either by default or our own preference (1 being of the highest priority).

    ```
    config classification: not-suspicious,Not Suspicious Traffic,3
    config classification: unknown,Unknown Traffic,3
    config classification: bad-unknown,Potentially Bad Traffic, 2
    config classification: attempted-recon,Attempted Information Leak,2
    ```

    These classifications will be used within the rule files within Snort. For instance:

    ```
    #    alert TCP any any -> any 25 (msg:"SMTP expn root"; flags:A+; \
    #          content:"expn root"; nocase; classtype:attempted-recon;)
    ```

4. In the next step, Barnyard's *dp_log* input plug-in read Snort's *spo_unified* output data from the /var/log/snort directory and passed it to the appropriate output plug-in. Barnyard's output plug-in, *log_dump*, then accepted the data and converted it into a human-readable format. The next step performed by *log_dump* is that the information is written to the Snort database. According to our *run* commands and our Barnyard configuration file, the processed ASCII packet dump file output file is

located in the /var/log/barnyard directory, and the file will be called youropfile.log.

What Are the Output Options for Barnyard?

Barnyard comes equipped with various output options. The Barnyard installation process creates a new directory to /snort called *output plug-ins*. This directory contains the information needed for Barnyard to accept data from the DPs and correlate that data into an acceptable format for the database we are using.

As mentioned earlier, the output plug-ins are included and enabled in the barnyard.conf file. In addition to manipulating the Snort rules to collect specific data, we can select the output plug-ins to present that data for our personal or business reporting needs.

Tools & Traps…

Switches to Try…

With all the various runtime switches from which to choose, there are a few that might be a little more standard for regular use, and yet others (*–g* and *–s*) that are mandatory for proper use. The following is an example of those switches and actually represents one command:

```
[root@localhost /bin]# barnyard -c /etc/snort/barnyard.conf\
-f /var/log/snort/file_to_process.log \
-L /var/log/barnyard \
-w /var/log/snort/waldo \
-g /etc/snort/gen-msg.map \
-s /etc/snort/sid-msg.map <enter>
```

Using the " \ " symbol creates a much nicer format to view and makes it easier to understand what will be taking place. In this example, Barnyard will use the information within the barnyard.conf file, located within the directory /etc/snort/barnyard.conf, to process the binary log

Continued

---

file as designated by the *–f* switch. The binary log file Barnyard will process is located at the -f /var/log/snort/ directory, and the file, previously created by Snort, is called file_to_process.log. The processed output will be stored in the -L /var/log/barnyard directory and recorded using the OP specified within the Barnyard configuration file. Using the *–w* option will indicate the location of your *waldo* file to monitor your transaction log. The *–g* and *–s* switches indicate the location for Barnyard to generate alerts and map to Snort rule IDs, respectively. These two switches must be used in order to find the appropriate file, or an error will occur. Without the *–o* option present, Barnyard will run in continuous mode. Any data provided by Snort will be processed as it comes in. The previously mentioned classification.config file will need to be moved (or copied) from the snort/etc directory so it resides within the barnyard/etc directory. There is currently no switch for providing a path to this file. If the file is not in the appropriate place, we will receive an error similar to:

```
ERROR => Unable to open Classification file
"/usr/local/barnyard/etc/classification.config": No such file or
directory
```

Some recent additions to the barnyard.conf file will allow us to actually run Barnyard without the *–g* and *–s* switches. These files can be preconfigured within the "configuration declarations" section of the barnyard.conf file. For example:

```
config generator-map: gen-msg.map
config signature-map: sid-msg.map
```

With these lines added to the barnyard.conf file, we could cut out the last two lines. The SourceForge's CVS Web site (mentioned next) constantly adds updates to Barnyard files, so check it often if you are an avid Barnyard user.

But I Want My Output Like "This"

Creating output plug-ins for Barnyard is basically straightforward; however, it could be very time consuming to all but a seasoned C programmer. Unfortunately, there are no templates deployed with Barnyard release 0.1.0. There is good news, however. We can download templates for Barnyard input plug-ins and output plug-ins at the SourceForge's Concurrent Version System (CVS) Web site (http://cvs.sourceforge.net/cgi-bin/viewcvs.cgi/barnyard/barnyard). These templates will take care of our output plug-in template needs.

For anyone new to the CVS concept, it includes information regarding various open-source code and application projects. The one we are concerned with here, of course, is Barnyard. We can find a wealth of information regarding the current creation of output plug-ins and the latest "preferred style" of code formatting. At this site, you can also read news regarding the future of Barnyard, written by the developers of Barnyard. This Web site also contains a message board where we can read about problems others have experienced and the resolutions to said problems in their respective follow-up messages, or we can post our own questions. The creator's of Barnyard are the most likely candidates to field our

questions and help us find a resolution.

On the CD-ROM accompanying this book, you will find the latest version of the *alert_csv* OP. The scalability of the *alert_csv* module will more than likely become the most popular output method used by Barnyard. Since the Comma Separated Values (CSV) format is so common to different operating systems, it will allow portability to Windows programs, such as Microsoft Excel and Microsoft Exchange, or allow Barnyard to report its output to a myriad of other software programs.

The following code is an output plug-in template created by Andrew Baker, one of the original developers of Snort. This output plug-in will give us a basis to better understand the structure and help us to create our own output modules. After the template, there is a quick guide to installing our newly created output plug-in so that it will be recognized by Barnyard. If this example isn't quite what you need, as mentioned earlier, you'll find it helpful to print this example out and another currently deployed Barnyard output module, and with highlighter in hand, compare the two files for similarities.

An Example Output Plug-In

The output plug-in consists of two files: the Header, or .h file, and the C, or .c file. ("C" represents the programming language used to create this file). These files are located in the /barnyard/src/output-plugins directory. Input plug-ins are located within the same parent directory as well. Here is an example of the op_alert_csv.h header file:

```
/* $Id: op_alert_csv.h,v 1.2 2003/01/30 13:29:53 andrewbaker Exp $ */
/*
** Copyright (C) 2001-2003 Andrew R. Baker <andrewb@snort.org>
**
** This program is free software; you can redistribute it and/or modify
```

```
** it under the terms of the GNU General Public License as published by
** the Free Software Foundation; either version 2 of the License, or
** (at your option) any later version.
**
** This program is distributed in the hope that it will be useful,
** but WITHOUT ANY WARRANTY; without even the implied warranty of
** MERCHANTABILITY or FITNESS FOR A PARTICULAR PURPOSE.  See the
** GNU General Public License for more details.
**
** You should have received a copy of the GNU General Public License
** along with this program; if not, write to the Free Software
** Foundation, Inc., 59 Temple Place - Suite 330, Boston, MA 02111-1307,
USA.
*/
/*
These statements will initialize the associated ".c" file for use.
*/
#ifndef __OP_ALERT_CSV_H__
#define __OP_ALERT_CSV_H__


int OpAlertCSV_Init();


#endif  /* __OP_ALERT_CSV_H__ */
```

The following is a representation of the ".c" file. For our purposes we included the op_alert_csv.c C file. This file is extremely long, so we only included enough of the file to get an understanding of the structure.

```
/* $Id: op_alert_csv.c,v 1.5 2003/02/28 23:55:18 andrewbaker Exp $ */
/*
** Copyright (C) 2001-2002 Andrew R. Baker <andrewb@snort.org>
**
** This program is free software; you can redistribute it and/or modify
** it under the terms of the GNU General Public License as published by
** the Free Software Foundation; either version 2 of the License, or
** (at your option) any later version.
**
```

```
** This program is distributed in the hope that it will be useful,
** but WITHOUT ANY WARRANTY; without even the implied warranty of
** MERCHANTABILITY or FITNESS FOR A PARTICULAR PURPOSE.  See the
** GNU General Public License for more details.
**
** You should have received a copy of the GNU General Public License
** along with this program; if not, write to the Free Software
** Foundation, Inc., 59 Temple Place - Suite 330, Boston, MA 02111-1307,
USA.
*/


/*
 * BUGS:
 *
 *    Strings are not properly escaped.   (embedded '"' will cause bad
things)
 *
 * TODO:
 *
 * Allow multiple timestamp printing formats
 *
 * Suggestions?
 *
 *
 * Keyword list:
 *   sig_gen          - signature generator
 *   sig_id           - signature id
 *   sig_rev          - signatrue revision
 *   sid              - SID triplet
 *   class            - class id
 *   classname        - textual name of class
 *   priority         - priority id
 *   event_id         - event id
 *   event_reference  - event reference
 *   ref_tv_sec       - reference seconds
 *   ref_tv_usec      - reference microseconds
 *   tv_sec           - event seconds
```

```
 *    tv_usec          - event microseconds
 *    timestamp        - prettified timestamp (2001-01-01 01:02:03) in UTC
 *    src              - src address as a u_int32_t
 *    srcip            - src address as a dotted quad
 *    dst              - dst address as a u_int32_t
 *    dstip            - dst address as a dotted quad
 *    sport_itype      - source port or ICMP type (or 0)
 *    sport            - source port (if UDP or TCP)
 *    itype            - ICMP type (if ICMP)
 *    dport_icode      - dest port or ICMP code (or 0)
 *    dport            - dest port
 *    icode            - ICMP code (if ICMP)
 *    proto            - protocol number
 *    protoname        - protocol name
 *    flags            - flags from AlertRecord
 *    msg              - message text
 *    hostname         - hostname (from barnyard.conf)
 *    interface        - interface (from barnyard.conf)
 */



/*  I N C L U D E S  ********************************************************/
/* These statements will distinguish the other "C" files that are
/* associated with this output plug-in.  It is much easier and less
/* time consuming to use code previously written, also known as "modular"
/*  programming.  This will also help avoid the "reinventing the wheel"
/*  anamoly and potential code errors that could otherwise occur.
*/
#include "parser.h"
#include "mstring.h"
#include "util.h"
#include "barnyard.h"
#include "by_errno.h"
#include "Dictionary/Class.h"
#include "Dictionary/ClassMap.h"
#include "Dictionary/Signature.h"
#include "Dictionary/SignatureMap.h"
```

```c
#include "op_plugbase.h"
#include "Event/EventRecord.h"

#include <sys/types.h>
#include <stdio.h>
#include <string.h>
#include <stdlib.h>
#include <syslog.h>
#include <errno.h>



/* KEYWORD DEFINES */
/* This area defines the keywords that will be used throughout the
*/ rest of the file.
*/
#define CSV_SIG_GEN             1
#define CSV_SIG_ID              2
#define CSV_SIG_REV             3
#define CSV_SID                 4
#define CSV_CLASS               5
#define CSV_CLASSNAME           6
#define CSV_PRIORITY            7
#define CSV_EVENT_ID            9
#define CSV_EVENT_REFERENCE    10
#define CSV_REF_TV_SEC         11
#define CSV_REF_TV_USEC        12
#define CSV_TV_SEC             13
#define CSV_TV_USEC            14
#define CSV_TIMESTAMP          15
#define CSV_SRC                16
#define CSV_SRCIP              17
#define CSV_DST                18
#define CSV_DSTIP              19
#define CSV_SPORT_ITYPE        20
#define CSV_SPORT              21
#define CSV_ITYPE              22
#define CSV_DPORT_ICODE        23
```

```
#define CSV_DPORT              24
#define CSV_ICODE              25
#define CSV_PROTO              26
#define CSV_PROTONAME          27
#define CSV_FLAGS              28
#define CSV_MSG                29
#define CSV_HOSTNAME           30
#define CSV_INTERFACE          31


/*  D A T A    S T R U C T U R E S  *************************************/
/*
/* This area will define the format and the method for storing data
/* to best work with our chosen output scheme.
*/
typedef struct _OpAlertCSVData
{
    char *filepath;
    FILE *file;
    int num_entries;
    u_int32_t *entry_defs;
} OpAlertCSVData;




/*  P R O T O T Y P E S  ***************************************************/
/*
/* We can notice the "OpAlertCSV" relates to the "OpAlertCSV_Init()"
/* from the header file.  These prototypes will indicate the specifics
/*  of the OP arguments and return values. This area also defines the
/* actual functions and how they will report the data collected.
*/
static int OpAlertCSV_Setup(char *args);
static int OpAlertCSV_Start(OpInstance *);
static int OpAlertCSV_Stop(OpInstance *);
static int OpAlertCSV_Destroy(OpInstance *);


static int OpAlertCSV(void *context, EventRecord *eventRecord);
```

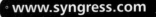

```
static int OpAlertCSV_ParseArgs(char *, OpAlertCSVData **);
static int OpAlertCSV_ParseCustomFormat(OpAlertCSVData *data, char *format);
static char *CSVEscape(char *);


/*
This area will make the OP available to the preprocessor directives.
*/
void OpAlertCSV_Init()
{

    OpRegister("alert_csv", OpAlertCSV_Setup);

    if(pv.verbose)
        LogMessage("AlertCSV registered\n");
}


/*
 * Output plugin opInstance setup
 * process arguments
 * Create a new output plugin opInstance
 * link in functions
 */
static int OpAlertCSV_Setup(char *args)
{
    OpAlertCSVData *data;
    OpInstance *opInstance;
    int rval = 0;

    if((rval = OpAlertCSV_ParseArgs(args, &data)))
        return rval;

    /* create a new output plugin instance */
    if((rval = OpInstantiate((void *)data, &opInstance)))
    {
        /* XXX free data */
        return rval;
    }
```

```
    /* attach functions */
    opInstance->startFunc = OpAlertCSV_Start;
    opInstance->stopFunc = OpAlertCSV_Stop;
    opInstance->destroyFunc = OpAlertCSV_Destroy;

    /* register event handlers */
    if((rval = OpInstallEventHandler(ALERT, opInstance, OpAlertCSV)))
    {
        /* XXX free instance */
        return rval;
    }

    return 0;

}

/*
 * start this opInstance.   Open files, network sockets, etc...
 */
static int OpAlertCSV_Start(OpInstance *opInstance)
{
    OpAlertCSVData *data;

    if(!opInstance)
        return -1;   /* EINVAL */

    data = (OpAlertCSVData *)opInstance->context;

    if(!data)
    {
        LogMessage("ERROR: Unable to find context for AlertCSV\n");
        return -1;
    }

    /* Open file */
    if(!(data->file = fopen(data->filepath, "a")))
    {
```

```
            LogMessage("ERROR: Unable to open file '%s': %s\n", data->filepath,
                    strerror(errno));
            return -1;
        }


        return 0;
}



/*
 * stop this opInstance.  Close files, network connections, etc.
 */
static int OpAlertCSV_Stop(OpInstance *opInstance)
{
    OpAlertCSVData *data;

    if(!opInstance)
        return -1;   /* XXX EINVAL */

    data = (OpAlertCSVData *)opInstance->context;

    if(!data)
    {
        LogMessage("ERROR: Unable to find context for AlertCSV\n");
        return -1;
    }

    /* close file */
    fclose(data->file);

    return 0;
}


static int OpAlertCSV_Destroy(OpInstance *opInstance)
{
    OpAlertCSVData *data = (OpAlertCSVData *)opInstance->context;
```

```
    if(data)
    {
        if(data->filepath)
            free(data->filepath);
        if(data->entry_defs)
            free(data->entry_defs);
    }

    return 0;
}


static int OpAlertCSV(void *context, EventRecord *eventRecord)
{
    int i = 0;
    Signature *signature = NULL;
    Class *class = NULL;
    char timestamp[TIMEBUF_SIZE];
    AlertRecord *record = NULL;
    OpAlertCSVData *op_data = NULL;
    FILE *file = NULL;
    char *escaped_string = NULL;

    if(!context || !eventRecord)
        return BY_EINVAL;

    if(eventRecord->type != ALERT)
        return 0;

    record = (AlertRecord *)eventRecord->data;
    op_data = (OpAlertCSVData *)context;
    file = op_data->file;

    if(op_data->num_entries == 0)
    {
        /* default output mode */
        fprintf(op_data->file,
            "%u,%u,%u,%u,%u,%u,%lu,%lu,%u,%u,%u,%u,%u,%u\n",
```

```
                    record->event.sig_generator,

                    record->event.sig_id, record->event.sig_rev,

                    record->event.classification, record->event.priority,

                    record->event.event_id, record->ts.tv_sec, record-
                        >ts.tv_usec,

                    record->sip, record->dip, record->sp, record->sp, record-
                        >dp,

                    record->protocol);

    }

/*

/* This area will run individual output data files through the

/* previously mentioned keywords until a match is found.

/* If no match is found within the keywords, a function will

/* either print out a "," or a return character (blank line).

/* This would then require some additional research.

*/


    for(i = 0; i < op_data->num_entries; ++i)

    {

        switch(op_data->entry_defs[i])

        {

            case CSV_SIG_GEN:

                fprintf(file, "%u", record->event.sig_generator);

                break;

            case CSV_SIG_ID:

                fprintf(file, "%u", record->event.sig_id);

                break;

            case CSV_SIG_REV:

                fprintf(file, "%u", record->event.sig_rev);

                break;

            case CSV_SID:

                fprintf(file, "%u:%u:%u", record->event.sig_generator,

                        record->event.sig_id, record->event.sig_rev);

                break;

            case CSV_CLASS:

                fprintf(file, "%u", record->event.classification);

                break;
```

```
case CSV_CLASSNAME:
    class = ClassMapLookupById(record->event.classification);
    fprintf(file, "\"%s\"",
            class != NULL ? class->name : "Unknown");
    break;
case CSV_PRIORITY:
    fprintf(file, "%u", record->event.priority);
    break;
case CSV_EVENT_ID:
    fprintf(file, "%u", record->event.event_id);
    break;
case CSV_EVENT_REFERENCE:
    fprintf(file, "%u", record->event.event_reference);
    break;
case CSV_REF_TV_SEC:
    fprintf(file, "%lu", record->event.ref_time.tv_sec);
    break;
case CSV_REF_TV_USEC:
    fprintf(file, "%lu", record->event.ref_time.tv_usec);
    break;
case CSV_TV_SEC:
    fprintf(file, "%lu", record->ts.tv_sec);
    break;
case CSV_TV_USEC:
    fprintf(file, "%lu", record->ts.tv_usec);
    break;
case CSV_TIMESTAMP:
    RenderTimestamp(record->ts.tv_sec, timestamp,
        TIMEBUF_SIZE);
    fprintf(file, "\"%s\"", timestamp);
    break;
case CSV_SRC:
    fprintf(file, "%u", record->sip);
    break;
case CSV_SRCIP:
    fprintf(file, "%u.%u.%u.%u",
            (record->sip & 0xff000000) >> 24,
```

```
                                (record->sip & 0x00ff0000) >> 16,
                                (record->sip & 0x0000ff00) >> 8,
                                record->sip & 0x000000ff);
            break;
        case CSV_DST:
            fprintf(file, "%u", record->dip);
            break;
        case CSV_DSTIP:
            fprintf(file, "%u.%u.%u.%u",
                                (record->dip & 0xff000000) >> 24,
                                (record->dip & 0x00ff0000) >> 16,
                                (record->dip & 0x0000ff00) >> 8,
                                record->dip & 0x000000ff);
            break;
        case CSV_SPORT_ITYPE:
            fprintf(file, "%u", record->sp);
            break;
        case CSV_SPORT:
            if((record->protocol == 6) || (record->protocol == 17))
                fprintf(file, "%u", record->sp);
            break;
        case CSV_ITYPE:
            if(record->protocol == 1)
                fprintf(file, "%u", record->sp);
            break;
        case CSV_DPORT_ICODE:
            fprintf(file, "%u", record->dp);
            break;
        case CSV_DPORT:
            if((record->protocol == 6) || (record->protocol == 17))
                fprintf(file, "%u", record->dp);
            break;
        case CSV_ICODE:
            if(record->protocol == 1)
                fprintf(file, "%u", record->dp);
            break;
        case CSV_PROTO:
```

```
            fprintf(file, "%u", record->protocol);
            break;
    case CSV_PROTONAME:
            fprintf(file, "\"%s\"", protocol_names[record->protocol]);
            break;
    case CSV_FLAGS:
            fprintf(file, "%u", record->flags);
            break;
    case CSV_MSG:
            signature = SignatureMapLookupById(record-
                >event.sig_generator,
                    record->event.sig_id, 0 /* rev */);
            if(signature)
            {
                /* XXX err check */
                escaped_string = CSVEscape(signature->message);
                fprintf(file, "%s", escaped_string);
                free(escaped_string);
            }
            else
                fprintf(file, "Snort Alert");
            break;
    case CSV_HOSTNAME:
        /* XXX err check */
        escaped_string = CSVEscape(pv.hostname);
        fprintf(file, "%s", pv.hostname != NULL ? escaped_string :
            "");
        free(escaped_string);
        break;
    case CSV_INTERFACE:
        /* XXX err check */
        escaped_string = CSVEscape(pv.interface);
        fprintf(file, "%s", pv.interface != NULL ? escaped_string :
            "");
        free(escaped_string);
        break;
    }
```

```
            if(i < op_data->num_entries - 1)
                fprintf(file, ",");
            else
                fprintf(file, "\n");
    }
    fflush(file);
    return 0;
}


/*
/* This area is where the Output Processor is actually started
/* and prepares the data for output for a single data type (instantiation).
*/
/* initialize the output processor for this particular instantiation */
static int OpAlertCSV_ParseArgs(char *args, OpAlertCSVData **data)
{
    OpAlertCSVData *tmp;
    char **toks = NULL;
    int num_toks;

    if(!(tmp = (OpAlertCSVData *)calloc(1, sizeof(OpAlertCSVData))))
    {
        return BY_ENOMEM;
    }

    if(args)
    {
        /* parse out your args */
        toks = mSplit(args, " ", 2, &num_toks, 0);   /* XXX error check */
        switch(num_toks)
        {
            case 2:
                if(OpAlertCSV_ParseCustomFormat(tmp, toks[1]))
                    goto error;
            case 1:
                if(!(tmp->filepath = strdup(toks[0])))
                    goto error; /* ENOMEM */
```

```
                    break;
                case 0:
                    if(!(tmp->filepath = strdup("csv.out")))
                        goto error; /* ENOMEM */
                    break;
                default:
                    LogMessage("ERROR %s (%d) => Invalid arguments for
                        AlertCSV "
                            "plugin: %s\n", current_file, current_line, args);
                    goto error;
        }
    }
    else
    {
        if(!(tmp->filepath = strdup("csv.out")))
            goto error;
    }

    if(toks)
        FreeToks(toks, num_toks);

    *data = tmp;

    return 0;

error:
    if(toks)
        FreeToks(toks, num_toks);

    if(tmp)
    {
        if(tmp->filepath)
            free(tmp->filepath);
        if(tmp->entry_defs)
            free(tmp->entry_defs);
        free(tmp);
    }
```

```
    return BY_ENOMEM; /* ??? */
}



int OpAlertCSV_ParseCustomFormat(OpAlertCSVData *data, char *format)
{
    char **toks;
    int num_toks;
    int i;
    toks = mSplit(format, ",", 128, &num_toks, 0); /* Error check */
    data->num_entries = num_toks;

    if(!(data->entry_defs = (u_int32_t *)calloc(num_toks,
sizeof(u_int32_t))))
    {
        return -1; /* ENOMEM */
    }

    for(i = 0; i < num_toks; ++i)
    {
        if(strcasecmp("sig_gen", toks[i]) == 0)
        {
            data->entry_defs[i] = CSV_SIG_GEN;
        }
        else if(strcasecmp("sig_id", toks[i]) == 0)
        {
            data->entry_defs[i] = CSV_SIG_ID;
        }
        else if(strcasecmp("sig_rev", toks[i]) == 0)
        {
            data->entry_defs[i] = CSV_SIG_REV;
        }
        else if(strcasecmp("sid", toks[i]) == 0)
        {
            data->entry_defs[i] = CSV_SID;
        }
```

```c
else if(strcasecmp("class", toks[i]) == 0)
{
    data->entry_defs[i] = CSV_CLASS;
}
else if(strcasecmp("classname", toks[i]) == 0)
{
    data->entry_defs[i] = CSV_CLASSNAME;
}
else if(strcasecmp("priority", toks[i]) == 0)
{
    data->entry_defs[i] = CSV_PRIORITY;
}
else if(strcasecmp("event_id", toks[i]) == 0)
{
    data->entry_defs[i] = CSV_EVENT_ID;
}
else if(strcasecmp("event_reference", toks[i]) == 0)
{
    data->entry_defs[i] = CSV_EVENT_REFERENCE;
}
else if(strcasecmp("ref_tv_sec", toks[i]) == 0)
{
    data->entry_defs[i] = CSV_REF_TV_SEC;
}
else if(strcasecmp("ref_tv_usec", toks[i]) == 0)
{
    data->entry_defs[i] = CSV_REF_TV_USEC;
}
else if(strcasecmp("tv_sec", toks[i]) == 0)
{
    data->entry_defs[i] = CSV_TV_SEC;
}
else if(strcasecmp("tv_usec", toks[i]) == 0)
{
    data->entry_defs[i] = CSV_TV_USEC;
}
else if(strcasecmp("timestamp", toks[i]) == 0)
```

```
{
     data->entry_defs[i] = CSV_TIMESTAMP;
}
else if(strcasecmp("src", toks[i]) == 0)
{
     data->entry_defs[i] = CSV_SRC;
}
else if(strcasecmp("srcip", toks[i]) == 0)
{
     data->entry_defs[i] = CSV_SRCIP;
}
else if(strcasecmp("dst", toks[i]) == 0)
{
     data->entry_defs[i] = CSV_DST;
}
else if(strcasecmp("dstip", toks[i]) == 0)
{
     data->entry_defs[i] = CSV_DSTIP;
}
else if(strcasecmp("sport_itype", toks[i]) == 0)
{
     data->entry_defs[i] = CSV_SPORT_ITYPE;
}
else if(strcasecmp("sport", toks[i]) == 0)
{
     data->entry_defs[i] = CSV_SPORT;
}
else if(strcasecmp("itype", toks[i]) == 0)
{
     data->entry_defs[i] = CSV_ITYPE;
}
else if(strcasecmp("dport_icode", toks[i]) == 0)
{
     data->entry_defs[i] = CSV_DPORT_ICODE;
}
else if(strcasecmp("dport", toks[i]) == 0)
{
```

```
        data->entry_defs[i] = CSV_DPORT;
    }
    else if(strcasecmp("icode", toks[i]) == 0)
    {
        data->entry_defs[i] = CSV_ICODE;
    }
    else if(strcasecmp("proto", toks[i]) == 0)
    {
        data->entry_defs[i] = CSV_PROTO;
    }
    else if(strcasecmp("protoname", toks[i]) == 0)
    {
        data->entry_defs[i] = CSV_PROTONAME;
    }
    else if(strcasecmp("flags", toks[i]) == 0)
    {
        data->entry_defs[i] = CSV_FLAGS;
    }
    else if(strcasecmp("msg", toks[i]) == 0)
    {
        data->entry_defs[i] = CSV_MSG;
    }
    else if(strcasecmp("hostname", toks[i]) == 0)
    {
        data->entry_defs[i] = CSV_HOSTNAME;
    }
    else if(strcasecmp("interface", toks[i]) == 0)
    {
        data->entry_defs[i] = CSV_INTERFACE;
    }
    else
    {
        LogMessage("ERROR %s(%u):  Unrecognized keyword in
            'alert_csv': "
                "%s\n", current_file, current_line, toks[i]);
        FreeToks(toks, num_toks);
        return -1;  /* EINVAL */
```

```c
        }
    }
    FreeToks(toks, num_toks);
    return 0;
}


char *CSVEscape(char *input)
{
    size_t strLen;
    char *buffer;
    char *current;
    if((strchr(input, ',') == NULL) && (strchr(input, '"') == NULL))
        return strdup(input);
    /* max size of escaped string is 2*size + 3, so we allocate that much
*/
    strLen = strlen(input);
    /* XXX improve error checking */
    buffer = (char *)calloc((strLen * 2) + 3, sizeof(char));
    current = buffer;
    *current = '"';
    ++current;
    while(*input != '\0')
    {
        switch(*input)
        {
            case '"':
                *current = '\\';
                ++current;
                *current = '"';
                ++current;
                break;
            case '\\':
                *current = '\\';
                ++current;
                *current = '\\';
                ++current;
                break;
```

```
        default:
            *current = *input;
            ++current;
            break;
    }
    ++input;
}
*current = '"';
return buffer;
}
```

When creating your OP, there are a few things to keep in mind. There are seven functions that are exported from every OP. These include *Init*, *Setup*, *Exit*, *Start*, *Stop*, *Restart*, and *Func*.

- The *Init* function is responsible for registering your OP, and runs at system startup or when the coupled OP is loaded.

- The *Setup* function is responsible for, oddly enough, setting up the plug-in. This function is responsible for registering other associated plug-in functions and processing the given arguments.

- *Exit* is the inverse of the Setup function. This function will stop an OP and free any memory that was being used by that OP.

- The *Start* function is responsible for starting the plug-in. This allows the plug-in to start processing data.

- The *Stop* function is the opposite of the Start function. It is responsible for stopping the plug-in.

- The *Restart* function manages the use of the Stop and Start functions.

- The *Func* function is responsible for processing the data record.

OINK!

This OP can be quite overwhelming to the beginner C programmer. To best understand the functions and relationships within the .c and .h files (and is also beneficial to any security enthusiast), it would be good to have a basic understanding of the C language.

Using plugbase.h and plugbase.c

Now, let's go over the methods for getting Barnyard to recognize our custom OPs. The plugbase.h file contains lists of where to find our header information so Barnyard can use our plug-ins. The plugbase.c file contains a list of where to find our plug-in code. Once we have created, or modified, an OP, we will need to update these two files in regard to the new input or OP. These files can be found within our output plug-ins (op-plugbase) and input plug-ins (dp-plugbase) folders, respectively.

Adding Output Plug-Ins to Barnyard

Once we familiar with the format of the OPs and have downloaded the latest upgrade from the CVS Web site, we can follow these steps to install our plug-in so that it will be recognized by Barnyard.

1. Once we have created a module and are ready to try it out, make sure to have it saved in the appropriate input or output plug-in folder.

   ```
   /usr/local/bin/barnyard/output-plugins/
   ```

2. Next, we will want to edit the plugbase.h file within the plug-in directory. Within the *#include statements* list, add the line for your plug-in.

   ```
   #include "op_your_plugin.h"
   ```

3. Now we will edit the plugbase.c file within the plug-in directory. Within the *Global Functions* list, add the line with our *init* routine name.

   ```
   YourOpPluginInit();
   ```

4. Now we will edit the makefile.am file in the barnyard install directory. Within the Barnyard Sources list, add the two files we created.

   ```
   op_your_plugin.h
   op_your_plugin.c
   ```

5. The last step is to recompile Barnyard.

   ```
   make && make install
   ```

What Do We Get from Barnyard?

Barnyard gives us eight, very useful, OP options from which to choose. These are all located within the barnyard/src/output-plugins directory. A good way to produce our own OP is to copy and rename one of these OPs to something rele-vant to what we want to accomplish, edit that file, and test that file. Then, we can make more modifications and test again until we come up with the desired results. As mentioned earlier, the creators of Barnyard (and various other contrib-utors) are constantly updating the files that combine together to make up Barnyard. While authoring this chapter; several files were updated, including the addition of OP and DP templates. The previous example, *op_alert_csv* was used for the detailed look of an actual working file. Once comfortable with the structures of creating original OPs, these templates will serve well as a starting point.

Summary

Barnyard will help to relieve Snort of the exhausting duties of verbose database writing. We can also feel confident that Snort will be free to work efficiently and effectively when placed on a high-traffic network. Since the developers have closely integrated it to work with Snort, we can perceive Barnyard as a highly reliable option. The software is continuously updated, and the latest files can be downloaded from the Snort Web site and the SourceForge CVS Web site. All queries on the Barnyard message boards are quickly replied to, and usually on the same day they are posted.

Numerous preferences can be customized within Barnyard. We can use the barnyard.conf file to specify certain environmental specifics on our systems, such as the monitoring interface and the location of certain files. This configuration file will also allow us to choose the type of input plug-ins we would like to use while reading data output from Snort. Our OPs are specified here as well. From the many options of OPs, we can select the ones that fit our needs and comment out (or delete) the others. The OPs provided with the Barnyard default installation are easily modified, and downloadable templates serve as a starting point for creating our own (of course we always recommend keeping the original kept as a backup). Other preferences are offered by Barnyard, such as the ability to launch a "one-shot" instance. We can set up the "one-shot" instance to retrieve specific data and handle it differently from the normal procedures, and, using another configurable function of Barnyard, report it to one of the many compatible database schemas.

Once we establish our desired preferences, we are ready for the actual Barnyard process to start creating our manageable information. Saving the Snort log data by using the unified-spooler plug-in indicated with the −b switch creates the fastest environment for Snort to work. Barnyard, running in one of three modes (one-shot, continual, continual w/checkpoint), will read the log files and translate that data into the previously designated database table. Now we're ready to put Barnyard to the test by creating our detailed reports that will help us to track and stop network intruders, and explain to our managers and directors why money needs to be spent on information systems security.

Solutions Fast Track

What Is Barnyard?

☑ Barnyard takes the complex and resource-intensive database writing labor away from Snort and allows Snort to run at full speed.

☑ Barnyard is an output utility used in conjunction with Snort's unified output spooler plug-in.

☑ Barnyard allows Snort to output to binary, the fastest output method, and creates files from that output for both alerting and logging.

Preparation and Installation of Barnyard

☑ The installation of Barnyard is fairly straightforward for the standard UNIX/Linux user. The first thing you need is to have Snort running on your system. You will also need to have a working database configured for Snort.

☑ You can find updates and recent, or future, changes to Barnyard at the SourceForge Web site, http://cvs.sourceforge.net/cgi-bin/viewcvs.cgi/barnyard.

How Does Barnyard Work?

☑ Snort's unified output spooler plug-in sends binary data to a spool file.

☑ Barnyard reads that file and creates legible information for the administrator to review.

☑ Parsing the barnyard.conf file, Barnyard will convert the specified binary output from Snort and create the user-specified output.

What Are the Output Options for Barnyard?

☑ The barnyard.conf file is used to configure specific input DPs and OPs.

☑ Barnyard options are closely integrated with certain Snort output options and can easily be modified by the user.

☑ We can specify our output to certain locations, such as directories that distinguish between alerts and log files.

But I Want My Output Like "This"

☑ Using the template, or a current module as a template, it is relatively easy to construct a module for our personal needs.

☑ New output options are being developed and some are included with the Barnyard installation. These files offer even more flexibility for output methods.

☑ For creating reports, the newly evolving CSV OP will be very versatile and portable.

Frequently Asked Questions

The following Frequently Asked Questions, answered by the authors of this book, are designed to both measure your understanding of the concepts presented in this chapter and to assist you with real-life implementation of these concepts. To have your questions about this chapter answered by the author, browse to **www.syngress.com/solutions** and click on the **"Ask the Author"** form.

Q: Why won't Barnyard recognize my database after installation?

A: By default, Barnyard will not recognize your database. You will need to use a *configure-time* switch to add database support. For example: *./configure —enable-mysql.*

Q: Is there a version of Barnyard for Windows?

A: At the time of this writing there is not. However, Windows support is included in the "TODO list for Barnyard" list. This list can be viewed at http://cvs.sourceforge.net, so keep checking.

Q: What version of Snort do I need to successfully use Barnyard?

A: Version 1.8.7 or higher will work with Barnyard; however, we recommend that you get the latest version and the current rules for Snort.

Q: Why should I use Barnyard and not some other tool?

A: Barnyard was created exclusively for Snort, and therefore they work very well together. Snort's future output architecture for high-speed networks will be focused on the unified spooler output. Barnyard uses that format brilliantly. The creators of Barnyard also provide support via e-mail and certain mailing lists.

Q: What databases does Barnyard support?

A: At the time of this writing, Barnyard supports MySQL, PostgreSQL, Oracle, and UNIX ODBC. Barnyard is being continuously updated and the latest changes are available on the SourceForge Web site, http://cvs.sourceforge.net/cgi-bin/viewcvs.cgi/barnyard.

Advanced Snort

Introduction

So far, we've discussed the concepts behind Snort, installation, configuration, and many other topics. While many of these topics covered some very elaborate and detailed information, this chapter is dedicated to the more advanced features of Snort and how it can be used to provide an even greater degree of information security.

Snort can perform the same extensive intrusion detection tasks for which many companies are charging tens of thousands of dollars. With proper and knowledgeable configuration, Snort can be used to increase the effective security in your organization while at the same time saving a great deal of money. This might seem in contrast to most information technology solutions, but that's the power of the open-source community.

In this chapter, we discuss *policy-based intrusion detection* and *inline intrusion detection*. These are additional functions that Snort is able to provide that work alongside its normal intrusion detection capabilities. By using some or all of these functions, you can leverage the capabilities of Snort to help make your systems even more secure.

Keep in mind that the technologies that we're using in this chapter are not really a different kind of IDS. After all, we're using Snort for both implementations. Policy-based intrusion detection and inline intrusion detection are simply variants of normal intrusion detection and differ only in their implementation. As always, intrusion detection is the concept of detecting intrusions on your systems or networks. Whether you're using standard *signature-based* intrusion detection techniques or *anomaly based* intrusion detection, the result is the same—a more secure network environment.

Policy-Based IDS

When defining rules or attack signatures for an IDS operating normally, you define what attack signatures you *don't* want to see on your network. For example, if a new attack comes out, you would add its signature to your IDS because you want to be alerted if a packet containing that signature is seen on your network. In other words, you don't want to see a packet with this signature on your network because it indicates that an attack of a specific type is being performed. Following this process and performing frequent rule updates allows your IDS to constantly watch for the latest attacks.

By operating in this fashion, your IDS is constantly playing catch-up with intruders. As a new attack is performed somewhere in the world, you have to wait for a signature for the attack to be determined, and then add it to the rules for your IDS. During this time, the attack could conceivably happen to your network and you wouldn't be aware of it. This is one of the principal problems with normal intrusion detection.

Policy-based IDS is almost a complete reversal of normal intrusion detection. With policy-based IDS, the IDS administrator defines what is normal and acceptable behavior for the network. This can include communication of specific types between specific hosts, specific protocols, and so forth. The benefit of defining this policy is that the administrator is able to set baselines of what "normal" operations for the network should look like. This information can then be used to determine what unusual behavior is.

The concept behind policy-based IDS is that whatever is not included as part of the list of acceptable behavior is potentially an intrusion. The IDS administrator goes through the often long and arduous process of determining what should *not* trigger an alert. Then, the IDS sends an alert on anything not previously defined by the administrator as acceptable traffic.

Using a policy-based IDS has several advantages over normal IDSs. A policy-based IDS can be used to determine whether your firewall is performing properly by checking the network to see if traffic that should have been blocked at the firewall has made it to the internal network. This provides an added layer of redundancy to your existing security system by allowing you to be notified in the event of an unexpected failure. This also works with other security systems in place besides firewalls, such as ensuring that switches have not become susceptible to an ARP spoofing attack, and so forth.

Another very beneficial aspect of using a policy-based IDS is that it can be used to detect new and previously undocumented attacks. Whereas a normal IDS is reactive based on its predefined rules, a properly configured policy-based IDS is proactive in that it will alert you to *any* unexpected activities on the network. This can allow you to diagnose a new form of attack that might not have been detected by a standard or typical IDS.

In many cases, a policy-based IDS can make you aware of an attack faster than a typical IDS can. Since there are typically fewer rules involved in defining acceptable traffic compared to the number of rules necessary to define all known attack signatures, a policy-based IDS can sometimes outperform a normal IDS. Additionally, sometimes the start of an attack might not necessarily match a known attack signature, but it might be flagged as unusual behavior to a policy-based IDS. This can allow you to head off an attack before it occurs.

Defining a Network Policy for the IDS

The first step in setting up a policy-based IDS is to define your network policy. This should be a *very* detailed policy specifying exactly what is allowable on the network. This can include communication between specific systems, the use of specific protocols on the network, and so forth. The main point to keep in mind when defining this policy is that *any* traffic that does not conform to your policy of allowable behavior will be considered suspicious and will trigger an alert. You don't want your policy to be so stringent that you get alerts every few minutes, nor so lax that you miss an actual attack. Getting this policy defined properly is the most difficult task in setting up your policy-based IDS.

When defining your policy, you can determine your allowable traffic based on IPs, protocols, ports, and so forth. As the first part of your policy definition, you need to be aware of what devices are communicating on your network and how they are communicating. For example, if you have a Web server communicating on your network, you will need to know what its IP is and the ports on which it is publishing. The best way to start this process is to inventory your systems and determine what their purposes are. Again, in a large enterprise, this is a *huge* task, but it can be fairly easy in smaller networks. For example purposes, we will create a fictional network with a number of servers and clients to demonstrate the definition of a network policy. Figure 12.1 is the network diagram illustrating our environment.

While the diagram in Figure 12.1 is fairly complex, it shows a very basic, well-designed network for a small office with a public Web presence and plans for future growth. The clients are connected to a dedicated switch, which is in turn connected to a router and another dedicated switch used for the environment's servers. A system functioning as a policy-based IDS is connected to SPAN ports on each of these switches, using two interfaces to perform IDS functions for both networks. The dedicated server switch has a few servers attached to it and a connection to the internal firewall. This firewall separates the DMZ from the internal network and functions as a router.

Within the DMZ, we have three publicly accessible Web servers. These servers and the externally facing port on the internal firewall are connected to a switch for the DMZ network. Also attached to this switch is the internally facing port on the external firewall. The externally facing port of the external firewall is connected to yet another switch that also has connections to the router for the CSU/DSU and a normal IDS.

Figure 12.1 Network Diagram

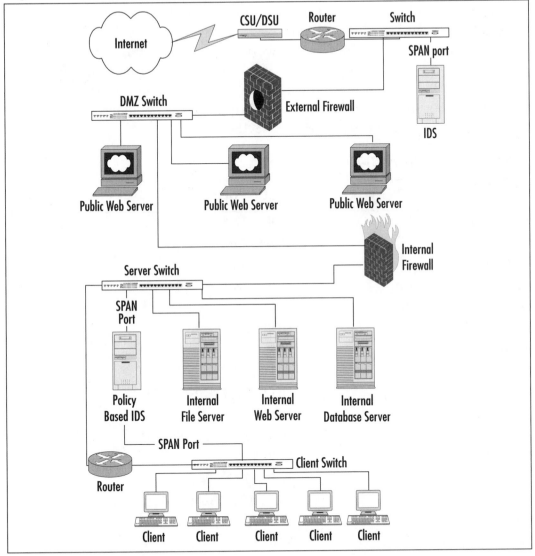

Many modifications can be made to this design to improve security, such as adding another firewall situated between the CSU/DSU and the switch; however, this design is fairly typical in most small organizations. Additional security usually involves additional funds that are not always available. For the purposes of example in this section, we will be referring back to this diagram regularly.

To design our policy, we'll assume that this diagram shows every entity connected to our network. In reality, there are usually a few rogue systems of which the administrators are not aware, but we'll discuss how to find those later in this section.

The next step in defining our network policy is to determine what traffic is acceptable between these known hosts. We'll start with the client/server communications. First, we have the internal network's file server. In this network, we'll assume that this is a standard Microsoft Windows 2000 server hosting a file share for the network. It is probably also performing authentication for the network to grant access to its files. Table 12.1 lists the ports used by a Windows 2000 server based on Microsoft Knowledge Base article 150543.

Table 12.1 Windows 2000 Server Ports

Function	Static Ports
Browsing	UDP:137,138
DHCP Lease	UDP:67,68
DHCP Manager	TCP: 135
Directory Replication	UDP:138 TCP:139
DNS Administration	TCP: 135
DNS Resolution	UDP: 53
Event Viewer	TCP: 139
File Sharing	TCP: 139
Logon Sequence	UDP:137,138 TCP:139
NetLogon	UDP: 138
Pass Through Validation	UDP:137,138 TCP:139
Performance Monitor	TCP: 139
PPTP	TCP: 1723 IP:47
Printing	UDP: 137,138 TCP:139
Registry Editor	TCP: 139
Server Manager	TCP: 139
Trusts	UDP: 137,138 TCP:139
User Manager	TCP: 139
WinNT Diagnostics	TCP: 139
WinNT Secure Channel	UDP: 137,138 TCP:139
WINS Replication	TCP: 42

Continued

Table 12.1 Windows 2000 Server Ports

Function	Static Ports
WINS Manager	TCP: 135
WINS Registration	TCP: 137
SMB	TCP,UDP: 445
ISAKMP (IPSec)	UDP: 500
ESP (IPSec)	IP: 50
AH (IPSec)	IP: 51
Kerberos	TCP,UDP: 88
RSVP	IP: 46

Based on the port information shown in Table 12.1, we can determine that the clients will need to be able to communicate to this server on a number of these ports. Now, let's assume that all of these services might be needed at some point. That leads us to the conclusion that the clients will need to communicate with the file server on the ports listed in Table 12.2.

Table 12.2 File Server Communication Ports

IP	TCP	UDP
46	42	53
47	88	67
50	135	68
51	137	88
	139	137
	445	138
	1723	445
		500

Now that we have determined the communication needs of the clients for connecting to the file server, let's work on the remaining servers. The next server in our diagram is an internal Web server. Assuming that all traffic to this server is using either HTTP or HTTPS on their standard ports, we'll simply need to allow traffic to TCP ports 80 and 443 on this server. Our last server is an internal database server, and we'll assume that it is running Microsoft SQL Server. If this is the case, communication to the server will take place over TCP port 1433 by default. Allowing traffic to this server on TCP port 1433 will take care of the client communication needs.

It looks like we have a handle on the communication from the clients to the servers, so let's look at communication from the servers back to the clients. In most cases when using Microsoft Windows, a client system will open a TCP or UDP connection to a remote system using a port between 1024 and 5000. This can be changed by modifying the Registry of the Windows client. Other operating systems use different standards, but for this example we'll assume that non-modified Windows clients are in use. Based on this, we will assume that any traffic between the server subnet and the client subnet on these ports is acceptable. In addition, some of the clients might be running some Windows services, so we'll also apply the port list from Table 12.2 to the client systems and the servers.

At this point, we have basically defined our network policy and just need to put it all together. We've defined communication with each device, so let's see what we have determined to be acceptable traffic.

- Clients to file server on ports defined in Table 12.2
- Clients to Web server on TCP ports 80 and 443
- Clients to database server on TCP port 1433
- Servers to clients on TCP and UDP ports 1024 through 5000
- Servers to clients on ports defined in Table 12.2

Anything outside this list will be deemed unacceptable traffic when we define the rules for our policy-based IDS. In truth, we certainly have not captured every port that will be used, but this will give us a baseline for determining what else is acceptable. We'll discuss the process of fine-tuning in the section *Policy-Based IDS in Production*.

An Example of Policy-Based IDS

Since we have now defined our basic network policy, we'll move on to how to actually use this information. Our first step is to translate this policy into actual Snort rules. As previously mentioned, using a policy-based IDS is really the reverse of normally running an IDS. Therefore, we have to pass a parameter to Snort to cause it to process the rules in a different order.

By default, Snort processes alert rules first, followed by pass rules. For our needs, we will have to force Snort to process pass rules before alert rules. Otherwise, we would receive an alert on all traffic, as Snort would not even check to see if it was acceptable based on our pass rules. Using the *-o* command-line parameter when starting Snort will cause it to process the pass rules before the alert rules. For example, you could start Snort like so:

```
./snort -c /etc/snort/snort.conf -o
```

We also need to add an entry to our snort.conf file to point to a new rule file. This is simply another *include* statement in the rules section of the snort.conf file. Add the following line to the file:

```
include $RULE_PATH/policy-based.rules
```

The policy-based.rules file will hold all of the rules we define for our policy-based IDS. The first part to defining this set of rules is to set up the alert rules. In this case, we want to generate alerts on any TCP, UDP, or IP-based traffic that is not explicitly defined in a pass rule. Figure 12.2 shows how we would configure these alert rules in the policy-based.rules file.

Figure 12.2 Alert Rules for the policy-based.rules File

```
# $Id: policy-based.rules,v 1.0 2003/02/08 16:00:00 jeremyfaircloth Exp $
# ----------------
# POLICY BASED RULES
# ----------------
# These rules are defined for policy based intrusion detection.
#
# Alert Rules
# This will alert on ANY TCP connections on these subnets
alert tcp any any <> [10.10.10.0/24,10.10.11.0/24] any
# This will alert on ANY UDP connections on these subnets
alert udp any any <> [10.10.10.0/24,10.10.11.0/24] any
# This will alery on ANY IP connections on these subnets
alert ip any any <> [10.10.10.0/24,10.10.11.0/24] any
```

In this rules file, we first define an alert for TCP traffic from any IP and any port going to or from two subnets on any port. These two subnets, 10.10.10.0/24 and 10.10.11.0/24, are our client and server subnets, respectively. We then duplicate the rule to cover the UDP and IP protocols. With the alert rules defined in this manner, we will receive an alert on every connection attempt in these two subnets.

Next, we have to transform our previously defined network policy into Snort rules. Let's go over our network policy again. We have five specific directives in our policy on what is permissible traffic:

- Clients to file server on ports defined in Table 12.2
- Clients to Web server on TCP ports 80 and 443
- Clients to database server on TCP port 1433
- Servers to clients on TCP and UDP ports 1024 through 5000
- Servers to clients on ports defined in Table 12.2

The first order of business is to define rules that allow the systems on the client subnet (10.10.10.0/24) to communicate with the file server (10.10.11.1) on the specific ports defined in Table 12.2. We'll begin with IP traffic, and then move on to TCP and UDP. For IP ports 46, 47, 50, and 51, we can define the pass rules in two lines and cover only these specific ports. We could cover the range of ports 46 through 50 in a single rule, but we want to be as restrictive as possible.

```
pass ip 10.10.10.0/24 any -> 10.10.11.1 46:47
pass ip 10.10.10.0/24 any -> 10.10.11.1 50:51
```

These rules tell Snort to allow any traffic from the 10.10.10.0/24 subnet from any port to 10.10.11.1 ports 46, 47, 50, and 51 to pass and not signal an alert. From here, we'll move on to defining the rules for TCP communication to the file server. We'll define the rules in the same manner, but use TCP rather than IP. These rules should look like the following:

```
pass tcp 10.10.10.0/24 any -> 10.10.11.1 42
pass tcp 10.10.10.0/24 any -> 10.10.11.1 88
pass tcp 10.10.10.0/24 any -> 10.10.11.1 135
pass tcp 10.10.10.0/24 any -> 10.10.11.1 137
pass tcp 10.10.10.0/24 any -> 10.10.11.1 139
pass tcp 10.10.10.0/24 any -> 10.10.11.1 445
pass tcp 10.10.10.0/24 any -> 10.10.11.1 1723
```

Again, these rules simply tell Snort to allow any traffic from the 10.10.10.0/24 subnet from any port to 10.10.11.1 on the specific ports defined to pass without generating an alert. We'll do the same for the UDP ports shown in Table 12.2.

```
pass udp 10.10.10.0/24 any -> 10.10.11.1 53
pass udp 10.10.10.0/24 any -> 10.10.11.1 67:68
```

```
pass udp 10.10.10.0/24 any -> 10.10.11.1 88
pass udp 10.10.10.0/24 any -> 10.10.11.1 137:138
pass udp 10.10.10.0/24 any -> 10.10.11.1 445
pass udp 10.10.10.0/24 any -> 10.10.11.1 500
```

We've now defined all of the rules necessary to achieve objective one of our network policy. Figure 12.3 shows all of these rules.

Figure 12.3 Network Policy Objective-One Rules

```
# Rules for Network Policy Objective One
pass ip 10.10.10.0/24 any -> 10.10.11.1 46:47
pass ip 10.10.10.0/24 any -> 10.10.11.1 50:51
pass tcp 10.10.10.0/24 any -> 10.10.11.1 42
pass tcp 10.10.10.0/24 any -> 10.10.11.1 88
pass tcp 10.10.10.0/24 any -> 10.10.11.1 135
pass tcp 10.10.10.0/24 any -> 10.10.11.1 137
pass tcp 10.10.10.0/24 any -> 10.10.11.1 139
pass tcp 10.10.10.0/24 any -> 10.10.11.1 445
pass tcp 10.10.10.0/24 any -> 10.10.11.1 1723
pass udp 10.10.10.0/24 any -> 10.10.11.1 53
pass udp 10.10.10.0/24 any -> 10.10.11.1 67:68
pass udp 10.10.10.0/24 any -> 10.10.11.1 88
pass udp 10.10.10.0/24 any -> 10.10.11.1 137:138
pass udp 10.10.10.0/24 any -> 10.10.11.1 445
pass udp 10.10.10.0/24 any -> 10.10.11.1 500
```

Now, let's move on to the second objective in our network policy. We need to define rules that allow the client systems to communicate with the internal Web server. We'll set the internal Web server IP as 10.10.11.11, and the client systems are still on subnet 10.10.10.0/24. Based on this information, these rules are very simple to define. Since we're just using TCP, we define the rules as follows:

```
pass tcp 10.10.10.0/24 any -> 10.10.11.11 80
pass tcp 10.10.10.0/24 any -> 10.10.11.11 443
```

Those two simple rules cover the second objective of the network policy and allow traffic originating from any port on the 10.10.10.0/24 subnet directed to ports 80 or 443 to pass without generating an alert. The next objective is just as easy and only requires one rule. We need to allow the clients to communicate with the database server on TCP port 1433. In this fictitious network, we'll put our database server at IP 10.10.11.21.

```
pass tcp 10.10.10.0/24 any -> 10.10.11.21 1433
```

Objective four of our network policy defines traffic going in the other direction, from the servers to the clients. For this objective, we need to allow the servers to connect back to the clients on TCP and UDP ports 1024 through 5000. These rules are fairly simple to define, as we can easily specify more than one source IP address.

```
pass tcp [10.10.11.1,10.10.11.11,10.10.11.21] any -> 10.10.10.0/24 1024:5000
pass udp [10.10.11.1,10.10.11.11,10.10.11.21] any -> 10.10.10.0/24 1024:5000
```

The rules we've defined now meet the first four objectives of the network policy. The fifth objective is a little trickier—we must allow the servers to communicate back to the clients on the ports defined in Table 12.2. We can do this in a number of ways. We could simply allow all communication between the server subnet and the client subnet on these ports to be allowed. Alternatively, we could define the specific server IPs and allow any traffic from the servers to the client subnet on these ports to pass. Finally, we could define the IPs of the servers and the clients and allow traffic from the specific server IPs to the specific client IPs on these ports to pass.

Since in our previous rules we allowed traffic from the entire client subnet to pass to the servers, we'll do the same here and take the second option. This allows for easier rule definition, yet gives us a good level of security. In addition, this allows for future growth in the number of client systems that is typically more likely than growth in server systems. Figure 12.4 shows the rules that we defined to meet this objective.

Figure 12.4 Network Policy Objective-Five Rules

```
# Rules for Network Policy Objective Five
pass ip [10.10.11.1,10.10.11.11,10.10.11.21] any -> 10.10.10.0/24 46:47
pass ip [10.10.11.1,10.10.11.11,10.10.11.21] any -> 10.10.10.0/24 50:51
pass tcp [10.10.11.1,10.10.11.11,10.10.11.21] any -> 10.10.10.0/24 42
pass tcp [10.10.11.1,10.10.11.11,10.10.11.21] any -> 10.10.10.0/24 88
pass tcp [10.10.11.1,10.10.11.11,10.10.11.21] any -> 10.10.10.0/24 135
pass tcp [10.10.11.1,10.10.11.11,10.10.11.21] any -> 10.10.10.0/24 137
pass tcp [10.10.11.1,10.10.11.11,10.10.11.21] any -> 10.10.10.0/24 139
```

Continued

Figure 12.4 Network Policy Objective-Five Rules

```
pass tcp [10.10.11.1,10.10.11.11,10.10.11.21] any -> 10.10.10.0/24 445

pass tcp [10.10.11.1,10.10.11.11,10.10.11.21] any -> 10.10.10.0/24 1723

pass udp [10.10.11.1,10.10.11.11,10.10.11.21] any -> 10.10.10.0/24 53

pass udp [10.10.11.1,10.10.11.11,10.10.11.21] any -> 10.10.10.0/24 67:68

pass udp [10.10.11.1,10.10.11.11,10.10.11.21] any -> 10.10.10.0/24 88

pass udp [10.10.11.1,10.10.11.11,10.10.11.21] any -> 10.10.10.0/24 137:138

pass udp [10.10.11.1,10.10.11.11,10.10.11.21] any -> 10.10.10.0/24 445

pass udp [10.10.11.1,10.10.11.11,10.10.11.21] any -> 10.10.10.0/24 500
```

The rules defined in Figure 12.4 are similar to the rules we defined for traffic coming from the client subnet to the file server. The main difference is that these rules define the source IPs of all of the servers and a destination IP of the client subnet. Otherwise, the port definitions are identical and the functionality of the rules is the same.

We've now covered all of the objectives of our network policy. Each of the five objectives has been translated into Snort rules and defined in our *policy-based.rules* file. The contents of this file are shown in Figure 12.5, and this file is included on the CD-ROM that accompanies this book.

Figure 12.5 policy-based.rules File Covering All Network Policy Objectives

```
# $Id: policy-based.rules,v 1.0 2003/02/08 16:00:00 jeremyfaircloth Exp $

# ----------------

# POLICY BASED RULES

# ----------------

# These rules are defined for policy based intrusion detection.

#

# Alert Rules

# This will alert on ANY TCP connections on these subnets

alert tcp any any <> [10.10.10.0/24,10.10.11.0/24] any

# This will alert on ANY UDP connections on these subnets

alert udp any any <> [10.10.10.0/24,10.10.11.0/24] any

# This will alery on ANY IP connections on these subnets

alert ip any any <> [10.10.10.0/24,10.10.11.0/24] any

#

#

# Pass Rules
```

Continued

Figure 12.5 policy-based.rules File Covering All Network Policy Objectives

```
# These rules define acceptable network traffic
# Rules for Network Policy Objective One
pass ip 10.10.10.0/24 any -> 10.10.11.1 46:47
pass ip 10.10.10.0/24 any -> 10.10.11.1 50:51
pass tcp 10.10.10.0/24 any -> 10.10.11.1 42
pass tcp 10.10.10.0/24 any -> 10.10.11.1 88
pass tcp 10.10.10.0/24 any -> 10.10.11.1 135
pass tcp 10.10.10.0/24 any -> 10.10.11.1 137
pass tcp 10.10.10.0/24 any -> 10.10.11.1 139
pass tcp 10.10.10.0/24 any -> 10.10.11.1 445
pass tcp 10.10.10.0/24 any -> 10.10.11.1 1723
pass udp 10.10.10.0/24 any -> 10.10.11.1 53
pass udp 10.10.10.0/24 any -> 10.10.11.1 67:68
pass udp 10.10.10.0/24 any -> 10.10.11.1 88
pass udp 10.10.10.0/24 any -> 10.10.11.1 137:138
pass udp 10.10.10.0/24 any -> 10.10.11.1 445
pass udp 10.10.10.0/24 any -> 10.10.11.1 500
# Rules for Network Policy Objective Two
pass tcp 10.10.10.0/24 any -> 10.10.11.11 80
pass tcp 10.10.10.0/24 any -> 10.10.11.11 443
# Rules for Network Policy Objective Three
pass tcp 10.10.10.0/24 any -> 10.10.11.21 1433
# Rules for Network Policy Objective Four
pass tcp [10.10.11.1,10.10.11.11,10.10.11.21] any -> 10.10.10.0/24 1024:5000
pass udp [10.10.11.1,10.10.11.11,10.10.11.21] any -> 10.10.10.0/24 1024:5000
# Rules for Network Policy Objective Five
pass ip [10.10.11.1,10.10.11.11,10.10.11.21] any -> 10.10.10.0/24 46:47
pass ip [10.10.11.1,10.10.11.11,10.10.11.21] any -> 10.10.10.0/24 50:51
pass tcp [10.10.11.1,10.10.11.11,10.10.11.21] any -> 10.10.10.0/24 42
pass tcp [10.10.11.1,10.10.11.11,10.10.11.21] any -> 10.10.10.0/24 88
pass tcp [10.10.11.1,10.10.11.11,10.10.11.21] any -> 10.10.10.0/24 135
pass tcp [10.10.11.1,10.10.11.11,10.10.11.21] any -> 10.10.10.0/24 137
pass tcp [10.10.11.1,10.10.11.11,10.10.11.21] any -> 10.10.10.0/24 139
pass tcp [10.10.11.1,10.10.11.11,10.10.11.21] any -> 10.10.10.0/24 445
pass tcp [10.10.11.1,10.10.11.11,10.10.11.21] any -> 10.10.10.0/24 1723
pass udp [10.10.11.1,10.10.11.11,10.10.11.21] any -> 10.10.10.0/24 53
```

Continued

Figure 12.5 policy-based.rules File Covering All Network Policy Objectives

```
pass udp [10.10.11.1,10.10.11.11,10.10.11.21] any -> 10.10.10.0/24 67:68
pass udp [10.10.11.1,10.10.11.11,10.10.11.21] any -> 10.10.10.0/24 88
pass udp [10.10.11.1,10.10.11.11,10.10.11.21] any -> 10.10.10.0/24 137:138
pass udp [10.10.11.1,10.10.11.11,10.10.11.21] any -> 10.10.10.0/24 445
pass udp [10.10.11.1,10.10.11.11,10.10.11.21] any -> 10.10.10.0/24 500
```

Policy-Based IDS in Production

At this point, you've modified the snort.conf file to include the new policy-based.rules file. You've also created the policy-based.rules file and the rules to implement our network policy. Now it's time to start Snort and put the rules into action.

We discussed previously that Snort has to be started with the *-o* parameter to cause the pass rules to be processed before the alert rules. Assuming that your snort.conf file is in /etc/snort, we start Snort using this syntax:

```
Snort -c /etc/snort/snort.conf -o
```

If your configuration is correct and there are no errors in the new rules, Snort should successfully start and begin scanning. It should be noted from the start screen (unless you're running in daemon mode) that Snort is indeed processing the pass rules before the alert rules, as shown in Figure 12.6.

Figure 12.6 Snort Start Screen

With Snort now actively scanning, you can now refine your rules based on the *reality* of the traffic on your network. While the rules that we have defined cover the expected traffic on your network, there is always unexpected traffic that

is probably acceptable. The process of actively monitoring your alert log during this burn-in period allows you to fine-tune your rules.

For example, during a review of your alert log, you see the following entries:

```
[**] Snort Alert! [**]
[Priority: 0]
02/09-15:49:03.042888 10.10.10.1:3137 -> 10.10.11.21:21
TCP TTL:128 TOS:0x0 ID:33435 IpLen:20 DgmLen:48 DF
******S* Seq: 0x57E7A50F  Ack: 0x0  Win: 0x4000  TcpLen: 28
TCP Options (4) => MSS: 1460 NOP NOP SackOK


[**] Snort Alert! [**]
[Priority: 0]
02/09-15:49:05.946778 10.10.10.1:3137 -> 10.10.11.21:21
TCP TTL:128 TOS:0x0 ID:33572 IpLen:20 DgmLen:48 DF
******S* Seq: 0x57E7A50F  Ack: 0x0  Win: 0x4000  TcpLen: 28
TCP Options (4) => MSS: 1460 NOP NOP SackOK


[**] Snort Alert! [**]
[Priority: 0]
02/09-15:49:11.963321 10.10.10.1:3137 -> 10.10.11.21:21
TCP TTL:128 TOS:0x0 ID:33848 IpLen:20 DgmLen:48 DF
******S* Seq: 0x57E7A50F  Ack: 0x0  Win: 0x4000  TcpLen: 28
TCP Options (4) => MSS: 1460 NOP NOP SackOK
```

These log entries indicate that one of the client systems is attempting to connect to the Web server using port 21. This is the well-known port used for FTP, so apparently someone is trying to use FTP to connect to the Web server. Following up on this, you might find that the Web content developer uses FTP to upload new content to the Web server. If management approves this operation, you'll need to modify your network policy to include this objective. In addition, you'll need to create a new rule to indicate that this is acceptable traffic for Snort. This rule could be defined as:

```
# Rules for Network Policy Objective Six
pass tcp 10.10.10.1 any -> 10.10.11.21 21
```

You will run into many of these exceptions during the burn-in period of your policy-based IDS. Tuning your IDS might take quite a while, depending on the number of systems on the network, the type of work being performed, and many other factors. Moreover, adding and modifying rules is a nonstop administrative effort. There will always be something new added to the network or some new service added to an existing system. The ongoing modifications of this system might be tedious, but they do offer a high level of security to your environment.

It should be noted that we did not remove any of the existing rules from Snort when we configured the system to operate as a policy-based IDS. When you are using a policy-based IDS, it is still important to process normal IDS rules as well. Many attacks could easily slip by the policy-based rules that we defined, but the normal IDS rules would catch these attacks. For example, our policy-based rules do not define any restrictions on ICMP traffic. That leaves the door open for an ICMP (ping) flood attack.

In addition, we are allowing traffic to port 80 on the Web server, but the policy-based rules are not scanning the content of those packets. There is a problem here in that the IDS is now configured to process pass rules before alert rules. That means that even if there is malicious content inside a packet destined for the Web server, the IDS will not generate an alert.

The only real solution to this problem is to run one IDS in policy-based mode and the other normally, or creating a new rule action. In our fictitious network design, we haven't done this because it's unlikely that someone would attack the internal Web servers from the internal network, but it could happen. To add an additional layer of security, you can simply add another IDS into the mix or create a new rule action in your rules file.

```
#####
ruletype passgood
{
    type alert
    output log_null
}


ruletype everything
{
    type log
    output log_tcpdump: suspicious.log
}


config order: alert passgood everything


# insert all your normal rules here
```

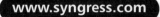

```
passgood tcp any any <> $HTTP_SERVERS $HTTP_PORTS

passgood tcp any any <> $SMTP_SERVERS 25

passgood tcp any any <> $DNS_SERVERS 53

passgood udp any any <> $DNS_SERVERS 53

everything ip any any <> any any
```

The primary disadvantage to implementing a policy based IDS is the amount of time and effort necessary to define the policy as to what acceptable behavior is. This is fairly simple in a small network, but in a large enterprise, it can be a very daunting task. Sometimes using a policy based IDS isn't feasible due to the size of the network or the amount of administrative effort required to maintain the IDS. Keep in mind that the combination of a policy based IDS and a normal IDS can provide for an incredibly high level of security, but it's not always possible to implement this strategy.

Inline IDS

An inline IDS is the latest technology in use within the *intrusion prevention* genre. Intrusion prevention is the next step in the evolution of intrusion detection. Whereas intrusion detection is designed to make the security administrator aware of potential attacks, intrusion prevention goes one step farther and works actively to prevent the intrusion.

The basic concept of intrusion prevention is to take the data gathered during intrusion detection and act upon it through an automated process. This provides for faster response than what could be provided by an on-call administrator. An example of intrusion prevention would be an active firewall that stops communication from a specific IP address when an attack is detected from that address.

Inline IDS acts in a manner similar to an active firewall, but does offer several advantages. First, as an IDS, it can be configured to respond to the latest available attack signatures. It also acts more intelligently than a firewall in that it does not simply block communication from a specific IP address or port. Inline IDS has the ability to drop the packets that contain the attack and allow normal traffic to go through.

Using an inline IDS affords you the capabilities of a good IDS and allows you to incorporate the data gathered from this system into an intelligent firewall. This gives you a great method of securing your network from intrusion.

Damage & Defense...

Using a Firewall Against Itself

One major problem with "intelligent" firewalls is their ability to automatically react to attacks without administrative intervention. While this might seem like a very useful feature of the firewall, it can easily be abused. For example, let's say that you have a firewall set up and configured to block access to a specific IP address if a portscan is detected from that IP. An intruder starts probing your network and performs a portscan from one of his systems. After a few moments, the intruder sees that he is no longer able to connect to your network from that IP. This makes it obvious that you are blocking his IP by using a firewall configured to block portscans. The next step for the intruder if they want to wreak havoc on your network would be to simply spoof the IP address of your upstream router and perform a portscan using this spoofed address. The firewall will detect the portscan and believe that it is coming directly from the upstream router. Therefore, the firewall does its job and blocks access to the IP address of your network's upstream router. Now your network can no longer send or receive data from your upstream router. External communications are now down for the network, and all because your firewall reacted "intelligently" to an attack.

Where Did the Inline IDS for Snort Come From?

Snort first had the capability of being an inline IDS because of a project called *Hogwash*. Hogwash is based on the Snort engine and was designed to operate inline with your Internet connection similar to a firewall. Rather than functioning like a firewall, Hogwash presents the ability to drop individual packets based on a set of rules similar to Snort's. These rules define the behavior of Hogwash and instruct it on which packets should be passed, dropped, or alerted upon.

The Hogwash implementation was designed to work at the Data Link layer of the OSI model (Layer 2) to offer a higher level of security to the system on which Hogwash is running. Because of this design, the machine running Hogwash does not even necessarily have to have an IP stack; therefore, it is invulnerable to IP-based attacks. This feature makes the system almost invisible to intruders.

There is now an effort underway to merge Hogwash back into the original Snort system, primarily because of the difficulties of keeping Hogwash up to date with changes in Snort. It makes more sense from a development point of view to integrate the advanced features available with Hogwash back into the base Snort application. This allows for Snort and Hogwash to be kept at the same build level without the requirement of a large maintenance effort.

This effort has led to the release of a Snort inline mode patch by Jed Haile. This patch is designed to merge the efforts of the Hogwash project back into Snort. It is currently available at www.snort.org/dl/contrib/patches/inline/ and is on the CD-ROM that accompanies this book. More information about Hogwash is also available at http://hogwash.sourceforge.net/.

Installation of Snort in Inline Mode

Before installing Snort in inline mode, you need to be aware of a few requirements. First, to run Snort in inline mode, you must give your system the ability to be inline with a network connection. This means that you'll be running your IDS as a bridge in one form or another. There are two options for this. You can either run your system as a normal network bridge, or you can bridge traffic and provide for network address translation (NAT) at the same time. For this example, we will be running our system as a normal bridge. Figure 12.7 shows a simple network with our system placed inline with a network connection to the Internet. Table 12.3 lists all of the software we'll need to install Snort in inline mode. This software is available at the referenced location and is on the CD-ROM that accompanies this book when a filename is referenced in the table.

Figure 12.7 Inline Network Diagram

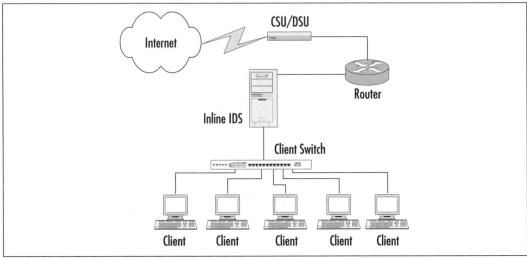

Table 12.3 Software Required for an Inline Mode Installation of Snort

Name	Location	Filename on CD-ROM
Red Hat 8.0 Linux Distribution	ftp://ftp.redhat.com/pub/redhat/linux/8.0/en/iso/i386/	(not included)
IPTables	www.netfilter.org/downloads.html#1.2.7a	iptables-1.2.7a.tar.bz2
libpcap	http://freshmeat.net/projects/libpcap	libpcap-0.7.1.tar.gz
Linux bridge patch	http://bridge.sourceforge.net/devel/bridge-nf/bridge-nf-0.0.7-against-2.4.19.diff	bridge-nf-0.0.7-against-2.4.19.diff.txt
bridge-utils	http://bridge.sourceforge.net/download.html	bridge-utils-0.9.6.tar.gz
Snort Inline Patch	www.snort.org/dl/contrib/patches/inline/	snort-inline.tgz
Snort Rules	www.snort.org/dl/rules/snortrules-current.tar.gz	snortrules-current.tar.gz
rc.firewall Script	www.honeynet.org/papers/honeynet/tools/	rc.firewall (Note: The included rc.firewall script is not the original, but is our modified version.)

In Chapter 3, "Installing Snort," we showed the installation of Snort on the Red Hat 8.0 distribution of Linux. Keeping with that, we will be performing our examples in this chapter on the same distribution. One of the features of the Linux 2.4 kernel build is that *IPtables* is included. This is an open-source stateful (or stateless) firewalling subsystem and replaces its predecessor, *IPchains*. IPtables is used for examining each packet based on a series of *chains* that you define. We'll discuss the specific IPchains functionality that we'll be using a little later.

Unfortunately, the Snort inline patch requires some additional library and header files for IPtables that are not included with the distribution. Therefore, you'll need to download IPtables 1.2.7a from the location listed in Table 12.3, or copy it from the accompanying CD-ROM. Once downloaded, extract this file into a temporary directory. Installation is a little different and requires that you have the Linux kernel source files available. Perform the install by issuing the following commands:

```
make KERNEL_DIR=/usr/src/linux-2.4.18-14
make install KERNEL_DIR=/usr/src/linux-2.4.18-14
make install-devel
```

These commands direct the compiler to your kernel source directory, install IPtables, and install the *libipq* libraries required by the Snort inline patch.

Tools & Traps...

Upgrades

Keep in mind that if you performed an upgrade to get to Red Hat 8, you might still have IPchains on your system. IPchains and IPtables are not compatible and will not run together. If you have any problems starting this IPtables service, you might have to stop the IPchains service.

Another requirement to running Snort in inline mode is *libpcap*. We discussed the installation of this software in Chapter 3, so we won't cover it again here. If you do not have this installed, follow the instructions in Chapter 3 to do so.

 By default, the kernel included with Red Hat 8 includes the ability to do bridging and firewalling, but not to do both at the same time. To do this, we're going to need to patch the kernel and recompile it. The Linux bridge patch can be found at the location shown in Table 12.3 or on the accompanying CD-ROM. Download this patch and place it in a temporary directory. Then, apply the patch using the following command:

```
patch -p1 < bridge-nf-0.0.7-against-2.4.18.diff
```

While the specific methods available to configure and recompile your kernel are beyond the scope of this book, we will cover the specific changes that you need to make to enable the features that we need on the system. After applying the bridge patch, we'll need to configure the kernel. You can do this by issuing one of the following commands in your kernel source directory:

```
make menuconfig
make xconfig
```

Your choice of configuration utilities will vary based on your preference of using the X Window system or a menu–based command-line tool. For our example, we'll be using *xconfig*, which is shown in Figure 12.8.

Figure 12.8 xconfig Linux Kernel Configuration

Go through the various menu options and ensure that the specific kernel options required for your system are enabled. In addition, the following options need to be enabled and compiled into the kernel for our bridging firewall to work:

- Code Maturity Level Options
  - Prompt for Development and/or incomplete code/drivers
- Networking Options
  - Network packet filtering (replaces ipchains)
  - IP: Netfilter Configuration
  - All options
  - 802.1d Ethernet Bridging
  - Netfilter (firewalling) support

Figure 12.9 shows how the Networking options section of xconfig should look when configured for Snort in inline mode. It is very important to go through these configuration options and confirm that the additional options required for Linux to run on your system are selected.

Your next step will be to recompile your kernel using the new patch and options. Again, this process is beyond the scope of this book, but the following syntax worked well for us and automatically placed a new entry into the *grub.conf* file for the new kernel:

```
make dep clean bzImage install modules modules_install
```

Figure 12.9 xconfig Networking Options Dialog

You'll also need the bridge-utils software to control the bridging features of your system. This software can be found at the location shown in Table 12.3. Extract the files from the source tarball into a temporary directory, and then install them using the following commands:

```
./configure
make
make install
```

Next, you'll need the Snort inline patch. Download this from the location shown in Table 12.3, or copy it from the accompanying CD-ROM. Then, decompress this patch into a temporary directory. If you have Snort running on the system on which you are installing the patch, it is best to stop Snort first. Keep in mind that although this is labeled as a patch, it is a full Snort install; therefore, having the normal version of Snort installed is not a prerequisite. Perform the patch installation by issuing the following commands in the directory to which you extracted the patch:

```
./configure --enable-inline
make
make install
```

One error you might run into is the Snort inline patch being unable to find your libpcap files. If this occurs, simply copy the files extracted from the libpcap archive into a directory called *pcap* within your Snort inline patch temporary directory.

If you don't already have them, you'll certainly want the latest Snort rules. These can be found at the location specified in Table 12.3 or on the accompanying

CD-ROM and just need to be placed in your Snort rules directory. You'll also need Rob McMillen's rc.firewall script. This is an IPtables script used for counting and controlling outbound connections and is available at the location listed in Table 12.3 or on the accompanying CD-ROM. To make the best use of this script, you'll want it to be started with your system, so copy the rc.firewall script to your /etc/rc.d directory and modify it using the following commands:

```
cp rc.firewall /etc/rc.d
chmod 700 /etc/rc.d/rc.firewall
```

After the file has been copied, you'll need to edit your /etc/rc.d/rc.local file using your favorite text editor and add the following lines at the bottom of the file:

```
if [ -x /etc/rc.d/rc.firewall ]; then
     /etc/rc.d/rc.firewall
fi
```

Now we need to start configuring all the software we've installed. The Snort inline installation will need to have the *snort.conf* file configured to suit your environment. This is identical to the configuration shown in Chapter 3, so please refer to Chapter 3 for further information on configuring this file.

Next, let's configure the rc.firewall script. Load the script with vi or your favorite text editor. Many changes are necessary to make this script work for a normal firewall rather than a honeynet firewall. First, add any systems that you want to be able to access the external interface to the line that reads *PUBLIC_IP="192.168.1.144"*. Multiple addresses can be added by placing a space between each. Next, ensure that the *INET_IFACE="eth0"* corresponds with the network interface that is facing externally. The following three variables should be changed to reflect your internal network. For example, if your internal network is 10.10.10.*, then you'll want to change the variables as shown here:

```
LAN_IFACE="eth1"                        # Firewall interface on internal
network
LAN_IP_RANGE="10.10.10.0/24"            # IP Range of internal network
LAN_BCAST_ADRESS="10.10.10.255"         # IP Broadcast range for internal
network
```

The next configuration change in the rc.firewall script will allow it to interface with Snort. Change the following setting as shown here:

```
QUEUE="yes"            # Use experimental QUEUE support
#QUEUE="no"            # Do not use experimental QUEUE support
```

The *Location of Programs Used by This Script* section lower in the file will need to be changed to suit your environment. For our installation, the following changes were necessary:

```
##############################################
# LOCATION OF PROGRAMS USED BY THIS SCRIPT #
##############################################
IPTABLES="/usr/local/sbin/iptables"
BRIDGE="/usr/local/sbin/brctl"
IFCONFIG="/sbin/ifconfig"
ROUTE="/sbin/route"
MODPROBE="/sbin/modprobe"
```

It is very important that you use the correct location for each of these, as you might have different versions loaded in different locations. For example, the Red Hat 8.0 Linux install has a binary for *iptables* located in /sbin, but this is an older version.

We also need to change the way in which the rc.firewall script uses IPtables. We will be using one simple IPtables command to cause Snort to be in charge of all packets being forwarded through the system. This command needs to used instead of all of the current rc.firewall IPtables commands:

```
$IPTABLES -A FORWARD -j QUEUE
```

If you want to see what the script is doing when you start it, simply go back to the beginning of the file and remove the # symbol from the beginning of the *#set −x* line. This should complete the modifications necessary to the rc.firewall script, but you can also do some optional things such as auto-starting Snort. Figure 12.10 shows the completely modified rc.firewall script should look like and includes commands to start Snort automatically (based on the snort.sh script from www.honeynet.org). This file is included on the CD-ROM that accompanies this book.

Figure 12.10 rc.firewall Script (rc.firewall)

```
#!/bin/bash
#
# rc.firewall, ver 0.6.1
# http://www.honeynet.org/papers/honeynet/tools/
# Rob McMillen <rvmcmil@cablespeed.com>
#
```

Continued

Figure 12.10 rc.firewall Script (rc.firewall)

```
# CHANGES:
# 14 Feb 2003: Modified extensively to support Snort Inline mode for
#               a bridging firewall.  Snort controls all packet decisions
#               and IPTABLES simply queues everything. - J. Faircloth



#### If you want to see all the commands or which command is giving your
#       problems, remove the comment below.
set -x



#*********************************************************************
# USER VARIABLE SECTION
#*********************************************************************


###############
# COMMON VARS #
###############


# The MODE variable tells the script to #setup a bridge HoneyWall
# or a NATing HoneyWall.
#MODE="nat"
MODE="bridge"

# A space delimited list of honeypots IPs (public IP)
# If you are in "bridge" mode, this is the list of your
# honeypot IP's that will be behind the bridge.  If you are
# in "nat" mode, this is the list of public IPs you will
# be using for IP address translation.  Still confused?  Its
# the list of IPs the hackers will attack.
PUBLIC_IP="10.10.11.100"



### Variable for external network
INET_IFACE="eth0"                          # Firewall Public interface
```

Continued

Figure 12.10 rc.firewall Script (rc.firewall)

```
### Variables for internal network
LAN_IFACE="eth1"                          # Firewall interface on internal
network
LAN_IP_RANGE="10.10.11.0/24"              # IP Range of internal network
LAN_BCAST_ADRESS="10.10.11.255"           # IP Broadcast range for internal
network


### IPTables script can be used with the Snort-Inline filter
### You can find the current release at
###   http://www.snort.org/dl/contrib/patches/inline/
QUEUE="yes"              # Use experimental QUEUE support
#QUEUE="no"              # Do not use experimental QUEUE support


PID=/var/run/snort_eth0.pid # Location for Snort's PID
DIR=/var/log/snort # Logging Directory
DATE=`date +%b_%d` # Date for creating log directories


######################
# END OF COMMON VARS #
######################


##########################
# VARIABLES FOR NAT MODE #
##########################
#  You use these variables ONLY if you are using NAT mode.
#  If you are in bridging mode, then these variables will
#  not be used.
#

ALIAS_MASK="255.255.255.0"          # Network mask to be used alias

HPOT_IP="192.168.0.144"          # Space delimited list of Honeypot ips
                                 # NOTE: MUST HAVE SAME NUMBER OF IPS
AS
                                 # PUBLIC_IP VARIABLE.
```

Continued

Figure 12.10 rc.firewall Script (rc.firewall)

```
#############################
# END OF NAT MODE VARIABLES #
#############################


######################################
# VARIABLES FOR MANAGEMENT INTERFACE #
######################################



# Interface for remote management.  If set to br0, it will assign
# MANAGE_IP to the bridge logical interface and allow its use
# as a management interface.  If you do not want to use a
#  management interface, set it to "none"
#MANAGE_IFACE="br0"
#MANAGE_IFACE="eth2"
MANAGE_IFACE="none"

MANAGE_IP="192.168.0.104"            # IP of management Interface
MANAGE_NETMASK="255.255.255.0"       # Netmask of management Interface

# Space delimited list of tcp ports allowed into the management interface
ALLOWED_TCP_IN="22"

# IP allowed to connect to the management interface
# If set to "any", it will allow anyone to attempt to connect.
# The notation ip/mask or a space delimited list of ips are
# allowed.
#MANAGER="any"
MANAGER="10.1.1.1 172.16.1.0/24"



####################
# END OF MANAGE VARS
####################
```

Continued

www.syngress.com

Figure 12.10 rc.firewall Script (rc.firewall)

```
###########################################################
# VARIABLES THAT RESTRICT WHAT THE FIREWALL CAN SEND OUT #
###########################################################

# This variable will limit outbound Firewall connections
# to ports identified in the ALLOWED_TCP_OUT and
# ALLOWED_UDP_OUT variables.  If set to yes, it will
# restrict the firewall.  If set to no, it will allow all
# outbound connections generated by the firewall.
# NOTE:  There must be a management interface in bridge
# mode in order to have a firewall interface to restrict.

#RESTRICT="yes"
RESTRICT="no"

ALLOWED_UDP_OUT="53 123"
ALLOWED_TCP_OUT="22"

##########################
# END RESTRICT VARIABLES #
##########################

#############################################
# LOCATION OF PROGRAMS USED BY THIS SCRIPT #
#############################################
IPTABLES="/usr/local/sbin/iptables"
BRIDGE="/usr/local/sbin/brctl"
IFCONFIG="/sbin/ifconfig"
ROUTE="/sbin/route"
MODPROBE="/sbin/modprobe"
SNORT="/usr/local/bin/snort"

####################
# END OF PROG VARS #
####################
```

Continued

Figure 12.10 rc.firewall Script (rc.firewall)

```
#**********************************************************************
# END OF USER VARIABLE SECTION (DO NOT EDIT BEYOND THIS POINT)
#**********************************************************************


#########
# First, confirm that IPChains is NOT running.  If
# it is running, clear the IPChains rules, remove the kernel
# module, and warn the end user.


lsmod | grep ipchain
IPCHAINS=$?


if [ "$IPCHAINS" = 0 ]; then
  echo ""
  echo "Dooh, IPChains is currently running! IPTables is required by"
  echo "the rc.firewall script. IPChains will be unloaded to allow"
  echo "IPTables to run.  It is recommened that you permanently"
  echo "disable IPChains in the /etc/rc.d startup scripts and enable"
  echo "IPTables instead."
  ipchains -F
  rmmod ipchains
fi


#########
# Flush rules
#
$IPTABLES -F
$IPTABLES -F -t nat
$IPTABLES -F -t mangle
$IPTABLES -X


echo ""


##########
# Let's setup the firewall according to the Mode selected: bridge or nat
```

Continued

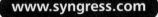

Figure 12.10 rc.firewall Script (rc.firewall)

```
#

if [ $MODE = "bridge" ]

then


    echo "Starting up Bridging mode."


    #########

    # Let's clean up the bridge.   This will only work if this script

    #    started the bridge.

    #

    $BRIDGE delif br0 ${INET_IFACE} 2> /dev/null

    $BRIDGE delif br0 ${LAN_IFACE} 2> /dev/null

    $IFCONFIG br0 down 2> /dev/null

    $BRIDGE delbr br0 2> /dev/null


    #########

    # Let's make sure our interfaces don't have ip information

    #

    $IFCONFIG $INET_IFACE 0.0.0.0 up -arp

    $IFCONFIG $LAN_IFACE 0.0.0.0 up -arp



    #########

    # Let's start the bridge

    #

    $BRIDGE addbr br0

    $BRIDGE addif br0 ${LAN_IFACE}

    $BRIDGE addif br0 ${INET_IFACE}


    # Let's make sure our bridge is not sending out

    #    BPDUs (part of the spanning tree protocol).

    $BRIDGE stp br0 off


    if [ "$MANAGE_IFACE" = "br0" ]

    then

        $IFCONFIG br0 $MANAGE_IP netmask $MANAGE_NETMASK up
```

Continued

Figure 12.10 rc.firewall Script (rc.firewall)

```
    else
        $IFCONFIG br0 0.0.0.0 up -arp
    fi

elif [ $MODE = "nat" ]
then

    echo "Starting up Routing mode and enabling Network Address
Translation."

    i=0
    z=1
    tempPub=( $PUBLIC_IP )

    for host in $HPOT_IP; do

        # Bring up eth aliases
        $IFCONFIG $INET_IFACE:${z} ${tempPub[$i]} netmask ${ALIAS_MASK} up

        # Ensure proper NATing is performed for all honeypots
        $IPTABLES -t nat -A POSTROUTING -s ${host} -j SNAT --to-source
${tempPub[$i]}
        $IPTABLES -t nat -A PREROUTING -d ${tempPub[$i]} -j DNAT --to-
destination ${host}
        let "i += 1"
        let "z += 1"
    done
fi

# Let's figure out dns
if [ $DNS_HOST -z ]
then
    if [ $MODE = "bridge" ]
    then
        DNS_HOST=$PUBLIC_IP
    else
```

Continued

Figure 12.10 rc.firewall Script (rc.firewall)

```
        DNS_HOST=$HPOT_IP
    fi
fi



#########
# Load all required IPTables modules
#

### Needed to initially load modules
/sbin/depmod -a

### Add iptables target LOG.
$MODPROBE ipt_LOG

### Add iptables QUEUE support (Experimental)
if test $QUEUE = "yes"
then
    # Insert kernel mod
    $MODPROBE ip_queue

  # check to see if it worked, if not exit with error
  lsmod | grep ip_queue
  IPQUEUE=$?

  if [ "$IPQUEUE" = 1 ]; then
    echo ""
    echo "It appears you do not have the ip_queue kernel module compiled"
    echo "for your kernel.  This module is required for Snort-Inline and"
    echo "QUEUE capabilities.  You either have to disable QUEUE, or compile"
    echo "the ip_queue kernel module for your kernel.  This module is part"
    echo "of the kernel source."
    exit
  fi
```

Continued

Figure 12.10 rc.firewall Script (rc.firewall)

```
    echo "Enabling Snort-Inline capabilities, make sure Snort-Inline is"
    echo "running in -Q mode, or all outbound traffic will be blocked"
fi


### Support for connection tracking of FTP and IRC.
$MODPROBE ip_conntrack_ftp
$MODPROBE ip_conntrack_irc

### Enable ip_forward
echo "1" > /proc/sys/net/ipv4/ip_forward


### Queue everything and let Snort figure out what to do with each packet.


$IPTABLES -A FORWARD -j QUEUE


##########
# Kill off old Snort and start a new instance

### Kill snort
if [ -s $PID ]; then
  PRO=`cat $PID`
  echo ""
  echo "Previous version of Snort running"
  echo "Killing Snort, PID $PRO"
  echo ""
  kill -9 $PRO
fi


# Make directory based on date, if already exists do nothing.
if [ -d $DIR/$DATE ]; then
        :
else
        mkdir $DIR/$DATE


fi
```

Continued

Figure 12.10 rc.firewall Script (rc.firewall)

```
# Snort options explanation
# -c configuration file
# -d log packet details
# -D daemon mode
# -l log directory
# -i interface in our case eth0, this option is required when using
#    the -Q option.
# -Q (used ONLY with Snort-Inline for QUEUE mode)


### Start snort for the Honeynet
$SNORT -D -d -c /etc/snort/snort.conf -Q -l $DIR/$DATE


Now, change to the /etc/rc.d directory and run the script by issuing the
following commands:
cd /etc/rc.d
./rc.firewall
```

You'll see a lot of data scroll across the screen as the script sets up the bridging functions and configures the firewall if you enabled *set −x* in your rc.firewall file. You'll probably want to scroll through this data just to make sure everything worked properly. At this point, you should have a functioning fire-walling bridge.

If everything appears to be functioning correctly, it's time to reconfigure Snort. The primary change we're going to make is in the rules files. All of the default rules are set to *Alert*. For our inline IDS to function, we'll need to change the actions on some or all of the Alert rules to Drop rules depending on your needs. This will cause Snort to drop the packet rather than issue an alert. Which rules you set to drop will differ based on the purpose of your IDS and the structure of your network. If you are running a honeynet, a good list of drop rules can be found at www.honeynet.org.

Modifying your rules files can be done manually by editing each rule file using vi or your favorite text editor. This will have to be done for any rules that you want to use as drop rules. The rules that you modify will depend on the needs of your network environment. If you use vi, you can issue the following command to quickly replace all instances of Alert with Drop:

```
:%s/alert/drop/
```

At this point, you should be ready to run Snort in inline mode. We'll need to restart Snort for the rules to take effect, so simply rerun the rc.firewall script to do so using the following command:

```
/etc/rc.d/rc.firewall
```

Snort should successfully start and begin monitoring the network traffic going across the bridge. Hopefully, you have an operational Snort inline installation at this point. If you run into any problems with the installation of software or their configuration, refer to the Web site from which the software was gathered. Moreover, don't forget some of the invaluable resources available on the Web for specific help in setting up an IDS or Snort. Table 12.4 lists some of the Web sites that we found to be very helpful in setting up Snort in inline mode.

Table 12.4 Web Resources

URL	Description
www.snort.org	The main source for Snort information and documentation.
http://groups.google.com	A search engine for newsgroups that can help you find a great deal of help on any subject.
www.honeynet.org	Information on honeynets and the configuration of an IDS for honeynets.
www.redhat.com	Information on the Red Hat Linux distribution.

Using Inline IDS to Protect Your Network

Now that we have a functioning inline IDS, we need to test it and see how it can be used to protect our network. We will continue to use the network diagram shown in Figure 12.7 for example purposes. This will allow us to configure some basic rules and see how the IDS reacts to them.

To recap, we have configured the Linux system to function as a bridge. The system has two network cards, with one facing the external network and the other facing the internal network. IPtables is being used to bridge between the network cards and route the traffic to a queue for processing. The Snort inline patch has been installed and configured to monitor this queue and determine the fate of all packets crossing the bridge. By configuring the rules files with *drop* statements, we can set specific packets to be dropped and not routed between the interfaces.

For our first test, we will set up a Web server on one of our client systems. This Web server will be configured without SSL and will be listening on port 80. To test this, we will need access to a system outside the protected network. For the purposes of this test, we will be using a freely available online port scanning site at www.securitymetrics.com/portscan.adp. If you run this test from the system hosting the Web server, you will receive a response similar to the one shown in Figure 12.11.

Figure 12.11 Portscan from Web Server

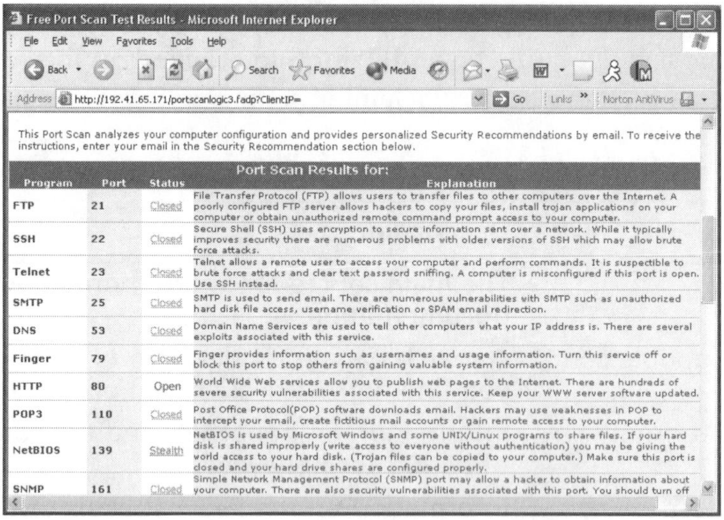

As you can see in Figure 12.11, port 80 has been detected as Open, which means that this port can be detected from an outside system. To prevent this, we're going to add a rule for Snort to drop packets destined for port 80 on the internal network.

Open the file "local.rules" in your rules directory using your favorite text editor. Add a rule similar to the following to configure Snort to drop traffic destined for this port:

```
drop tcp any any -> 10.10.10.0/24 80
```

This simple rule will make your IDS drop any traffic destined for port 80 on your internal network. Ensure that the "local.rules" line has been uncommented in your "snort.conf" file, and then restart Snort to make this rule take effect. If you repeat the portscan from the remote system, you should receive the result shown in Figure 12.12.

Figure 12.12 Portscan from Web Server with Snort Filtering

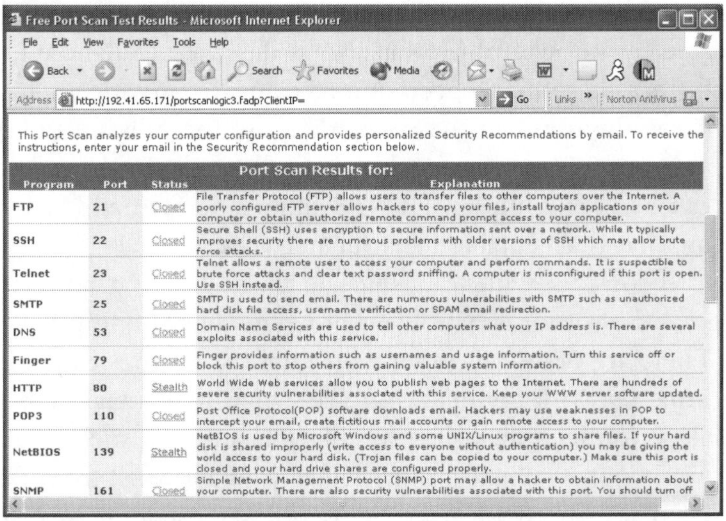

As you can see, it is extremely easy to configure Snort to drop packets after the software has been properly configured. A more complex example would be to make Snort drop packets based on both their port and their content. This is just as easy to do, and as previously mentioned, can be accomplished by simply changing the current Snort rules to drop instead of alert. For example, the following rule would drop *any* packet going across the bridge via an established TCP connection containing the text "nudie pictures":

```
drop tcp any any -> any any (msg:"Adult Content"; content:"nudie pictures";
nocase; flow:to_client,established;)
```

Creating Snort rules is discussed in Chapter 5, "Playing by the Rules," so refer to that chapter for further information on rule definition. The basic change in the rule definitions is that you use the *drop* command instead of *alert*.

Is Inline IDS the Tool for Me?

Inline IDS is not always the best protection for your network. If you are working in a large corporate environment, running an inline IDS can slow your network traffic to an unacceptable level. In addition, if the IDS has not been configured properly or is malfunctioning, the possibility exists that the IDS could interrupt normal network functionality. Valid traffic could be mistakenly dropped, or communications in their entirety could be stopped. The proper use of tools such as this is an important skill for a security administrator to learn.

If you are running a typical corporate network, chances are that you have one or more high-speed Internet connections going into your network. These are typically protected by a powerful firewall that is designed to handle the amount of data received from these high-speed connections. To provide an acceptable quality of service to the users on the network, these firewalls are typically configured with rules that process traffic quickly and efficiently. In the case of inline IDS, the rules can be very complex, and the actions performed by the IDS might take longer than what is acceptable for your network.

One option to consider with the use of an inline IDS is a honeynet implementation. A great deal of information on honeynets can be found at www.honeynet.org. There are occasions when you might want to set up a honeynet beside your normal network connection to see what new attacks are being performed or to allow you to tune your firewall. In a situation such as this, an inline IDS would be very appropriate to both protect your network from devastating attacks and to keep your network from being used as a staging area to launch further attacks.

There is a great deal of liability in setting up a honeynet, and you need to ensure that an intruder cannot use your honeynet to attack other systems. An inline IDS can help to prevent this by blocking outgoing malicious packets or by rewriting outgoing packets.

Another useful purpose for an inline IDS would be to implement it in a position where only a specific portion of a network is behind the IDS. This can provide an extra layer of security to systems containing highly confidential data. By using the content of the packets as a guide, you can configure your IDS to ensure that confidential data can only be accessed by specific entities that are explicitly granted access to the data.

Whatever your intentions, put some thought into both the advantages and disadvantages of installing an inline IDS onto your network. There are many situations in which this type of security device can be very useful, but just as many where it can be devastating to your user community.

Summary

In this chapter, we covered some of the more advanced features of Snort. We began by discussing policy-based intrusion detection. With policy-based intrusion detection, all acceptable traffic on the network is defined in advance by the security administrator, and a network policy is developed. This network policy is then translated into Snort rules, and Snort is configured to monitor the network for traffic that does not comply with the network policy. Policy-based intrusion detection can be used in smaller networks or in very high security environments to ensure that all traffic flowing across the network complies with the approved network policy.

Next, we reviewed the concepts behind an inline IDS. An inline IDS is an IDS that functions between two portions of the network by bridging traffic between two interfaces. This allows the IDS to take action on traffic flowing between its interfaces before the traffic gets to its destination. Using Snort in inline mode allows you to selectively drop individual packets based on their intended host, port, or content. By using a combination of several different pieces of software working together, Snort can actively protect your network from attack rather than just alert you to attacks in progress.

Solutions Fast Track

Policy-Based IDS

☑ A policy-based IDS operates in the reverse of a normal IDS by allowing previously defined acceptable traffic and dropping everything else.

☑ Snort can easily be configured to work as a policy-based IDS by simply configuring *pass* rules to allow acceptable traffic, and *alert* rules for all other traffic.

☑ For Snort to process these rules properly, it must be configured to use pass rules before alert rules by using the −*o* parameter.

Inline IDS

☑ An inline IDS runs inline with the network and bridges the traffic between two interfaces to allow it to selectively drop packets.

☑ An inline IDS has a major advantage over a normal firewall in that specific packets are dropped rather than blocking connections.

☑ Running Snort in inline mode requires a great deal of additional software and configuration, but is possible and can function in either NAT or bridge mode.

Frequently Asked Questions

The following Frequently Asked Questions, answered by the authors of this book, are designed to both measure your understanding of the concepts presented in this chapter and to assist you with real-life implementation of these concepts. To have your questions about this chapter answered by the author, browse to **www.syngress.com/solutions** and click on the **"Ask the Author"** form.

Q: If I run a policy-based IDS, why should I run a normal IDS as well?

A: Running a policy-based IDS will alert you to any traffic going across your network that does not comply with your predefined rules. The problem with this is that many attacks can be performed that actually comply with your network policies. To detect these attacks, it is necessary to run a normal IDS.

Q: Is a policy-based IDS a viable solution for most networks?

A: It depends on the size of the network and the level of security necessary for the network. For a large network, a policy-based IDS is probably not the best solution for the network as a whole because of the administrative effort. However, a policy-based IDS could still be used on a smaller portion of the network that has a higher security requirement.

Q: Is running Snort in inline mode better than running a normal firewall?

A: Depending on the type of firewall in use, yes. Some attacks can take advantage of a firewall's ability to dynamically block an IP address because of attacks originating from that address. With Snort in inline mode, only the offending packets are dropped, not the ability to connect to or from the remote address.

Q: Why would I want to use my Snort inline IDS as a bridge instead of using NAT?

A: Using a bridge rather than NAT is very useful in DMZ or honeynet environments. In these situations, you might not need address translation, either because it has already been done prior to the packet reaching the IDS, or because you want your systems to be accessible to intruders to log their activities.

Index

*(asterisk)
  in content string, 165
  defined, 167
  with *rpc* option, 177
: (colon), 144
..\ (dot dot slash), 10, 12
! (exclamation point), 156, 167
- (minus sign), 167
-> operator, 116, 159
| (pipe character), 162
? (question mark), 165
; (semicolon), 161, 191
143 Traffic Rule, example, 190
21, 116
3D linked list, 114–115, 118–119

A

-*a* (directory) switch, 426
AB (ad hoc benchmark), 395
abort_invalid_hex option, 221
ACID (Analysis Console for Intrusion
    Databases), 311–332
  alert display of, 322–324
  alert groups, 326–329
  Barnyard configuration and, 421
  configuration of, 319–322
  description of, URL for, 40
  features of, 311
  features supported by, 133
  graphical features of, 329–330
  installation of, 312–319
  managing alert databases, 330–332
  for output plug-ins, 300
  overview of, 348
  querying database with, 324–326
  upgrading, 372
  using, 349
ACID tables, 320–321
ACK field, 170–171
acquisition plug-ins, 139
action events, 179
action field, 326

activate rule, 159–161
activate rule action, 152
activates object, 160
activation rules, 122
active monitoring, 41
active response option, 177
ad hoc benchmark (AB), 395
add-ons, Snort, 39–40
+ (addition sign), 167
addition sign (+), 167
ADODB library, 316
Aggregate, 184
AIDE, 56
AirCERT, 311
alert, 116
alert databases, ACID, 330–332
alert facility, 129
alert groups, 326–329
alert log, 476
alert notification, 337
Alert notification screen, IDScenter, 346
alert option, 132
alert rule action, 151
alert rules
    configuring for inline mode, 496
    in policy-based IDS, 468–469, 475, 501
alert_csv output plug-in, 424, 432
alert_fast output plug-in, 422–423
alertfile instruction, 146
alert_html processor, 424
alerting/logging component
    defined, 59
    plug-ins for, 60
    process of, 37, 38, 39
Alerting mode options, 129
Alertmail screen, IDScenter, 346
alert_odd_protocols parameter, 233
alerts
    ACID, graphical features for, 329–330
    archiving in ACID, 319
    Barnyard for, 413
    defining action events, 179
    displayed in ACID, 322–324

S

Version 2, June 1991

Preamble

The licenses for most software are designed to take away your freedom to share and change it. By contrast, the GNU General Public License is intended to guarantee your freedom to share and change free software—to make sure the software is free for all its users. This General Public License applies to most of the Free Software Foundation's software and to any other program whose authors commit to using it. (Some other Free Software Foundation software is covered by the GNU Library General Public License instead.) You can apply it to your programs, too.

When we speak of free software, we are referring to freedom, not price. Our General Public Licenses are designed to make sure that you have the freedom to distribute copies of free software (and charge for this service if you wish), that you receive source code or can get it if you want it, that you can change the software or use pieces of it in new free programs; and that you know you can do these things.

To protect your rights, we need to make restrictions that forbid anyone to deny you these rights or to ask you to surrender the rights. These restrictions translate to certain responsibilities for you if you distribute copies of the software, or if you modify it.

For example, if you distribute copies of such a program, whether gratis or for a fee, you must give the recipients all the rights that you have. You must make sure that they, too, receive or can get the source code. And you must show them these terms so they know their rights.

We protect your rights with two steps: (1) copyright the software, and (2) offer you this license which gives you legal permission to copy, distribute and/or modify the software.

Also, for each author's protection and ours, we want to make certain that everyone understands that there is no warranty for this free software. If the software is modified by someone else and passed on, we want its recipients to know that what they have is not the original, so that any problems introduced by others will not reflect on the original authors' reputations.

Finally, any free program is threatened constantly by software patents. We wish to avoid the danger that redistributors of a free program will individually obtain patent licenses, in effect making the program proprietary. To prevent this, we have made it clear that any patent must be licensed for everyone's free use or not licensed at all.

The precise terms and conditions for copying, distribution and modification follow.

TERMS AND CONDITIONS FOR COPYING, DISTRIBUTION AND MODIFICATION

0. This License applies to any program or other work which contains a notice placed by the copyright holder saying it may be distributed under the terms of this General Public License. The "Program", below, refers to any such program or work, and a "work based on the Program" means either the Program or any derivative work under copyright law: that is to say, a work containing the Program or a portion of it, either verbatim or with modifications and/or translated into another language. (Hereinafter, translation is included without limitation in the term "modification".) Each licensee is addressed as "you".

Activities other than copying, distribution and modification are not covered by this License; they are outside its scope. The act of running the Program is not restricted, and the output from the Program is covered only if its contents constitute a work based on the Program (independent of having been made by running the Program). Whether that is true depends on what the Program does.

1. You may copy and distribute verbatim copies of the Program's source code as you receive it, in any medium, provided that you conspicuously and appropriately publish on each copy an appropriate copyright notice and disclaimer of warranty; keep intact all the notices that refer to this License and to the absence of any warranty; and give any other recipients of the Program a copy of this License along with the Program.

You may charge a fee for the physical act of transferring a copy, and you may at your option offer warranty protection in exchange for a fee.

2. You may modify your copy or copies of the Program or any portion of it, thus forming a work based on the Program, and copy and distribute such modifications or work under the terms of Section 1 above, provided that you also meet all of these conditions:

a) You must cause the modified files to carry prominent notices stating that you changed the files and the date of any change.

b) You must cause any work that you distribute or publish, that in whole or in part contains or is derived from the Program or any part thereof, to be licensed as a whole at no charge to all third parties under the terms of this License.

c) If the modified program normally reads commands interactively when run, you must cause it, when started running for such interactive use in the most ordinary way, to print or display an announcement including an appropriate copyright notice and a notice that there is no warranty (or else, saying that you provide a warranty) and that users may redistribute the program under these conditions, and telling the user how to view a copy of this License. (Exception: if the Program itself is interactive but does not normally print such an announcement, your work based on the Program is not required to print an announcement.)

These requirements apply to the modified work as a whole. If identifiable sections of that work are not derived from the Program, and can be reasonably considered independent and separate works in themselves, then this License, and its terms, do not apply to those sections when you distribute them as separate works. But when you distribute the same sections as part of a whole which is a work based on the Program, the distribution of the whole must be on the terms of this License, whose permissions for other licensees extend to the entire whole, and thus to each and every part regardless of who wrote it.

Thus, it is not the intent of this section to claim rights or contest your rights to work written entirely by you; rather, the intent is to exercise the right to control the distribution of derivative or collective works based on the Program.

In addition, mere aggregation of another work not based on the Program with the Program (or with a work based on the Program) on a volume of a storage or distribution medium does not bring the other work under the scope of this License.

3. You may copy and distribute the Program (or a work based on it, under Section 2) in object code or executable form under the terms of Sections 1 and 2 above provided that you also do one of the following:

a) Accompany it with the complete corresponding machine-readable source code, which must be distributed under the terms of Sections 1 and 2 above on a medium customarily used for software interchange; or,

b) Accompany it with a written offer, valid for at least three years, to give any third party, for a charge no more than your cost of physically performing source distribution, a complete machine-readable copy of the corresponding source code, to be distributed under the terms of Sections 1 and 2 above on a medium customarily used for software interchange; or,

c) Accompany it with the information you received as to the offer to distribute corresponding source code. (This alternative is allowed only for noncommercial distribution and only if you received the program in object code or executable form with such an offer, in accord with Subsection b above.)

The source code for a work means the preferred form of the work for making modifications to it. For an executable work, complete source code means all the source code for all modules it contains, plus any associated interface definition files, plus the scripts used to control compilation and installation of the executable. However, as a special exception, the source code distributed need not include anything that is normally distributed (in either source or binary form) with the major components (compiler, kernel, and so on) of the operating system on which the executable runs, unless that component itself accompanies the executable.

If distribution of executable or object code is made by offering access to copy from a designated place, then offering equivalent access to copy the source code from the same place counts as distribution of the source code, even though third parties are not compelled to copy the source along with the object code.

4. You may not copy, modify, sublicense, or distribute the Program except as expressly provided under this License. Any attempt otherwise to copy, modify, sublicense or distribute the Program is void, and will automatically terminate your rights under this License. However, parties who have received copies, or rights, from you under this License will not have their licenses terminated so long as such parties remain in full compliance.

5. You are not required to accept this License, since you have not signed it. However, nothing else grants you permission to modify or distribute the Program or its derivative works. These actions are prohibited by law if you do not accept this License. Therefore, by modifying or distributing the Program (or any work based on the Program), you indicate your acceptance of this License to do so, and all its terms and conditions for copying, distributing or modifying the Program or works based on it.

6. Each time you redistribute the Program (or any work based on the Program), the recipient automatically receives a license from the original licensor to copy, distribute or modify the Program subject to these terms and conditions. You may not impose any further restrictions on the recipients' exercise of the rights granted herein. You are not responsible for enforcing compliance by third parties to this License.

7. If, as a consequence of a court judgment or allegation of patent infringement or for any other reason (not limited to patent issues), conditions are imposed on you (whether by court order, agreement or otherwise) that contradict the conditions of this License, they do not excuse you from the conditions of this License. If you cannot distribute so as to satisfy simultaneously your obligations under this License and any other pertinent obligations, then as a consequence you may not distribute the Program at all. For example, if a patent license would not permit royalty-free redistribution of the Program by all those who receive copies directly or indirectly through you, then the only way you could satisfy both it and this License would be to refrain entirely from distribution of the Program.

If any portion of this section is held invalid or unenforceable under any particular circumstance, the balance of the section is intended to apply and the section as a whole is intended to apply in other circumstances.

It is not the purpose of this section to induce you to infringe any patents or other property right claims or to contest validity of any such claims; this section has the sole purpose of protecting the integrity of the free software distribution system, which is implemented by public license practices. Many people have made generous contributions to the wide range of software distributed through that system in reliance on consistent application of that system; it is up to the author/donor to decide if he or she is willing to distribute software through any other system and a licensee cannot impose that choice.

This section is intended to make thoroughly clear what is believed to be a consequence of the rest of this License.

8. If the distribution and/or use of the Program is restricted in certain countries either by patents or by copyrighted interfaces, the original copyright holder who places the Program under this License may add an explicit geographical distribution limitation excluding those countries, so that distribution is permitted only in or among countries not thus excluded. In such case, this License incorporates the limitation as if written in the body of this License.

9. The Free Software Foundation may publish revised and/or new versions of the General Public License from time to time. Such new versions will be similar in spirit to the present version, but may differ in detail to address new problems or concerns.

Each version is given a distinguishing version number. If the Program specifies a version number of this License which applies to it and "any later version", you have the option of following the terms and conditions either of that version or of any later version published by the Free Software Foundation. If the Program does not specify a version number of this License, you may choose any version ever published by the Free Software Foundation.

10. If you wish to incorporate parts of the Program into other free programs whose distribution conditions are different, write to the author to ask for permission. For software which is copyrighted by the Free Software Foundation, write to the Free Software Foundation; we sometimes make exceptions for this. Our decision will be guided by the two goals of preserving the free status of all derivatives of our free software and of promoting the sharing and reuse of software generally.

NO WARRANTY

11. BECAUSE THE PROGRAM IS LICENSED FREE OF CHARGE, THERE IS NO WARRANTY FOR THE PROGRAM, TO THE EXTENT PERMITTED BY APPLICABLE LAW. EXCEPT WHEN OTHERWISE STATED IN WRITING THE COPYRIGHT HOLDERS AND/OR OTHER PARTIES PROVIDE THE PROGRAM "AS IS" WITHOUT WARRANTY OF ANY KIND, EITHER EXPRESSED OR IMPLIED, INCLUDING, BUT NOT LIMITED TO, THE IMPLIED WARRANTIES OF MERCHANTABILITY AND FITNESS FOR A PARTICULAR PURPOSE. THE ENTIRE RISK AS TO THE QUALITY AND PERFORMANCE OF THE PROGRAM IS WITH YOU. SHOULD THE PROGRAM PROVE DEFECTIVE, YOU ASSUME THE COST OF ALL NECESSARY SERVICING, REPAIR OR CORRECTION.

12. IN NO EVENT UNLESS REQUIRED BY APPLICABLE LAW OR AGREED TO IN WRITING WILL ANY COPYRIGHT HOLDER, OR ANY OTHER PARTY WHO MAY MODIFY AND/OR REDISTRIBUTE THE PROGRAM AS PERMITTED ABOVE, BE LIABLE TO YOU FOR DAMAGES, INCLUDING ANY GENERAL, SPECIAL, INCIDENTAL OR CONSEQUENTIAL DAMAGES ARISING OUT OF THE USE OR INABILITY TO USE THE PROGRAM (INCLUDING BUT NOT LIMITED TO LOSS OF DATA OR DATA BEING RENDERED INACCURATE OR LOSSES SUSTAINED BY YOU OR THIRD PARTIES OR A FAILURE OF THE PROGRAM TO OPERATE WITH ANY OTHER PROGRAMS), EVEN IF SUCH HOLDER OR OTHER PARTY HAS BEEN ADVISED OF THE POSSIBILITY OF SUCH DAMAGES.

END OF TERMS AND CONDITIONS

How to Apply These Terms to Your New Programs

If you develop a new program, and you want it to be of the greatest possible use to the public, the best way to achieve this is to make it free software which everyone can redistribute and change under these terms.

To do so, attach the following notices to the program. It is safest to attach them to the start of each source file to most effectively convey the exclusion of warranty; and each file should have at least the "copyright" line and a pointer to where the full notice is found.

one line to give the program's name and an idea of what it does.
Copyright (C) *yyyy   name of author*

This program is free software; you can redistribute it and/or
modify it under the terms of the GNU General Public License
as published by the Free Software Foundation; either version 2
of the License, or (at your option) any later version.

This program is distributed in the hope that it will be useful,
but WITHOUT ANY WARRANTY; without even the implied warranty of
MERCHANTABILITY or FITNESS FOR A PARTICULAR PURPOSE. See the
GNU General Public License for more details.

You should have received a copy of the GNU General Public License
along with this program; if not, write to the Free Software
Foundation, Inc., 59 Temple Place - Suite 330, Boston, MA 02111-1307, USA.

Also add information on how to contact you by electronic and paper mail.

If the program is interactive, make it output a short notice like this when it starts in an interactive mode:

Gnomovision version 69, Copyright (C) *year name of author*
Gnomovision comes with ABSOLUTELY NO WARRANTY; for details
type `show w'. This is free software, and you are welcome
to redistribute it under certain conditions; type `show c'
for details.

The hypothetical commands 'show w' and 'show c' should show the appropriate parts of the General Public License. Of course, the commands you use may be called something other than 'show w' and 'show c'; they could even be mouse-clicks or menu items—whatever suits your program.

You should also get your employer (if you work as a programmer) or your school, if any, to sign a "copyright disclaimer" for the program, if necessary. Here is a sample; alter the names:

Yoyodyne, Inc., hereby disclaims all copyright
interest in the program `Gnomovision'
(which makes passes at compilers) written
by James Hacker.

signature of Ty Coon, 1 April 1989
Ty Coon, President of Vice

This General Public License does not permit incorporating your program into proprietary programs. If your program is a subroutine library, you may consider it more useful to permit linking proprietary applications with the library. If this is what you want to do, use the GNU Library General Public License instead of this License.

Syngress: *The Definition of a Serious Security Library*

Syn·gress (sin-gres): *noun, sing.* Freedom from risk or danger; safety. See *security*.

Check Point Next Generation Security Administration

Cherie Amon and Doug Maxwell

The Check Point Next Generation suite of products provides the tools necessary for easy development and deployment of Enterprise Security Solutions. Check Point VPN-1/FireWall-1 has been beating out its competitors for years, and the Next Generation software continues to improve the look, feel, and ease of use of this software. *Check Point NG Security Administration* will show you the ins and outs of the NG product line.

ISBN: 1-928994-74-1
Price: $59.95 USA $92.95 CAN

Special Ops: Host and Network Security for Microsoft, UNIX, and Oracle

Erik Pace Birkholz

"Strap on the night vision goggles, apply the camo pain, then lock and load. *Special Ops* is an adrenaline-pumping tour of the most critical security weaknesses present on most any corporate network today, with some of the world's best drill sergeants leading the way."
—Joel Scambray, Senior Director, Microsoft's MSN

"*Special Ops* has brought some of the best speakers and researchers of computer security together to cover what you need to know to survive in today's net."

ISBN: 1-928994-74-1
Price: $69.95 USA $108.95 CAN

Stealing the Network: How to "Own the Box"

Ryan Russell, FX, Joe Grand, and Ken Pfiel

Stealing the Network: How to Own the Box is NOT intended to be an "install, configure, update, troubleshoot, and defend book." It is also NOT another one of the countless Hacker books out there now by our competition. So, what IS it? *Stealing the Network: How to Own the Box* is an edgy, provocative, attack-oriented series of chapters written in a first hand, conversational style. World-renowned network security personalities present a series of chapters written from the point of an attacker gaining access to a system. This book portrays the street fighting tactics used to attack networks.

ISBN: 1-931836-87-6
Price: $49.95 USA $69.95 CAN

SYNGRESS®